Winner of the Jules and Frances
Landry Award for 1992

TUMULT
AND
SILENCE
AT
SECOND
CREEK

TUMULT AND SILENCE AT SECOND CREEK

An Inquiry into a Civil War Slave Conspiracy

WINTHROP D. JORDAN

LOUISIANA STATE UNIVERSITY PRESS
BATON ROUGE AND LONDON

1294 3005

First printing
02 01 00 99 98 97 96 95 94 93   5 4 3 2 1

Designer: Amanda McDonald Key
Typeface: Trump Mediaeval
Typesetter: Graphic Composition, Inc.
Printer and binder: Thomson–Shore, Inc.

Library of Congress Cataloging-in-Publication Data

Jordan, Winthrop D.
　　Tumult and silence at Second Creek: an inquiry into a Civil War
　slave conspiracy /　Winthrop D. Jordan.
　　　　p.　　cm.
　　Includes index.
　　ISBN 0–8071–1762–5
　　1. Slavery—Mississippi—Adams County—Insurrections, etc.
　　2. Afro-Americans—Mississippi—Adams County—History—19th century.
　　3. Plantation life—Mississippi—Adams County—History—19th
　century.　4. Adams County (Miss.)—Race relations.　I. Title.
　　F347.A2J67　1993
　　976.2'2600496073—dc20　　　　　　　　　　　　　　　　92–22138
　　　　　　　　　　　　　　　　　　　　　　　　　　　　　　　　CIP

This publication has been supported by a grant from the National Endowment for the Humanities, an independent federal agency.

The paper in this book meets the guidelines for permanence and durability of the Committee on Production Guidelines for Book Longevity of the Council on Library Resources.⊗

Maps: Mott Jordan

To Cora

CONTENTS

ILLUSTRATIONS

NOTE OF APPRECIATION AND THANKS

A friend once cautioned me about borrowing paper clips, on grounds that the name of the donor might well end up having to be listed in the "acknowledgments" at the beginning of one's book. Since then, paper clips have blossomed into an array of colors, yet the warning remains apt. Accordingly, in this note of appreciation and thanks (rather than acknowledgment) I remain acutely aware that I cannot possibly thank everyone who has been of assistance with this book and also that, alas, I have no doubt overlooked the names of several people who ought to be included.

I am, nonetheless, very grateful to Beth Allen, Ira Berlin, Ed and Ardis Berry, Judy Bolton, Rebecca Bowers, Gene Brucker, Sim Callon, Bob Campbell, Miles Campbell, Don Carleton, Hodding Carter III, Bill Cate, Amanda Cook, Michael Craton, Ronald Davis, Ginger Delk, Susan Ditto, David Fischer, Eugene Genovese, Fredonia Hairston, Laura Harper, Evans Harrington, Dwight Harris, Robert Haws, Nancy Hendershot, Nancy Horton, Rhys Isaac, Tony Jenkins, Mary Jordan, Charles Keller, Lucy Kerman, Kim King, Michael Landon, Catherine Landry, Ann Lanneau, Bazile Lanneau, Bazile Lanneau, Jr., Frederick Laurenzo, Ann Lipscomb, Carol McKibben, Mrs. Charles McNeil, Bruce Mactavish, Betty Mauney, Henry Miles, Stoney Miller, Sheila Moore, Philip Morgan, Dave Mudavanha, Deborah Northart, James Oakes, Elaine Owens, Harry Owens, Faye Phillips, Lynn Pierson, John Price, Armstead Robinson, David Rosenberg, Morton Rothstein, Charles Royster, David Sansing, Richard Shrader, Kenneth Stampp, Mark Stegmaier, Martha Swan, Lil Taiz, Theo Von Laue, Debbie Wahl, Lance Walters, Lillie Ward, Rob Waters, Michael Wayne, Bill West, Virginia Williams, Fay Wimberly, Katie Wood, Robert Wood, Jr., Vicki Woodall, the late James Wooldridge, and Bertram Wyatt-Brown.

Mott Jordan has skillfully done the maps for this book. I especially appreciate the personal and collegial friendship of James Kettner, Charles Joyner, and Robert Middlekauff, who read and gave good counsel on the manuscript. In my opinion its remaining faults ought in justice be assigned entirely to them, but apparently custom dictates a different view of such matters.

Many years ago, the assistant archivist at the LSU Archives, Margaret Fisher, brought to my attention and transcribed the document that has proved so central to this book. We thought it might be the basis for an interesting article. Now, as Margaret Dalrymple and editor-in-chief at the LSU Press, she has patiently presided over publication of what has turned into a somewhat longer study than originally anticipated. Also at the Press, Gerry Anders has greatly improved the text with remarkably astute editorial skill. Phil Holman, of the University of Mississippi, has persistently ferreted out and checked a great deal of often elusive information, including many empty holes, always with acuity, precision, and good humor.

I am very grateful also to the person to whom this book is dedicated. The reasons for my gratitude to Cora Jordan are better paraded on another ground, even though we do trade paper clips now and then.

ABBREVIATIONS AND NOTATIONS ON SOURCES

References in the footnotes to lettered Documents (Documents A, B, C, etc.) are to the individual documents printed in the Appendixes.

ADAMS LAND   Adams County Land Assessment Rolls, extant in the period 1850–1865 for 1850, 1853, 1857, 1861, microfilm in MDAH. Except where indicated, citations are to all these four years. Last names were alphabetized by first letter only, but this procedure at least lumped all the names beginning with the same letter on only one or two pages. Each annual list was separately paginated; thus pages are not cited.

ADAMS PERSONAL   Adams County Personal Property Assessment Rolls, extant in the period 1850–1865 for 1852, 1858, 1859, 1861, 1862, microfilm in MDAH. Citations are to all these five years except where indicated. These rolls were organized in the same way as the Adams Land Rolls, immediately above, and are cited in the same manner.

CAL. VA. STATE PAPERS   William Palmer, Sherwin McRae, and H. W. Flournoy, eds., *Calendar of Virginia State Papers and Other Manuscripts, 1652–1869, Preserved at the Capitol in Richmond* (11 vols.; 1875–1893; rpr. New York, 1968), (Vol. IX, ed., Flournoy).

CENSUS   U.S. MS census data are cited simply as Census with the county unnamed if it is Adams County, the date, and the schedule (Free or Slave or Mortality). Since pagination of the free population schedules was sometimes haphazard in Adams County, household numbers are used. Since the slave schedules usually have two page numbers on a single page, one preprinted and a different one by hand, MS pp. are so indicated. Occasionally there is no pagination at all. U.S. MS census returns are at the National Archives and can be purchased on microfilm. In several instances where films are unclear, the original returns have been consulted.

DARDEN DIARY   Susan Sillers Darden Diary, 2 vols., both a MS and a very incomplete typescript copy, in Darden Family Papers, MDAH. All references and quotations are to Vol. I of the MS version.

DUL   Special Collections Department, William R. Perkins Library, Duke University, Durham, North Carolina.

GOODSPEED'S   *Goodspeed's Biographical and Historical Memoirs of Mississippi Embracing an Authentic and Comprehensive Account of the Chief Events in the History of the State and a Record of the Lives of Many of the Most Worthy and Illustrious Families and Individuals* (2 vols.; Chicago, 1891).

JENKINS DIARY   Typescript (no MS available), in John C. Jenkins and Family Papers, LSU. The typescript has many errors, especially with proper names; these have here been silently corrected where the meaning is certain. Some of the entries appear to be by Jenkins' friend and manager, Dr. Samuel L. Grier.

JOHNSON'S DIARY   William R. Hogan and Edwin A. Davis, eds., *William Johnson's Natchez: The Ante-Bellum Diary of a Free Negro* (1951; 2 vols.; rpr. Port Washington, N.Y., 1986). The index is unreliable.

JNH   *Journal of Negro History.*

JSH   *Journal of Southern History.*

LSU   Louisiana and Lower Mississippi Valley Collections, Louisiana State University Libraries, Hill Memorial Library, Baton Rouge.

MDAH   Mississippi State Department of Archives and History, Jackson.

RAWICK, *AMERICAN SLAVE*   George P. Rawick, ed., *The American Slave: A Composite Autobiography* (41 vols. [the first to be published were in two series with a total of 19 vols. numbered consecutively; then came Supplement 1 (12 vols.) and Supplement 2 (10 vols.)]; Westport, Conn., 1972–79). Various libraries have catalogued these volumes in various ways, but the catalog main entry is usually *American Slave.*

ROAD DUTY, MDAH   "Adams County, List of hands liable to road duty, 1855–1856; list of labor done on public roads . . .

1st May 1855 to 4th Monday in April 1856" (Bound MS vol. in 2 Parts, in MDAH). The rolls were taken in the summer months and usually signed by the owner, overseer, or agent. Part 1 is the original, from which a contemporary copy was made for 1855 in the volume cited immediately below. Part 2, "labor done," is not copied in the UTA volume, and is a list grouped by individual owners of the number of hands and days of labor actually worked. The lists were compiled in the name of the superintendent of roads and bridges; they include, purportedly, all male and female slaves aged fifteen to fifty, listed by plantation (only sometimes named), with names of the owner, of the slaves, and often of overseers or agents. There are, of course, some omissions and arithmetical errors.

ROAD DUTY, UTA   "Slaves Subject to Road Duty, Adams County, Mississippi, 1850–1857" (Bound MS in Natchez Trace Slaves and Slavery Collection, Barker Texas History Center, University of Texas at Austin). The year 1851 is not included, and 1857 is a fragment. 1855 is a revised but accurate copy from the volume at MDAH listed immediately above. Otherwise the lists are similar to the ones in Road Duty, MDAH, except for the lack of actual signatures. The initial table of contents is far from complete.

UNC   Southern Historical Collection, Library of the University of North Carolina at Chapel Hill.

UTA   Natchez Trace Slaves and Slavery Collection, Barker Texas History Center, University of Texas at Austin.

VIRGIL STEWART   H. R. Howard, *The History of Virgil A. Stewart, and His Adventure in Capturing and Exposing the Great "Western Land Pirate" and His Gang . . . Also of the Trials, Confessions, and Execution of a Number of Murrell's Associates in the State of Mississippi During the Summer of 1835* . . . (New York, 1837). The latter part of this is the same as Thomas Shackleford, ed., *Proceedings of the Citizens of Madison County, Mississippi at Livingston, in July, 1835, in Relation to the Trial and Punishment of Several Individuals Implicated in a Contemplated Insurrection in This State* (Jackson, 1836).

WAILES DIARY   Diary, Benjamin Leonard Covington Wailes Collection, DUL

TUMULT
AND
SILENCE
AT
SECOND
CREEK

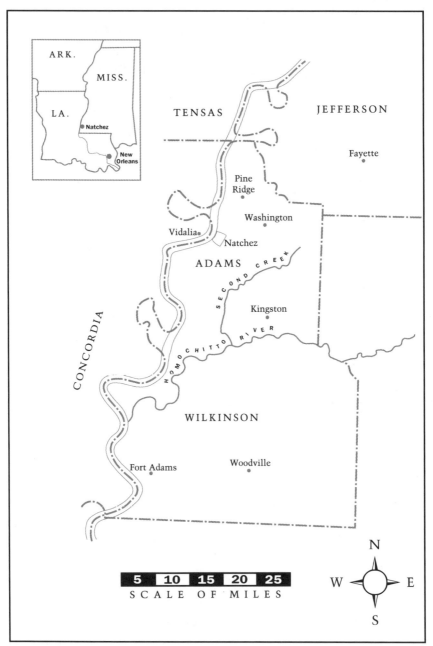

Southwestern Mississippi and Eastern Louisiana *ca.* 1861

INTRODUCTION

I don't credit the story of the extension of the [Nat Turner] Virginia insurrection, tho' I have great apprehension that we will one day have our throats cut in this county. We have here 5 blacks to one white; and within 4 hours march of Natchez there are 2200 able bodied male slaves. It behooves to be vigilant—but <u>silent</u>.

—Stephen Duncan to Thomas Butler,
Natchez, October 4, 1831

It is kept very still, not to be in the papers. . . . don't speak of it only cautiously.

—S. H. Hunt to her niece, near Woodville,
October 15, 1861

He that has no character is not a man, only a thing.

—Charles Williams,
formerly a slave in Adams County, to a
Federal Writers' Project interviewer, 1937

This book is a story, but at the same time it is not. Stories require sequence, the ineffable logic that is conveyed by the sheer fact that specific events happen either before or after others. All make-believe stories have this quality, and so do the ones that are called real. Indeed our sense of sequence is essential to our lives as human beings. Merely on a day-to-day basis—the phrase itself is so naturally sequential—we cannot function without knowing that some things happen after others. Even our language does not work without this sense.

The story of what happened at Second Creek is hobbled by our not being able to find out exactly what happened when. It is a pretty poor tale that cannot tell us whether the horse galloped off before or after the rider got on. In this case, though—the one at Second Creek—there is at least a modicum of known sequence, and by clutching onto it we are saved from being totally lost. It is known that certain events took place before others. Without that knowledge there might be a bit to tell, but surely not enough worth the telling. So we are limited, handicapped, but not completely helpless in the face of the towering silence that shrouds the tumult that demonstrably took place there.

At least we know the year, an artificial but vitally serviceable crutch to our need for sequence, and within that calendrical limit we have enough sequential information to construct *something* of a story, but what finally results has more the nature of a tapestry, a textural and visual object that can, but does not necessarily, convey a series of events. Tapestries are often regarded as works of art, and they may well be. But they are also often perceived as telling a story, and some famous ones have been acclaimed as telling a great deal about big stories. Here is a small one, with events woven and interwoven. I use this image partly by way of asserting that these events have not been made up, as the saying goes, out of whole cloth.

Historical tapestries, whatever their merits, lack voice—at least in the most literal sense of that term. Though they are often described as speaking to us, they do not fill us with sound. Today we live with more sound than ever before in human experience. Often we denounce it as noise or racket, but most of us have to hear it. We live with a phenomenon new in human history, the ability to re-create sounds almost exactly as they transpired—an instrumentality that modern professional historians have not been thoroughly attuned to, let alone associating it with the German professor's famous injunction, a century ago, that history should be written "exactly as it happened."

Surely there were sounds at Second Creek. There were smells too, which fact merely furnishes us with the irony that the most redolent of our animal senses is the least recoverable from the past. We do not seem to yearn for such smells (partly because we find most of them noxious, but also because we have been otherwise socialized and trained, and as well because we presume they have a persistent similarity through time), and we have both a stronger urge toward and a better chance of recovering things that touch the ear.

Usually we regard tapestries with the eye, and think of them as primarily visual in nature. In studying some past cultures, historians have benefited from luxuriously informative visual artifacts of the time—for example, paintings from the seventeenth-century Netherlands or bronze sculptures from sixteenth-century

Benin. Mid-nineteenth-century Adams County was a great deal less productive of magnificent or even of crudely informative visual evidence. There remain a few very conventional portraits of individuals, and several photographs of street scenes in Natchez, but none of the rural countryside. Natchez itself still has the most impressive concentration of antebellum mansions in the entire southern United States, but most of the rural housing structures out in the county have long since burned or otherwise joined the soil.

Indeed, when viewed visually, present-day rural Adams County is deceptive as to its history. In the late twentieth century much of the land looks like virgin forest interspersed (in the flatter parts) with meadows and an occasional parklike pasture. There are few cultivated fields. It requires conscious effort to translate the present sight of densely vine-tangled woods on the sloping hills into the gully-scarred cotton fields and cornfields that once spread over those grounds. In the early autumn, which was the time of the "examinations" of slaves at Second Creek in 1861, there is still a prevailing color on the land, but it is now darkly and deeply green, and the old fundamental brown is gone. Today, the land has reverted to the verdant shades that prevailed before the arrival of cotton.

There is less than an overabundance of surviving evidence about the local crisis that took place in 1861. All of the most directly pertinent material I have found is printed toward the end of this book. While trying to understand the crisis, I have relied mostly on listening to written documents—with an eye and ear to understanding what people in the past, now all dead, were saying. Others listeners, reading now, will hear different things, different messages. But, by way of excusing the cumbersome title of this book, let me urge that readers approach the matter with an ear open to the silence that lies like a smothering tarpaulin on the mountain of pain in Adams County, Mississippi, in 1861.

A conspiracy among slaves took place there. They wanted freedom, and they wanted to define freedom in their own terms, though they sometimes disagreed about what those terms should be and how to reach their ultimate goal. The events we now know most about took place on a group of plantations near Second Creek where that little stream still bends directly south, which is about ten miles south-southeast of the county seat of Natchez. The Second Creek plot may possibly have been connected to a smaller one in northerly neighboring Jefferson County and almost certainly was to one in Natchez itself.

The phrase "we now know about" seems appropriate because this slave plot was kept so quiet at the time that it has since remained virtually unknown, or at least not written about by historians, or (so far as can be discovered) even spoken of by living descendants of the antagonists.

For both the black and the white participants, the revolt, the plot, the uprising, the insurrection, the conspiracy—most commonly, "the Plan"—was in a sense a collaborative effort, with people on both the black and the white sides cooperating collectively amongst themselves and, without fully knowing it, with each other because both shared assumptions about what was possible, what was likely, and what was right. It was as much a matter of culture as of technology that this particular Mississippi tragedy prefigured the "face-to-face" battles on "common ground" during the American Civil War. It was very much a nineteenth-century, not a twentieth-century, conflict. It involved not only intimacy of scale, but also intimacies of acquaintanceship and affect.

The Plan began very shortly after the war broke out. The bombardment of Fort Sumter had begun at four-thirty in the morning on April 12 (1861) and had ended thirty-six hours later with the Charleston harbor island fort in shambles but miraculously no one killed in all the one-way cannonading. News about this event reached some slaves on Second Creek less than a week later. Although the new electric telegraph was magically rapid, the much older grapevine transfer of news from Natchez to the slave quarters of Second Creek was not slow, and it was more efficient in conveying the emotional impact of information.

Serious talk about the possibility of war between the North and the South had been going on for at least ten years. Of course, it is impossible to say who in that locality knew what about the various crises of the 1850s that have become staples in American history textbooks. Yet surely it would be rash for us to suppose that Mississippians, white and black, had not heard about, say, the pistols dropping on the floor of the House of Representatives during the prolonged struggle over the speakership two years previously.

The stridency of all the talk had reached a still higher pitch after the presidential campaign and the election of a man the southern newspapers persistently called a "Black Republican." What meaning that ironic phrase conveyed in the slave quarters is open to question, though it is certain that by the winter of 1861 slaves near Second Creek knew the name Lincoln and that he was an enemy of those who claimed to own them. It is an open question also how many slaves in the cotton South knew about the state of Mississippi seceding from the federal Union in February and joining a new confederacy, or indeed, how much they cared. Yet there is no doubt at all that they regarded word of this actual war between white people as an opportunity for their own ambitions. They did not know that a major war was coming, but neither did the white people. Political leaders in Washington were calling for three-month volunteers, a posture toward the conflict that found further expression when carriageloads of finely dressed observers wheeled and cantered southward from the older nation's capital to view the first and presumably final performance at the theater of Bull Run/Manassas in June of 1861.

No one had any way of knowing then that there would be another battle on that site fourteen months later. Slaves had little reason to speculate about the possible duration of the conflict that was now indisputably under way. No one—white or black—expected it would last four long years. Although the Plan at Second Creek was triggered by word of the outbreak of warfare, the Civil War as such did not cause this tragedy in Mississippi.

What happened was that a certain group of slaves heard of fighting between groups of white people and learned about political and ideological differences between the antagonists that seemed to them very much pertinent to their own situations as slaves. This knowledge loosed a pile of accumulated anger among some slaves in a particular neighborhood, which drew a reaction of frightened, determined vengeance from the local master class.

That September of 1861, and long into the chilling weather that came in November, panic spread into Natchez itself. In all, at least twenty-seven slaves—and very probably more—were hanged. The Confederate provost marshal at Natchez reported early in 1862 that forty slaves had been hanged within the previous year and that as many remained in irons. We will never know the exact number of black people killed at Second Creek or in Adams County as a whole. The state government did not reimburse owners of slaves executed at the orders of extralegal courts, and no official accounting was ever made. In Adams County the "examination" or "vigilance" committees kept things as quiet as possible, and no one involved shared our present predilection for counting bodies after disasters.

By modern standards, what took place in Adams County in 1861 may seem unimportant. If judged numerically in comparison with many other slave, serf, and peasant revolts throughout the world's history, it was a small affair. Some three dozen blacks and no whites were killed. Yet if compared with other notable episodes in the United States—with New York in 1712 and 1741; with Stono, South Carolina, in 1739; with Gabriel's, Vesey's, and Turner's rebellions in 1800, 1822, and 1831; and even with the larger uprising outside New Orleans in 1811—the events at Second Creek were not minor. Very little is known about the crises in 1712 and 1811, but there is opportunity to draw comparisons with the others. Each of the three revolts that were named after individual leaders, for example, produced a volume of evidence that dwarfs what is available about Second Creek.

Yet a good deal can be ascertained about the events in Adams County, even though the evidence is fragmentary and often ambiguous. In assessing what is known, we will have to resort to the realm of probability, utilizing a mode of thought historians employ much more often than they usually acknowledge or care to admit. Even those historians who do not "quantify"—and I am one of them—actually do so when they employ such ordinary and innocent terms as *may have, probably, might have, certainly, nearly always, rarely, often, occasionally, sometimes, perhaps, presumably,* and even *never* and *always*. Most such terms refer either to frequency of occurrence or degree of certainty. Of course, even though they seem to emanate from original documents, their genesis also lies in the minds of the assessors.

Indeed, all such language *can* be quantified in terms of percentages, or at least ranges of percentages, but many of us feel uncomfortable saying "ninety to ninety-five percent of the time" instead of "nearly always." We rightly sense that numbers impose an exactitude that is inappropriate when applied to what are often very mushy historical "facts." The same difficulty arises when we give unwarranted numerical shape to data that are essentially sloppy in the way they were generated. Yet we often see data mathematically manipulated in ways that convey a totally unjustified impression of precision, the most notoriously egregious instance pertinent to this study being the assertion in *Time on the Cross* that American slaves received 1.4 whippings per year. Thus it *could* be said, but will not be, that a slave hauled before the Second Creek Examination Committee had a 97-percent chance of being hanged. We simply do not know and never will. But we *can* say that slaves knew that being summoned before the Committee was very likely to be followed shortly by death and that this awareness greatly affected their lives.

Apart from probabilities, and especially for the events at Second Creek, there is need to ward against difficulties from another quarter, for in the United States the subject of slave resistance has been heavily freighted with ideologies for at least two centuries. This study skirts those ideologies, which have a long and important history of their own that deserves separate inquiry. Yet skirting that history does not fully avoid entanglement with its difficulties, because at Second Creek as much as anywhere, expectations about what people should and would do powerfully shaped what individuals planned and said and did. Setting those problems aside for the moment, it seems to me that the people involved in these most particular events need to be taken seriously as individuals with their own agendas and concerns, living as they did in situations very different from ours and, indeed, participating in a culture that, no matter how much it influenced our own, no longer exists.

It is in this light that the historical evidence has been gathered and interpreted. It is 99-percent certain that I have not found all extant source materials that bear upon the matter at hand. More important, it is a truism that no two historians would interpret the evidence presented here in exactly the same way. Yet so far as I can see the matter, not all interpretations are equally valid in their conformity with available historical sources or even—and this is a related but separate problem—in their essential aims. I ought to say, therefore, that despite the apparent narrowness of its subject matter, this tapestry is woven, however roughly, not only as the story of Second Creek, but also with the intention of exploring certain generic problems about the nature of historical inference.

CHAPTER 1

AN EPISODE IN MAY

If one were to transform a map of Adams County into a pond and drop a pebble onto the Mosby place, one would have a fairly good overview of the geographical spread of the Second Creek Plan. The widest ripples reached at least to Natchez, some eight miles to the north and a bit west. They may have touched near the hamlet of Kingston, about the same distance in a nearly opposite direction, to the southeast. There were several thousand slaves and a few hundred whites living within a few miles of Mosby's Brighton. The plantations were lovingly and sonorously named, often with the earlier bucolic and sylvan character of the neighborhood in mind: Retirement, Cherry Grove, Fair Oaks, Bottany Hill, and (though more than an hour's ride from navigable water) Anchorage. By contrast, a free Negro who owned a flourishing barbering business in Natchez named the initial tract of farmland he bought, in swampy country near the river, Hard Scrabble. With the planters, always the same name applied to both the land and the big house, connecting them in organic union. The whole ground and all its buildings were referred to as a "plantation" or "place," never (perhaps to avoid pretentiousness and emphasize equality despite great variations in size) as an "estate."[1]

In the antebellum period the area was sliced south-north by the main road up from New Orleans, Baton Rouge, and Woodville to Natchez, a road today relocated closer to Second Creek and greatly widened, split by a median, bridged, paved with asphalt and concrete, and otherwise modernized, with a route number, Mississippi 61.[2] At the time, that artery of dirt to Natchez both did and

---

1. In the United States, the latter term was commonly applied only to sugar plantations, perhaps by extension from the West Indies, where Anglophilia persisted desperately amidst a sea of blacks. Hard Scrabble is in *Johnson's Diary,* I, 36–39; II, 530, 745, and *passim.* The quotations heading the previous introductory chapter are from Butler Family Papers, LSU; Hughes Family Papers, UNC; and Rawick, *American Slave,* Suppl. 2, Vol. I (Ala. [etc.] Narrs.), 189.

2. The very recent four-laning of the route makes it seem even more historically anomalous than when, only a few years ago, it was a rural blacktop.

did not play a role in the Plan. The mutineers did not mention it, or at least were not queried about it at their examinations. Yet everyone knew where it went if taken north and, more vaguely, that the other way led eventually to New Orleans. Some slaves had ridden or walked it to Natchez and back, and therefore knew that it led easily and directly to that important town despite the difficulties of the fording places. It was not a sightseeing road; long stretches had been deliberately planted with hedges of Cherokee rose, whose thick curtains of leaves prevented travelers from even glimpsing the fields on either side. Newly arriving visitors sometimes spoke of it as if they had been traveling through a roofless tunnel.[3]

By comparison the smaller roads in the area were rough, narrow, and often muddy; they were mere feeders for the plantations. Yet they were wide enough for wagons and carriages. Wagons had important economic functions, whether they were driven by a slave or a white teamster; they served as transportation for all manner of goods. Buggies and "cabs" were sometimes used by white people for short, casual trips. But "luxury" or "pleasure" carriages (as they were variously called) were the only vehicles assessed on the property tax rolls. They had weighty social implications.

Carriages implied high status and dignity for everyone involved—their owners, passengers, and drivers. Ordinary white people could not afford to maintain one. The cotton planters could and did, but customarily they did not ride in them. Wealthy men preferred to ride singly on horseback alongside these carriages, and they trained their sons in the same taste and skill. Often their wives and daughters used the carriage with no other escort than the slave who drove it. The ladies relied upon their carriages mainly for visiting, as much to one another's houses as to town.

Some of these vehicles were luxurious, but others were neither showy nor elegant. Some were entirely unpainted, great lumbering affairs, heavily built to withstand the jarring of holes, tree roots, fallen branches, and stones. Their towering wooden wheels were rimmed with untreaded bands of iron to resist cuts, and were wide enough not to sink too far into mud. Those huge wheels

---

3. One of the best descriptions is Frederick Law Olmsted, *A Journey in the Back Country* (New York, 1860), 34–35. The hedges had several functions: they were thought to be attractive; they provided privacy; and they were thick enough to keep large animals and even hogs both in and out.

stood taller than the occupants of the carriage itself, chiefly so the axles and the floorboards would remain above water at the fords across the smaller creeks and even Second and St. Catherine's creeks at times when the water was not too high.

No matter how crude, the various roads formed a crucial network throughout the area. County officials kept annual inventories of all able-bodied slaves aged fifteen to fifty on each plantation expressly in order to know which planters were to furnish how many slaves for certain days of public maintenance work. The superintendent of roads and bridges was paid a salary of $1,500 in 1850—a substantial sum, reflecting the post's importance, though often an assistant actually compiled the lists.[4]

Abutting Adams County some twelve miles upriver from Natchez, Jefferson County had similar topography but less wealth and (though it was a "river county") no appreciable port. Its seat, Fayette, lay at its geographical center, linked by a stagecoach over some twenty-five miles of road southwest to Natchez.[5] It was the same route that continued south through the Second Creek area to Woodville in Wilkinson County, then through the sugar country of East Feliciana Parish to Baton Rouge and thence eventually to the largest city in the South, commonly and almost affectionately abbreviated N.O.

On May 10, 1861, about when the weather was beginning to warm into summer, Susan Darden wrote in her diary that the slaves "had been talking a great deal about Lincoln freeing the servants. David Harrison's carriage Driver had been taken up. They had been forming plans about an insurrection. He has a great many carriage drivers connected with it."[6] That was exactly four weeks

4. For more on Road Duty books see pp. xvi–xvii of the Abbreviations and Notations on Sources herein. The salary is noted in *Johnson's Diary*, II, 718. Tax valuations on luxury or pleasure carriages were quite various, but normally not less than $200; see Adams Personal. I am indebted to Mrs. Douglas H. MacNeil for showing me her family's old carriage at Elms Court in Natchez and explaining its functions.

5. The stage may not have been very regular; it is mentioned in Darden Diary, July 3, 1859. Other, more immediately relevant entries in this diary are in Document C herein.

6. Darden Diary, May 10, 12, 1861, Document C. James Oakes generously brought these two particular passages to my attention. The identity of Fed, the man who was doing the talking, is not clear, although Mrs. Darden's husband "whipped" and "discharged" him, after which he remained around, "sick" (from

after South Carolina authorities had ordered the shelling of Fort Sumter in Charleston harbor.

News of the firing reached Natchez rapidly, since the town had been linked to the nation's growing telegraph network—one of the "wonders" of the age—for more than a dozen years. There was as yet no railroad connection, attempts in Natchez to tap the interior of the state having petered out some twenty-five miles east of town.[7] Natchez' principal highway for travel to and from the outside world was still the Mississippi River. The Natchez *Daily Courier* published two special editions on the bombardment, one at 10 A.M. and a second at 4 P.M. that Saturday, April 13, and people in Fayette learned about it late that evening.[8] The next day or perhaps even that night, news of the dramatic events seven hundred miles to the east began spreading among the people on Jefferson County plantations.

Susan Sillers Darden mentioned a number of those people in her diary, which she wrote at her home three miles southwest of Fayette on the Salem Church road. Her circle of family and friends lived near each other outside the county seat and often attended the Presbyterian and other churches together. They all were at least moderately wealthy in slaves, land, and personal property— as the husbands and male friends of southern women who kept diaries tended to be. Susan Darden's husband owned 45 slaves,

---

the whipping) for two days. He was probably a slave hired from another owner, but perhaps a free black man; *ibid.*, esp. January 17, 1861. White employees could be discharged but not whipped by their employer, unless of course they were very youthful.

7. Jenkins Diary, November 9, 1848, noted that this "wonder" (the telegraph) had brought news of Zachary Taylor's presidential victory only one day after the election. The railroad had actually carried small amounts of cotton to the Natchez bluff from William Minor's plantation, which will be encountered in another connection. In January, 1860, after years of financial struggle and physical effort, a north-south line was completed from New Orleans through Jackson to Kentucky. Natchez was not even near it. Water and rail transportation are discussed in John Hebron Moore, *The Emergence of the Cotton Kingdom in the Old Southwest: Mississippi, 1770–1860* (Baton Rouge, 1988), Chap. 7.

8. At least on Tuesday, April 16, the newspaper claimed to have done so. A regular Saturday edition had no such news. Neither of the special editions seems to have survived, and the paper was not published Sundays and Mondays. Saturday night Mrs. Darden noted that a "Telegraphic Dispatch came that they were fighting at Fort Sumpter," but there were so many "false reports" she was uncertain whether to credit the news. She did not allude to military conflict for another five days. Darden Diary, April 13, 18, 1861.

which placed him barely in the top third of slaveholders in Jefferson County, but well within the top 5 percent of the South as a whole. Her two brothers-in-law each owned slightly more than 50 slaves. The two neighbors whose drivers were implicated, David Harrison and P. K. Montgomery, owned 79 and 139.[9] The material fortunes of these planters had been on the upswing. Owing to the burgeoning prosperity and consolidation of land holdings during the previous decade, of six hundred dwellings in the county, more than thirty were declared by the 1860 census marshal to be unoccupied.[10]

Such numbers may do little to illuminate what took place concerning this alarming plot, but numeration can provide approximate dimensions. An examination committee was gathered and the slaves questioned. At least four carriage drivers were hanged. Other slaves may well have been involved. As was frequently the case in such times of crisis, white men were also suspected. On May 14, J. D. L. Davenport wrote the governor from Fayette saying that "three Negroes" had already been hanged, adding, "We have at this time five white men and one negro in our jail who will doubtless pull hemp." He continued ominously: "There are others who we have not yet succeeded in arresting." One of the white men, a married father of three children, was tried, as Susan Darden put it, "for helping negroes to insurrection"; but the evidence was ambiguous, and a mass meeting voted 165 to 142 to confine him to jail rather than hang him, a verdict that left "the people living in his neighborhood very much dissatisfied." Mr. Frank Higdon's Negro was shot and then hanged when he resisted being taken up. Mr. Sam Scott's slaves were "engaged in the Rebellion" and had pistols and knives, though their purported buried gunpowder could not be found. Mrs. Darden summarized the situation: "It is dreadful state affairs certain."[11]

9. Darden Diary, May 10, 11, 1861, Document C. Some of the important individuals in her diary were her husband, Jessie Darden, and her brother-in-law Buckner Darden, who had married her sister Sarah. Madison was the son of the latter couple. Samuel Darden was married to Anna, who will be mentioned in another connection. The families are in Jefferson Census, 1860 Free, pp. 31, 32, 33, 36, 48; 1860 Slave, MS pp. 74–75, 79–80, 80–81, 88–90, 129.

10. Herbert Weaver, *Mississippi Farmers, 1850–1860* (1945; rpr. Gloucester, Mass., 1968), tables on pp. 79, 80, 81, 101, 115; Jefferson Census, 1860 Free, *passim.*

11. J. D. L. Davenport to Gov. [John J.] Pettus, May 14, 1861, in Governors Papers, MDAH, Document E (James F. Wooldridge first kindly pointed out this reference); Darden Diary, May 13, 16, 18, 23, 1861.

Davenport had two reasons to inflate the figures in his report: He was neither the first nor the last person to discover that his civic duty and self-interest coincided exactly. The younger white men of Jefferson County were already gathering to fight the northern enemy, and this sapping of strength came from what he described as "a population of 650 voters surrounded by 11,000 slaves." A company of one hundred " 'Charley Clark Rifles' " was "already in the field," and three other companies were mustered and "awaiting your call." The domestic danger, he confided, "has set me to thinking where I could be of the most service to my Country, at home or in the army." The answer was clear, at least in his own mind: his letter was essentially an inquiry about substituting someone else for his military service.[12]

In keeping with his request, Davenport launched into a description of the internal danger that reads now almost like a caricature of white fears about slave insurrection. "You will see that nothing but eternal Vigilance will keep down the enemy at home. . . . The plans as developed are of the most diabolical character." As he fleshed out the formula, "The white males were all to be destroyed—such of the females as suited their fancy were to be preserved as Wives." To fit this long-standing scenario with the new circumstances, he added that the slaves "were to march up the river to meet 'Mr. Linkin' bearing off as booty such things as they could carry."[13]

The same day, another Jefferson County planter, Howell Hines of Home Hill near Fayette, wrote the governor in much the same vein, though without Davenport's self-serving suggestion about serving his country against the domestic enemy. By Hines's account, information about "an organization by the negros" had come from across the river in Tensas Parish, where David Harrison's children had been visiting their uncle. The "discovery" had been made when Mr. Isaac Harrison, "being aware that the negros all knew of the war and what it was for, . . . secreted himself under the house and heared the conversation" among some male slaves. They had "the purpos of riseing on the 4th of July next at which

12. Davenport to Pettus, May 14, 1861.
13. *Ibid.* Some planters could be more disinterested and level-headed about the danger. From Jaspar County the captain of the Home Guards wrote, "Rumours are rife that the negroes of the surounding neighborhoods are making preparations to raise an insurrection, 'headed by white men' as soon as our Volunteers leave." John B. Harnley to Gov. Pettus, May 4, 1861, in Governors Papers, MDAH.

time they had been induced to believe Lincons troops would be here for the purpos of freeing them all." More specifically (and so excitedly that he omitted either one or two crucial verbs), Hines reported "that when Lincons came down each one was to kill his master and that they would later the fine houses and the white women."[14]

At the time Hines wrote, May 14, one Tensas slave had "paid the penalty" and another was "still in durance vile." In Jefferson County, Mr. Darden's "boy" and one of Mr. Montgomery's had been "hung by the Gentlemen of the neighbourhood."[15] The titular designations of the participants—"boy" and "Gentlemen"—were in a sense as important as the activity, though obviously not for the individuals involved. The term *gentlemen* was the ordinary courtesy title, even though much of its precision and power had drained away since earlier, more deferential times. Whites in the Natchez region, in common with whites throughout the South, used the word *boy* for male slaves and indeed all male blacks (except the occasional elderly "uncle"). This intentionally demeaning term as applied to blacks has proved to be notably persistent through time, but it was then only a few generations old, not having been commonly used in the eighteenth century. And in the antebellum era, blacks used the term when talking about themselves, often with a meaning of camaraderie rather than self-condemnation. As will become apparent, the small group of men on the Mosby place used the term that way, with connotations not very different from those among western cowboys and other work gangs. Thus in southern plantation society the word clearly had a strong racially derogatory dimension, but others as well. It did not in peacetime have the military flavor associated with the long-standing militia age of sixteen and the "boys" of "Yankee Doodle" or those who later bravely charged in the myriad battles of the

14. How[ell] Hines to Gov. J. J. Pettus, May 14, 1861, in Governors Papers, MDAH, Document D. Hines, whose name has been variously rendered by historians, is in *Cohen's New Orleans and Southern Directory, for 1856* (2 vols.; New Orleans, 1855–56), II, 31.

15. Hines to Pettus, May 14, 1861. The reaction of the governor to Hines's and Davenport's letters (if he ever saw them) is not known, but one can imagine a possible scenario from the observation on one occasion by a visiting reporter from the London *Times* that the chief magistrate of Mississippi let go "a portentous plug of tobacco juice just outside the spittoon, with the air of a man who wished to show he could have hit the centre if he liked." Recounted by William Howard Russell, *My Diary North and South,* ed. Eugene H. Berwanger (Philadelphia, 1988), 195.

Civil War, including the black men who fought at Fort Wagner and Milliken's Bend.[16]

It is doubtful that carriage drivers would have used the term about themselves. They stood apart—above being one of the boys. As far as their owners were concerned, they were valuable, not merely in monetary terms (some about $2,000) but as accoutrements of elevated station. There is no way of counting the cost of the Jefferson County hangings to the confidence and self-esteem of the owners. Both Susan and Jessie Darden were deeply distressed by the affair. Ten days after David Harrison's driver had been taken up, she noted that her brother-in-law "is not satisfied about Davy's being guilty."[17] As usual, though, planters and their families were well aware that even if the authorities had cut out the most dangerous of the disaffected, the cancer may have spread—especially in this time of talk about Lincoln.

There was great excitement in the whole Natchez district, as there was throughout the slave South. Little "troops" of volunteers were already drilling for war. Their names gave good indication of how they came into being. In addition to the Charley Clark Rifles of Adams and Jefferson counties, there was the Washington Troop at the tiny hamlet of that name seven miles east of Natchez. The Adams County Light Guard Battalion left in May for Corinth, in the northeast corner of the state, supported at least in part by private monetary contributions.[18] The organizing of these military units had begun before the firing on Sumter: in March a group of Home Guards had been organized in Washington.[19] Some forty men of the Quitman Light Artillery, with Captain W. S. Lovell

16. *Boy* as used derogatorily by whites was remarked on by a New England newcomer to Adams County; see [Joseph Holt Ingraham], *The South-West. By a Yankee* (2 vols.; 1835; rpr. Ann Arbor, 1966), II, 194n.

17. This despite her previous notation that "Mr Montgomery told Mr Darden that Davy died with a lie in his mouth." Darden Diary, May 16, 20, 1861.

18. Jeannie Marie Deen, ed., *Annie Harper's Journal: A Southern Mother's Legacy* (Denton, Miss., 1983), 10; Steven Power, *The Memento: Old and New Natchez . . . 1700–1897* (1897; rpr. 2 vols. [under the name Major Steve Power]; Natchez, 1984), II, 90. For example of private support, see $25 receipt from James A. Sleete to Benjamin Roach, May 27, 1861, in Benjamin Roach Papers, UTA.

19. Receipt from O. M. Blanton to Benjamin Roach, March 27, 1861, in Roach Papers.

commanding, left hurriedly by boat from Natchez on April 14, seen off by "a brilliant and numerous gathering of the populace" high on the bluff overlooking the river and by the hardier and more curious people, both white and black, who jounced down to notorious Natchez-under-the-Hill to cheer them off and then at last zigzagged back up the steep slope that led to Natchez proper. The *Courier* reported proudly that "the whole population appeared to turn out." For the next several weeks the town's two newspapers carried extensive accounts about some five local companies that were organizing to go off to war. Financial support came from public subscriptions, and the ladies sewed new flags and greatly various uniforms. In due time, some or all these little units became known as the Adams Troop, which in turn eventually became part of a larger Mississippi unit in the Confederate army.[20]

In addition to the men preparing for battle against the northern adversary, vigilante committees were forming to keep an eye on "domestic enemies"—meaning blacks and abolitionists. (Indeed, such committees were forming all over the South.) It is possible that alarms about slave insurrection had arisen locally nearly a year earlier, well before the election of Lincoln. William T. Martin, a young Natchez lawyer who became a Confederate general, recalled long after the war that he had helped organize proper countermeasures in the late spring and early summer of 1860. He contended that it had then been feared that slaves both in Adams County and in Concordia Parish, across the river, "might resort to that sort of warfare common to half-civilized people, such as burning, robbing, insulting women, and all that kind of thing," and that there had been "proposed a company of cavalry . . . belonging to the best families." William Martin was not a man to underestimate the importance of his own role in this activity. Money had been raised among the "wealthier people" of the area, and in particular "one wealthy lady" had subscribed the cost of one hundred sabers (at $6 apiece), which Martin personally had purchased in Springfield, Massachusetts. The principal difficulty with these recollections is that no one else (so far as has been discovered) seems to have thought there was slave unrest in Concor-

20. Natchez *Daily Courier,* April 17, 1861. The other paper was the *Free Trader.* Each military unit consisted of fifty to eighty men, most of whom were proudly named in the newspapers.

dia or in Adams in 1860, or that white men were, at that time, making unusual efforts to organize troops.[21]

As far as events after Sumter are concerned, it is not known whether the episode of servile plotting in Jefferson County was connected directly with what happened in the Second Creek neighborhood in Adams County, a day's ride through Natchez to the south. Certainly the affair at Second Creek had its own beginnings and its own energy generated there on home ground, sufficient to thoroughly alarm the white inhabitants of that old and prosperous neighborhood.

Yet that summer of 1861 seemed quiet. Louisa Quitman Lovell, daughter of a prominent planter-politician, kept up her frequent correspondence with her husband Joseph, a captain in the army at the front in Virginia. From Monmouth, on the outskirts of Natchez, she assured him (and herself) that all was well at home. The servants, she wrote at the end of July,

> have all behaved extremely well, indeed I cannot utter the least complaint of them, they are deeply interested and very sympathizing with us all. They often speak to me about the war and there was great rejoicing in the kitchen at the news of our recent glorious victory in Virginia. What would those miserable abolitionists say to such manifestations of devotion and affection on the part of the poor maltreated slave, whose heart, according to them, is only the abode of hatred and revenge against their master—They know nothing of the bond that unites the master and servant[,] of its tenderness and care on the one side, and its pride fidelity and attachment on the other.[22]

21. Martin's statements are remarkable for two qualities, their specificity and their self-inflation. Thus they are difficult to interpret, since the two attributes both do and do not fit with one another, as is clear in Testimony of William T. Martin, Washington, D.C., December 12, 1877, Claim (No. 7960) of Katherine S. Minor, Settled Case Files, 1877–83—Mississippi, Adams County, Records of the Southern Claims Commission, Records of the General Accounting Office, RG 217, National Archives, Document P.

22. Louisa Lovell to Joseph Lovell, July 28, 1861, in Quitman Family Papers, UNC. The family is listed in Census, 1860 Free, household 816; 1860 Slave, MS p. 33. *Goodspeed's* (I, 1152–54), customarily worshipful in its biographical sketches, explained retrospectively that the successes in life of Joseph's brother, Captain William S. Lovell of the Quitman Light Artillery, "have been attained rather by the force of native talent and culture than by tact."

Mrs. Lovell was not writing for any public but herself and her husband. She believed what she wrote. But within a few months she was to change her mind.

Word of these developments in Jefferson County of course spread to neighboring communities, especially along the road to Natchez in Adams County. Benjamin L. C. Wailes, living outside the tiny village of Washington on that road, summarized what he had heard in his diary. "It seems an intended insurrection near Fayette, Jefferson County," he wrote, "planned by some white men, foreigners, Germans it is said has been detected and some two or three white men and as many negroes have been executed." As was so often the case with such events, the news included speculation about wider involvement. As Wailes put it, "Further discovery has been made extending into Franklin County."[23] Franklin bordered Adams on the east. His diary contained nothing about alarms in his own neighborhood or any part of his county. Not then, at least. Not until September.

23. Wailes Diary, May 19, 1861, Document F.

CHAPTER 2

EVIDENTIARY SOUNDS AND VOICES

It is impossible to replicate exactly the voices and other sounds of the long past. They are gone. When we spell out speech by word in either standard or dialecticized English vocabulary, we miss the nuances of sound. We can never recapture the nearly infinite variety of human inflections and accents as they resonated in different places, situations, and times. We can indeed attempt to recreate old cadences of speech, but we will never fully succeed. Speech itself is too idiosyncratic, too fragmentary, and too sensitively reflective of specific social settings.

As elsewhere in the South, the sounds of speech among slaves in Mississippi melded with the sounds of song, so thoroughly that there was no clear dividing line between what many other Americans then (and today) regarded as two distinct modes of expression. Today those sounds cannot be recaptured. Something of their timbre and rhythm can be appreciated by listening to twentieth-century audio electromagnetic recordings, but there is always danger in listening backward in time by a process of extrapolation from the sounds of later years. Related problems plague the writing down of spoken words. As many historians have discovered, there are peculiar problems with written documents generated fifty years ago in which interviewer-writers attempted to set down on pages the speech of elderly former slaves, using a process that despite attempts at faithfulness often ended up with a bewildering collection of added, dropped, and altered letters, with the words generously sprinkled with apostrophes.[1] There are few such problems with the written evidence about the Second Creek Plan, though there are others that become apparent immediately and often refuse to disappear.

Other kinds of sounds were as much a part of the atmosphere at Second Creek as human voices, and we are on much firmer

---

1. Most conspicuously with interviews of elderly former slaves in the 1920s and 1930s. Most historians have elected to retain the awkward and inconsistent forms used in the original typescripts.

ground listening to them, even though they are more than a century past. Presumably the scratching of a heavy hoe, the squeaking of a wooden wheel, the whining of mosquitoes, and so on sounded then very much as they do today. Yet even this certainty is muddied by the fact that such noises carried different affective freight than they do today. Sounds are heard in specific social contexts, even if only one person hears them. The noise of metal upon metal made by the movement of the links of a chain "sounds" very different depending whether the chain is part of a mule's harnessing and hitches or the shackling of a twenty-pound ball to the neck and legs of a human being. We use different terms for the same noises in such distinct situations: in the one case the chain "rings" or "jangles"; in the other, it "scrapes" or "clanks."

We may also assume that the various birds have not changed their cries and melodies, with the possible exception of the mockingbird, whose remarkable repertoire of mimicry extends to human as well as avian voices.[2] Yet on the old Second Creek plantations the quality and volume of background noises were very different than they are on many modern farms. During the day, the cocoon of quiet was alive with the various barnyard noises of hogs, hens, roosters, hounds, horses, mules, and human beings. The river was too far away for the noise of steamboats to break the air. At dawn (with the awakening call of the conch) and then again after dusk, one could hear the bumping and clanging of hoes and plows being taken down or put up, the whap of axes and the rasp of saws for firewood, and the slop of emptying buckets. In the day, the buzzards circled silently. With so much of the forest gone, the chattering of the gray and black squirrels had become occasional. The moccasins kept their customary quiet, as the rattlesnakes did except upon chance encounter. At night, unless during thunderstorms, the loudest ordinary sounds came from the owls, which many slaves had learned to imitate. Rarely, more at night than at day, one could hear howling wolves and the responsive baying

2. Not surprisingly, John James Audubon included birds in his remarks about "Natchez in 1820." He remarked on the "White-headed eagle," the "Fishing Hawk," the "Carrion Crow," and "Vultures," the latter without using the word *buzzard*. He reserved comment on ornithological sounds to "our deservedly famed Mocking Bird" which "sang and danced gratis to every passer by." John James Audubon, *Delineations of American Scenery and Character*, intro. Francis Hobart Herrick (1926; rpr. [New York], 1970), 332–34. Yet there were still wild turkeys in the woods near the swamplands bordering the river, though probably few slaves heard or saw them: see Jenkins Diary, December 19, 1851.

from the hounds. A very few panthers still ranged the wilder reaches of the county, their screams sounding (as an elderly Mississippian remembers them) "like an old woman being murdered in the woods."[3]

In the evenings during the picking season, the loudest noises came from the steam-driven cotton gins, though there were few of them in the county.[4] The scraping, thumping, and hissing of those machines could be heard a long way away. Many plantations did not use steam power at all. Even the sounds of household living were different from today. Neither slave nor master knew the humming and burring of electric appliances, or the far sweeter sound of water splashing from a faucet or a toilet tank. Slaves had all grown up with the crackling of fireplaces, and some had heard the same noise muffled in the stove of the big-house kitchen. In the cabins of the quarter, or "street," the wobbly wooden doors and windows creaked and banged when moved by the wind or by human or canine agency. Wood spoons scraped quietly against iron kettles as well as wooden and earthenware bowls, even though on some plantations the youngsters were slopped outdoors without utensils at a common trough. If there were stools or even chairs in the cabins, their scraping was nearly noiseless on dirt floors but resonant where the board flooring was raised off the ground. When the wind was up, it whistled in the chimney, in the cracks around the planked window and door, and through the shingles of the roof and the chinks between the boards or logs of the ceiling and walls. At night the dried corn shucks in mattresses made dried-corn-shuck sounds under the movement of human bodies.

The human sounds in the neighborhood of course varied so

3. General conversation with a group of older white men in a café, Oxford, Miss., October 3, 1983. The description must actually have long been a folk commonplace: in the 1830s the scream was "like a female in the death-struggle from sudden violence" in James R. Creecy, *Scenes in the South and Other Miscellaneous Pieces* (Washington, D.C., 1860), 93. In Mississippi (and in the Deep South generally) the large, widely ranged *Felis concolor* was known as a panther (in some localities pronounced "painter"); elsewhere the same animal has been called a cougar, cantamount, mountain lion, and puma. Unlike the Old World leopard or panther (*Felis panthera pardus*), it has no black phase (chiefly Asian rather than African), and hence could not serve as an exact model for the name of either the Alabama or national political organizations of the 1960s. It is now extinct in Mississippi except for several defanged pets and in the Jackson zoo.

4. "Evening" is still often defined in Mississippi as the period between the midday meal and the last one of the day, after which comes "night."

widely that they cannot be adequately conveyed by the standard written words even of the local dialects of the British American and Afro-American English languages.[5] There is always difficulty in rendering human sounds on paper. Our attempts to do so seem contrived, as with *ahem*s, *ouche*s, and *harrumph*s, and even with rational commands to draft animals such as *gee, haw,* and *whoa.* There is even difficulty with such a standard southern word as *y'all* (variously spelled), the exceedingly useful rendering of the second-person-plural pronoun that is no longer so much a contraction as a single word. All such terms fail to impart the exact weight of meaning they actually carry. And, of course, human sounds generated under conditions of great psychic and physical intensity lie beyond the scope of our standard vocabulary. It is not possible fully to convey the sounds a man or woman may make under the lash.

We can fully understand words and other sounds only if we ascertain their context. This truism is particularly applicable to the expressions that serve as much of the evidence about the historical episode that is the focus of this study. They need to be considered not only in their very specific social contexts, but also within the wider realms of plantation slavery, race relations, and prevailing religious, family, and political values and practices in the Second Creek area of Adams County, Mississippi, in particular, and in the southern United States as a thoroughly variegated whole. How else are we to interpret the name of a person who seems to have played a crucial role in the affair, "Mas Benny"? Yet this par-

5. This statement assumes that Mississippi slaves of that era did not speak standard English. Yet there is no evidence to suggest problems of intelligibility between the races. The speech of whites was far from uniform, for the region had been settled by the Natchez Indians, who were displaced by the French, and then by Anglo- and Celtic-Americans and a much smaller number of Choctaw Americans, as well more recently by Irish and Germans. Nor did Mississippi African Americans have a completely standardized pattern of speech. Most Adams County slaves were immigrants or the children, grandchildren, or great-grandchildren of immigrants from various older southern states. They may have spoken much like the blacks of eastern Virginia, since many had come from that region. Social, historical, and demographic circumstances had combined to prevent development of an English-based creole language of their own, such as happened especially in the South Carolina and Georgia low country and in such areas as British-dominated Jamaica and Surinam.

ticular Plan needs also to be viewed in broader contexts still, as an episode in the opening of the American Civil War, during the waning Jacksonian-*cum*-mid-Victorian period of the history of the United States, and as an instance of conflict between bound laborers and their owners, a species of conflict that of course was never restricted to New World racial slavery but has characterized the relationship between agricultural workers and landowners, between rural oppressors and oppressed, throughout the history of much of the entire world.

All the evidence specifically bearing on the Plan itself comes to us in written form, unless one counts as evidence the significant *absence* of any currently accessible oral traditions about the affair. For the descendants of the whites involved in the Second Creek affair, a curtain seems to have been drawn long ago. At least three lineal descendants of planters who owned rebel slaves do not now recall ever having heard any word about the conspiracy or the hangings that followed. It is virtually certain that nothing was passed down to them even in the most guarded or sweetened terms. Admittedly, the tragedy took place 130 years ago, but events of such huge magnitude in a small locality might easily have created a persistent even if sotto voce oral tradition among aristocratic people who possessed and still retain a powerful sense and actual knowledge of family history. Their great-grandparents had good reason—more so than the slaves—to draw an opaque and impermeable veil across what they regarded as a troubling, even tragic, affliction much more than a triumph.

As for the descendants of the slaves involved, there may very well exist old family traditions about the awful affair. If they do indeed exist, they have probably been altered considerably as they have been transmitted through generations of memory and recapitulation. Today they may in fact be more common in Chicago than in Adams County; put less narrowly, a great many blacks have left the county and Natchez for other parts of the United States and even for other parts of Mississippi. And there are great difficulties for anyone, black or white, making inquiries about such a sensitive matter. It is impossible to ask questions about the Second Creek Plan without first providing information about it, information that is bound to elicit either ignorance of the matter, deliberate denial, fanciful elaboration, or a complete reversal of roles between interviewer and interviewee. In any case, as will be seen with Charlie Davenport in 1937, the mists of time can thicken to dense fog as the years go by, and we are left to deal with evidence that has to be read rather than heard. Still, we must listen, as we do when we hear from someone by letter.

When considered today, the written evidence appears to be of two kinds. Some was originally written at the time, rather than spoken, with the intention of its being read rather than literally heard. With the private letters, the presumptive readers were the addressed recipients and perhaps also their relatives, friends, and in the case of government officials, other government officials. Of course, such letters may have been heard—that is, read aloud to third and fourth parties at the time. They may also have been, in more recent times, read silently or aloud by persons not a part of their intended audience, especially descendants of the original recipients, holograph collectors, archivists, historians, and readers of this book. There is nothing in any of these letters to suggest that they were written with posterity in mind. As with most of the evidence in this affair, we are eavesdropping.[6]

With diaries the case is somewhat different and more problematical. As written documents they were usually composed for the eyes of the writer. Yet some of them were aimed also toward other living individuals, descendants, and/or posterity in general. Of the diaries pertinent here, one can only say that they clearly were not recorded with posterity uppermost in mind. The Second Creek area had no Mary Boykin Chesnut.[7]

Another possible kind of written voice from the past was in this instance silent. Many newspapers were being published at the time, including the *Courier* and the *Free Trader* in Natchez. Given the nature and customary practices of mid-nineteenth-century American newspapers, one would scarcely expect stories based on interviews with participants or even with indirect observers of the Plan.[8] Yet contemporary newspapers did not even

6. Another genre of "private" letters, not directly pertinent here, are those dictated to an amanuensis or read aloud by him. See the remarkable correspondence between William S. Pettigrew and his two slave overseers, Moses and Henry, carried on through a semiliterate white man, in Pettigrew Family Papers, UNC, and widely quoted in a variety of modern works.

7. C. Vann Woodward, ed., *Mary Chesnut's Civil War* (New Haven, 1981). Prior to this edition, published versions of her "diary" did not make clear that she very consciously drafted it for publication.

8. Though the requisite technology existed, there are no extant photographs (so far as I can determine) of *anything* in the rural portions of Adams County at that time, not even one of a great house. There are, however, formal paintings of a few of the white slaveholders indirectly involved. Mrs. Charles H. McNeil kindly showed me several of her Surget family portraits. A photograph *ca.* 1860 of a street

hint about it, allude to it, let alone discuss it. The reasons for this silence are sufficiently obvious. Fighting against a powerful enemy had already begun. Southern planters, and indeed white southerners generally, had to no wish to see word of serious slave discontent spread across the pages of the nation's press. They knew perfectly well that if either of the Natchez newspapers published anything on the subject, it would soon be picked up and flaunted in such papers as Horace Greeley's *Tribune* in New York City.

For whites, several considerations urged complete silence in the local press. One was fear of bolstering morale in the North. Many white southerners would not admit the fact, but most white northerners would have condemned the conspiracy. On the other hand, northern public opinion would have welcomed any sign of weakness in the Confederacy. Another consideration was internal, and thus even more disturbing. For more than a generation defenders of slavery—and now proponents of the southern nation—had contended publicly with apparent great conviction that blacks were naturally servile and content in their bondage. Contented people could not be perceived as seething in rebellion, not publicly or actually even if they really were. A third line of thinking was not so important as might be supposed. A few slaves could read, and any interesting disclosures in the newspapers would be rapidly passed along. Yet the planters knew that important news spread rapidly by word of mouth in their society. They recognized, at times, that their own conversations had a way of passing from the dinner table to the quarters. They were aware that their servants did not have to rely on written documents to discover what was going on, and that newspapers did not circulate easily (to say the least) among their work force. For slaves, possession of such documents was both dangerous and unnecessary.

It was for these reasons that a white women wrote in a private letter about the affair, "It is kept very still, not to be in the papers. . . . don't speak of it only cautiously."[9]

in Natchez-Under-the-Hill is in D. Clayton James, *Antebellum Natchez* (Baton Rouge, 1968), opp. p. 179. See also David G. Sansing, Sim C. Callon, and Carolyn Vance Smith, *Natchez: An Illustrated History* (Natchez, 1992).

9. S[ophia] H. Hunt to Jennie [Hughes], October 15, 1861, in Hughes Family Papers, UNC, Document I. Such thinking was not new. Concerning a plot by some Virginia slaves to link up with British troops should hostilities break out, James Madison had written, "It is prudent such attempts should be concealed as well as

In addition to the silence in the press, there were also no political speeches, official messages, or pamphlets about the Plan, such as there had been after Gabriel's, Vesey's, and Turner's. The Mississippi legislature passed no laws aimed at preventing repetition of the events, or any acts of financial compensation to the owners of the executed slaves. More than anything, this silence in the *public* record explains why historians have not included the Adams County plot in their customarily rather standardized brief catalogs of American Negro slave revolts and conspiracies.

A final principal category of written voices from Second Creek in 1861 consists of those that were originally spoken so as to be heard rather than read. For differing and sometimes puzzling reasons they were written down at the time or shortly after they were spoken. In every case here (though it is not the only conceivable one) the words were set to paper by someone other than the speaker. In turn, such documents can gather accretions through time, as when a lineal descendant of Lemuel P. Conner wrote a covering note on the most important document—Conner's record of some of the examinations—addressed to her children and urging them to save it. In a chronologically more contemporaneous passage, a Union army officer wrote down the gist of his conversation with a white woman about the suppression of the Plan, three years after it had taken place. More immediately still, two gentlemen wrote to the governor about hearing of a slave plot in Jefferson County while it was still being exposed. Almost certainly their information came to them by word of mouth rather than in writing, although then as today one could "hear" from someone in writing as well as by oral communication.

The central document, Lemuel Conner's written record of what some slaves said, or did not say, at some of the examinations, is crucial to our learning something about what went on at Second Creek. Without it there could not be even a partially coherent story. If we relied solely on all the other evidence, we would be left knowing little more than that the white people of the Second Creek neighborhood thought they were having serious difficulties with some of their slaves in the year 1861.

On its face, Conner's document is straightforward. It is printed in two forms in the Appendixes to this volume, first as a literal

---

suppressed." Madison to William Bradford, November 26, 1774, in *The Papers of James Madison*, ed. William T. Hutchinson *et al.* (17 vols.; Chicago and Charlottesville, Va., 1962–91), I, 129–30.

transcription and then in somewhat augmented form. It appears to be a verbatim transcript of answers given by some slaves to queries about a planned revolt against their masters. It is undated, but it furnishes more information about the thoughts and aims of a group of rebel slaves than any other single document in American history. As such it deserves informed and careful reading. We need to keep steadily in mind what we have here: the central document is a written record, produced by a white planter in his own handwriting, of what he thought he heard some slaves say under unusual and extremely stressful circumstances. We are not listening to these slaves directly but rather through the ears and hand of an individual who (aside from the fact that he was also a human being) was emphatically not one of them.

CHAPTER 3

OF WATER, LAND, AND WORK

The Plan began while several of the Mosby and Mitchell boys were fishing down at the creek on a Sunday early in May. Except during heavy rains and much rarer snowstorms, the banks of upper Second Creek stood only some fifteen to twenty feet apart. In most places the low-lying edges of the stream were so well watered that one had to scuff or trample the tall grass and plants in order to find a place to sit for pole fishing. The water in the creek was an almost rusty brown, bearing the color of the higher hills at a distance on the eastern side and the lower ones on the west. Years earlier, perhaps three generations before, the stream had been so clear that on the brightest days its few unshaded stretches appeared nearly to match the brilliant blue of the sky. That was before all the plowing had been pushed onto the hills. Now it looked downright muddy. Like any silted stream, it had few good fording places, not ones that would solidly brace a horse's hoof or the wide wheels of a wagon or a carriage. Yet it remained more a hindrance than a barrier to travel, and one could talk across it easily. Despite its color, it was still clean enough for the bottom-dwelling catfish to thrive, and even for people to drink.

From the large bend near where the men were sitting, Second Creek slowly ambled southward into the Homochitto River, which in turn emptied into the Mississippi some twenty miles to the southwest. Because the Homochitto originated in a less friable geological formation many miles to the east, it was a clearer stream. At low water it showed its huge, shifting white sandbars, but was usually sufficiently deep to permit shallow-draft steamboats to carry cotton down to the real river for shipment to New Orleans.

The Homochitto—supposedly "red-big" in the Choctaw language—was broad and deep enough to have a regular ferry.[1] Like

1. George R. Stewart, *American Place Names: A Concise and Selective Dictionary for the Continental United States of America* (New York, 1970), 209; Frederick Law Olmsted, *A Journey in the Back Country* (New York, 1860), 25; Springfield Plantation Account Book, Vol. I, *passim*, in John A. Quitman Papers, MDAH.

other arteries in the region it also had snag problems, and both slave and free laborers were worked at clearing fallen trees and branches from the channel. It was not an easy job to pull a large fallen tree out of the shifting muck, especially if the tree was still rooted in the bank. Some slaves were forced to this toil, and they worked alongside white laborers. Usually the principal source of power was a team of oxen. The knowledge of effective techniques with ropes, pulleys, and chains came from the men who had somehow to do the job. Many of these same men were used during harvest to drive wagon teams to Natchez. It is no wonder that the phrase "Homochitto teamsters" came out at the trials, almost as if these men were a breed apart.[2]

The Homochitto River appears today on retrospective maps as a "navigable" waterway, a concept that appeals more readily to mapmakers than it did to shallow-draft-steamboat captains, who knew from experience that stretches with a clear channel one week might well not have one the next.[3] By contrast, Second Creek could normally float only rowboats or little rafts. It was, however, one of the places where the Plan began, when Nelson (Mosby) and some other slaves were down there fishing on that Sunday in mid-spring.

The low hills of Adams County rolled along as slowly and gently as the water in the creek. John James Audubon called the land "gently undulated." In the very western portions of the county, though, marshes formed a barrier parallel to the Mississippi River. Some of that land, known locally as Butler's Swamp or simply as "the Swamp," was under cultivation, but the farms there were small, and the constantly spreading and receding

2. In one sense the term *trial* is not entirely appropriate, as will become clear, but in another it certainly was. As will later become apparent, some people used the term at the time, especially one of the victims.

3. Alan Dee Morrison, *The American South: Historical Atlas* (3 vols; Athens, Ohio, 1965), Vol. III, Pt. 2, map 570, shows navigable rivers. A generation earlier, a company had been formed for clearing the river, enabled by a general act of the state legislature: see Company Commissioners to Gov. Gerard C. Brandon, October 22, 1831, in Gerard C. Brandon Papers, MDAH. Cypress logs that would have immediately jammed in the creek could be floated down the Homochitto: see B. L. C. Wailes, *Report on the Agriculture and Geology of Mississippi, Embracing a Sketch of the Social and Natural History of the State* ([Jackson], 1854), 347–48. The potability of Second Creek is suggested but not certain in Jenkins Diary, July 29, 1851. Ten years later, on hot days, it may well have been thought foul but drinkable. In fact it may have been bacterially dangerous for years, but no one at the time would have known. The usual source of drinking water for everyone at Second Creek was a cistern.

patches of standing water were large enough to support a flourishing population of alligators.[4] It is doubtful that many Second Creek slaves had ever seen the great river except perhaps on a visit to Natchez.

On the hills, many of the trees had long since been felled for the plow. In some spots, found too steep for cultivation, new stands were struggling upward, competing for the sun with creeping and climbing vines and knots of bushes and grasses. Yet the easier slopes were still given over to cotton and corn and to other, less important crops such as peas, beans, watermelons, orchard fruits, sweet potatoes, various "greens," and sorghum cane. There were still forested acres left, and in the mid-1830s an English traveler had found "the country beautifully diversified; a succession of hill and dale, with timber trees of the noblest kind" and the "magnolia grandiflora . . . in groves absolutely, and . . . forty to fifty feet high." But even by the time of his visit some of the steeper grounds were bare of greenery and scarred with gullies, having long since lost their protective blankets of vegetation. An Episcopal clergyman from Maine who settled in the county in those same years described the appearance of the land in very different terms. "Every plough-furrow," he wrote, "becomes the bed of a rivulet after heavy rains. . . . By degrees, acre after acre, of what was a few years previous beautifully undulating ground, waving with the dark green, snow-crested cotton, presents a wild scene of frightful precipices, and yawning chasms." He went on to note, "There are many thousand acres within twenty miles of the city of Natchez . . . which are now lying in this condition, presenting an appearance of wild desolation, and not unfrequently," he added with fine Victorian literary flourish, "of sublimity."[5]

4. John James Audubon, *Delineations of American Scenery and Character,* intro. Francis Hobart Herrick (1926; rpr. [New York], 1970), 332–33. Hunting and farming in the Swamp were described in the 1830s and 1840s by an active participant: see *Johnson's Diary, passim.*

5. Tyrone Power, *Impressions of America; During the Years 1833, 1834, and 1835* (2d American ed., 2 vols.; Philadelphia, 1836), II, 112; [Joseph Holt Ingraham], *The South-West. By a Yankee* (2 vols.; 1835; rpr. Ann Arbor, 1966), II, 87. See also Wailes, *Report on the Agriculture and Geology of Mississippi,* 198. Even more than the playwright Power, Ingraham was a man of literary aspirations: he went on to write several novels as well as a book of magnolia-drenched "letters" purportedly "edited" by Ingraham, *The Sunny South; or, The Southerner at Home, Embracing Five Years' Experience of a Northern Governess . . .* (1860; rpr. New York, 1968). Its account of Natchez and Adams County reflects little besides his having adopted residence there and his determination to show that Mrs. Stowe's *Uncle Tom's Cabin* had things all wrong.

The great majority of visitors to Natchez first saw Adams County from the river, though some hardy travelers did come up from New Orleans by road or from the North down the Natchez Trace. In the 1830s a northern woman aboard a steamboat pushing slowly up from New Orleans was struck by the "cotton trees" (cottonwoods) lining the banks above Fort Adams, not far upstream from the Wilkinson County line. From the river, Adams County below Natchez did not look very grand, since the planting country was several miles inland. "The fine plantations that have all along appeared so beautiful," she wrote, "begin to be exchanged for wild forests, here and there broken by a new settlement, with its log cabins, and—long piles of wood." She went on to describe the "astonishing" speed with which this carefully chopped fuel was placed on board. The wood had been cut by slaves or by white workmen, but the transfer was done by "the deck passengers, of whom it is expected as part of the consideration for their passage." Only the ladies and the (other) cabin passengers enjoyed complete leisure as the steamboat challenged the river.[6]

The planting neighborhood along Second Creek was a mere corner of the vast Mississippi drainage basin, and it was totally invisible from the great river. Every rainfall in that corner contributed real estate to southern Louisiana, courtesy of Second Creek, the Homochitto, and the Father of Waters. Geologically, the Gulf of Mexico was the residual legatee of Adams County, Mississippi, as well as of more than a thousand other counties across the nation from New York State to what would soon become the Montana and Wyoming territories.[7]

Adams was the only county in the entire South named for the first president from Massachusetts, an irony that might have been thought an affront in South Carolina but was a mere historical

6. Jane North Lewis Travel Diary, 1835–1836, p. 13, in John M. Bishop Collection, Indiana Historical Society, Indianapolis. Nancy Hendershot kindly provided this reference. Lengthy descriptions of travel on river steamboats were more commonly written going upriver than down.

7. Redrawing of Territorial boundaries suddenly became common in the years from 1861, when the South no longer had much influence in Congress. They are readily followed in Charles O. Paullin, *Atlas of the Historical Geography of the United States*, ed. John K. Wright (Baltimore, 1932), plates 64, A, B, C.

circumstance in Mississippi. Until nearly 1820 it had been the foremost cotton-producing county in the state. During the next decade it lost ground to newer counties northward in the areas around Vicksburg and east to Jackson. The long-term trend was not merely relative, since Adams produced fewer bales in 1860 than it had in 1820. Still, the Adams County lands remained productive, and the plantations much larger than most in the cotton South.[8] Adams was the seat of what by Old Southwest standards was an old aristocracy. As late as the 1830s the value of its lands was greater than in any other county in the state. A more telling indicator was the disproportionate value (on the tax lists) of its "pleasure Carriages"—disproportionately high not only relative to land values, but even more so in relation to the size of the white population.[9]

Most of the enormous sums of money generated by the cotton plantations went into buying more lands and more Negroes, but some went into construction of elegant mansions in Natchez and its outskirts. Natchez was the county seat, a historic town with an important port that was nationally notorious as a den of iniquity. Despite its widespread reputation, with a total population of 6,600 in 1860, Natchez was not among the 102 of the nation's cities and towns that numbered over 10,000 (the smallest of which was Waterbury, Connecticut).[10] Yet it was the center of an important region and the focal point of some of the oldest monied fortunes in the new cotton South. It may actually have been true that, as some said, Natchez had more millionaires than any city in the country.

The town remained an important center of the domestic slave trade. Mississippi's most important slave depot stood on the eastern outskirts of town at the Forks of the Road, but that mart served much more as a way station for slaves headed for other parts of the state and across the river than for local trading. Though there was still some local buying and selling, the county's

8. The largest plantations of all were in coastal South Carolina and Georgia, under long-staple cotton and rice, and in southern Louisiana, which was sugar country. There are extremely helpful maps pertaining to many matters in this chapter in Sam Bowers Hilliard, *Atlas of Antebellum Southern Agriculture* (Baton Rouge, 1984): see esp. maps no. 49–53.

9. A table of tax evaluations by county and category of wealth is in *Journal of the Senate of . . . Mississippi, at an Adjourned Meeting Thereof . . .* (Jackson, 1837), 23–24.

10. The list is in U.S. Bureau of the Census, *Statistics of the United States . . . in 1860 . . . Eighth Census . . .* (Washington, D.C., 1866), xviii–xix.

plantations were already well stocked with human merchandise, and the black population of the county as a whole was statistically more likely to be Adams-born than was the white.[11]

Natchez boasted (as it did not about the slave mart) numerous conspicuously elegant dwellings, if that humble word may be used in connection with the pillared mansions that graced the town and in a real sense dominated it more than the courthouse, the Episcopal and Presbyterian churches, and the several hotels. Many of these houses were on the outskirts of the old part of town, which itself was divided in two. Low down, on the river itself, was a narrow strip of shops, warehouses, wharfs, tippling establishments, and brothels known locally and throughout the great valley as Natchez-under-the-Hill, a name inevitably shortened by certain classes of people to "Natchy-under-hill."[12] Its lifeline was the river, and a good part of its heavily male population literally floated in and out. It was a mecca for boatmen. For the respectable, it was a way station to and from the central grid of streets laid out high on the bluff above, sometimes called (with half-intentional duality of meaning) "Natchez proper."

Much of the center of the town, with its many offices, hotels, stores, shops, banks, stables, houses, and apartments, its churches, markethouse, courthouse, and jail, its fenced yards, chicken coops, sties, cisterns, and privies, had been rebuilt after the disastrous tornado of 1840. In addition to destroying many

11. The importance of Natchez as a slave-trading center is clear in Frederic Bancroft, *Slave Trading in the Old South* (1931; rpr. New York, 1959), 304–309, but the ultimate destinations are not, and the only one mentioned is Waterproof, in Concordia Parish. The mart was earlier described, almost romantically, in [Ingraham], *South-West*, II, 192–204. Later it was more matter-of-factly portrayed by Isaac Stier, who was born a slave next to the "Montgomery place" in Jefferson County, partly as being where his father had been traded when he had arrived from Tennessee: see Rawick, *American Slave*, Vol. VII (Okla. and Miss. Narrs.), Pt. 2, pp. 143–44. In 1902, Bancroft interviewed an elderly lawyer who had been adjunct to the trading and who described huge gangs and three large buildings at the Forks. This William T. Martin was the man who in 1877 made the somewhat doubtful claim of having bought sabers to meet insurrectionary threats as early as 1860 (see chap. 1). The statistical conclusion is drawn from more general demographic sources. The nature of the interstate slave trade has been greatly clarified by Michael Tadman, *Speculators and Slaves: Masters, Traders, and Slaves in the Old South* (Madison, Wisc., 1989).

12. Not surprisingly, the less formal version was rarely used in written descriptions, but see Power, *Impressions of America*, II, 113. An interesting description of the town is in Edwin B. Bronner, ed., "A Philadelphia Quaker Visits Natchez, 1847," *JSH*, XXVII (1961), 518–19.

brick and board buildings, that storm had ripped out the beautiful China trees that had lined the main streets. At night these streets were lighted only by flickering shafts cast from windows, portable torches, and an occasional celebratory bonfire—except on those disastrous occasions, common then in many towns and cities, when fire swept through entire buildings and even whole blocks. The rectilinear thoroughfares, and even the sidewalks, in the center of town were surfaced with gravel, and they sometimes became so dusty that they were wet down by order of the town authorities. Alleys and outlying streets and lanes tended to become either dusty or muddy, since the soil was so friable. Everyone was accustomed to stepping carefully, of course, with an eye out for animal ploppings.

Apart from its myriad commercial activities, Natchez had several schools, an orphan asylum, several Masonic lodges, and other "cultural" organizations. The five best-established church denominations were Episcopal and Presbyterian (the two wealthiest), Methodist, Baptist, and Roman Catholic. The latter served the more devout of the town's foreign-born residents, who made up a third of the population and were mainly German and (especially) Irish. Though the two newspapers were read widely beyond the limits of the town, the Democratic *Free Trader* had a subscription list three times as large as the Whig *Courier*'s, since the town itself had been heartily for Andrew Jackson and his less monumental successors.

Natchez had a decidedly male tone. Indeed, in 1860 only about 40 percent of its residents were female. Favorite entertainments included the traveling circuses, which were thrilling to everyone, and there were touring singers and a steady diet of horse racing at the track on the east edge of town, where the aristocracy pitted their famous horses against one another and where even men of modest means could enter their nags in secondary contests with much less money at stake.[13] Betting was endemic—wagers were made on every conceivable variable, from the results of the many target-shooting contests to the sex of foals, from the arrival times of steamboats to (very much most especially) the outcomes of elections. Elections per se drew most attention when national

13. Horse racing was referred to frequently in *Johnson's Diary.* Earlier the clerical visitor from Maine wrote that "the planter's character . . . will never be perfectly understood until he is seen, booted and spurred, with his pocket-book in one hand, and bank bills fluttering in the other, moving about upon the turf." [Ingraham], *South-West,* II, 220.

candidates such as William Henry Harrison or Zachary Taylor had appeared in town, but the betting went on with or without the stimulus of visiting celebrities, and there were enough electoral contests to satisfy gamesmen of all classes and colors. National and state races drew little more attention than local elections, including those of such various officials as judges and road inspectors. Militia musters were as much social gatherings as drills, and membership in the Guards and the Fencibles was dominated by the aristocrats. So, too, were the balls, where there really were iced drinks and crinolined belles. Since most of Adams County's free blacks lived in the town, there were also "darkey balls," which the respected and successful free mulatto barber, William Johnson, carefully noted in his famous diary but could not lower himself to attend.

One of the most striking aspects of that diary, apart from its abrupt termination when Johnson was murdered by a man of disputed race in 1851, is the appalling level of violence in the town. Gentlemen sometimes went across the river for formal duels, since dueling was illegal in the state. But horrendous fights took place all over town, under the Hill of course (where they often went unrecorded), but also in hotel bars, in the streets, even on the steps of the courthouse. Lawyers were not above biting and gouging, whipping and shooting, in the wake of incautious words exchanged in the courtroom. Men were maimed and killed in these fights. Sometimes someone was convicted of a crime, and sometimes not; many murders went unsolved or unprosecuted. As for legal punishments, whipping was normally reserved for blacks, slave and free, but there was a jail and even a state penitentiary. The level of violence was not regarded as unusually high. Yet for a town of that size, there was (by today's standards) a great deal of mayhem.

About one-third of the people of Adams County lived in Natchez. The contrast between town and county was so great that a majority of Adams County whites actually lived in Natchez, and whereas the county as a whole (including the town) was about three-quarters black, the rural portions were overwhelmingly black and slave. The county as a whole had by far the largest number of free blacks in the state, but nearly all were residents of the town itself.[14] Though the aristocracy owned Natchez financially

14. D. Clayton James, *Antebellum Natchez* (Baton Rouge, 1968), 163; Joseph C. G. Kennedy, comp., *Population of the United States in 1860; Compiled from the Original Returns of the Eighth Census . . .* (Washington, D.C., 1864), 267. Of the county's 225 free blacks, 208 lived in Natchez.

and dominated it visually, their strength lay in the county, especially in the suburbs and the richer portions like Second Creek valley. There, amid their masses of slaves and servants, they reigned in supposedly unquestioned supremacy over a world of plantations.

That spring, before the Plan began, the fields in the county had already been fresh plowed and planted. The grounds around the cabins and outbuildings had also been turned with plows and heavy hoes and set with the customary variety of vegetables. Both of the really important field crops were nearly knee high, the corn already shooting out leaves and the cotton stalks tall enough for thinning.[15]

Cotton was planted in rows, the seeds pressed into the soil with the foot, but so thickly that later the shorter shoots had to be chopped out. In that region, "cutting out cotton"—the thinning process sometimes called "scraping"—ordinarily took place in early May and lasted for about two weeks. It has relevance to our understanding of the timing of what went on, as well as what slaves were forced to do. Today the procedure is obsolete, since modern seeding machines and improved seeds permit nearly automatic spacing of successful plants.

By the middle of August, before the steaming heat of the summer months began almost imperceptibly to recede, both corn and cotton began to ripen. Corn first. There are scores of accounts by former slaves throughout the South about the joy of the corn-shuckings, usually at night with music. Such recollections did not attach to bringing in the cotton crop—a longer, more continual, and harder job that had a different connotation for all concerned. Since the cornfields had been planted at staggered times, gathering could seem to have no end, what with picking, hauling, pulling fodder, shucking, pounding the kernels, and cooking in various ways. Yet corn was food, the mainstay food. For slaves, cotton was not even indirectly edible.

But from late August until nearly Christmas the cotton fields billowed with their white foam. It had to be picked—not a matter of simply pulling, but of carefully extracting the small-fist-sized blossoms of fibers from their stubbornly grasping brown leaves.

15. The same planter whose diary noted the Jefferson County episode, Benjamin L. C. Wailes, had earlier produced his fine, quasi-official *Report on the Agriculture and Geology of Mississippi*, which is still very useful.

Both hands had to be used, and the stalks and stiff sharp leaves tore on the fingers. It had to be done while dragging a canvas or burlap sack by a long shoulder loop. The contents of the bag had to be emptied into large baskets at the ends of the rows. Some fields had to be picked over twice. Always things *had* to be done.

Sometimes at midday and always at the end of every picking day on most plantations, every slave's gatherings were weighed, often by torchlight, and inspected for "trash." That term, which already had negative connotations when applied to human beings, included mainly leaves, stalks, and dirt (not stones as in many parts of the South because the soil of the Second Creek valley was primarily windblown loess). In this case what we might consider to be detritus, everyone at the time regarded as significant evidence of human behavior. Probably more slaves in the Deep South were whipped for "picking trashy cotton" than for "running away," which was the other customary reason for standard punishment.[16]

Before turning to the plans of some Second Creek slaves to overturn this regimen, it would be well to look more closely at what these slaves ordinarily *did*, which at least in terms of hours, week after week, year after year, was chiefly to perform forced agricultural labor. Recently, historians have emphasized both the joyous and grieving "cultural" activities of American slaves, such as dances, games, storytelling, and musical and religious exercises both celebratory and funereal. Slaves did indeed carve out something of an independent life for themselves, including quarreling and making love, but it is important to bear in mind that their main exertions went into very long hours of very hard work. This work became routine, but of course underlying the routine— at its very bedrock—was the ever-present element of force and violence. For many years historians have known a great deal about the general outlines of those rounds of labor as they prevailed in various parts of the slave South.

Fortunately, it is possible to scan the annual work cycle as it operated on one of the Second Creek planting units. A "plantation

16. In 1854, Wailes, in *Report on the Agriculture and Geology of Mississippi*, 154, wrote that on Mississippi cotton plantations cotton from the fields was weighed at noon and at night. Weighing times were not recorded at Aventine; the practice may have been less general than he thought.

diary," kept by two overseers seriatim in 1857 and 1859, affords details about the agricultural work at Aventine, very near but not bordering on the creek itself. As we listen for the sounds of those men and women and children at work, we need to keep in mind that the written record has had its own particular quirks of generation and preservation, and as always we need to exercise care in translating such a document.

With marvelous fortuity, the annual cycle of work on cotton plantations coincided with the calendar year. It was the nature-bound timing of the principal crop that made the week from Christmas to New Year's a holiday for so many slaves, and the beginning of January the start of the overseers' contractual annual hiring and commitment (though some contracts ran only from month to month). Thanks to the businesslike temperament of the owner of Aventine Plantation, it is possible to follow that cycle as it was recorded for a single Second Creek plantation in 1857 and 1859—years that were notable there (for the owner and management at least) mainly for the high price of cotton.[17]

Gabriel B. Shields was the wealthiest of four sons of the prominent and wealthy William Dunbar Shields, who had come from Delaware and risen to a position on the first supreme court of the state. Gabriel had only recently bought (or been given) Aventine, for it had previously belonged to his father-in-law. He did not live there, but Aventine steadily furnished supplies to Montebello, Gabriel's homeplace in the southeastern suburbs of Natchez.[18] Major Gabriel Shields was the sort of man who was referred to in different ways by different people and on different occasions. He appears in historical records variously as Mr. Shields, Major Shields, Gabriel B. Shields, G. B. Shields, Esq., and even Gabe Shields.

No matter how much he was open or subject to casual informality, Shields laid down strict requirements for his overseers at

17. Aventine Plantation Diary, 1857–59, in MDAH. The extant manuscript has daily entries by Patrick Francis McGovern, January 13, 1857–January 23, 1858, and by Charles Sauters, January 3–December 31, 1859. The latter concludes with some summary lists, including an account of supplies purchased for the year, a record of visits by the doctor, and a list of the slaves' names and clothing dated May 1, 1859. The earlier Jenkins Diary is also useful but less informative about the labor of slaves. For cotton prices, John Hebron Moore, *Agriculture in Ante-Bellum Mississippi* (1958; rpr. New York, 1971), 179–80.

18. See the plantation map, pp. 122–23. The term *suburb* perhaps sounds anachronistic, but it was used at the time, as in [Ingraham], *South-West*, II, 74.

Aventine.[19] The man he employed was expected to keep an exact record of the work done there, at any neighboring plantations, and on the public roads, as well as lists of purchases made, crops produced, livestock and poultry, special punishments, sick slaves, and doctor's visits. He was also expected to record the to-ing and fro-ing of anyone, white or black, who crossed the plantation's boundaries for visiting or (more usually) for purposes of work. Shields demanded a daily record of what was going on, together with a cumulative accounting of the amount of cotton picked, ginned, and baled. Evidently this record was sent to him on a somewhat regular basis, carried by a slave from Second Creek to Montebello. Gabriel Shields or his brother Thomas sometimes came by at Aventine, but not with any regularity.

Given these requirements, Aventine was a tightly run operation. The overseers called the roll of slaves daily. Each Sunday they carefully noted having that day called it three times—a highly unusual practice in the South. On March 13, 1859, for example, Charles Sauters made his nearly rote weekly notation: "Roll called 3 times, quarter and yard cleaned out every morning, clean clothes put on Monday and Thursday." Many Sabbath entries included "bed clothes aired."

The beds of course were in the cabins in the quarter, and nearly the only descriptive data about slave housing in the Second Creek area come from Aventine. They are not informative. The roofs were reshingled by slave carpenters in September, 1859. One of the slaves there recalled that "our houses wuz clean en snug."[20] If each was a single cabin and not atypical of the cotton South, it was the size of a modern middle-class living room. A sixteen-by-eighteen-foot cabin would have been a bit more spacious than average in the South, and it might be a mistake to assume that greater wealth in Adams County led to larger cabins, especially on absentee plantations. Some large cotton-belt plantations had

19. At least he was absentee as of the fall of 1861: Adams Land, 1861. He may have had a home built there shortly thereafter, since the Aventine Plantation Diary refers to slaves working on a pond on the "big house lot," though there was (at least as yet) no big house there: July 4, 5, 6, 7, 1859. By Second Creek standards, Aventine was relatively large with assessed acreage of 1,142. For the Shields family: Mary Conway Shields Dunbar, *My Mother Used to Say: A Natchez Belle of the Sixties*, ed. Elizabeth Dunbar Murray (Boston, 1959), 79–80.

20. Aventine Plantation Diary, September 14–16, 1859; Rawick, *American Slave*, Vol. VII (Okla. and Miss. Narrs.), Pt. 2, p. 36, and Suppl. 1, Vol. VII (Miss. Narrs.), p. 560, Documents Y and Z.

double cabins, with a shared chimney in the middle or one at each end of the structure. Less common still were cabins with lofts or more than two rooms. Whether such larger structures existed at Second Creek is an open question. At Elgin—about the same size as Aventine—the owner had maintained a "hospital" for slaves, but there are no other specific references to such buildings at Aventine or anywhere else in the county.[21] When the United States assistant marshal took census, he merely put an arabic numeral in the column indicating number of slave cabins. It was as much description as the census forms wanted and, probably, as he thought suitable to give.

In 1859, Charles Sauters was overseer at Aventine for the entire year. A native of the kingdom of Württemberg, one of the southwestern German states, he was in process of becoming a United States citizen. Now in his mid-thirties, he had a wife and young children, none of whom appeared in the record he kept for his employer. In the plantation book he recorded some conspicuous, but not frequent, disciplinary problems with the slaves, including running away, for which the remedies were the plantation "jail house," confinement in "the stock" by either the legs or the neck, and/or whipping up to the traditional (because scriptural) thirty-nine lashes.[22] His predecessor in 1857, Irish-born Patrick Francis

---

21. Jenkins Diary, November 28, December 2, 1851. The lack of references to hospitals may be merely a reflection of documentary generation and survival, for there are only three extant plantation diaries for the county (so far as has been ascertained), one of which was a record of operating a ferry more than of a plantation. Yet Isaac Stier remembered a hospital on his large place in Jefferson County, in his same interview in Rawick, *American Slave*, Vol. VII (Okla. and Miss. Narrs.), Pt. 2, p. 144. At the Jenkins absentee River Place in Wilkinson County, white carpenters built six new "double cabins," which "will enable us to give a room to each family now on that place." At Elgin, Jenkins ordered a new structure, thirty-eight by forty feet, which had a "kitchen," "Ironing room," "wash room," and "servents dining room" on the first floor, and a "school room" and three "servents sleeping apartments" on the second. The arrangement suggests how closely his own children were thrown in with the "house" slaves. Jenkins Diary, June 1, 7, 13, 1853.

22. Thirty-nine so as not to exceed the strict limit of forty in Deut. 25:2–3; also 2 Cor. 11:24. On some plantations some slaves suffered many, many more at a time. Sauters may in fact have restricted himself to thirty-nine, but he was unlikely to have recorded a larger number even if he had inflicted them. Much the same caution needs to be observed when assessing the common legal prescriptions of thirty-line lashes for certain offenses. Court judges (despite Deut. 25:2) and legislators were not in the habit of standing watchfully by during actual punishments. On occasion they handed out sentences of thirty-nine lashes per day for several days.

McGovern, recorded virtually no "offenses" or punishments, which may have meant that he ran either a happier or a more cowed plantation than Sauters or (alternatively) that he was less inclined to keep his employer informed of difficulties. Employers like Shields regarded whipping as necessary on occasion but a sign of poor management as much as anything.[23]

No matter what the overseer's temperament, the agricultural cycle governed what the slaves had to do, as it did on most plantations. There were sometimes nearly a hundred slaves at Aventine, but the number of hands varied considerably because from time to time some were pulled off the work there and sent to other of Shields's plantations. Yet the overseers' logs at Aventine give good indication of the annual cycle of hard labor.[24]

In January and February, mule teams hauled manure and the hands racked it up. The hands ("h^{ds}," as Sauters referred to the grown people on the place) were busy shelling and shucking corn, hauling fence rails, and putting up a fence. They were set to clearing the cornstalks by plowing them under or burning them up. Four hands chopped down willows in the bottoms. Others were chopping weeds, hauling cottonseed, and cleaning out the ditch in the bottom of No. 8 field. While Allen, one of the few skilled slaves, was repairing harrows and sharpening ploughs, twenty-four hands were rolling logs, picking up chunks and brush in the deadening, stopping up washes and making a levee in the bottoms of No. 2. Several cleaned the gutters on the gin, while five sickly hands were picking wool.

In March and early April, some of the winter work continued, but preparations for the warming weather got fully under way. While Allen and Dixon were fixing a gate and making hoe handles, the ordinary hands were dropping and covering corn. While two hands were hewing sills for repairing the cotton house,

23. McGovern's birthplace is a guess, based on his name; he is not in the 1860 census. Sauters' application for citizenship on April 21, 1857 is in Record of Naturalization, 1854–1905, p. 81, in Adams County Circuit Court Clerk's Office, Natchez. He was listed in Census, 1860 Free, household 1045.

24. Some phrases and words in the following several descriptive paragraphs are actual quotations from the Aventine diary without being so indicated; as a whole, activities are mentioned in seasonal but not necessarily daily sequence.

others were getting and framing timber for the press. The term "hands" did not ordinarily include the children, but the youngsters were not at play, as instanced by "9 hands and the children racking down weeds and corn stalks" and two hands setting out cabbage and "all the children toting seed." As the days lengthened, twenty-four hands were "putting cotton seed on the corn hills," while two were belting trees.

In 1859, on April 12, "7 ploughs" were "breaking up peoples patches." Two days later, forty of the forty-nine hands were out "putting manure to the corn." The last brief early morning frost that year came late, on April 17. Planting cottonseed took only three days, beginning April 20. Only two weeks later, May 4, hoe hands began "cutting out cotton" and the plows "baring off cotton." On May 13, Sauters carefully noted, "finished cutting out cotton in 11 ¾ days."

The late spring meant continued work on the money crop, but also a variety of tasks that went with cotton planting. In mid-May, while some plows were molding cotton, other hands were cutting down plum trees that were either nearly dead or their land needed for other purposes. On May 20, "Three teams to Natchez, returned at 9 o'clock P.M. with 100 sacks of corn." Others were "sheering sheeps" and "washing wool." The plows were still hilling corn. After a bad storm, some hands were "chopping off and picking up in the big new ground," and then "piling up." Two men worked at cleaning out the spring in the hogs' pasture. Teams were sent to Natchez, returning with loads of 18,000 shingles at a time—60,000 in all, as Sauters totaled them. By the middle of June some hands were chopping down weeds, others hauling basket timber and making baskets. What was becoming a relatively slack period was marked by a rare half-holiday on a Saturday. On several other Saturdays after dinner the hands were "working their own corn." One of Sauters' Saturday journal entries put the matter in a way that made clear what he considered work: "stopped working at dinner, afternoon the women washing, the men working in their patches."

On July 15: "The road overseer was here today"; a gang worked not only on the public road, but on the private ones on the place as well. Meanwhile, the real crops were coming along, and were not badly in the grass. In mid-July, the cotton was "bolling very good," and by the twenty-third the corn was already tall enough for "pulling fodder." Patience had her baby on the eighteenth (without having been previously put on the daily list of "sick," nonworking hands), and she was "laying in" through Sunday the thirty-first. She was "sick" again on August 4, but doing light picking thereafter. There had been no need to call upon Dr. Foster, the physician who administered to the slaves in difficult cases. On the Saturday after Patience's baby, Sauters recorded "nine pigs and two lambs dropped last week."

In early August, Lucy was still making shirts, two hands were plowing peas, and four men were repairing fences and putting up a new one around the cow pen. Cotton picking began on August 8, 1859, with eleven children starting the work. Soon Sauters set "5 complaining hands trashing cotton"—presumably in response to complaints of illness brought on (he felt) by the picking season. Two black carpenters were at work on the "cotton house," and a "teamster," probably white, helped with building the scaffold and began hauling off daily loads of cotton. It was a busy time. One Sunday morning, all the hands pulled fodder for Dr. Foster from five o'clock until ten.

The picking, trashing, ginning, pressing, and hauling went on into September. And on, and on. Picking was not the only work. The carpenters shingled "the childrens house." The teamster hauled three loads a day but found time to make oxbows. Some hands were "scraping weeds, vines and grass," while others were pulling, loading, and cribbing corn, picking peas, digging out sweet potatoes. On days with heavy rain, they trashed, ginned, and ground corn. Fanny was punished severely, but she continued to have her crazy "fits." On September 18: "Davenport in the stock and gave him 39 lashes with the strop for ~~saucing and~~ being saucy and clinching his hands against the overseer." Davenport— a name that will come up again—was on the list of the "sick" for several days. The first white morning frost came on October 29.

On November 3, Sauters noted with evident satisfaction, "Finished pulling and hauling corn." Less than a week later he wrote in large, bold letters, "Major G. B. Shields visit Aventine." It was the owner's first visit in months. Three days after that great event, Sauters recorded the crop to date: 167 bales, or 382,400 pounds. As the month went by and the picking and ginning went on, there was time to have a ditch in a cornfield cleaned out. Jacob "got a good flogging" and a night in the stock for an offense Sauters chose not to record. The last "scattering cotton" was picked December 14. The hands "kept holiday" from December 24 until work began again on Wednesday the thirtieth.

There had also been time, late that fall, for the hands at Aventine to mend the hedges bordering on fields owned by Mr. Mitchell and Mr. Surget—names that two years later were to keep coming up in connection with a plan made not by Second Creek owners and overseers, but by some slaves themselves.

CHAPTER 4

OF THE PLANTING CLASSES

Adams County, together with its seat in Natchez, was and is a special place, or as it is described by people with any sense and feeling, "particular" or even "peculiar." Today, almost any reasonably well-educated Mississippian will be quick to explain that Natchez is not like the rest of Mississippi. In fact the people who "matter" there have a great deal in common with FFVs and with Beacon Hill and its various neighboring branch offices. One knows one's great-aunts and second cousins twice removed. Faulkner's Yoknapatawpha County (Lafayette, in the north central part of the state), where cousinhood was (and still is) important, bears roughly the same relationship to Adams and Natchez as Peoria does to Suffolk and Boston. Unlike in most of Mississippi, in Natchez the important people are Episcopalians and Presbyterians, not Baptists or even Methodists. For some, the important thing about money is the dust on it.[1]

Even as early as 1840, Adams County had taken on the flavor of old wealth. At least so it seemed to James Silk Buckingham, an English visitor who wrote a book about his own lecture tour of the United States. "The environs of Natchez abound with fine mansions and well-cultivated plantations; and the most wealthy and longest-settled families reside in these." "My lectures," he went on in his self-congratulatory tone, "which were delivered in the Presbyterian Church, were chiefly attended by this class, and a few of the principal families in town; and though not so numerous as the audiences at New Orleans and Mobile, it was among

---

1. During the interracial turmoil of the early 1960s, the Ku Klux Klan was strong in Adams County precisely because so many of the old elite were unwilling to support an active Citizens' Council, since doing so would have altered their positive civic-minded commitments in a negative and unbefitting (and for some, totally wrong) direction. The opposite situation prevailed in the newer (and much larger) capital city of Jackson, where a very active Citizens' Council meant that the local Klan remained relatively weak. Today, efforts are being made to open some of the papers of the Mississippi Sovereignty Commission to the public, and it is possible that more will be known about these contrasts.

the most elegant, both in dress, appearance, and ease and polish of manners, that I had yet seen in the United States."[2]

One of the wealthiest county families on the eve of the war, the Surgets, had its roots in the late eighteenth century when French Louisiana was under Spanish rule. Pierre Surget arrived from France in the 1780s and bought up sizable tracts of land. In 1860 the heirs of the recently deceased Francis Surget owned thousands of acres and nearly a dozen plantations in Adams County.[3] During the prosperous 1850s the larger planters increased their holdings by buying up land from marginally small farmers. By 1860 the average Adams County "farm" was worth more than $10,000. Animated by ambition, crowding, and soil erosion, the most successful owners purchased huge tracts directly across the river in Concordia Parish, where the flat swampy forested floodplain stretched as far as the eye could see.[4] They moved Negroes and overseers onto that enormous blue-green-gray expanse to drain and clear the land and to plant cotton.[5] Some of the wealthiest bought plantations in more northerly Tensas and Madison parishes, in Arkansas, and even sugarcane plantation-factories below the isothermal line that permitted that crop in the southern half of Louisiana. A small number of younger sons of the Adams planters seem to have actually taken up residence across the river, but most remained at or near home. A few of the very wealthy took off for places like New York, where they had financial ties, and a handful of disaffected sons ventured to California. Yet whereas many slaveholders in Mississippi had been born in northern

2. J. S. Buckingham, *The Slave States of America* (2 vols.; London, [1842]), I, 458.

3. The Surget family is discussed more fully in chap. 7. For the earlier history of the region, see Robert V. Haynes, *The Natchez District and the American Revolution* (Jackson, Miss., 1976).

4. When the French arrived in the late seventeenth century, they found this enormous swampy floodplain from three to twenty-five miles wide and fifty miles long. Ronald L. F. Davis, *Good and Faithful Labor: From Slavery to Sharecropping in the Natchez District, 1860–1890* (Westport, Conn., 1982), 24. The flooding by the Tensas, Black, and Mississippi rivers was of course periodic. Even today if one drives near the Tallahatchie on the north-south Mississippi interstate one can often see living trees growing out of what look like shallow lakes.

5. Many of these slaves were not from Adams County but, rather, had been purchased in Natchez at the slave mart at the Forks of the Road, where they had been assembled from downriver at New Orleans or from overland coffles from the east. Apparently there "never was" a slave market in Concordia: Robert Dabney Calhoun, "A History of Concordia Parish, Louisiana," *Louisiana Historical Quarterly*, XVI (1933), 95.

states, Adams County (with the obvious exception of Natchez) was numerically dominated by slaveholders native not only to the state but to the county itself.

Immediately to the west, the newer lands were governed by the arbitrary eminent domain imposed by the great river system. In Concordia, for example, the land was nearly flat and the rich top-soil twelve to fifteen feet deep thanks to periodic flooding and contributions of soil from two-thirds of the nation's terrain. Today in that region, patches of previously plowed acres produce if left fallow what looks like thick young virgin forest in four or five years. The weather permits "double-cropping" of winter wheat and cotton and soybeans, but of course in 1861 planters considered and planted only cotton as a commercial crop, especially the Petit Gulf variety that had proved itself for a quarter century.[6]

Largely owing to emigration, during the 1850s Adams County (if one excludes the incorporated county seat) actually lost population (if one includes slaves).[7] Huge amounts of money poured back from the floodplain to the west, though of course some was siphoned off at Natchez and down the river by brokerage and shipping fees. Most of the new Louisiana plantations were named as such-and-such a "place"—as in Francis Surget's "Cheripa place." Home plantations in Adams County were sometimes referred to in the same manner—by blacks especially, but by whites as well—but more often simply by their old name. Montrose and Bottany Hill and so on needed no further elaboration.

Despite the steam ferry that plied the river between Natchez and the village of Vidalia, older Adams planters and the baronial capitalists of Natchez seem not to have even visited their Louisiana holdings. The river was more a psychological than a physical barrier. William Johnson, the prosperous free Negro barber and businessman in Natchez, crossed it many times for fishing in Concordia Lake; he sometimes went by skiff but recorded one steam ferry trip as four minutes over and seven-and-a-half min-

6. For cotton, as well as planting more generally, John Hebron Moore, *Agriculture in Ante-Bellum Mississippi* (1958; rpr. New York, 1971), esp. chap. 2. I am greatly indebted to Ed and Ardis Berry for showing me their 1,300-acre farm near Waterproof, Concordia Parish, which he inherited from his father, as well as for answering many questions about its operation.

7. D. Clayton James, *Antebellum Natchez* (Baton Rouge, 1968), 162. Incorporated Mississippi towns (including tiny hamlets as well as county seats) were and are part of the county in which they are located, though possessing certain separate jurisdictional powers.

utes back.[8] From old Mississippi, Concordia seemed a distinctly different world. And indeed it was, with blacks outnumbering whites eight to one, and one-third of the improved land owned by absentees living mainly in Adams County.[9]

Given this situation, it is arresting that alarm about the Plan, and evidently the Plan itself, did *not* leap across the river. It is arresting also, though perhaps less surprising, that Lemuel P. Conner seems more than anyone else to have straddled the river in his activities, to have been as much a resident of Concordia Parish as of Adams County. In the 1860 census of Adams County, he was listed on July 29 as the head of household No. 855, together with his large family. But there is no way of discovering which side of the river he was living on when the Examination Committee gathered at Second Creek in September of 1861.

The Adams County planters lived at the historical core of the great southwestern cotton empire. Adams was the oldest county in the state and until some year between 1810 and 1820 produced more cotton than any other. It had boasted the original territorial and state capital, located at times in Natchez itself and at times eight miles east in the hamlet of Washington, with its tiny and struggling Jefferson College. As cotton and Anglo- and Afro-American settlement pushed north and east, however, Natchez and its environs were left in a geographical and political corner. The capital was eventually relocated in Jackson, intentionally in the west central part of the state and close to what was becoming its center of population. Upriver, with a successful railroad to the interior, Vicksburg outstripped Natchez as an economic hub. When the Quitman Light Artillery departed for the expected battlefront on April 14, they took a steamboat from Natchez to Vicksburg, and then a train east.[10]

Yet the Natchez region remained a seat of prestige, power, monied elegance, and (like the rest of the state) deep commitment to slavery. In 1860 the population of Adams County was three-quarters black, with many of the whites concentrated in Natchez itself. Over the previous decade there had been a pronounced tend-

8. *Johnson's Diary*, I, 186 and *passim*. In all other sources collectively, direct references to individual Adams planters' venturing to plantations across the river are rare.

9. Davis, *Good and Faithful Labor*, 36, 27; Joseph Karl Menn, *The Large Slaveholders of Louisiana—1860* (New Orleans: Pelican Publishing Co., 1964), 196–211.

10. Natchez *Daily Courier*, April 17, 1861.

ency toward more slaveholding farms and more large plantations. From 1850 to 1860 the proportion of nonslaveholding families dropped from 31 to 10 percent. The size of slaveholding aggregations grew dramatically. By 1860, 63 percent of Adams County farming units had twenty or more slaves and 38 percent had more than fifty. By a wide margin the modal size was from fifty to a hundred slaves; plantations of that size outnumbered nonslaveholding farms by more than two to one.[11] These huge proportions were utterly atypical when compared with those in the rest of the upland cotton South. Concomitantly in the last decade before the war, there was an increase in the size of individual landholdings—though not thereby in the size of individual plantations, since an increasing number of planters owned more than one.[12]

Planters and merchants laid out huge sums for construction of magnificent mansions, both in the city and out in the county.[13] Customarily, the suburban and country plantation houses stood hidden from public view at the end of long, winding drives that ran through what an English geologist called "wild forests." In the 1840s this distinguished visitor was charmed by these "country-houses," which he thought "elegant." Many were shaded by China trees, garlanded by flowering vines, with "some of the gardens belonging to them laid out in the English, others in the

11. Calculated from the table in Herbert Weaver, *Mississippi Farmers, 1850–1860* (1945; rpr. Gloucester, Mass., 1968), 39.

12. James, *Antebellum Natchez,* 149. Modern attempts to manipulate the census data statistically often give the impression of greater accuracy than is warranted, as when one scholar announces that .536 percent of free white males aged twenty and over owned fifty or more slaves. This stunning precision is accomplished by ignoring ownership of slaves by women and by trusteeships, and (a matter of importance in Adams County) the fact that many large planters owned more than one plantation located in different counties and even different states and were thus listed two or more times in census aggregations. See Lee Soltow, *Men and Wealth in the United States, 1850–1870* (New Haven, 1975), 134–36. The more general assertions in Kenneth M. Stampp, *The Peculiar Institution: Slavery in the Ante-Bellum South* (New York, 1956), 29–33, are in fact more accurate by virtue of their imprecision.

13. Today Natchez itself, with expanded boundaries, has the greatest concentration of such mansions in the United States, owing to the combination of wealth, the tornado of 1840 (which encouraged new building), little destruction during the war, and locally powerful historical pride. In Second Creek valley, however, only a handful of antebellum manor houses still stand. Most have burned accidentally.

French style." The hedges were "made of . . . the Gardenia florida
. . . others of the Cherokee rose, with its bright and shining
leaves." [14]

Elegant mansions presented lines and dimensions befitting the
elevated status of their owners. They were constructed on foundations made with bricks that were themselves made locally, or
sometimes of large stones, usually without a "cellar" or what
would elsewhere be called a "basement." Many were arrayed with
picture-book neoclassical columns supporting the roof over the
veranda, which sometimes totally belted the house. Inside, towering windows on the first floor had movable latticed blinds to
protect against the sun and let in the breeze, enormous doorways,
and ceilings three and four times the height of the tallest occupants. Much of the furniture and some of the furnishings were
imported through New Orleans, chiefly from England. Outbuildings in back often included a separate kitchen, servants' rooms,
and of course, several privies.[15]

Many of these elegant structures—those that are still standing—have today become tourist attractions. The big houses with
their supporting staffs of slaves were indeed—as the matter would
be phrased by some of these tourists—nice places to entertain.
They were certainly used for that purpose, though more for
friends and relatives than for strangers. Frederick Olmsted, the famous northern traveler and commentator on slavery and other
southern customs, was warned about the prospects for travelers
by a dyspeptic companion during supper at a hostelry near Woodville. Olmsted was curious, since he was headed for Natchez, and
he was told that "beyond the ferry [across the Homochitto] . . . , a

14. Sir Charles Lyell, *A Second Visit to the United States of North America*
([2d ed.], 2 vols.; New York, 1850), II, 153. See also the description in [Joseph Holt
Ingraham], *The South-West. By a Yankee* (2 vols.; 1835; rpr. Ann Arbor, 1966), II,
108–13.

15. In the 1830s an English traveler described the "mansion" belonging to
"Mrs. M[ino]r" not far from town as "having on either front very deep porticoes
opening into a capacious hall, with winding stairs of stone outside leading on to a
gallery twenty feet wide, which is carried round the building on a level with the
first-floor story, and is covered by a projecting roof supported by handsome pillars:
by this means the inner walls are far removed from the effect of either sun or rain,
and the spacious apartments kept both cool and dry. The kitchen and other offices
are detached, forming two sides of a quadrangle, of which the house is the third,
and the fourth a garden." Tyrone Power, *Impressions of America; During the Years
1833, 1834, and 1835* (2d American ed., 2 vols.; Philadelphia, 1836), II, 116–17.
This was in fact Concord, later presided over by a Minor son who wrote about the
crisis at Second Creek and Natchez.

man might die on the road 'fore he'd get a lodging with one of them. . . . Yes sir; just so inhospitable as that—swell-heads! swell-heads, sir, every plantation." [16] Among the wealthy planters them-selves, there was much visiting and the occasional grand party. At Elgin in 1850, a "soiree" for 150 people included sea-turtle soup, oysters, and fruits—brought up by steamboat—and a musical trio (two violins and a string bass), also from New Orleans. The fol-lowing day the host noted, "Servants clearing off the wreck from Party of last evening." The cost of the food alone was $341.50.[17] But some of the less exotic fare was locally grown, and of course the labor of the servants was without noticeable cost—at least to their owner.

Socializing among the aristocracy encouraged intermarriages among families, producing eventually such a complex network of interrelatedness that genealogists still have difficulty sorting it out. Today there are a number of Adams County residents who do not have complete sets of thirty-two different great-great-great-grandparents. At the time, the topics of business, family, friends, and politics—subjects not necessarily distinct from one an-other—were of primary interest. In addition there was always the *weather*, which was a concern for all agriculturalists, even those of great wealth, who lived in the sticky heat and unpredictable rainfall of the southern Mississippi Valley summers and then in the winter had to deal with frost and occasional ice and snow. More than today, the weather was likely to affect fortunes.

In many dining rooms an enormous slab of wood, smoothed and polished to show the gorgeous grain, hung suspended narrow-edge-down over the great central table. These punkahs were rigged with ropes and pulleys so they could be swung back and forth as a fan over the diners, their noiseless energy coming from the retro-

16. Frederick Law Olmsted, *A Journey in the Back Country* (New York, 1860), 25–26. Olmsted's democratic sensibilities were offended by the social ambience of Natchez and environs. He recounted at great length comments by the traveling critic of the "swell-head" families that "if they had a reputation for hospitality . . . it could only be among their own sort," and further, that "they made it a point to have a great deal of company; they would not have any thing to do if they didn't." The first points were on target, but the last greatly understated the time planters put it on their business. Despite his high reputation for accurate reporting, Olmsted asserted the population of Natchez to be three times what it actually was. He declared the huge suburban villas "not remarkable"—an assessment of taste that in his day was as widely in error as his statistic about the town. *Ibid.*, 32, 40, 35.

17. Jenkins Diary, May 20, 21, 1850.

active motion of an arm attached to the body of a young slave standing discreetly in a corner or by the door. The cooling effect of such a device is not great when the temperature is 95°F, but it was real and welcome enough when one was dressed from neck to floor in broadcloth or crinoline. We may conjure up the rustling of that crinoline and the gentle tones of china, crystal, and silverware, though few of today's tourists do so. We can listen also to the cacophony of voices at table in 1861, knowing that there was talk of cotton, horses, neighbors, politics, and war. The silent slave pulling on the rope was (we may say in all probability) not deaf or blind. Neither were the several other well-dressed servants who waited on such tables. It would have been a wonder if slaves had not heard of Lincoln and even one or two of his most public generals.

The Adams planters did not welcome war. Many were decidedly tepid about secession, and more than a few were outright opposed, but their political representatives had been roundly outvoted by men from newer areas of the state who had far less to lose in any possible armed conflict. The great majority of these outsiders were not risking scores of slaves and the elegant lifestyle those slaves supported. Immediately after Lincoln's election, the majority of Adams County voters were willing to wait him out, to test his frequently reiterated disclaimers of any federal power to interfere with slavery where it already existed. These planters had no visions of moving westward into the territories when there was plenty of fine land for cotton in a slave state just across the river. Why should their sons? Born to their roles as lordly masters, and able in myriad ways to exercise and display mastery every day, they saw slavery as a natural and very comfortable way of life, not as a threatened institution that needed shrill defense. Why should they jump on the lurching bandwagon of secession? Like many Americans, South and North, they held the Union dear. It had nurtured them better than most people.

Not that the planters lacked stomach in the face of possible violence. Indeed, the ones on Second Creek displayed cool aplomb—among other, less attractive qualities—when faced by the projected horrors of the Plan. They were withy in the face of storms. They were strengthened by all their possessions—their slaves, lands, and families—and also by that peculiarly aristocratic buttress, couth. They would have and did put the matter differently, especially those at the apex of a class that had, after all, its own important internal gradations. "Recollect dear Son," wrote one plantation mistress, "you have a name to preserve." Yet, in a crisis, self-preservation could become more literally at stake, and distinguished names muted, though not forgotten, in a common cause.[18]

At the local political polls there were few signs of outright, wholesale hostility toward the great planters, but there were abundant indications that some whites resented their wealth and economic power. Horse racing, a favorite sport of the planters, seems to have divided men of the county more than it bonded them. So far as can be ascertained, the poor white farmers who held no slaves were less aggravated by the grandees than were the so-called second planters, who owned from several to a dozen or fifteen or twenty or so.

In Adams County, members of planting families greatly outnumbered the members of families owning fewer than ten slaves, even if that group were combined with the even smaller number of rural whites who owned none at all. In most parts of the slave South, a man or woman owning some twelve to twenty slaves would not have been regarded as a "small" slaveholder. That term, indeed, seems to have been invented retrospectively by twentieth-century historians attempting to describe the structure of southern slaveholding. In doing so, they have reified a dividing line based on numbers that was not thus recognized at the time. The line was real enough, perhaps, but seen much more in public manner and style than in numeric terms.[19]

18. The admonition is from R[ebecca] A. Minor to James [Minor], December 21, 1859, in Minor Family Papers, UNC.

19. The MS census of 1860 listed no "planters" in all of Adams County. Even the largest slaveholders were termed "farmers" in the occupation column. Several historians have intruded their own assumptions into this data by making up their own often glaringly inconsistent nomenclatures. In fact, A. D. Pickens was not eccentric among Mississippi census marshals in 1860, since the terms *planter* and *farmer* were used without precise meaning. In neighboring Wilkinson County, virtually every landowner outside Woodville was a "planter." In counties where both terms were used, "planter" usually implied larger holdings, but Jefferson Davis was a "farmer" (Warren Census, 1860 Free, household 1397; Slave, MS p. 175). Pickens was a twenty-three-year-old "clerk" who owned only one slave, and he was paid for his census services, as were all 4,417 such marshals throughout the country. See Carroll D. Wright and William C. Hunt, *The History and Growth of the United States Census* (Washington, D.C., 1900), 50–52; U.S. Census Office, Eighth Census, *Instructions to U.S. Marshals. Instructions to Assistants* (Washington, D.C., 1860). Pickens and his farmer father (whose property the census taker did not record), are listed in Census, 1860 Free, household 647; Slave, MS pp. 7, 31 (one slave, listed twice). The younger man's rising prosperity can be traced in Adams Personal, 1858, 1859, 1861, 1862; Adams Land, 1861—records compiled by A. D. Pickens as

Yet it is the case that in 1861 anyone who owned ten or fifteen slaves was decidedly not poor, unless in the unlikely event that most of his (or sometimes her) slaves were infants, over fifty, blind, or otherwise disabled. Depending on age, gender, health, disposition, and occupational skill, a group of ten slaves was likely to be worth from five to ten thousand dollars in prewar currency. Some artisans in town owned that many and more, including Steve Odell, a gunsmith who, as it later developed, greatly attracted the interest of the rebels.

The contemporary term *second planters* as used in the county denoted a relative, rather than an absolute, standard of wealth and social status. Second planters' houses were far from grand.[20] The group's members constituted a separate class—and evidently were conscious of doing so—not merely because of the prodigious wealth of the great planters but much more because they lacked the ties of intermarriage that bound the first families together in such an intricate web. A twenty-five-year-old planter with only sixteen slaves was scarcely to be thought of as a second planter if he already owned a thousand acres of unimproved land in Concordia, his father owned three hundred slaves on four plantations, and his new bride's father was similarly situated.

Yet accumulated and accumulating wealth was bound to attract public attention. Looking from the relatively detached distance of Natchez itself, one critic laid out the case against the grandees on economic grounds that carried more than a whiff of resentment concerning aristocratic style. "The large planters," he wrote in 1842 to the *Free Trader* (the Jacksonian-Democratic paper), "— the one-thousand-bale planters—do not contribute most to the prosperity of Natchez." Their money went elsewhere: "They, for the most part, sell their cotton in Liverpool; buy their wines in London or Havre; their negro clothing in Boston; their plantation implements and supplies in Cincinnati; and their groceries and fancy articles in New Orleans." By way of contrast, in the face of the then-prevailing economic depression, lesser men contributed to the local economy: "The small planter hoards no money in these times; he lends none at usurious rates of interest; he buys up the property of no unfortunate debtor for a few dollars; but he

---

tax assessor. His duality of function resulted in a rare, but for the historian most happy, harmony between the census estimates of property and the tax assessment rolls.

20. So far as can be discovered, none still stand and there were no contemporary descriptions of them.

lays it all out for the purchase of supplies, and thus directly contributes to the prosperity of our city." [21]

Evidently some whites and perhaps a few slaves saw these two groups of whites as having distinct interests, but the racial bond among whites was a powerful one, and slaves knew about that bond from unforgettable imprints of experience. If we were to say that the second planters were envious and hostile toward the first families, we would be wrong only if we stopped there, for they were also awed, or at least thoroughly impressed. They lacked knowledge and curiosity about theoretical explanations for their own and the great planters' status. If anything, most of what passed for relevant theory in their culture told them merely that some people could prosper handsomely in this world and that others did not—though some day, of course, they might. Hope for that someday was bound to be strongest among those who were climbing up the mid-part of the ladder of success—partway up, as they saw it, not partway down. Especially during the prosperous years of the 1850s, many had done very well; they had tested the ladder and found it strong and upright but somehow lacking access to the topmost rungs. Many of those perches had been appropriated long before, in territorial days at the turn of the century.

Underlying this division between the larger and smaller slaveholders—between the haves and the have-not-as-yets—lay a bedrock of fundamental common interest. They all owned slaves, and they all knew at heart and would have asserted if asked that discontent among one person's slaves might well spread to others. In the event or even the possibility of slave violence, they all stood together without regard to the price of cotton or who could bet how much on a racehorse.

They felt this common bond despite their sharing in the nearly universal tendency among slaveholders to think of serious slave discontent as emanating from someone else's place rather than one's own. In addition, for a generation since the hydra of "fanaticism" had first fully personified itself in such demonic shapes as David Walker, Nat Turner, and William Lloyd Garrison, most of these slaveholders had been inclined to think on the one hand that their slaves were thoroughly contented and, on the other, that

21. Natchez *Mississippi Free Trader*, April 14, 1842, quoted in James, *Antebellum Natchez*, 145–46. That there was good basis for this view is clear in Morton Rothstein, "The Natchez Nabobs: Kinship and Friendship in an Economic Elite," in Hans L. Trefousse, ed., *Toward a New View of America: Essays in Honor of Arthur C. Cole* ([New York], 1977), 97–112.

slave unrest must surely be owing to outside agents of abolition, not to the slaves themselves. Some of this feeling was linked to sectional proslavery rhetoric; it formed an important element in the relatively new siege mentality of the region. Yet on another level, most slaveholders knew perfectly well that "misbehavior" could and would arise at home without nurture from external agitation. When William Russell visited New Orleans as a reporter for the London *Times* in May of 1861, he noted: "None of the Southern gentlemen have the smallest apprehension of a servile insurrection. They use the universal formula 'our negroes are the happiest, most contented, and most comfortable people on the face of the earth.' " Russell went on to "admit I have been struck by well-clad and good-humoured negroes in the streets, but they are in the minority; many look morose, ill-clad, and discontented." Evidently there had just been some sort of alarm: "The patrols I know have been strengthened." Yet, he continued, "I heard a young lady the other night, say, 'I shall not be a bit afraid to go back to the plantation, though mamma says the negroes are after mischief.' " [22] As a perceptive foreigner, Russell seems to have caught the pervading ambivalence very well.

Normally, neither class of Adams County slaveholders put much energy into thinking about possible slave conspiracies. They simply assumed that they would have trouble with their laborers from time to time, especially with certain known individuals, but they did not really think of themselves as sitting on a powder keg of servile discontent. During the ominous election campaigns of 1860, they seem to have been immune to the sort of panic that was breaking out in Texas and in equally nouveau localities in their own state.[23] They were well aware that most sizable groups of slaves included at least a few malcontents. In 1859, Susan Darden recorded the use of slave-catching dogs without special remark, even when the runaways were badly bitten.[24] The planting classes had good reason for this view. "Running away"

22. William Howard Russell, *My Diary North and South*, ed. Eugene H. Berwanger (Philadelphia, 1988), 161–62.

23. For Texas, see chap. 5. Nearer to home, rumors of a revolt supposedly " 'headed by white men' " in Jasper County, in the southeast central piney woods of Mississippi, seem to have created no stir in Adams: see John B. Harnley to Gov. J. J. Pettus, May 4, 1861, in Governors Papers, MDAH. Harnley, captain of the "Home Guards," himself placed the phrase about white men in quotation marks. See also Adrienne C. Phillips, "Responses in Mississippi to John Brown's Raid" (Ph.D. dissertation, University of Mississippi, 1983), 171–75.

24. Darden Diary, August 30, 31, September 21, 1859.

was such a common problem not because a great many slaves took off without leave, but because those who did so were likely to do it again and again. One of the "worst" of the Second Creek rebels was probably just such a recidivist.

With running away, as with other matters of slave discipline, slaveholders looked to one another for support. They also expected that other right-thinking white men would rush to plug any breach in the wall of racial discipline. In normal times they got the backing they expected. Yet most of the time the slave "patrols" were much more impressive on paper than in practice. In Natchez itself the two militia companies—the Guards and the Fencibles—were more often engaged in protecting property and keeping order among the notoriously "riotous" Irish and other fractious elements than in disciplining the Negroes, though perhaps most of their time was spent in what might be called social drilling. The slave patrol served as a once-a-week constabulary to clear the town of county slaves when the courthouse bell rang at four o'clock on Sunday evenings.[25] Except in winter, that bell gave Second Creek slaves time enough to reach home before dark.

In the countryside, the patrols rode on Sundays and at night, though not on a regular basis. Depredations by runaways, suspicious fires, and unusual gatherings of slaves were the most common causes for assembling patrols, so slaves often knew where and when they were likely to run into them. Still, traveling off one's place without a written pass was always a chancy business. Without a pass, a slave could expect a severe flogging by men whose whips were not in the slightest restrained by acquaintanceship or paternal feelings—which in any event were often not restraints at all. The great planters and their sons rarely rode patrol except at times of special alarm. Even at such times, most were not enthusiastic, as was clear in Susan Darden's diary during the local Jefferson County crisis in 1861: "May 25 . . . Mr. Darden was commanded to patrol to night, he went." "May 26 . . . Mr. Darden got Capt. Jacob Stampley to excuse him." Many planters were ambivalent about the patrols: they acknowledged the necessity, but they made very clear to their overseers and slave foremen that the "paterollers" were not ordinarily to be permitted to search the cabins of the quarter. Planters were well aware of the impact of invasiveness upon slave morale and of the possibilities of sexual and other physical abuse. Though they may not have thought so

25. *Johnson's Diary, passim;* [Ingraham], *South-West,* II, 72–73.

consciously, the idea of such an intrusion violated their pride of ownership and exclusive authority.

We know little about those men who rode the patrols, if only because such men were somehow disinclined to sit down after a night's riding to write about their experiences. Some were not slaveowners. Yet in Adams County, the number of white men who owned no slaves was small enough that at least some slaveholders, perhaps even second planters, participated out of necessity. No doubt some men regarded nightriding as a boring obligation to be dodged if possible. Others seem to have found it welcome relief from the tedium of farming life—a chance to get out and ride around with the boys, get a bit liquored up, and catch a few nigras and educate them. The patrol "system" was also, in effect, a school; it established a tradition of nightriding that was used after the war to deal with blacks (particularly male) who got too uppity. As yet, though, there was no occasion for white sheets. All that was needed was a horse, often a gun, and a length of cowhide. There was little danger: about the worst that ever happened was being thrown from a horse by a rope or vine that had been strung across the path.[26]

Though the planters relied on such activities to maintain their hegemony, they spent their time on other concerns—particularly, before the war and the Plan, on the more genteel and exciting battlefields of cotton pricing, horse racing, and most especially politics. Before May of '61, they had no special reason to discuss the mood of their bondsmen.

26. A vivid example, of repeated ropes across a bridge in Alabama, is in Rawick, *American Slave.* Vol. VII (Okla. and Miss. Narrs.), Pt. 2, p. 129. As a general matter, the system may be capsulized for whites by two Sunday entries in the diary of a smallish slaveholder in South Carolina: "Mr. Leadbetter preached full attendance of White and not very full of blacks. Rode Patrol at 3 oclk"; "Mr. T. Leadbetter preached a very full attendance. Patroled in the afternoon nothing of importance occured whipped Chance." Charles Graves Plantation Diary, December 24, 1854, January 7, 1855, in South Carolina Historical Society, Charleston.

CHAPTER 5

OF ONE KIND OF POLITICS

In terms of formal electoral politics, the Plan developed in the face of weakness, not strength. Despite all their wealth, the Adams County planters had long since lost their political clout in the state of Mississippi.

Had that state existed as a British colony in the eighteenth century, its socioeconomic structure would have easily supported the same kind of aristocratic politics that had prevailed in colonial Virginia and South Carolina. Slaveholding elites had controlled the domestic political life of those two colonies until about the time of the American Revolution. By the time war broke out in 1775, challenges to the power of these groups were clearly evident. Though not identically rooted in both cases, this defiance interwove in complex ways with the reverberating spirit of that glorious year. In both colonies, geographical factors and long-standing patterns of settlement had combined to concentrate large-scale slaveholding in the eastern sections along the seaboard. This concentration was far more pronounced in South Carolina, so much so that visitors sometimes thought the low country resembled the West Indian islands. But both colonial Virginia and South Carolina prefigured the later "colony" of Mississippi as it became a territory and, at last, a state in 1817.

The earliest Anglo-Afro-American settlements in Mississippi had been in the Old Natchez District, in the southwest corner of what became officially a United States territory in 1798. At first, that little area flourished as a conspicuous blossom of westward-expanding empire. By the 1820s, though, black and white settlers had moved northward and also into a large pocket of fertile land in the eastern part of the state, their way cleared by treaties with the Choctaw and Cherokee Indians—treaties usually made in the wake of interloping settlement. By this time, the small Natchez tribe was long since gone, wiped out by the weapons and diseases of the French, though a few Choctaws lived in some back parts of

Second Creek valley.[1] As the rest of the state developed, the Natchez district planters found themselves politically engulfed by a wave of "democratic" sentiments and voters.

The triumph of both the democracy and Jackson's political party came more suddenly and with greater force in Mississippi than in most parts of the country. In 1832 a state convention adopted a new constitution that liberalized the residence requirement and abandoned the old tax-paying qualifications for voting; the effect was to throw open the polls to every free white man aged twenty-one "or upwards."[2] During the next few years representatives from thirty new counties came storming into the legislature—an invasion the Vicksburg *Register* likened to a scalping attack by Indians—and the proud eminence of Natchez and Adams County shriveled in the arena of state politics.[3]

By the light of developments twenty-five years later, the sputterings and lamentations of the southwestern planters were ironically instructive. Outnumbered by new white settlers in their own state, they deplored the triumph of "Brownism, demagogism, and repudiation," and announced that they might secede. If Louisiana would not have them, they would establish a separate state with a "respectable name, no repudiation, and no taxation without representation."[4]

More directly stated, political sectionalism in Mississippi revolved around such issues as banking, the state debt, representation, and "internal improvements"—the latter the catchword of

1. In 1937 former slave Charlie Davenport (then very approximately one hundred years old) recalled, "De Choctaws lived all 'roun' Secon' Creek. Some of 'em had cabins lak settled folks. I can 'member dey las' chief." Rawick, *American Slave*, Vol. VII (Okla. and Miss. Narrs.), Pt. 2, p. 36; very similarly in Suppl. 1, Vol. VII (Miss. Narrs.), Pt. 2, p. 560, Documents Y and Z. None of the other documents pertaining to the conspiracy mention Choctaw people, nor do most histories bearing on the area.

2. *Code of Mississippi: Being an Analytical Compilation of the Public and General Statutes of the Territory and State . . . 1798–1848*, comp. A. Hutchinson (Jackson, 1848), 41. The more stringent requirements dated from the first state constitution of 1817, and are *ibid.*, 25.

3. D. Clayton James, *Antebellum Natchez* (Baton Rouge, 1968), 116–17.

4. Percy Lee Rainwater, *Mississippi: Storm Center of Secession, 1856–1861* (Baton Rouge, 1938), 9–10. In this case the term "Brownism" did not derive from the seventeenth-century Robert Browne in England, whose views on church order were considered dangerously radical, but from Albert G. Brown, the able Mississippi Democratic party leader of the 1840s.

the times for state and federal aid to land and water transportation. Political discourse and practice came to turn upon what many people thought of as an eternal struggle between Democrats and Whigs, with increasing numbers of men imbibing their political allegiances in their cradles. In Mississippi, Whigs were usually in the minority. The state as a whole voted for Jackson three times, starting with his first campaign in 1824, and for Democratic candidates thereafter except for the Whig log-cabin-and-cider year of 1840. Adams County was one of only three that voted Whig in every presidential election from 1840 until 1856, though that record disguised the fact that voters in the town of Natchez remained heavily Democratic.[5]

Large planters in Adams County, even more than in the rest of the Old District, became Whigs at birth or perhaps even at conception. People of entrenched wealth very often develop steady political habits, especially when they feel isolated and threatened. The Adams planters were able to dominate their own county's politics until close to the end, despite their having the support of only one of the two Natchez newspapers and being outnumbered by Democrats in the town itself. So far as one can tell from their public silence, at the state level they operated politically in a detached orbit of ineffective and unrequited hauteur.

During the national crises of the 1850s the planters on Second Creek seem to have been well aware that if they spoke out they would be brooming at the waves of a rising, raging tide.[6] The first issues that really struck home were major segments of the Compromise of 1850. Looking at the package as a whole, most white Mississippians thought they had been subject to a humiliating defeat. A free California, the status of slavery in the pertinent territories left to their white inhabitants, the slave trade abolished in the nation's capital—all were northern victories. Only the stringent new Fugitive Slave Law could be held in balance, and Mississippi whites found their suspicions confirmed by outcries of protest against that law in the North, by violent slave "rescues," and

5. See the map in Rainwater, *Storm Center of Secession*, 15. James, *Antebellum Natchez*, 128–35, rightly emphasizes the political split between the town and the county; many previous historians lumped all the Adams County votes together and assumed the town voted Whig. On the subject earlier and more generally, see Edwin A. Miles, *Jacksonian Democracy in Mississippi* (Chapel Hill, 1960).

6. The extant record is one of deafening silence and presents no positive proof except for the diary of B. L. C. Wailes, which reflects gloomy exasperation. See Wailes Diary.

by counteractive personal liberty laws passed by states where fanaticism held sway.[7]

There was talk of secession in 1850 and 1851. With each crisis
of the following decade, the calls for separation grew louder, more
strident, more vitriolic, more threatening, more bombastic, and
more defensive. The Adams planters found themselves being rapidly swept toward the falls of disunion. Viewing the South as a
whole, one gains little sense of inevitability about this process except, of course, with the help of hindsight. In Mississippi, however, one does indeed detect a feeling of hopeless fate: that short
of a miracle, Mississippi was going out—peaceably perhaps, but
fighting if necessary, and not a bad thing either.[8]

During the four years of James Buchanan's presidency the issue
was kept on tentative hold in terms of action but not of rhetoric.
The election campaigns of 1860 began in 1856. In that earlier year
the great planters of Mississippi were trounced at the polls. With
the old Whig party defunct, they opted for Millard Fillmore on the
ticket of the American—the Know-Nothing—party, whose platform included temperance (which was welcome to the Baptist element) but whose anti-Catholicism and anti-immigrant nativism
(however welcome in theory) had little appeal in Mississippi. The
Democrats carried the state.[9]

Certain aspects of that decade of hullabaloo in Mississippi are
worth attention in light of ensuing developments on Second
Creek. The disunionists regarded themselves as good Americans,
loyal to the founding principles of the nation. In important ways,
they were. They defended the rights of private property, and they
had a good case even with the sort of property that was peculiar to
the fifteen states of the slave South. The main plank of the new

7. Some had been passed much earlier: see Thomas D. Morris, *Free Men All:
The Personal Liberty Laws of the North, 1780–1861* (Baltimore, 1974); also Stanley
W. Campbell, *The Slave Catchers: Enforcement of the Fugitive Slave Law, 1850–
1860* (Chapel Hill, 1968).

8. The long historical background is discussed in William W. Freehling,
Secessionists at Bay, 1776–1854 (New York, 1990), Vol. I of William Freehling, *The
Road to Disunion*, 2 vols.

9. Rainwater, *Storm Center of Secession*, 15, 39n. There had been a small Roman Catholic church in Natchez for years, without friction except about slaves'
dancing on Sunday, a matter commented on by the London *Times* traveling reporter, William Howard Russell, *Pictures of Southern Life, Social, Political, and
Military* (New York, 1861), 93–96. State politics are discussed in Glover Moore,
"Separation from the Union, 1854–1861," in *A History of Mississippi*, ed. Richard
Aubrey McLemore (2 vols.; Hattiesburg, 1973), I, 420–46.

Republican party would deny them their constitutionally protected right to take their property with them or to transfer it into
territories of the United States. Such denial would render them
(though certainly not their peculiar property) second-class citizens. This was to make "war upon the South and Southern institutions."[10] Jefferson Davis, widely and correctly regarded as a
moderate man, confided to a large audience that he hoped never
to see the day the South would "unresistingly bow her neck to the
yoke of bondage and oppression"—a phrase that may have been
interesting to the handful of Mississippi blacks who heard or
read it.[11]

Thus the spokesmen for disunion rallied for the cause of freedom and appealed to the nation's "brave and noble revolutionary
fathers."[12] The Founders had in fact pledged their lives and sacred
honors to protect, among other things, private property. For many
of them property in human beings had been an awkward embarrassment, even a millstone around their necks, and they would
have been happy to be rid of it. Yet few had thought it possible
to do so.

On various occasions in the 1850s, both sides referred to secession as "revolution." Yet disunionists had to be cautious with that
term, since they also held that secession was a decidedly non-
revolutionary constitutional right. Lacking much sense of irony,
they felt free to announce that Unionists should be treated like
"Tories in the Revolution." They called upon the "ministers of
God" to don the mantles of the "preachers in the days of '76."[13] In
February of 1858, Natchez' Democratic *Free Trader* urged the
southern states to follow the example of the thirteen colonies and
declare their independence on the next Fourth of July. In reply, the
Natchez *Courier* could proffer only the lame request that the editors of the *Free Trader* "put a curb on your horses."[14]

All white southerners, as well as many other Americans, were
troubled by the emergence of a political party based exclusively in
one section of the nation. Nearly from its inception, the new
northern coalition became known in the South as the Black Republican party—a designation often personalized into "Black Re-

10. Speech of W. Barksdale, *Congressional Globe*, 34th Cong., 1st Sess., Appendix, 1182.
11. Jackson *Daily Mississippian*, December 1, 1858. The words may have been
the newspaper's paraphrase of Davis' remarks.
12. Natchez *Free Trader*, November 28, 1860.
13. *Ibid.*, December 4 and following issues, 1860.
14. Quoted in Rainwater, *Storm Center of Secession*, 50, 52.

publicans." Linking the two words must have struck a profound chord, for it was done very frequently. Occasional offhand combining of the two terms would scarcely attract our attention; but the prevailing inability to disjoin them ought to. No doubt *black* served to suggest the sheer nefariousness of the northern threat, and no doubt also the future of blacks was a crucial issue for the Republic. But a powerful inner force in the phrase may be heard by reversing it: Republican blacks.[15]

The children and grandchildren of '76 had good reason to associate republicanism with revolt against "slavery"—a term very commonly used by Revolutionary patriots when referring to the insidious design of the British ministry to "enslave" them. The "horrors of St. Domingo"—a catchphrase still commonly used in the 1850s—had shown that black slaves could also seize the sword and adopt republicanism as their own. For white Americans, then, the meaning of black revolt was deepened by its links with the very founding of the nation.

For some thirty years prior to the American Civil War, white Mississippians had tried their best to purge themselves of such thoughts by denying that black slaves had either reason or inclination to rebel. In their public expressions they wholeheartedly embraced the novel proposition that slavery was a "positive good," a benefit to whites, to blacks, to the southern states, just as it had been to such illustrious societies as ancient Greece and Rome. The Founding Fathers would have been flabbergasted.

In Mississippi, as in the South generally, the shift came rapidly in the early 1830s.[16] It was so pronounced and rapid as to be a genuine reversal of public opinion. It may be epitomized by the views of Seargent S. Prentiss, a lawyer and state representative and

15. With a somewhat similar play on words, the day of the 1954 Supreme Court school-integration decision rapidly became known throughout much of the white South as Black Monday.

16. A few younger men of the early Republic, such as William Laughton Smith of South Carolina and James Jackson of Georgia, had already moved in this new direction. My view of the 1830s as turning point is different from Alison Freehling, *Drift Toward Dissolution: The Virginia Slavery Debate of 1831–1832* (Baton Rouge, 1982); Larry E. Tise, *Proslavery: A History of the Defense of Slavery in America, 1701–1840* (Athens, Ga., 1987); and more generally William Freehling, *Secessionists at Bay*, Pts. 2–5. See also the Introduction and Bibliography of Drew Gilpin Faust, ed., *The Ideology of Slavery: Proslavery Thought in the Antebellum South, 1830–1860* (Baton Rouge, 1981), 1–20, 301–306. At the time, some of the many triggers of the change were three editions of a book, by a free black man in Boston, which called for slave revolt; see Herbert Aptheker, *"One Continual Cry": David Walker's Appeal to the Colored Citizens of the World, 1829–1830: Its Setting and Its Meaning* (New York, 1965).

later congressman for Natchez, who wrote to his brother on July 25, 1831—a month before the Turner rebellion—that there could be "no doubt" that "slavery is a great evil. . . . At present, however, it is a necessary evil, and I do not think admits of a remedy." Only five years later Prentiss introduced a well-publicized resolution in the legislature: "That the people of the state of Mississippi look upon the institution of domestic slavery, as it exists among them, not as a curse, but a blessing."[17]

From the 1830s onward, public dissent on the question of slavery became downright dangerous in Mississippi. In 1835 a dramatic ritual solemnized the thoroughness of the new commitment. The notorious slave insurrection scare of that year provided the seal of faith. Rumors of widespread slave plotting swept through several counties in the west central portion of the state, and without benefit of trials or even investigation some fifteen slaves were strung up. So too were a half dozen white men thought to be secret agents of abolition. Of all the supposed slave insurrections in the United States, this one has most frequently been regarded by historians as an instance of panic among whites rather than of actual plotting by slaves, even though whites did have real cause for some of their fears.[18]

During the 1850s defenders of slavery mounted a counteroffensive (as they saw it) against northern aggression. By doing so they inevitably confirmed northern suspicions of a monstrous conspir-

17. [George Lewis Prentiss], ed., *A Memoir of S. S. Prentiss* (2 vols.; New York, 1856), I, 107; Woodville (Miss.) *Republican*, April 21, 1838, which quotes the 1836 resolution. As was (and is) commonly the case, some of the difference in Prentiss' two remarks may have been owing to the nature of his audience, one private, the other public. The point may perhaps be permitted to stand here, but of course any study focusing primarily on such changes in opinion needs to track such statements through time with that distinction kept constantly in mind.

18. There will be reason to refer again to this famous set of events. The principal studies, some of which emphasize mob rule, lynching, and vendettas in a quasi-frontier social environment, are Edwin A. Miles, "The Mississippi Slave Insurrection Scare of 1835," *JNH*, XLII (1957), 48–60; William Freehling, *Secessionists at Bay*, 110–13; Davidson B. McKibben, "Negro Slave Insurrections in Mississippi, 1800–1865," *JNH*, XXXIV (1949), 73–90; Christopher Morris, "An Event in Community Organization: The Mississippi Slave Insurrection Scare of 1835," *Journal of Social History*, XXII (1988), 93–111; James Lal Penick, Jr., *The Great Western Land Pirate: John A. Murrell in Legend and History* (Columbia, Mo., 1981); Lawrence Shore, "Making Mississippi Safe for Slavery: The Insurrectionary Panic of 1835," in *Class, Conflict, and Consensus: Antebellum Southern Community Studies*, ed. Orville Vernon Burton and Robert C. McGrath (Westport, Conn., 1982), 96–127. The crucial primary source is *Virgil Stewart*.

acy on the part of the slaveocracy. Many southern politicians were enticed by the idea of expanding the present territories of the nation so as to make more room for their special institution. Some called for a policy of vigorous southward expansion. What was needed, Congressman O. R. Singleton told the House of Representatives, was to "expand in that direction and thus perpetuate it [slavery]—a hundred or a thousand years it may be." [19] On the eve of Lincoln's election the Vicksburg *Weekly Sun* predicted with the air of inevitability that is usual with such claims, "The Southern States once constituted as an independent Republic, the acquisition of Mexico, Central America, San Domingo, and other West India Islands would follow as a direct and necessary result." Thus, in geopolitical terms, "the Gulf of Mexico will be simply a Southern lake." [20]

Proposals for territorial acquisition in the West Indies flew directly in the face of widely recognized history. The very term "St. Domingo" (variously spelled) had long been a synonym for slave rebellion, ever since the massive and successful revolt in that French colony in the 1790s. Toussaint L'Ouverture was one of the best-known French names in the United States, a man who epitomized the bloody overthrow of white dominion. In 1802 Haiti had become the second independent *republic* in the New World— though in 1861 it had still not been accorded diplomatic recognition by the United States. To talk about "taking" St. Domingo was dangerous nonsense. Napoleon had lost an entire army trying to do so. An aroma of unreality and desperation clung to all these propositions, as when the able Mississippi Congressman A. G. Brown announced: "If we want Central America, the cheapest, easiest, and quickest way is to go and take it, and if France and England interfere, read the Monroe Doctrine to them." [21]

The suggestions for reopening the Atlantic slave trade were no more realistic. In an age when Western opinion regarded that traffic as the epitome of inhumanity, it was necessary to stretch the

19. Speech of O. R. Singleton, entitled "Resistance to Black Republican Domination," *Congressional Globe*, 36th Cong., 1st Sess., Appendix, 47–54 (quotation p. 53).

20. Vicksburg *Weekly Sun* quoted in Natchez *Free Trader*, October 29, November 24, 1860. The same striking imagery arose two generations later when U. S. imperialism was said to be turning the entire Caribbean into "an American lake."

21. Michael W. Cluskey, ed., *Speeches, Messages, and Other Writings of the Hon. Albert G. Brown* . . . (2d ed.; Philadelphia, 1859), 594. Brown made no mention of any possible objection or interference from the benighted inhabitants of that region.

case to the breaking point in order to make it at all. Brown, having found to his satisfaction that slavery was a social and moral blessing, publicly urged its propagation "like the religion of the Divine Master to the uttermost ends of the earth."[22] So much for "world opinion" (then confined, of course, to Europe and some of its overseas extensions); and so much, too, for the world's largest navy, which patrolled the coast of West Africa for the express purpose of suppressing the Atlantic slave traffic.[23]

Since there never actually were any realistic prospects for legalizing the trade, discussion tended to turn to smuggling. Proponents whistled brightly about how easily Negroes might thus be obtained, especially through Cuba. Some smuggling was in fact going on along the Gulf and even the Atlantic coastline. How much was open to question, and the estimates then were as widely variant as they are today. No one really knew at the time, and historians might do well to cease their "estimates" and admit that they do not know either and never will. In Mississippi, there is no good evidence of appreciable African immigration in the 1850s. On Second Creek there is no such evidence at all.

Certainly there were African-born slaves on some Mississippi plantations in 1861, just as there were in every state of the cotton South. In all probability most of them were elderly, since Africans had been legally imported in massive numbers into South Carolina for several years prior to the federal ban that took effect January 1, 1808. Unlike blacks in heavily African societies such as Jamaica's, they were not giving their children African names, or at least they did not admit to doing so. Many slaves had been brought from South Carolina into Mississippi (though many more from Virginia, where imports from Africa had stopped at the time of the Revolution). In Concordia Parish the United States assistant marshal, A. R. Kilpatrick, gratuitously entered the word "African" after his entry of several elderly slaves on his 1860 slave schedule. Perhaps he deliberately avoided doing the same for younger ones, although given his proclivity for commenting on the character of individual plantations, this possibility seems unlikely.[24] A. D. Pickens, assistant marshal for Adams County, made

22. *Ibid.*, 595.

23. Ronald T. Takaki, *A Pro-Slavery Crusade: The Agitation to Reopen the African Slave Trade* (New York, 1971); W. E. Burghardt Du Bois, *The Suppression of the African Slave Trade, 1638–1870* (New York, 1896).

24. Naming among slaves was a complex matter. In Jamaica, African-born slaves were simply assigned English or classical names, but then some themselves

OF ONE KIND OF POLITICS

no such entries or other comments beyond the minimum lists required.[25] If African-born slaves had been active in the Second Creek Plan, it seems likely that such participation would have come out at the trials. No such evidence emerged. Thus the conspiracy lacked a feature important in many West Indian and Brazilian revolts—the collective participation of distinct African ethnic groups.[26] At Second Creek the white planters were dealing with other Americans, many of them with a background of six or eight generations in the New World.[27]

What mattered more than the actual presence of an unknown but very small number of Africans were the specters they raised. A prominent Mississippi politician, Henry S. Foote, sketched them vividly in a speech at Yazoo City where he and his audience stood on a bluff that looked westward over the prosperous plain of the Mississippi Delta, over lands where four-fifths of the people were of African descent. Foote launched his diatribe against renewed African immigration from the solid ground of economic self-interest. Too many Negroes, he said, would result in a fall of cotton prices owing to overproduction. Then, so as to have things

---

implanted African names on their children so firmly that bookkeepers (overseers) accepted their use.

25. In 1870, when southern African Americans were for the first time listed by name and with their state of birth, two Adams County blacks were listed as born in Africa, a seventy-six-year-old nurse and a seventy-year-old "mulatto." Probably they had been in the county ten years earlier. Census, 1870 Population, MS pp. 45, 46. An older study of slave names, heavily based on Mississippi lists but especially Lowndes County rather than Adams, found less than 1 percent African names. See Newbell N. Puckett, "Names of American Negro Slaves," in *Studies in the Science of Society Presented to Albert Galloway Keller . . .* , ed. George Peter Murdock (New Haven, 1937), 471–94. Mythologizing about old Africans had attractions for people of both races, as for example, in Ethel L. Fleming, "Old Servant of Marshall Family" (Typescript ca. 1937, in folder "Adams County, Cemeteries," Box 215, Works Progress Administration, Adams County, RG 60, MDAH), and the similar account by the same author in Rawick, *American Slave,* Suppl. 1, Vol. X (Miss. Narrs.), p. 2206.

26. Among many studies, good introductions are Monica Schuler, "The Ethnic Slave Rebellions in the Caribbean and the Guianas," *Journal of Social History,* III (1970), 374–85, and the same author's "Akan Slave Rebellions in the British Caribbean," *Savaçou,* I (1970), 8–31.

27. Plantation documents and the recollections of former slaves suggest that most modern estimates of illegal smuggling are inflated. Joe G. Taylor, "The Foreign Slave Trade in Louisiana After 1808," *Louisiana History,* I (1960), 36–43, has sketchy data pertinent to Mississippi and stresses the decline of illegal imports after the War of 1812.

both ways, he argued that if the rapid natural increase of slaves failed to meet demand, more "could be easily obtained from Virginia and Maryland, and other slave-breeding States." *But* (and here he began his river-planter sketch), importation of "thousand[s], and perhaps millions of wild and savage Africans" would inevitably hazard the advancement of "our slave population." Such a flood would "greatly retard their advancement in moral and religious culture, diminish their happiness and inevitably degrade both the classes of masters and slaves." A torrent of immigrants from Africa would result in "altogether uprooting the present kindly relations existing between these classes, making a more rigid and penal discipline indispensable, and involving the whole white population in the danger of being demoralized and brutified."[28]

Here was the eloquent public warble of the Mississippi statesman. For political purposes, at least, divisions among southern whites must be ignored because society is otherwise properly divided into two sorts, white and black. Under suitable tutelage the quondam savages have advanced in happiness, morals, and religion. Any disturbance of this relation would make whites, like blacks, "demoralized and brutalized." Should such unhappy misfortune transpire, blacks would become unfortunately but "indispensably" both the objects and subjects of "a more rigid and penal discipline." Henry Foote might well have been describing what later happened with whites and blacks during the violent episode in Adams County.

As a United States senator in 1850, Foote had listened attentively to the great speeches that soon turned out to be nearly the dying words of the three giants who had dominated that chamber for so many years. Like many Americans he had felt—with the deaths of John C. Calhoun and Henry Clay and Daniel Webster— a sense of passing into unchartered waters with the old pilots gone. Whatever might happen in the national capital, and although he opposed secessionist rhetoric, Henry Foote's deepest attachment was to his home state. In 1852 he outpolled his fellow Democrat Jefferson Davis for the Governor's Mansion.[29] Indeed, on the floor of the Senate he had spoken for his state by inviting New Hampshire's Senator John P. Hale to bring his abolitionist

28. Yazoo City *Banner* quoted in Natchez *Daily Courier,* June 3, 1859.

29. The building in Jackson has been expanded, but the original portion is now elegantly restored as the official and actual residence of the governor.

views to Mississippi, where he "could not go ten miles into the interior before he would grace one of the tallest trees of the forest, with a rope around his neck." Having figuratively called in the good ole boys, Foote rose to a loftier posture. Such lethal retribution, he declared, would deserve "the approbation of every virtuous and patriotic citizen." Finally, with a swoop of dignity not yet fully mastered, Foote announced that "if necessary"—by which he made plain it would not be—"I should myself assist in the operation."[30]

Behind the storm clouds of misguided philanthropy and fanaticism lurked the possibility of slave rebellion. Actual events seemed to confirm such fears. On the floor of the House of Representatives, L. Q. C. Lamar excoriated Black Republican members for abetting John Brown's raid at Harper's Ferry. In the wake of that shocking event, Susan Darden appears to have really believed reports that "there was a Map found designating different places in different States . . . marked with a Cross," including several places in southwest Mississippi.[31] During the election summer and fall of 1860 there were numerous local panics in the southern states, seemingly without any particular pattern but certainly with vengeance taken on the lives of assertedly dangerous villains both black and white. In Texas outraged rumors about slave rebellions resulted in the hanging of more whites than blacks.[32] The political crisis of 1860–1861 brought panic about slave unrest and white disloyalty home to Mississippi. Newspapers, private letters, and conversations spread the word. There were several hangings of both whites and blacks.[33]

Until May, Adams County seemed quiet. It had remained so

30. *Congressional Globe,* 30th Cong., 1st Sess., Appendix (Vol. XIX), 502. Foote later regretted his remarks. He left for California after political defeat in 1854, and for Europe during the war. New Hampshire's Hale was in fact strongly antislavery; he was the presidential candidate of the Free-Soil party in 1852. As senator he was instrumental in the abolition of flogging (and grog) in the navy.

31. Darden Diary, November 3, 1859.

32. Herbert Aptheker, *American Negro Slave Revolts* (New York, 1943), 353–58; William W. White, "The Texas Slave Insurrection of 1860," *Southwestern Historical Quarterly,* LII (1949), 259–85. See also Wendell G. Addington, "Slave Insurrections in Texas," *JNH,* XXV (1950), 408–34; Wesley Norton, "The Methodist Episcopal Church and the Civil Disturbances in North Texas in 1859 and 1860," *Southwestern Historical Quarterly,* LXVIII (1965), 317–41; Donald E. Reynolds, "Smith County and Its Neighbors During the Slave Insurrection Panic of 1860," *Chronicles of Smith County* [Texas], X (1971), 1–8.

33. McKibben, "Negro Slave Insurrections in Mississippi," 87–88.

throughout a decade of oratorical volleys within the state and throughout the nation. Then, a few weeks after the real shooting began seven hundred miles away, men who were black field hands began talking down on the creek. Carriage drivers started doing the same, in Jefferson County as well as Adams. In the Second Creek area there was also talk on the Dunbar plantation and at Mosby's, where Nelson learned that "young missus wanted black to fight for her." And Orange, who was absent without leave from the Mosby place, was turning up everywhere with talk of the Plan.

But evidence about what black slaves were saying in the Second Creek neighborhood, about *their* politics, is harder to come by than what was going on in the halls of Congress.

CHAPTER 6

THE TRIALS

What the Second Creek conspirators had done, according to their own testimony, constituted a capital felony according to Mississippi law. As codified in 1857 in the *Laws of Mississippi*, "Chapter XXXIII—An Act in Relation to Slaves, Free Negroes and Mulattoes," their offense was clearly spelled out as one of the most serious slave crimes that could be contemplated by the judicial system. In fact, conspiracy to rebel or to murder was the first-named capital offense. The other capital offenses can easily be guessed at, and their inclusion and definitions were not peculiar to Mississippi. The list of such offenses, after conspiracy "to make insurrection," did little to conceal the racial dimension of the Mississippi slave's legal status. It named as capital the "murder of any human being," and thereby treated murder as a racially neutral crime. But it also provided the death penalty for: maiming of "a white person"; rape or attempted rape of "any white woman"; having or attempting "carnal connexion with any white female child" under the age of fourteen "with or without her consent"; "manslaughter of any white person"; and "maliciously burning or setting fire" to a detailed list of buildings ranging from dwelling houses to gins and barns to outhouses, or to being "an accessory to any such offence." Also included were burglary (or accessory thereto) if "some white person" was present in the house at the time, and also robbery. The latter offense was without explicit racial specification of the victim, presumably because legislators could not easily contemplate the possibility of one slave committing such a crime against another. Included as well was "assault upon any white person with intent to kill, upon express malice, and not in necessary self-defence." Yet such malice was not necessary to prove a capital offense if the victim was the slave's own "master, mistress, overseer or employer," or if the assault took place as part of "resistance of legal chastisement." Finally, the list concluded with the other crime (besides arson) most widely and deeply feared throughout the slave South—poisoning.

Attentively complete and without notable peculiarities, the

Mississippi list took greatest care with its first concern. Indeed, its definition of rebellion was concise but embracive:

> If any slave shall at any time consult, advise or conspire with any other slave, or with any other person whatever, to rebel, or to make insurrection, or shall plot or conspire with any slave or any other person, to murder any free white person, he shall be deemed guilty of felony, and . . . shall suffer death.[1]

There is little doubt that a number of Second Creek slaves were guilty under the law.

Yet they were *not* legally tried. The extant testimony was given before an "Examination Committee," sometimes referred to as the "Vigilance Committee," and eventually as simply "the Committee." The same paragraph of the code that defined conspiracy to rebel provided that indictments for such a capital crime—and, indeed, all felonies—be brought "in the circuit court." Such courts existed then (as they do today) as the highest criminal judicial authority in each Mississippi county.[2] But no contemporary documents refer to the Adams County Circuit Court as exercising any jurisdiction in the matter. The circuit court was certainly very much functioning, for at about the time the excitement about Second Creek died down, it tried and convicted one Adams County slave for murdering another owned by the same master.[3]

1. The entire act is in *The Revised Code of the Statute Laws of the State of Mississippi* (Jackson, 1857), 234–56, the section on capital punishments, pp. 248–50. Use of the word *conspiracy* in connection with these events relies partly on common usage and on the *Oxford English Dictionary, s.v.* "conspiracy," meaning 2: "A combination of persons for an evil or unlawful purpose; an agreement among two or more persons to do something criminal, illegal, or reprehensible (especially in relation to treason, sedition, or murder); a plot." The common law did and does not require realistic prospect of success as a criterion. The word *plan*, which the slaves used and their accusers acquiesced in, more strongly implies the element of construction: *OED, s.v.* "plan" (noun), meaning 3: "A formulated or organized method according to which something is to be done; a scheme of action, project, design; the way it is proposed to carry out some proceeding."

2. For capital slave trials, see Michael Wayne, "An Old South Morality Play: Reconsidering the Social Underpinnings of the Proslavery Ideology," *Journal of American History,* LXXVII (1990), 838–63, which cites several studies covering the South more generally. Mississippi offered slaves much greater procedural protection than some other states, notably Virginia and South Carolina, as is clear in Daniel J. Flanigan, "Criminal Procedure in Slave Trials in the Antebellum South," *JSH,* XL (1974), 540–45. Fortuitously, the most notable nineteenth-century slave conspiracies took place in these two older states.

3. Natchez *Daily Courier,* November 12, 1861.

Conspiracy against whites apparently was regarded as an altogether different matter. The statutory act concerning slaves required masters either to furnish legal counsel for any of their chattels accused of a capital crime or, if failing to do so, to pay the costs of such counsel assigned by the court. There is no evidence whatsoever that the Second Creek slaves received this mandatory legal defense.

There is not much direct evidence as to who sat on the Committee. We may safely assume that all its members were men and not women, that they were of adult age, and that they were slaveholders. The Committee may have formed itself on the model provided by statute for the trial of slaves for noncapital offenses, which was two justices of the peace and five slaveholders summoned by the convening justice—the so-called slaveholders court. They may have recalled the murder of an overseer near Kingston four years before, when the examinations had been handled by an *ad hoc* gathering of young planters, sparked by two very wealthy older planters in the neighborhood. That affair had initially been dealt with in a manner nearly indistinguishable from the gatherings during the more general crisis of 1861, though it had been concluded with a legal trial according to statutory procedure.[4] The extralegal procedure used in Jefferson County that May was simple self-assembly of "the Gentlemen of the neighbourhood."

In Adams County this special committee was one more instance of all the extemporaneous organizing that took place throughout the Deep South during the secession crisis. The political atmosphere was aggravated by the prolonged drought that had struck southern Mississippi and Alabama that summer.[5] News-

4. Wayne, "Old South Morality Play," 843–60.
5. William L. Barney, *The Secessionist Impulse: Alabama and Mississippi in 1860* (Princeton, 1974), chap. 4, which is entitled "Exploiting the Fears." John K. Bettersworth, *Confederate Mississippi: The People and Policies of a Cotton State in Wartime* (Baton Rouge, 1943), 25, claimed that such committees existed "in nearly every community." Earlier, during the great excitement about slave stealers and slave insurrection in nearby Madison and Hinds counties in 1835, the "Committee of Safety" was probably larger, perhaps owing to the larger geographical area thought to be involved. It was composed of thirteen freeholders with "a regular secretary and chairman," and was supposed to (but did not) meet "every day" from 9 A.M. to 4 P.M. See *Virgil Stewart*, 235.

papers were filled with reports of men gathering on their own to form groups to deal with local emergencies, so the planters of Adams County had no sense of embarking on an unprecedented or unparalleled procedure. Not all whites were happy about this development. A plantation owner in Louisiana noted privately, "The Vigilance Committee Killed two men, a poor Harmless man in Paincourtville this morning—A very cowardly act." In Alabama a Whig planter wrote dolefully of the excitements created by "great prejudice against northern people" and by "political discussions." He lamented that "vigilance committees have been formed in every neighborhood." Yet in the same area a vigilance committee authorized its executive council to proceed with dire cases because "the law is too tardy in its course, even if it could be effectual in its process."[6] After sectional warfare seemed imminent and then broke out, such activity could easily meld with wartime mobilization. It did so in Adams County and in neighboring Jefferson, where Susan Darden took comfort amidst the awful reports about the drivers by telling herself, "The Minute men are investigating the matter."[7]

Formation of such committees stemmed not only from fear and the need for self-reassurance, but also from the fact that Mississippi, like a number of other southern and western states, had a well-established tradition of vigilante justice.[8] The famous Mississippi slave insurrection scare of 1835, which included the hanging of slaves, white gamblers, and "steam doctors" (practitioners of hydrotherapy), had involved extralegal committees rather than the legal courts. One "Committee of Safety" was reassuringly described as being made up of "persons, conspicuous for wealth and intelligence, and distinguished for integrity and energy." As with many other such panics, published evidence included not only lurid details, but also sweeping and totally unsupported generalizations. After two blacks had been taken up a second time "and confessed that they had been drawn into it by white men," they "were seized by the populace and hanged." Not content with these purported facts, the Washington (D.C.) *United States Telegraph* went on to explain to its readers that "a plot of a most extraordinary

6. Plantation Diary, May 30, 1861, in Alexander F. Pugh and Family Papers, LSU; James Mallory Diary, August 28, 1860, in UNC; Natchez *Semi-Weekly Mississippian*, October 9, 1860.

7. Darden Diary, May 10, 1861, Document C.

8. See esp. John Hebron Moore, "Local and State Governments of Antebellum Mississippi," *Journal of Mississippi History*, XLVI (1982), 119–22.

and diabolical character was developing itself." The plan was nothing if not widespread: "It was ascertained that a general disaffection and the plan of an insurrection had been spread among the negroes, by a band of desperadoes that infested not only that section of the United States, but the whole country from Maryland to Louisiana." Long after the war, William T. Martin, the Natchez lawyer who had risen to the rank of general in the Confederate army, made a similar claim about "uneasiness showing itself among the negroes" in Concordia and Adams during "the Spring of 1860," complete with "emmissaries . . . both white and black," whom he recalled as being "such, because they were provided with money from some point." In a revealing summary of the matter, he concluded, "We captured some of those negroes, but the whites escaped."[9]

Overwrought reporting about interracial matters was common in that era, but it should be borne in mind that the nation as a whole was developing a ravenous appetite for conspiracies of nearly any sort, conspiracies mounted by groups so diverse as Roman Catholics, Masons, Mormons, abolitionists, the British government, and the "monster" Bank of the United States. There is also need for caution in generalizing about the South as a whole. In the older parts of the country, especially those with many whites who owned no slaves but which were dominated by self-consciously paternal planters, evidence of slave plotting was likely to be handled very differently. On the eve of Lincoln's election a prominent North Carolina planter wrote privately about the situation in and near Plymouth. Some twenty Negroes were said to have "intended to collect together 300 who would join them, . . . murder and destroy all they might encounter on the road, set fire to the town, kill all of the inhabitants that might oppose them, seize . . . money . . . ammunition and weapons." Several were imprisoned to await trial in the duly constituted Inferior Court. Only a few people in town "thought those charged should have been hung without Judge or Jury." On the other hand, "Some of the country people were said to have been so much ex-

9. All newspaper quotations are from the Washington, D.C., *United States Telegraph*, October 6, 1835. That newspaper offered unusually extensive coverage of events in Mississippi: see also the issues of July 28, 31, August 3, 4, 5, 8, September 8. For 1860, see Testimony of William T. Martin, December 12, 1877, in Claim (No. 7960) of Katherine S. Minor, Settled Case Files, 1877–83—Mississippi, Adams County, Records of the Southern Claims Commission, Records of the General Accounting Office, RG 217, National Archives, Document P.

cited and alarmed as to avow themselves ready to slaughter the negroes indiscriminately." As one benevolent planter to another, William Pettigrew said he agreed "that in case of panic on the subject of insurrectionary designs, the negroes are in much more danger from the nonslave holding whites than the whites are from the negroes." As for his own plantations and those of his neighbors, he thought, "There is not the slightest ground for apprehension here." His patronizing views may have been reinforced by the fact that these rebels were "Swamp" or "Lake" Negroes, who worked quite independently at what amounted to the wood industry, and he normally had no contact with them at all.[10]

Obviously, in Adams County in 1861 the danger seemed more imminent and to justify immediate action unencumbered by apology or by the letter of the law. The planters proceeded without an eye to financial costs. They were forgoing recompense from the state, since the law provided that the owner of a slave legally condemned to execution by a court be paid half the value of such a slave.[11] Similar compensation was common throughout the South, and had been in the southern colonies before the Revolution. The rationale was that masters should have no financial motive for concealing serious crimes committed by their slaves.[12] Even at the peak of slave prices in 1860, however, with "Extra No. 1 men" (field hands aged nineteen to twenty-five) selling at about $1,800, such considerations were scarcely of primary concern to Adams planters.[13]

10. William S. Pettigrew to James C. Johnston, October 25, 1860, in Pettigrew Family Papers, UNC.

11. The actual amount was to be assessed and certified by five slaveholders summoned before the court by the sheriff. *Revised Code*, 250.

12. In times of major crisis, payment of full value could place a real strain on a colony's or state's treasury, which was a principal reason why "transportation" was sometimes used in preference to execution. By this time, however, frugal sale of convicted slaves to the West Indies was no longer a viable alternative, and had not been since general emancipation in the British islands in the 1830s.

13. A mule cost about $160. The much-used chart in Ulrich B. Phillips, *American Negro Slavery* . . . (1918; rpr. Gloucester, Mass., 1959), opp. p. 370, gives the peak of $1,800 for prime field hands at New Orleans in 1860, but prices dropped sharply late that year in the face of the sectional crisis. See the tables in Michael Tadman, *Speculators and Slaves: Masters, Traders, and Slaves in the Old South* (Madison, Wisc., 1989), 287–91. For mules and horses (which were less subject than slaves to speculation but more to local conditions), see Darden Diary, June 4, 1859, January 19, February 8, March 8, 1860. According to Frederic Bancroft, *Slave Trading in the Old South* (1931; rpr. New York, 1959), 309, in January, 1861, "No. 1 Men" from Kentucky and Missouri were being advertised in Natchez "from

Only one of the white people who wrote anything about the proceedings dealt with the formation of the Second Creek Committee. The diary of Benjamin L. C. Wailes, the bookish planter living near the hamlet of Washington, suggests that wartime military preparations against the northern enemy smoothly paved the way for suppression of serious threat at home. On September 21 he wrote that "it seems there has been a meditated negro insurrection on Second Creek extending to Natchez and neighborhood" and that "a Committee of Citizens of different parts of the County composed in part of the Officer of the two military companies of Pine Ridge and this place have been closely engaged for several days past in making investigation."

Wailes had already had more direct experience with such situations, since several months earlier he had commented on the presentation of a flag "to the 'Washington Troop' on the College Campus by the ladies of the vicinity," and had gone on to note his "being invited with a few others not members of the Company by Capt Middleton to be present at a meeting of the Company when a report was to be presented in relation to the establishment of a patroll and formation of a Vigilance Committee all to be appointed by three person the Captain with the power of life and death." Nearly three weeks later Wailes had been named to a judicial committee of seven that was authorized by the Washington troop "to try in cases of immergency and last resort when our courts cannot in consequence of invasion or other unavoidable causes act efficiently, such persons white or black as may be detected in causing or engaged in insurrection." Wailes was willing to serve on such a committee despite having strong qualms: "This is a very delicate and dangerous power to exercise but self preservation may justify it." [14]

Such qualms were not common. Benjamin Wailes was a planter, though he owned only eighteen slaves in Adams County

---

$1,600 to $1,650," and "Virginia and South Carolina slaves were still more valuable there" at the Forks. There seem to be no extant records from the Natchez slave mart itself, which was a holding pen and a place for person-to-person transactions rather than a brokerage operation. Prices given in the newspapers may not have reflected prices actually paid for slaves, just as they often do not today for other kinds of property. A fine introduction to the complex problem of comparing prices over long periods of time is John Steele Gordon, "The Problem of Money and Time," *American Heritage*, XL (1989), 57–65.

14. Wailes Diary, September 21, June 8, 26, 1861, Document F.

and his chief planting interests and profits involved two plantations farther north, in Warren County.[15] But he was also a professor at tiny Jefferson College in the decaying little village that had
once been the capital of the Mississippi Territory. Despite this in-
auspicious post, he was in fact one of the state's most learned
men, well known as the author of the finest study of Mississippi's
agriculture, geology, and social and natural history. Most other
planters did not give the formation of examination committees a
second thought; if there was the slightest possibility of slaves in
the neighborhood being out of line, a committee ought to take
charge.

In the Second Creek neighborhood, the Examination Committee
seemed to form itself by spontaneous generation. Wailes was as
vague about its membership as about its creation. He noted that
the chief officers of two military companies were included on the
Committee, one from Pine Ridge and the other from Washington.
Both of these hamlets were miles from the scene of the supposed
conspiracy. Wailes also noted that the members were drawn from
"different parts of the County," which suggests that most or perhaps even all the examiners were not known personally by the
slaves being examined.[16] This composition of the panel may well
have been a matter of deliberate policy. Most consciously, the
planters may have assumed that it was better not to have the
slaves examined solely by their owners and others who knew
them at least by local reputation. It also may have been thought
desirable to have broad representation on the Committee in the
event the conspiracy turned out to have spread to other parts of
the county.

Benjamin Wailes and several other planters in *his* neighborhood became unhappy either with this arrangement itself or with
the way it was working out. On Sunday, September 22, there was a
meeting of the Washington Troop at the college. The gathering
was, as Wailes put it, "convened in view of the proceedings of the
Committee on Second Creek." Evidently members of this assemblage at Washington thought that the people at Second Creek were

15. Charles S. Sydnor, *A Gentleman of the Old Natchez Region: Benjamin
L. C. Wailes* (Durham, N.C., 1938), chap. 4.
16. Wailes Diary, September 21, 1861.

proceeding with too much rigor, for the Washington Troop sought "to claim the right of deciding on cases of accused slaves who may be arrested by our own Committee to secure the innocent from wanton severity and to give the accused the benefit of trial by those to whom they are best known." [17] Resolutions were adopted, no doubt without untactful references to "severity," but word about them apparently reached Second Creek and were found offensive. That Wednesday another meeting of the Washington Troop was called, "at which," Wailes noted, "it is proposed to reconsider the resolutions of Sunday, which it seems Capt Middleton and Lieut Roware assumed the responsibility of witholding least some offense might be given to the people of Kingston and Second Creek." [18] Clearly there could be touchy disagreement among members of the planting class as to how human property should be treated under such trying circumstances.

The day before, on Tuesday, ten Second Creek slaves had been hanged "by order of the Committee." [19]

Some of those slaves had been examined at Captain Jacob Surget's home plantation, Cherry Grove, and they probably were hanged there, though perhaps there were also hangings at Brighton Woods, more than a mile to the west.[20] Today, Cherry Grove is a stretch of meadows and woodland with the creek flowing along its southeast border, the landscape grey in winter but green during the longer part of the year. Its fine mansion was rebuilt on the original foundations when the old one burned accidentally just after the war. It affords no evidence of its own as to what tran-

17. *Ibid.*, September 22, 1861. The "from wanton" in the quotation is an almost conjectural reading, since Wailes's handwriting faltered or flurried at that point. Usually his hand was very steady.

18. *Ibid.*, September 25, 1861. The reference to Kingston and a similar allusion made at the Second Creek trials raise the possibility that a separate examination committee was meeting in that hamlet southeast of Second Creek, but there is no such indication in other documents. The Adams Troop had drilled there for at least a week in May, as was reported in Natchez *Daily Courier*, May 8, 15, 1861.

19. Not from Wailes but from a much wealthier planter, William J. Minor Plantation Diary, September 25, 1861, in William J. Minor and Family Papers, LSU, Document H.

20. A descendant's note on an envelope filed with Conner's transcript says "there were *ten* Slaves hung in Brighton Woods and Cherry Grove," Documents A and B.

spired there in 1861. Jacob Surget's "home place" was then at least partly under the plow, since it was relatively flat and the soil tired but not worn out. Seven of the ten slaves hanged that Tuesday belonged to Captain Jacob Surget.[21]

The Examination Committee seems probably to have met in several places, and certainly it summoned the presence of slaves from various plantations. Its members may have chosen to meet at other plantations where numerous slaves seemed to be involved.[22] But obviously the Committee was not roving about conducting itinerant interviews. Lemuel P. Conner noted that before Alfred Mosby testified, certain other slaves were "sent for," and Conner wrote down their names. In all, a total of nineteen slaves were examined at least once. They belonged to seven different owners.[23]

Some days later, on Monday, September 30, when suspicion was growing among whites that blacks in Natchez were involved, William J. Minor noted that the Committee began meeting "at race track"—the popular gathering place next to St. Catherine's Creek on the eastern edge of town, where A. L. Bingaman and Minor himself were the most prominent turfmen. Wherever Conner may have written his two-day record, it was almost certainly earlier and not at the racetrack, since his extant transcript does not mention what Minor had heard on the day the ten men were hanged. On that Wednesday (the twenty-fifth) Minor wrote that he thought it was "clearly proved that there was a plot between a number of negroes on several plantations in the neighborhood of 'Second Creek' and Negroes in Natchez . . . to rise to murder their master some day this month, and then to take possession of their mistresses and all property."[24]

21. The quoted term is in Minor Plantation Diary, September 23, 1861; for the hangings, September 25, 1861. I am grateful to the owner of Cherry Grove, Mrs. Douglas H. MacNeil of Elms Court, Natchez, for graciously showing and informing me about important aspects of the house and grounds.

22. Frederick (Dr. Scott's) twice spoke of "here," but he seems to have been referring to the Second Creek neighborhood in contradistinction to New Orleans. His first reference to "here" must otherwise and rather strainedly be interpreted as meaning not Dr. Scott's place but Mosby's, and the second, Dunbar's.

23. Seven different owners: Dunbar, Grier, Henderson, Mitchell, Mosby, Scott, Surget. Conner recorded responses for two separate examinations of three slaves: George, Harvey, and Harry Scott. Other slaves probably examined twice (at least) were: Alfred, Dick [Dunbar], George, Nelson, and Obey. A full list of those examined is provided in a headnote to Document B.

24. The quotation is in Minor Plantation Diary, September 25, and his return noted September 23.

Perhaps Conner never heard this testimony, which was taken at the Surget plantation. Indeed, we may conclude that Conner's transcript deals with a relatively early and narrowly gauged stage of thinking about what the plot or plots consisted of. In turn, Minor did not mention and may not have heard of Orange, prominent as that Mosby runaway had been when Conner wrote his record. Orange may possibly have already been caught and hanged before Minor's return from a trip to New Orleans at midnight on the twenty-second, but more probably, as will appear, he was still at large.

One of the most puzzling questions is why Conner bothered to write down his transcript of various slaves' responses to the Examination Committee. Neither he nor the Committee were under any legal obligation to do so. Clearly Conner did not attend all sessions of all such committees that met in Adams County that fall. He wrote down the testimony of two apparently complete days and perhaps parts of others—presumably on the spot, since he let stand his own crossings-out when he took his transcript home. Possibly he was a member of the Committee. Perhaps, as a well-established planter with experience in Concordia as well as Adams and with none of his own slaves apparently involved, he seemed to the Committee a likely person to serve as "secretary" and keep a record. But why should the Committee want a record, especially since they already had such a good (though approximate) idea of what they were going to hear? If Conner wrote down the record only for himself—and there is no evidence that he shared it with anyone—why did he do so? He certainly was no Mary Boykin Chesnut, privily composing (and recomposing) a diary with an eye toward dissemination to a wide posterity, for he did not bother or choose to record even the place and date of his transcriptions. He surely knew the heat of the fire he was dealing with—and quietly folded it in two envelopes together with his other papers. He dated them November 11, without any year and with no consciousness that that day was the thirtieth anniversary of the hanging of Nat Turner.

Both a lot and little is known about Lemuel Parker Conner. His grandfather had come to the area from South Carolina about 1790, when the territory was still in dispute between the United States and Spain. Born in 1827, he grew up as a boy either at Berkley (on the creek not far from the Homochitto) or at Clifford Plantation,

George

which his grandfather and father had founded in the low hills about three miles east of the creek's southward bend. In 1840 his widowed mother bought Linden, just outside the eastern edge of town. The oldest son among nine children, Lemuel attended Yale and then studied law in Natchez. He married young and used his inheritance to establish himself as planting gentleman. By 1860 he and Fanny were the parents of eight children, the oldest twelve and the youngest (as properly enumerated by the census marshal on July 29) "³⁄₁₂."[25]

Conner was both an insider and an outsider to Second Creek and Adams County. He had strong connections there, and he was listed in the census as living in Natchez itself. His small property of seventy-three acres was actually on the edge of town, and he lived the life of a suburban squire, doing without an overseer to supervise his recently expanded staff of twenty-four slaves. He (or rather they) maintained four "pleasure" carriages—an uncommonly large number. Now, in 1861, he was only thirty-four years old.[26]

Conner also had numerous relatives in Adams County, including his mother and siblings and other Conners and the "Mr. Young" mentioned in the testimony of Frederick and Simon. Yet he himself was shifting some of his worldly engagements to Concordia, where in 1860 he owned 256 slaves and two plantations, together worth $240,000, and he was referred to as being "at the bar of Vidalia."[27] He may have owned a house in that little village

25. D. Clayton James, *Antebellum Natchez* (Baton Rouge, 1968), 148; Mary Conway Shields Dunbar, *My Mother Used to Say: A Natchez Belle of the Sixties,* ed. Elizabeth Dunbar Murray (Boston, 1959), 82–83; Natchez *Democrat,* Pilgrimage "Pink" ed., 1959, p. 18.

26. Adams Census, 1860 Free, household 855; Slave, MS p. 39; Adams Land; Adams Personal, 1858, 1859, 1861, 1862.

27. Herbert Weaver, *Mississippi Farmers, 1850–1860* (1945; rpr. Gloucester, Mass., 1968), 109, gives the $240,000. Conner was not listed in Concordia's MS Free Schedules, but was on the MS Agricultural Schedules (Schedule 4) as owning two plantations, one with 122 slaves, the other with 134. See Joseph Karl Menn, *The Large Slaveholders of Louisiana—1860* (New Orleans: Pelican Publishing Co., 1964), 196, 202–203. Two other Conner brothers, H.[enry] L.[egrarer] and W.[illiam] G.[ustine], were bracketed with him as being of Concordia in *Cohen's New Orleans and Southern Directory, for 1856* (2 vols.; New Orleans, 1855–56), II, 19. *Goodspeed's,* I, 580–82 has pertinent data, including the "bar" quote. Sometimes different courts of much the same jurisdictional level met at the same time in Vidalia and in Natchez, despite the pronounced difference in the legal systems. See *Johnson's Diary,* I, 419. See also Mrs. Robert Young, "A Tradition of Second Creek Valley, A.D. 1772 to 1820" (Beau Prés Plantation, 1905); typescript copy in author's

across the river, and in 1856 had headed the building committee for a new parish courthouse there.[28] He had been a levee district inspector for Concordia, a position which—given the nature of that low-lying floodplain—was not merely honorific. In January, 1861, he had taken an active part in Louisiana's secession convention. On April 19 he was appointed to an emergency "Military Committee" and either then or later became its chairman. Yet with all these auspicious minor offices, Lemuel Conner was the sort of man who when away from home (in St. Louis) and writing to his wife was careful to add, "Howdy to the servants."[29]

During the war he was active in fund raising, and then joined the army as a colonel on the staff of General Braxton Bragg, perhaps through the influence of his sister's husband, who was one of Bragg's higher officers.[30] There were difficulties with some of his Concordia slaves during the great conflict; and afterward, with his other property officially "restored," he had problems with the management of free laborers. In 1866 and 1867 he borrowed heavily and ended up in bankruptcy. After further hard times and failure to obtain minor political appointments, he recouped somewhat by joining his son's law practice in Vidalia. Lemuel P. Conner died in 1891.[31]

Though he was said to have weighed 225 pounds, Lemuel P. Conner was an energetic and active man. He had entered public affairs, and unlike some Adams planters had enthusiastically sup-

possession of original owned by Mrs. Douglas H. MacNeil, Natchez). I am grateful to Mrs. Bazile R. Lanneau for giving me a copy of this document.

28. James, *Antebellum Natchez*, 148.

29. Lemuel P. Conner to "Fanny" [Frances Elizabeth Conner], March 4, 1861, in Lemuel P. Conner and Family Papers, LSU.

30. William T. Martin, the Natchez attorney, who has been mentioned before and who will be encountered again in another context.

31. His official appointments are in Robert Dabney Calhoun, "A History of Concordia Parish, Louisiana," *Louisiana Historical Quarterly*, XV (1932), 623–26, and XVI (1933), 99–100. A conspiracy among his slaves and its betrayal are in Undated Testimony, Conner Papers, LSU; on other difficulties with his slaves, see Lemuel P. Conner to Fanny Conner, n.d., in Conner Papers. Restoration of property is in Order by G. D. Reynolds, September 30, 1865, Natchez sub dist[rict] lists of property, Mississippi, Records of the Bureau of Refugees, Freedmen, and Abandoned Lands, RG 105, National Archives. Postwar labor problems are discussed in Ronald L. F. Davis, *Good and Faithful Labor: From Slavery to Sharecropping in the Natchez District, 1860–1890* (Westport, Conn., 1982), 92–94, 101–102. Other information is in Michael Wayne, *The Reshaping of Plantation Society: The Natchez District, 1860–1880* (Baton Rouge, 1983), 67, 82–83, 121.

ported secession. So had his brothers. When Lemuel Conner recorded the slave testimony on Second Creek in September, 1861, he was a young, wealthy planter and a vigorous supporter of the Confederate cause. What appears to differentiate him most conspicuously from so many others of his class and peculiar region was that he had a foot firmly planted on each side of the river.[32]

Though he would scarcely have appreciated the fact, Lemuel Conner's most important contribution to history was that he liked to keep good records and helped generate a family who liked to preserve them. In addition to all his other papers, Conner wrote down what he thought some Second Creek slaves said when answering questions posed by the Examination Committee. This fact—his creation of a "historical" document—raises the troublesome question of why these slaves said anything at all. Under the circumstances, they knew they were condemning themselves and their fellows to death, so why did these men talk?

We need to address that question in a particular context—within the framework of a specific culture and social situation that no longer exists but that nonetheless had features that were generic to hostile human confrontations. We know that men in power often employ organized violence on people they are dominating, especially at times felt to be fraught with crisis and danger. We assume that there is something in the very nature of humankind that causes men (and less often women) to do this, since throughout time and geographical space such behavior has been and is very common. It is often called "brutality"—our way of trying to distance ourselves from animality—but, as is well known, it nonetheless occurs frequently in the species homo sapiens.

In this particular instance, there is a question that ought to precede inquiry as to why these slaves talked. We can readily see why there was great tension about slaves throughout the white South in 1861. We can also see with equal readiness why some slaves might have wanted to rebel and have detected an unusual opportunity to do so in 1861. But what triggered a crisis among these

32. His weight is asserted in Calhoun, "History of Concordia Parish," XV (1932), 625. Lemuel and Fanny were probably married in Concordia, since their names are not in the Adams records; see Irene S. and Norman E. Gillis, *Adams County Mississippi Marriages, 1802–1859* (Shreveport, La., 1976).

particular slaves and slaveowners? In one sense we will never know, since we will never know enough about the individuals involved. Certainly we will need to keep an eye on the peculiar sociology of Adams County—and by all accounts it was peculiar, in relation to both the rest of Mississippi and the rest of the American South. But where was the element that triggered the tragedy? Why did some Second Creek masters begin hauling some Second Creek slaves before a quasi-official board of inquiry and start asking questions? Put more mundanely, perhaps, how did the planters learn about the Plan and thus even think of making serious inquiries? Planters did not ordinarily go about polling their slaves as to whether they were planning to revolt.

Many other American slave conspiracies were exposed before fruition because whites were told by some slave, that is, as the result of deliberate "informing"—loyalty or disloyalty, according to one's lights. The case with Second Creek was different. Surprisingly, it is possible to conclude with near certainty how whites learned about the Plan.

According to Harvey, whose father, Orange, was also owned by John S. Mosby, several slaves discussed the Plan while in the presence of someone Harvey referred to as "Benny." Orange said that "whipping colored people would stop," and according to Harvey, "Benny asked why." The response to Benny's question must have referred to what would happen to the white folks, because "Alfred said the resting place would be in hell." Benny remained "present" while the business was discussed by Louis, who was a Metcalfe driver, and Nelson, another Mosby slave.

After Harvey was examined, the next man to talk was Alfred, who also was owned by Mosby, and several of his answers were thoroughly congruent with Harvey's: "Orange said the whipping business would stop." Then, "Mas Benny asked why," and Alfred responded with "a resting place in hell."

Thanks to the national census enjoined by the Constitution for every tenth year, it is possible to discover who Mas Benny was. His full name was Benjamin H. Austen; he was a young white boy; and his father was the overseer employed by Dr. James Metcalfe, the planter who headed the large Metcalfe clan.

Benny Austen was only eight, or possibly nine, and attended a school when it was held during the winter. He may have been familiar with the Mosby place, since Mosby's school was on the property. He was young enough that the Mosby slaves had no fear of him, but old enough to be curious and later to talk about what he had heard. We do not know whom he talked to. We do know that he was the only white person named Benjamin in the immediate locality, and that he was at an age when most boys like to roam around their neighborhoods. He heard black men discussing some very strange things about Lincoln and whipping being stopped, though he had left by the time discussion turned to plans for going to Dr. Scott's, to Dr. Orrick Metcalfe's, and to Mrs. Dunbar's. Benny's father and mother lived on the senior Metcalfe's plantation, together with his older brother and sister and his younger brother. His father's employer was an extremely wealthy man who owned 325 slaves on several plantations in Adams County. Montrose was Dr. Metcalfe's home plantation, about three miles downstream from Cherry Grove.[33]

It is scarcely surprising that Benny should have been visiting on the Mosby place, since it was only about two miles from home and he may well have been in the company of Louis, a driver belonging probably to one of the Metcalfe clan and perhaps not attached full-time to any single Metcalfe plantation. Louis seems to have had the trust and personal leverage to go off his place even without a pass. Benny must have found it comfortable and fun to be allowed to go along with his big friend. Certainly Benny felt free to "ask why" when puzzled by the conversation among Louis and some of the Mosby slaves. The young were curious about such exciting matters, as Benjamin Wailes had occasion to observe elsewhere and several weeks later when he wrote that open discussion about his Vigilance Committee "seemed indiscreet there being several dozens small boys present," and "these children will mingle before night and converse freely if not indiscreetly with our servants."[34]

It does not necessarily follow that Benny went running home to blab to his parents or older siblings at Dr. Metcalfe's place that Louis was a troublemaker; Benny may well have not fully realized what the trouble *was*. But it seems very probable that the matter somehow came up at least tangentially—at supper or sweeping

33. James Metcalfe in Census, 1860 Free, household 950; Slave, MS pp. 61–65; Adams Land, 1861; Adams Personal, 1861. Benny's schooling is extrapolated from the census schedule's column headed "Attended School within the Year." In 1860, at age seven, he was not so indicated, but his eight-year-old sister was. The large Metcalfe family is discussed more fully in the next chapter.

34. Wailes Diary, June 8, 1861, Document F.

the porch, perhaps—and his wide-eyed mother and father began to probe with questions. No doubt Benny was upset. No doubt his parents were too.

Of the twenty-two or twenty-three examinations noted by Conner, one disclosed what he described as "00" and two others "nothing." In all probability he was not present at all the examinations. Still, most of the slaves he named did talk—most, but not all. He also recorded several testimonies as virtually worthless and at the end of his transcript seems to have given up taking full notes. Yet according to his account, nineteen or twenty slaves gave information, and three of the Mosby slaves, Nelson, Harvey, and Alfred, were nearly voluble.

It is not certain whether the examiners conducted their business in or out of doors, though the latter seems more likely, as will become apparent. It seems very probable that each slave examined was alone, without his friends, standing before or within a battery of white men who were obviously gentlemen of quality and grimly determined to get answers. This was exactly the procedure that the wealthy planter Alexander K. Farrar had helped organize when investigating the murder of an overseer near Kingston in 1857.[35] Now, as then, each and every slave faced the twin specters of the whip and the gallows.

Perhaps it would be more accurate to say that these specters stood *within* each slave. The probability of being whipped for a serious or even casual offense was not a matter for calculation; it existed as a certainty of life, a certainty that derived from experiential knowledge. One did not have to have experienced the pain on one's own back, though many had. Whipping had been seen; it had been heard. It was a palpable indicator of their condition. It was a fixture of life as real as rain, and like rain it would happen again because it had happened before and it was about as predictable and in such a time as this about as easy to stop and this time it's me for sure and they always do it when pushed and we sure have pushed them and now I'm here and it's me.

Orange had put his finger on the matter; he had said "the whipping business would stop."

35. Alexander K. Farrar to H. W. Drake, September 4, 5, 1857, in Alexander K. Farrar Papers, LSU.

Today we may speak from distant ground about the psychology of the victim, about self-destructive internalization of values, about socialization of deference from childhood years, about infantilization of personality, and about the psychological effects of totalism and hegemony—and we would not be wrong. It would be a mistake, however, to underestimate the power of the ingrained habit of telling the boss white man what he wanted to hear. That habit had indeed been imprinted by the slave's parents and by all the older people he had known when growing up. As habits go, it was not a bad one, for experience told him that it usually worked and was always safer than talking back. Here he was talking back in a different sense because the man was asking different questions. So he talked back to his questioners, told them what they wanted to hear. What they wanted to hear was not in doubt. The questions may have been—and often clearly were—very pointed, and the required answers were known to everyone long before they were asked. Yet beneath the fear and habitual deference lay a bedrock of pride. They had made a Plan, and revealing its details permitted a man to assert that they had done so—which was to assert oneself.

And why *not* answer. They and their friends were going to die anyway, whether they answered or not. After all that had happened they were going to die—which was a fact of life as real as the rain. Things had gone so far, far too far. There was no point in trying to get out. The time was long past for creative stories, for shuffling, for staring at the ground, for scratching the head. Why not give the man the details, since now it didn't make any difference. Not to oneself, not to one's friends. They had been taken up and would all be treated the same way—which rather oddly meant that everyone was equal—which wasn't really all that odd because they all were niggers. And probably most of their friends had already told the man about the Plan, or if they hadn't they certainly would when they get caught in the trap jaws I am in now.

But we are left with the fact: Obey "says nothing" and Billy "says nothing," and Harry Lyle "says 00." (The latter may not have been equivalent to "nothing," as will become apparent in the next chapter.) Under similar circumstances a few men—not many— have proved themselves capable of holding out in silence. Obey and Billy were young men belonging to one of the most prominent slaveholders in the county, but that old man had been gone far off for a long time. Their co-silence may have been just that, a function of living together on the same place. Their legal owner's immense wealth was of no concern to them. Certainly they had no hope of support from Captain Surget, whose plantation would in fact shortly be the site of more examinations. He was living in New York City and would not have been sympathetic no matter where he was living. After their silence, Obey and Billy were hanged too, unless of course they had already died from the whipping.[36]

There are hints but no direct assertions in the documents that the slaves summoned before the Examination Committee were examined under the lash. If this was the case, as seems very likely, it may explain in part why so many slaves talked, though it would greatly oversimplify matters to say that they were tortured into confessing. Clearly most men "talk" under the pressure of great pain, but just as clearly not all men do.

It is very possible that some of the men about to be examined were forced to watch and listen to such torture, at least at a distance. Whippings as punishments were traditionally and deliberately public affairs, sometimes administered before an assemblage of slaves at which attendance was required, the spectacle being closed only to white women and children. But whippings for the object of gaining information were more grimly purposeful.

Whipping as a *method* of inflicting pain was endemic in the culture as a whole and common in Western Europe and its overseas extensions. In the United States it was not confined to interracial situations. Most white children had experienced it, usually in mild forms at the hands of parents, schoolteachers, and others in authority. Flogging had recently been legally abolished in the United States Navy, though it still was sometimes practiced aboard naval vessels. The close vote in the Senate for ending the practice had been strictly sectional: with the exception of two Border State senators, the South had voted solidly for continuance of Navy flogging, in the face of northern contentions that it was a "slavish" practice that robbed sailors of their "manhood."[37]

36. Obey was later examined a second time, and again remained silent. There is no direct proof of their deaths, but they could scarcely have survived the affair. Both men had been named by others under examination and at least seven Surget slaves were executed. For Jacob Surget in New York, see James, *Antebellum Natchez,* 154.

37. James E. Valle, *Rocks and Shoals: Order and Discipline in the Old Navy, 1800–1861* (Annapolis, 1980), esp. 83; Myra C. Glenn, *Campaigns Against Corporal Punishment: Prisoners, Sailors, Women, and Children in Antebellum America* (Albany, 1984), chap. 7; Harold D. Langley, *Social Reform in the United States Navy, 1798–1862* (Urbana, 1967), chaps. 6–7.

Whatever the irony of that criticism, public standards in such matters—or perhaps public tastes—had changed greatly since the previous century. Burning alive and other such tortures were no longer regarded as acceptable public spectacles, though public burning of black slaves took place occasionally in the decades before the war. A generation after that conflict, the practice became popular entertainment during the wave of racial hatred that began to sweep the South.[38] Yet on the eve of the American Civil War, whipping followed by hanging was simply standard, normal procedure.[39]

Throughout the slave states, entirely explicit written references to whipping as a means of obtaining confessions were not nearly as common as the actual practice, which was often hinted at in veiled language. Thus a correspondent of the Macon *Daily Telegraph* in Georgia was unusual in his frankness when he wrote that he had examined five slaves. With the first, "I examined him under the whip." Then so on with the others, except that "one without the whip told the same."[40] Another Georgia newspaper noted concerning a different incident, "Several were arrested and whipped for the purpose of drawing from them a confession."[41] During a panic in the iron district of Tennessee in 1856, "some of

38. Joel Williamson, *The Crucible of Race: Black-White Relations in the American South Since Emancipation* (New York, 1984), 183–89. For burning in the eighteenth century, see Winthrop D. Jordan, *White Over Black: American Attitudes Toward the Negro, 1550–1812* (Chapel Hill, 1968), 106, 116, 118, 392, 398, 473, which mistakenly suggests that burning alive ended (until after the Civil War) in the early 1800s. See also Lowry Ware, "The Burning of Jerry: The Last Slave Execution by Fire in South Carolina?" *South Carolina Historical Magazine*, XCI (1990), 100–106, for an 1830 case that resulted in legislation making hanging the only legal method of capital punishment. There were at least several instances of mob burnings during the antebellum period. One across from Natchez is in *Johnson's Diary*, I, 386. In 1854 the New York *Daily Tribune* reported that a slave in Tennessee had been tortured to confess rape and three murders, and then had been burned "in the presence of a thousand or more persons"; Charles E. Beveridge and Charles Capen McLaughlin, eds., *Slavery and the South, 1852–1857* (Baltimore, 1981), 421n, Vol. II of [various editors], *The Papers of Frederick Law Olmsted*, 5 vols.

39. Hanging was the legally prescribed method of capital punishment in Mississippi. *Revised Code* (1857), 625.

40. Macon *Georgia Weekly Telegraph*, November 15, 1860.

41. Columbus (Ga.) *Daily Sun*, September 3, 1860. The brief article, entitled "The Negro Insurrection Movement in Dalton," was taken from the Dalton (Ga.) *Times*, August 30, 1860—an instance of the usually acknowledged borrowing common among eighteenth- and nineteenth-century newspapers, now largely supplanted by news services.

the favorite servants, (at the Iron Works,) who have been greatly indulged . . . had to be whipped very severely before they would reveal any thing." One man "received four hundred lashes before he would speak a word."[42] In 1835 in Mississippi, in Madison County, not far from Adams, slaves were (according to a published account) "put under the lash" to make them confess. In 1860 (after the election of Lincoln) citizens of Batesville in the northern part of the state whipped "a negro mechanic in the neighborhood of Sardis, who . . . upon being whipped, admitted" he and others planned to "murder his master" and then "escape."[43] Indeed, as one rereads the documents in connection with Second Creek, the term *examine* takes on the stench of euphemism for physical brutality.

Both procedures—whipping as punishment and examining under the whip at times of crisis—clearly served as rituals of confirmation. What was being confirmed, in the eyes of most participants on both sides, was the order of dominance and the role of dominance in the social order. Pain became the badge of power and powerlessness, and pain generates its own memories and clears space for its own private inner domination. Seventy-five years after the war, an old man in Texas, Andy J. Anderson, still recalled being whipped at the orders of a new owner: "So he ties me to de stake and every half hour for four hours, dey lays tm lashes on my back. For de first couple hours de pain am awful. I's never forgot it. Den I's stood so much pain I not feel so much and when dey takes me loose, I's jus' 'bout half dead. I lays in de bunk two days, gittin' over dat whippin', gittin' over it in de body but not de heart. No, suh, I has dat in de heart till dis day."[44]

The pain suffered while being "examined" may have been

42. Memphis *Daily Appeal*, December 5, 1856, quoted in Charles B. Dew, "Black Ironworkers and the Slave Insurrection Panic of 1856," *JSH*, XLI (1975), 329.

43. *Virgil Stewart*, 226–27, 231; James Lal Penick, Jr., *The Great Western Land Pirate: John A. Murrell in Legend and History* (Columbia, Mo., 1981), 111–13. The Batesville affair was reported in the *Panola Star* (Miss.), December 20, 1860. Other instances of "torture" for confessions in Mississippi, in 1857 and 1860, are cited in Moore, "Local and State Governments," 120n.

44. Rawick, *American Slave*, Suppl. 2, Ser. 2, Vol. II (Tex. Narrs.), Pt. 1, pp. 52–53; and another version of the same interview, *ibid.*, Vol. IV (Tex. Narrs.), Pt. 1, p. 15. Willie Lee Rose, *Rehearsal for Reconstruction: The Port Royal Experiment* (Indianapolis, 1964), 110, wrote that on some Sea Island plantations (in the 1860s) "nearly every" slave bore whip marks—an assertion that has been repeated elsewhere, with due citation but without the "nearly." Whipping was the most common punishment for contemporary Russian serfs; see Steven L. Hoch, *Serfdom and Social Control in Russia: Petrovskoe, a Village in Tambov* (Chicago, 1986), chap. 5.

rather different. Partly it was punishment for wrongdoing, but partly it required cerebral calculation by both parties because precious information was involved. Perhaps we ourselves are reluctant to acknowledge that the slash of the whip was an integral part of a dialogue. And when such dialogues take place on the threshold of expected death, they take on qualities not likely to appear in the more customary rituals of slave discipline and punishment. Andy Anderson was whipped because he accidentally broke a whippletree on a wagon. The Second Creek slaves were whipped (probably) because they plotted to kill their masters and take the young white women, and whites wanted information.[45]

Other contemporary documents hint strongly that their testimony was at least in part coerced by infliction of physical pain. Benjamin Wailes noted that some whites outside his own neighborhood thought the proceedings of the Second Creek Examination Committee were such that "the innocent" needed protection from "wanton severity."[46] On October 15 a white woman from neighboring Wilkinson County wrote to her niece that "they have been threatened with quite a formidable Insurrection in Adams County, Miss. Natchez 40—miles from here." She added, "The investigation is still going on. . . . The head one is not yet executed[.] They still hope to make him tell."[47]

45. Whipping of slaves has been discussed by many historians. What is most striking in the sources is how much more whipping actually took place than was recorded. Bennet Barrow, a Louisiana cotton planter, is famous among specialists on slavery precisely because he seems to have been the only planter to keep anything like a log of whippings. Modern attempts to quantify his punishments not only say more about our mentality than his, but (with less excuse) ignore the entries in his diary where Barrow states that he "had a general Whiping Frollick." Edwin Adams Davis, ed., *Plantation Life in the Florida Parishes of Louisiana, 1836–1846, as Reflected in the Diary of Bennet H. Barrow* (New York, 1943), 98 and *passim*. Attempts to quantify such matters seem to me rather like describing the weather by counting clouds. Some whites thought whipping an unfortunate necessity, but others used it with casual unconcern. One Louisiana planter gratuitously inserted in the middle of a letter without additional comment: "My negroes are getting healthy—but have to be licked like blazes—they are awful lazy." John Hamilton to William S. Hamilton, September 21, 1859, in William S. Hamilton Selected Letters, LSU.

46. Wailes Diary, September 22, 1861, Document F.

47. S[ophia] H. Hunt to Jennie [Hughes], October 15, 1861, in Hughes Family Papers, UNC, Document I. I am grateful to Stoney Miller for this reference. James L. Roark, *Masters Without Slaves: Southern Planters in the Civil War and Reconstruction* (New York, 1977), 74–75, quotes part of this letter very briefly and somewhat inaccurately, nearly dismissing it by saying that its writer had "heard a rumor." Taken as a whole, the letter suggests more substantial grounds of information.

More than two years later, while the war was still dragging on, a white woman in Natchez talked about the affair with an officer in the Union forces that had occupied Natchez—this time permanently—without the firing of a shot. Relations between the northern white troops and the local populace were more cordial than in most southern cities. A captain in the 12th Wisconsin Infantry noted in his diary a conversation after attending Sunday services at the Presbyterian church: "Called on Mrs. Henry in the evening and heard her version of the servile insurrection of 1861." Mrs. L. A. Henry was a Natchez widow whom Bennett described as "a very intelligent and pleasant lady, a teacher by profession." She evidently told him more than had been spoken of (so far as the documents convey) at the time. Captain Bennett was shocked: "The outrages committed on the poor, unfortunate Negroes who were suspected of evil designs surpass any thing I ever heard or read of." What she told him confirmed the worst he had been taught to expect from slavery, and he wrote bitterly, "The cruelty of the chivalrous gentry of Natchez would put to blush the warmest advocates of the Spanish Inquisition as practiced in the dark ages of Popery. Mrs. H. is a native of this town so the usual cry of 'educational prejudice' has no force whatever. We can never know half the evil."[48] Though clearly not without prejudices of his own, Captain Bennett had no reason to invent this conversation for his private diary.

Perhaps the most telling evidence of physical brutality lies in the Conner transcript itself. After entering Obey's name, Conner placed a dash before he wrote, "says nothing." He did not do so with Billy, probably because the precedent for saying nothing had just been established. This dash—this mere punctuation mark—strongly suggests there was a lapse of time after the beginning of Obey's examination before it became clear that he would not speak. Yet a dash of punctuation would be a weak reed for such a conclusion were it not for the way Conner's transcript ends, or nearly ends.

48. Diary of Van S. Bennett, January 10, 1864, in State Historical Society of Wisconsin, Madison, Document L. Charles Royster kindly provided this reference. Bennett's regiment had arrived in Natchez August 16. This was not his first time at that church, and he had called at Mrs. Henry's home with several other officers on September 25. She had probably been married to the prominent merchant frequently mentioned in the Jenkins Diary, which also noted (February 21, 1855) paying her "tuition" for Jenkins children. Other than the passage quoted here, Bennett's diary showed no interest in the fortunes of the local inhabitants, black or white.

Conner's record comes to a stop with Harry Scott's revelations about literacy and guns, and then with unrecorded examinations (or expectations of examining) of Harry Scott's son Alfred and two of the Dunbar slaves, George and Dick. But prior to these entries, Conner had assumed matters were at an "end," for he marked his notes with that word. He was beginning to tire and to lapse into boredom, and for the first time he began to scribble nonsense with his pencil. The earlier portions of his record were free of such doodles, so it is clear that the pace of revelations (or at least his interest in them) had slowed appreciably.[49] Harvey Mosby had just testified for the second time and had very plainly and directly implicated Captain Surget's Obey. Then Nelson (another of Mosby's) seems to have been called, but failed to say anything (in Conner's lights) worth recording. Conner then several times wrote down the full formal name of a man neither mentioned by the slaves nor a resident of the county nor apparently previously known to Conner—a name that remains without further identification. All that can be said about John O. Fenall is that he was somehow associated with Obey's continued obdurate refusal to say anything at all.[50]

Surely Conner did not write Obey's name repeatedly (a total of eleven times) for random reasons. Obey had been previously implicated and had refused to talk. Now he had been implicated again, damningly so by Harvey, who quoted him as saying, "I will join them too to help kill the white folks." So Obey was again "examined" at length and again refused to say anything. Clearly he was a hard case as far as Conner and the Committee were concerned. One almost detects a whiff of grudging respect as one watches Conner spell out Obey's name repeatedly. Perhaps one can also discern a sense of disgust and frustration, possibly even horror, as Obey continued to hold out in silence. Surely Obey was

49. No attempt has been made to re-create these markings in Documents A and B.

50. See the endings of Conner's transcript, Documents A and B. The possibility of Fenall's being a semiprofessional "slave breaker" cannot be ruled out, but this is sheer speculation. Conner's handwriting was very clear with the middle initial and last name, so John O'Farrell was surely not the man. As a fifty-two-year-old Natchez merchant dealing in "Plantation Goods, &c," owner of three house lots and four slaves, and an outright Unionist, O'Farrell was an unlikely candidate as a participant or for confusion arising from an oral introduction to Conner. See Census, 1860 Free, household 625; Slave, MS p. 13; A. Mygatt and Co.'s New Orleans Business Directory . . . (New Orleans, 1857), 267.

being whipped and perhaps tortured in other ways.[51] Indeed it is more than possible that when Conner wrote "end" after his repeated *Obey, Obey, Obey*'s, he was referring to Obey's complete, sagging unconsciousness or to his death under the lash.

Such an interpretation is made more than merely possible by the fact that Conner's record did not in fact end at that point. Yet in the record itself there is a sense of denouement—of the writer wrapping things up—as Conner finally records the names of three previous testifiers without noting what, if anything, they said. Probably most of the planters there felt things had gone on long enough and indeed too long, and that it was time to move on to the hangings, which it was hoped would put a stop to the business and which in any event ought not be delayed. After all, hangings were a crucial part of the whole proceedings.

At that time of year in Adams County the stifling heat of the summer begins to moderate. Rain comes less often, but more commonly by thunderstorm. It was still early on in the picking season. There was work to be done. Some of the Second Creek slaves thought so too, but they had different business in mind.

---

51. Two contrary and perhaps equally plausible arguments concerning another possible torture can be constructed: (1) that desperate and furious planters ordered any means they thought necessary, including "dismemberment," *i.e.*, castration; and (2) that castration had not often been practiced for generations (though it would later be revived, especially during lynchings, after the war), and that it would have seemed futile and also not fitting for the dignity of the Committee (furthermore, no one had implicated Obey in taking ladies). Heated irons, thumbscrews, etc., etc., were of course other possibilities.

CHAPTER 7

THE REBELS

When we inquire who the conspirators were, we are in essence asking about their motivation. We sense that if we were to know everything about the other aspects of their lives, we would know why they chose to plot against their masters. Obviously if we knew a great deal about these men we would think ourselves a long way toward explaining why they became involved in such a dangerous undertaking.

But of course we do not know all about them, and indeed cannot discover much. What we do know is largely shaped by what we know of their owners, and is thus distorted. As is usual with the history of the "inarticulate," when faced with a solid wall of absence of information, historians of slavery have tended to throw up their hands and lapse—sometimes to the point of repose—into a posture that owes more to their own ideological predispositions than to historical analysis. Here it ought to be remembered that historians today are themselves immersed in a long historiographical stream, a flowing collage of ideology and feeling that has had an active and influential history of its own.

Much of what has been written about slave conspiracies in the last half century has been shaped by the felt necessity of refuting the notion that American slaves were contented in their bondage. Many of these refutations have proceeded apace without consideration of the sheer peculiarity of that notion. Members of the master class in most slave cultures have not assumed or asserted that slaves actually *liked* being slaves. Yet assertions that African American slaves did so have been especially strong in the United States, much more than in most other slave cultures. Such assertions have a history of their own, and that history is sufficiently complicated and important as to need full treatment in another place. Put baldly for present purposes, that perception dominated white views of slaves for only about one century out of three and a half of substantial black-white contact in North America.

In more recent years, historians have countered these asser-

tions with a presumption more palatable to altered tastes. They
have decided that slaves hated their condition. More often, they
advance the revealingly negative proposition that slaves were *not*
contented. They have found it easy to prove by ordinary canons
that some slaves malingered and sabotaged, ran away, poisoned
and burned, and otherwise afforded evidence that they were not
the happy-go-lucky, lovable ol' darkies of magnolia-blossom historic legend.

It is indeed very easy to demonstrate that the vast majority of
slaves yearned to be free. But—and this point is greatly to our purposes here—it is not easy to prove that certain particular slaves
boldly planned a revolt *because* slaves in general did not like
slavery.

To answer the question implied here, we are forced to stare at
the thick curtain formed by lack of specific evidence. Yet if we go
on something of a diet concerning data and become patient with
very small and occasionally uncertain portions, we may learn
something about why some of these Second Creek slaves thought
and acted the way they did. If we do not do this, we are left treating
a specific slave conspiracy as part of a trend or movement more of
our making than of the slaves involved.

The Mosby boys were central to the Plan. At least as recorded by
Conner, Nelson was the first slave to be examined by the Second
Creek Committee, and he talked about contacts with men on the
Mitchell, Dunbar, Henderson, and Scott places. The men at Mosby's had become involved early on. When asked at the outset of
his examination when the business had started, Nelson responded that the "Plan began on the creek fishing in May" with
"our boys and Mitchell's." Evidently the Mosbys had only recently heard about the war. They had learned about it from
"young missus," probably seventeen-year-old Anna B. Mosby or
one of her two younger housemates, Fanni and Bessie. Apparently
the young lady had asked one or several of the slaves for protection
against the Yankees or, as they seem to have been known to Nelson, the "abolitionists." Perhaps reflecting initial confusion
among some slaves as to what abolitionists wanted, Nelson said
that two of the Mitchells, Edward and John, would join such a
fight. Orange Mosby clearly took a different view of abolitionists,
for he and his son were talking with friends at the Dunbar, Hen-

derson, and Surget places, setting the Plan (Nelson said) for "when Abolitionists come."

By Adams County or indeed any standards, Mosby's place was not a run-of-the-mill planting establishment. Located on prime land near but not on the southward turn of the creek, Brighton (of which the abutting Brighton Woods place may once have been a part) was only 180 acres, much smaller than most in the area. John S. Mosby owned about twenty slaves and had only a moderate amount of personal property. Unlike many of the real planters, he did not own enough gold- or silver-plate to concern the tax assessor. He was able to maintain one carriage, the usual minimum for a planting family; in all probability he drove it himself. In large part his status hinged on the fact that he had for years run Elva Academy, a school on his place where wealthy planters who chose not to hire a tutor at home were willing to send their sons. Indeed, the school seems to have become something of a social center. Dr. John C. Jenkins, a neighboring wealthy planter and a "scientific farmer," made note in his diary, "The examination of pupils at Mr. Mosby's school came off to day and quite a large attendance and in the evening the boy's gave a cotillion party to which most of the young girls in the neighborhood attended."[1] This was a Friday in June of 1855—and not the last such occasion in that area and many others where the "prom" as an institution has proved more durable than any single school. Apparently no one at the time saw any irony in using the term *examination* in connection with the accomplishments of young scholars and also with the forced extraction of information from slaves.[2]

Born in Virginia in 1801, John Mosby probably lived in Natchez when he first came to Adams County. William Johnson, the gossipy free black diarist there, noted Mosby's marriage to the widow Frances B. Babbitt in 1837. She already had three young children

1. Jenkins Diary, June 15, 1855. Young Johnnie Jenkins attended the school, and his father noted with pride hearing him "speak" at the (semi)annual "examination." See *ibid.*, December 15, 1854; also January 9, March 9, 1854, January 24, September 11, 1855. Dr. Grier, Jenkins' manager and friend, who kept the Elgin plantation journal when Jenkins was away, attended the school examination several years earlier, as was noted June 21, 1850, also October 23, 1851. Jenkins traded fruit with the Mosbys, and the relationship between the owner of three sizable plantations and the schoolmaster-*cum*–second planter may be summarized by Jenkins' reference to "Mr. Mosby our neighbour," April 30, 1853, also September 23, 1851.

2. The term was used for schoolgirls as well as schoolboys. See Darden Diary, July 26, 27, 1859, June 12, 1861.

of her own, and the new couple became parents of seven more, some perhaps by adoption. By 1840, at least, they had moved out into the county near Second Creek where the Woodville road actually cut through the edge of their property. During the 1850s Mosby managed to maintain a work force but not to expand it or buy more land. By the end of that decade he had fewer mouths to feed, for the Mosbys had lost one of their own children, and two of his stepchildren and several of their own had grown up and left the household. By 1861, with one exception, all who remained were teenagers, three females and a male. Still living with them also was Mosby's stepson, Charles W. Babbitt, now twenty-five, who had become a civil engineer and was perhaps acting part-time as overseer on the place. It was this enterprising young man who later became county surveyor in the 1860s and much later still was responsible for a plantation map of the county that is crucial for our understanding of the area. At the time of the Plan, Mr. and Mrs. Mosby probably welcomed the shrinkage of their household, for he was about sixty years old and his wife fifty-five.[3]

Mosby was thus a reasonably prosperous but not a wealthy man, far less well-off than his neighbors. For at least twenty years he had been, by one short definition, a "second planter," but with unusual social connections through his school. His wife was visited by Mrs. Annis Dunbar Jenkins and her children— immediate

3. Census, 1850 Free, household 136; Slave, unpaginated and confusingly microfilmed, but the 37th left page, column 2; 1860 Free, household 1011 (which gives ages of the couple as one and two years older than extrapolation from 1850 would indicate, but was generally more accurate); Slave, MS pp. 133–34. In 1839, Mosby and his wife had sold a house lot in town. Adams County Deeds, Book AA, p. 465, in Chancery Clerk's Office, Natchez. The 1850 census placed him in the county, not in town, and called him a "Teacher." The mortality schedule of that year showed that he had lost two valuable slave men during the year preceding. Census, 1850 Mortality. In 1860, still in the county, he was called (as were most agricultural owners in Adams County) a "Planter." For the school, see *Goodspeed's*, II, 309, and *Johnson's Diary*, II, 456. Bazile R. Lanneau, of Fair Oaks, recalls seeing the old school building as a boy, when it was a two-room tenant's shack. For Mosby's marriage, see *Johnson's Diary*, I, 208, and Irene S. and Norman E. Gillis, *Adams County Mississippi Marriages, 1802–1859* (Shreveport, La., 1976), 40, also 62. His property was listed in Adams Land and Adams Personal. By 1870, C. W. Babbitt (or Babbit) had started a family of his own, as listed in Census, 1870, household 3996. Throughout this book, the number of slaves owned is taken (when available) from the property rolls of 1861 (the preferable date), rather than the census of 1860. The personal tax rolls did not include slaves over age sixty, so they often slightly undercount the number actually owned. There is unusual consistency between the 1860 census figures and the 1861 assessment rolls for Adams County, no doubt because they were both compiled by the same person, A. D. Pickens.

neighbors to be sure, but Dr. Jenkins was a man of wealth and connections.[4] In contrast, based solely on the number of his slaves, Mosby was (barely) in the top one-fifth of southern whites, but only at the top of the bottom third of agricultural slaveholders in Adams County.[5]

With several exceptions, we do not know much about the man in his role as ruler of a medium-sized slaveholding cotton domain. From a gratuitous entry in William Johnson's diary, we have access to one particular side of his temperament. Twenty years before, Mosby had gotten into some sort of altercation in Natchez. Johnson recorded the incident as his entire entry for January 17, 1841. His coda is hard to interpret, since Johnson was sometimes sarcastic and sometimes very direct. There seem to be no other records concerning what happened, legal or otherwise.

> Nothing new. Mr Moseby, the man that married the widow Babbit, Killed a Mr Jones To Night—He Shot Jones with 15 Buck Shot through the Stomach—Self Defence—of Course.[6]

It was twenty years later when for different reasons some of Mr. Mosby's slaves decided to kill him.

These slaves lived in a relatively small group, slightly smaller than the majority of slaves in the South as a whole and far smaller than the rural Adams County average. The eighteen slaves had to deal with difficult conditions for family relationships, since they were crammed into three cabins. Ten years earlier, in 1850, the list of Mosby's slaves by a different census marshal had revealed a

4. Jenkins Diary, September 23, 1851. See Albert Garrel Seal, "John Carmichael Jenkins: Scientific Planter of the Natchez District," *Journal of Mississippi History*, I (1939), 14–28. Among his other misstatements about Adams County, Frederick Law Olmsted recounted without demurrer an informant's claim that there were no schools between Woodville and Natchez, in his *A Journey in the Back Country* (New York, 1860), 25. Olmsted in fact passed very close to Mosby's schoolhouse the next day on his road north to Natchez.

5. The distribution of slaves among agricultural owners in Adams County is given in Herbert Weaver, *Mississippi Farmers, 1850–1860* (1945; rpr. Gloucester, Mass., 1968), 39. Weaver's figures have rightly been questioned in the sophisticated methodological study by Frederick A. Bode and Donald E. Ginter, *Farm Tenancy and the Census in Antebellum Georgia* (Athens, Ga., 1986), but they are sufficiently on target for the purpose here.

6. *Johnson's Diary*, I, 315. Johnson did not know John Mosby, who is not to be confused with the William Mosbey (variously spelled) frequently mentioned in the diary. (John Mosby's name is only one of many not in the *Diary*'s index.) A technical note on the violence: shotguns were muzzle-loading and the "15" refers to one firing of fifteen fragments, not to fifteen separate, slow, reloaded shots.

marked surplus of women of childbearing ages but not many children. Apparently Mosby had purchased a labor force with hopes that it would increase naturally. If these figures were at all accurate, the slave women on the Mosby place did not bear as many healthy children as he had hoped.

And at times he seemed to be short of cash. In 1847 he was forced to sell ten of his slaves, his carriage, and five horses. The time of year suggests the pressure he was under—May 5— cutting-out time.[7]

Mosby had to struggle to make his school pay, but apparently he received some support from nearby parents. In 1852, Dr. John C. Jenkins noted in his Elgin plantation diary, "The ladies fair came off this evening at Mr. Mosby's School room," though there was "but a small attendance." His wife, Annis, spent nearly all next day at the fair, two days before Christmas, and her husband carefully noted his suitably generous expenditures of $40 for her, $10 for their children, and $35 for himself.[8]

Yet the "small attendance" and perhaps the fair itself were actually signs of trouble. Earlier that year of 1852 an Adams County physician used news about the problem as a vehicle for admonitory advice to his son:

> Mr Mosby's School is now quite small. He unfortunately fell into a big frolic last summer that broke his school up for a while. He is now steady and struggling to establish the past reputation of his school. This I fear (for the interests of his family) he will fail to do; as no man in whatever station in life, can expect the confidence of the Community if he is addicted to drunkenness.[9]

Nor (he might have added but of course did not) could such a man expect that his slaves would themselves expect to receive customarily fair and consistent treatment.

7. The 1850 Adams County census, by A. D. Meade, appears to have been done less carefully than 1860's. The earlier slave schedule has many entries about slaves that lapse into the assertion, "Refuses to give any Information." In 1850 there were six women between twenty-five and thirty-five and only five children under twelve on the Mosby place. His slaveholdings appear to have increased by at least two between the summer of 1860 and the fall of 1861, whether by birth or purchase is not known, but for age and gender the 1860 figures have to be used. The sale is recorded in Adams County Deeds, Book GG, p. 5, Chancery Clerk's Office, Natchez.

8. Jenkins Diary, December 22, 23, 1852.

9. James Foster to John Sanderson Foster, September 3, 1852, also January 10, 1852, in James Foster and Family Papers, LSU.

John Mosby seems to have recovered, at least temporarily. There is no direct evidence about the impact of his habit upon his slaves. It becomes clear, however, that by the end of that decade— on the eve of the war and of the Plan—he was flirting with financial disaster that might affect them directly and profoundly. How much the slaves knew about his and hence their situation is a matter of conjecture. It seems unlikely they knew nothing at all. Whatever their knowledge, John Mosby was borrowing heavily and putting up some of his slaves as collateral. In the late 1850s he began signing a series of promissory notes, rising from $2,750 to $4,400 at 10 percent, each backed by a group of his slave women (whose value he inflated by claiming they all had household skills) and their children.[10] Finally, in 1860, the last year before registry of such deeds stopped (or was lost) during the war, Mosby made a major sale to a Natchez slave-trading firm. For $8,631.25 he sold three middle-aged women, four children without designation of their parents, and Harriet (a cook) and her four children, including Wesley, aged twenty-one. A curious codicil to the deed substituted a woman named Maria for Harriet, which meant that Nelson's wife was not to be sold after all, but their children were to go.[11] Perhaps the sale was not fully consummated, since Wesley, at least, remained on the place—as will soon become clear.

A final intriguing hint about Mosby's financial wriggling emerged in the 1862 county personal tax assessment. He was listed as still owning a $75 watch. All the other Mosby personal property, including the reduced number of twelve slaves, was in the name of Frances B. Mosby.[12] It is not known whether the arrangement with his wife had been amicable or otherwise.

The Mosby men seem to have constituted something of a fraternity. According to the census of 1860, Mosby owned six slaves who could have participated in the Plan, with the youngest evidently too young at age fourteen.[13] Thus it is clear that when Fred-

10. Adams County Deeds, Book LL, 535, Book MM, 273, 443.

11. *Ibid.*, Book MM, 619. C. W. Babbitt was a legal witness to this transaction. Mosby may well have deliberately falsified ages of his slaves on more than one occasion.

12. Adams Personal, 1862. In 1861 he had owned twenty slaves. The land rolls for 1862 are not available. This helps explain Nelson's assertion, "O. says he would kill Master 1st — kill Mrs to get the money."

13. "Too young" may sound odd unless it is borne in mind that boys, as well as girls, matured sexually later then than today. For obvious reasons, there are no

erick Scott claimed there were "5 at Mosby's," he was correct in saying in effect that all the fully adult Mosby men were involved in the plotting. And whether the Mosby men knew everything about it, some or all of their wives and children were under threat of sale. Certainly they knew their master to be an imprudent, intemperate, impecunious man. Some of their families may actually have been sent to a trader the previous spring.

Thanks to the existence of "road duty" rosters kept by county authorities, it is possible to trace certain names in John Mosby's work force during the 1850s.[14] At the beginning of that decade he owned (or at least admitted to owning according to the road and bridge superintendent) only three male slaves between the ages of fifteen and fifty, two of whom (Orange and Nelson) later played major roles in the Plan. By the time of that crisis, the other man (Henry) had probably either been sold or hired out, or had died, or had run away successfully. Of the five men referred to by Dr. Scott's Frederick at his examination in 1861, three more (Harvey, Wesley, and Alfred) first appeared on the road gang lists for the year 1854. The first two had fathers on the place, and the other's father (Harry Scott) lived very close by. Uncertainties about ages in the census records make it impossible to be sure, but it seems probable that these five men had been owned by Mosby for at least ten years and perhaps a good deal longer.[15]

---

statistical data on the matter, but the assertion can stand on the basis of diet alone. On the other hand, most slaves were put to adult field work well before they matured.

14. Road Duty, UTA; Road Duty, MDAH. UTA covers slaves liable in 1850 and from 1852 to 1856; MDAH covers slaves liable in 1855 (the original from which UTA's 1855 is a copy) and work actually performed in 1856. The lists were compiled in the name of the superintendent of roads and bridges; they include, purportedly, all male and female slaves aged fifteen to fifty (Road Duty, UTA, 107), listed by plantation with names of the owner and of the slaves—and with, of course, some omissions and arithmetical errors. The Mosby slaves are listed in Road Duty, UTA, 98, 172, 277, 345, 449, 460, and Road Duty, MDAH, Pt. 1, p. 177, Pt. 2, p. 6. In Road Duty, MDAH (1855), the enumerations were often actually signed by the person giving the names, usually the owner but sometimes the overseer or agent. Some plantations were much harder hit (at least in 1856) by the corvée than others, and there seems to have been no particular logic underlying the greatly various number of days of labor actually performed by slaves from different plantations. The Mosby gang spent two days on the roads that year, which was an approximately modal amount.

15. It is impossible to reconcile the ages of the Mosby slaves when the two decennial censuses are compared. Mosby may have done some selling and buying

At some point early that summer of 1861, two of the most ubiquitous rebels, Mr. Mosby's Orange and Dr. Scott's Harry Scott, attended a Friday night dance over at Mrs. Dunbar's, probably at the large plantation abutting Brighton Woods on the east. The Forest Plantation slaves had given dances before.[16] Evidently the social affair was not closely supervised, for Orange took with him a runaway, Dave Bradley. Dave (perhaps owned by Mr. Robert Bradley) was apparently not previously known to the others at the dance. He was being hidden by day in Harry Scott's henhouse, and he and another runaway had double-barreled guns. Dave may well have come originally from Louisiana, since very few if any Adams County slaves "talked French" as he did. That language was not well known immediately across the river, but farther south some slaves spoke French as their native tongue.[17]

No doubt Mrs. Mary G. Dunbar was unaware of this socializing among her slaves at Forest, the old Dunbar family seat. She was in close touch with her mother-in-law, Martha W. Dunbar. Eighty-one years old and the dame of an old and awesomely prominent and extensive Adams County family, the senior Mrs. Dunbar lived at Dunbarton, nine miles east of Natchez on the upper reaches of the creek. She had been widowed in 1828, but over the years she seems to have been able to run her plantations effectively and

---

in that decade, but the Road Duty Books suggests considerable continuity. Unfortunately, the purported ages of Mosby male slaves in the census of 1860 do not permit determination of who was how old. Indeed, the ages in 1860 (fifty-nine, fifty-five, forty, thirty-nine, eighteen, thirteen, nine) are suspiciously high, being not only inconsistent with both Road Duty Books and the 1850 census, but also suspect considering what is known about the familial relationships among the men—yet not, despite these difficulties, conclusively incorrect. Presumably Wesley was the one listed at eighteen. It is conceivable, though very unlikely, that these filial relationships were adoptive, or in an anthropological sense, fictive.

16. Jenkins Diary, January 2,1852, noted attending with his family and many of his slaves a "party . . . given by Forest negroes." Though Jenkins was a native of Pennsylvania, his marriage to Annis Dunbar had long provided connections with other people in the neighborhood. A brief and otherwise unexplained entry June 19, 1846, reads: "Went to Forest in carriage—All the Foresters at Mrs. Mosby's at the Annual examination."

17. Ex-Slave Narratives, WPA Source Materials, in Louisiana State Library, Baton Rouge; Ronnie W. Clayton, ed., *Mother Wit: The Ex-Slave Narratives of the Louisiana Writers' Project* (New York, 1990), 52–53, 61, 166, 189. Dave's owner may have been Robert Bradley, owner of sixty slaves in Adams County (Census, 1860 Free, household 886; Slave, MS p. 84), but if so he was too young (or had been bought too recently) to be listed in Road Duty, UTA, 347, 410–11, 462 (1856). As is well known, runaways tended statistically to be young males.

with profit. She employed a New York–born overseer and for some reason boarded an illiterate young man from Mississippi. In the early fall of 1861, she owned eighty-nine slaves at Dunbarton, which was an unusually self-sufficient plantation. Her widowed daughter-in-law, Mary G. Dunbar, probably did not live with her, but at Forest. At that plantation Mary Dunbar in her own right owned about as many slaves as her mother-in-law had at Dunbarton. They worked there under the patently not very watchful eye of another overseer, a native of Kentucky. The younger Mrs. Dunbar's two daughters, both in their early twenties, lived with her. There were no white teenagers or children at either Dunbarton or Forest. If lumped together (as for some odd reason they were by the census marshal) the Dunbar ladies constituted a wealthy household, worth in land, slaves, and other property more than 200,000 in 1860 dollars. More to the point concerning the Plan, there were no white male Dunbars at either Forest or Dunbarton. It was the responsibility of the resident overseer to discover that the slaves at Forest were doing all that talking.[18]

Forest Plantation consisted of a thousand acres of fertile, valuable land lying between Dr. Jenkins' Elgin and the creek itself, with Brighton Woods on its western border and Surget's Cherry Grove just to the east. It was about seven miles downstream from Dunbarton and a very short walk from the Mosby place. As recorded by the Pennsylvania physician at Elgin who had married into the Dunbar clan, "The family Mansion House at the Forest," built around 1816, had "burned to the cellars" on January 13, 1852, the fire having started early that morning next to a flawed

18. Their nearby neighbor and relative, William H. Dunbar, was also a person of substance. See Census, 1860 Free, household 925 (Martha W. Dunbar), household 828 (William H. Dunbar); Slave, MS pp. 103–104 (Martha W.), 105–106 (Mary G.), 35–36 (William H.); also Adams Land, 1861; Adams Personal, 1859, 1861. In addition, see esp. Gabriella Means Bondurant, "The Dunbars: Dunbarton, 1863," in Mary Conway Shields Dunbar, *My Mother Used to Say: A Natchez Belle of the Sixties*, ed. Elizabeth Dunbar Murray (Boston, 1959), 186–91, as well as Gillis and Gillis, *Adams County Marriages*, 16. For Forest, see Natchez *Democrat*, Pilgrimage "Pink" ed., 1959, p. 19, and Mrs. Robert Young, "A Tradition of Second Creek Valley, A.D. 1772 to 1820" (Beau Prés Plantation, 1905), typescript copy in author's possession of original owned by Mrs. Charles MacNeil, Natchez. Further evidence about the two Mrs. Dunbars is in Testimony of Polly Bell Taken by E[nos] Richmond, June 6, 1879, p. 27, in Claim (No. 7960) of Katherine S. Minor, Settled Case Files, 1877–83—Mississippi, Adams County, Records of the Southern Claims Commission, Records of the General Accounting Office, RG 217, National Archives, and Claim (No. 19810) of Wm. H. McPhecters and Wm. H. Dunbar, executors of Martha W. Dunbar, *ibid.*

chimney. The same day, the last surviving son of the Thomas Dunbar who had built the house died from a fall from his horse.[19] The house was not rebuilt, at least not in the immediate wake of these calamities, but the younger Mrs. Dunbar seems to have maintained some sort of residence at Forest, since the property itself was taxed for a "pleasure Carriage" and such standard residential items as watches, clocks, and gold- and silver-plate, as well as slaves. Though some slaves from Dunbarton may also have attended the dance, the Mosby slaves talked with Dennis, Peter, George, Dick, Paul, Simon, Albert, and Harry—slaves all belonging to Mrs. Mary Dunbar who were planning to kill her and several other white people.[20]

Three Dunbar slaves were questioned before the Examination Committee, and another five were named. When word of the hangings reached the Mrs. Dunbars, they must have agitated about where things were going to stop. Clearly they could no longer trust their servants. Previously the Dunbar slaves had been more than trusted. In addition to the dances, discipline had been so lax that at least two slaves, Simon and George, had acquired firearms. The elder Mrs. Dunbar had hired a Presbyterian minister to provide her slaves religious instruction—a highly unusual effort in the valley of Second Creek.[21] For Presbyterians especially, such instruction sometimes included reading, and it was probably this minister who was responsible for several Dunbar slaves' learning how. At least it is the case that the only literate rebels (so far as is known) were Dunbar slaves. Unlike the slaves of the neighboring schoolmaster, three of the Dunbars had that skill. One was Dick, a man probably at least fifty years old and the only

19. Jenkins Diary, January 13, 1852.
20. Road Duty, MDAH, Pt. 1, pp. 129, 173, Pt. 2, pp. 4, 15; Road Duty, UTA, 247, 331, 347, 435, 466, 478. Ownership of property is in Adams Land; Adams Personal. The 1861 (and also 1862) list shows a drastic drop in the number of slaves assessed for taxes at Forest, far below the number in the assessment of 1859 and the census in 1860. Pickens signed the 1861 list on October 7, so a small part of the drop may be assigned to hangings, but probably much more either to sale or to shifted ownership within the Dunbar family. "Forest Plantation" was sometimes listed separately (under the F's, not the D's), uniquely so as a taxpaying entity in its own right, and it is not (and may not have been) clear which Mrs. Dunbar actually owned it. With only half the acreage of Dunbarton, it was assessed at the same dollar amount. At the time of the crisis, it was known that at least one Dunbar slave was hanged and that he belonged to the younger Mrs. Dunbar; see William J. Minor Plantation Diary, September 25, 1861, in William J. Minor and Family Papers, LSU.
21. Bondurant, "The Dunbars," 190.

rebel singled out as being a "religious man." The others were Dick's son, Peter, who was at least in his twenties, and Dick's brother, George. According to Conner's record, George was examined twice, and perhaps it was his literacy that attracted the special attention of the Examination Committee. Or very possibly he was summoned again (at a time when Conner's interest in note taking was beginning to flag) because Harry Scott had just revealed that George not only knew how to read, but had a gun.[22]

Harry Scott was something of a sparkplug and a go-between, a lively man but not forceful. In his fifties, he was the oldest of Dr. Scott's slaves and well past his physical prime. Normally he lived at the only slave cabin on the Scott place, crammed in with two women and four other men. There were no slave children there, even though the two women were of childbearing age. Most or all the Scott slaves had been purchased by the rising physician only within the past two or three years. Dr. John T. Scott was thirty-five years old. Four years earlier he had begun his switch from town to county, where he had bought Waverly, a small property of only seventy-five acres between Mosby's Brighton and the creek. With only seven slaves, he was considerably less well-off even than John Mosby, and by Second Creek standards barely comfortable. But unlike some older physicians in the county, he was just getting started with the business of planting. He had already reached the critical threshold of owning a carriage.[23]

22. Peter and George were listed at Forest in Road Duty, MDAH, Pt. 1, p. 129, also p. 173, and Road Duty, UTA, 466 (1856), but Dick was not. The tone of Dick Dunbar's testimony fits an older man; and his not being listed in the Road Duty books suggests that he was over fifty a half dozen years earlier, or at least that he and/or the overseer were able to pass off his age as over the legal cutoff for being liable for road duty. In general planters were under incentive to keep their slaves off the road-duty roster so as to keep them at home for work. Dick was unlikely to have been purchased recently or to have been a runaway two summers in a row on the particular day the assistant superintendent of roads and bridges dropped by.

23. Census, 1860 Free, household 1060; Slave, MS p. 140. Dr. Scott's marriage was noted in Jenkins Diary, April 3, 1855. The term *middle age* was not in common use; men of Harry Scott's age were regarded as becoming old. As census marshal, A. D. Pickens had valued Dr. Scott's real property at $3,000, but a year later, as county tax assessor, he listed it as $2,500, which is what the tax assessment had been when Pickens took over that job; see Adams Land, 1857, 1861. The difference probably reflected an error or an adjusted physician's fee. Scott's rise can be traced *ibid.* and Adams Personal, 1858, 1859, 1861. His work force of only three slaves

Dr. Scott was merely one of many physicians in the Deep South who as soon as they could went into the business of planting. This career shift was remarkably common in Adams County, and like many others Scott may have continued medical practice at least for a while. But cotton paid much better than patients and owners of patients. His wife was only twenty-two, and he had at least three youngsters to support. Thus it was probably for financial reasons that the Scotts boarded an Episcopal clergyman from New Jersey, the Reverend Mr. Thomas A. Ogden. There is little evidence that Ogden's preaching did much to spread the gospel among the slaves at Waverly or elsewhere in the neighborhood, but that question needs to await another context.

Harry Scott had a generally acknowledged last name, which was unusual but by no means rare for slaves in Adams County and in the South generally. His son Alfred lived at the neighboring Mosby place, and according to George Dunbar, young Alfred was insistent that his own last name was Scott.[24] Perhaps this self-identification had been pressed upon Alfred by his father; certainly Alfred claimed it, though possibly Harry used a surname partly because there were two other Harrys nearby.[25]

Harry Scott himself was a pushy, enterprising, but persistently tedious man. None of the slaves claimed he was going to have one of the white ladies: he or his comrades (or both) may have thought he was too old for such interests—though age did not stop Dick Dunbar or Nelson Mosby in this respect. Harry was bold enough to hide the runaway Dave in his henhouse and to usher Dave over to the dance at the Dunbars'. Evidently he was a frequent visitor at the Dunbar place and impressed his friends there with his re-

---

was first listed in Road Duty, UTA, 474 (1856); Harry Scott was not one of them, presumably because he was too old. Dr. Scott may have been the only person in the county assessed for a clock worth only two dollars—perhaps after all he did indeed know Pickens.

24. Harry Scott was the only Scott slave old enough to have been Alfred Mosby's father. At Scott's, the assistant marshal was unable to get exact slave ages, and he rounded them off to the nearest five years—a procedure common in most censuses (in the American South even with whites but especially with blacks), yet remarkably unusual in the Adams County census of 1860. The ages of the Scott slaves were given as fifty, twenty-five, twenty-five, twenty, and fifteen for the men, forty and thirty for the women. Pickens' unusual rounding in this case suggests he took considerable care in most others.

25. Harry Lyle belonged to James H. Mitchell. The third Harry, distinguished by Dennis as "Harry old," lived on the Dunbar place.

petitive enthusiasm: according to George, "Every time Harry Scott comes he says, 'Hell kicking Up.' " We can hear the voice of an older man—of long-withheld hopes—when "Harry Scott said we were all bound to be free." It was the same voice that claimed (with a thoughtful caution unusual among the rebels) he would "go to the back country" and begin the killing when Union forces reached Natchez. We can also hear the silence of a disappointed father upon listening to his son disingenuously propose to him, "Let us collect a company and whip old Lincoln out." Perhaps Alfred was testing to see where his father stood. At any rate, Alfred claimed that his father "never told me he would join" and that he, Alfred, had only learned of his father's commitment to the enterprise from Orange.

Harry Scott had long been accustomed to chipping away at the rigid day-to-day boundaries of the slave system. When he and Orange had boldly brought the runaway Dave Bradley (the "slim lame" one who "talked French") over to the dance, Dave seems to have promised to bring at least one accomplice the next night, a man described as also having a double-barreled gun. Harry harbored one of the runaways in the relative safety of his henhouse, although probably that man had long since taken off by the time of the trials in September. The henhouse was described by George Dunbar as "Harry's," and as "his house" (meaning Harry's), a description of some importance since Harry had no cabin to himself and the terminology suggests either that Dr. Scott permitted Harry to maintain his own henhouse or that as a partially superannuated slave Harry had been put in charge of *the* henhouse on the Scott place. In any case, it must have been a relatively safe refuge, since there was no overseer on the place and young Mrs. Scott, the only white woman there, was no doubt very busy with three little boys of her own.

Some three or four months later, on the Saturday before they were taken up and examined, Harry Scott carried a "dispatch" over to the Dunbar place. He may well have been unable to read it himself, but he was intensely aware of its explosive power, for he assured the others "there was 'Hell in that paper.' " In recognition of its value and ownership, Dick Dunbar paid him a dime for the dispatch and proceeded to read it. Dick's brother, George, also read it—at least so Harry later testified; George defensively claimed to have only "read of it a few words." Since Dick's son Peter also knew how to read, he too must have learned of its contents firsthand. The Examination Committee seems not to have probed into the dispatch's authorship or how it came into Harry Scott's possession. Its contents remain unknown, and all that may be asserted with confidence about this lost historical document is that it must have been very interesting indeed to those who read and heard it.

Its existence was no doubt of interest to members of the Examination Committee, and of course they examined George twice. Yet despite their fear of literacy among slaves, they seem not to have regarded that skill as crucial to their present danger. Perhaps these planters, in common with many others throughout the South, underestimated the number of their slaves who could read. Yet they may have had good basis for retaining unusual confidence in the letter-ignorance of their slaves, since they were correct in assuming that evangelical religious ideas and practices had made few inroads on their plantations. Everyone knew that enthusiasms of that sort often led to reading. Probably no one was rude or bold enough to make public remarks about the misguided religious beneficence of the elderly Mrs. Dunbar.

Two other Scott slaves were involved in the Plan. Frederick (sometimes known as Fred) and Mose were also in on it.[26] Harvey Mosby and his father, Orange, seem not to have talked with either of those two men, but both Alfred and Nelson Mosby did. Frederick reportedly told Nelson something about an otherwise mysterious "army at Kingston," the tiny village about seven miles to the southeast.[27]

At Second Creek, Dr. Scott had a next-door medical colleague, Dr. Orrick Metcalfe, who had made a similar career switch but was much wealthier and (unlike Scott) had well-established family in the neighborhood. As planter, Dr. Orrick Metcalfe lived at Fair Oaks, a small plantation bordered by the creek, Dr. Scott's, Mr. Mosby's, and Mrs. Dunbar's Forest. He may have carried on an active medical practice. A relative newcomer to the immediate

26. Neither was listed in Road Duty, UTA, 474 (1856); they may have been more recently purchased and/or have been the younger men listed as fifteen and twenty in the census of 1860.

27. Conceivably Frederick's master had been in that neighborhood on medical or other errands. It is unlikely but possible that Dr. John T. Scott is the same as the J. S. Scott listed on the grand jury that convicted three slaves near Kingston for murder of their overseer in 1857, for whom no information was found in the census by Michael Wayne in his highly pertinent article, "An Old South Morality Play: Reconsidering the Social Underpinnings of the Proslavery Ideology," *Journal of American History*, LXXVII (1990), 854–55.

neighborhood, he was nonetheless listed by the census marshal as a "farmer," yet the slaves called him a doctor. He was indeed a physician, educated at Yale, and then a professor at Jefferson College before going into planting. Aged thirty-seven, Dr. Orrick Metcalfe did without an overseer (at least when the census marshal came around that summer) for his eighty-four slaves. More eccentrically, he had given up maintaining a carriage several years earlier, but he and his young family lived elegantly ensconced in the low but spreading Fair Oaks plantation house, with their slaves living only three people (on average) to a cabin.[28] The Metcalfe slaves seem not to have been involved in the Plan; at least none of them were named in Conner's record. Indeed, Orrick Metcalfe was remembered in his family as unhappy with the ownership of slaves. At the time of the plan, Dr. Orrick was in fact away in the army with the Adams Troop.[29] Yet according to both Alfred Mosby and his father, Harry Scott, the doctor and his wife (the former Helen Gillespie, of Egypt Plantation, across the creek) were explicitly targeted for killing by the Mosby rebels as well as by those at the Dunbars'.

Dr. Orrick Metcalfe had numerous close family members nearby. His father, Dr. James Metcalfe, had arrived from Kentucky as a well-to-do young man about 1814 and after a few years in Natchez had established himself several miles farther south on the creek, at Montrose Plantation. He had done very well, for he owned more than three hundred slaves in the county. He had fathered six sons; in addition to helping them into the planting life, he had purchased Hutchins Landing Plantation and two others near the bend of the Mississippi west of his home. Now he was a widower in his early sixties and either living alone among his servants at Montrose or, if elsewhere, probably with one of his sons. One of them, Henry L. Metcalfe, owned more than a hundred slaves under the supervision of an overseer at The Grove, adjoin-

28. Census, 1860 Free, household 981; Slave, MS pp. 136–37; Adams Land, 1857, 1861; Adams Personal, 1858, 1859, 1861, 1862 (not to be confused with another Metcalfe listed as O., Oren, or Orin). Other details are in Charles S. Sydnor, *A Gentleman of the Old Natchez Region: Benjamin L. C. Wailes* (Durham, N.C., 1938), 216n, and *Goodspeed's*, II, 301. The doctor had earlier and perhaps still owned slaves at "Carina" on the river (possibly Corinna; see plantation map), as is indicated in Road Duty, UTA, 495 (1856). His Fair Oaks plantation was not included in that last extant Road Duty roster. Mr. and Mrs. Bazile R. and Ann Metcalfe Lanneau most graciously showed me through Fair Oaks, one of the very few houses directly pertinent to this affair still standing.

29. William H. Ker to Mary S. Ker, October 27, 1861, in John Ker and Family Papers, LSU; Dunbar, *My Mother Used to Say*, 84, 116–17.

ing both Fair Oaks and Brighton to their south. Another, James W. Metcalfe, had established his livelihood outside the county but now lived next to Forest at little Ingleside Farm, which at eighty acres—by far the smallest of the Second Creek plantations—had no overseer and only fourteen slaves.[30]

To manage Montrose, the elder Dr. Metcalfe relied on the services of a thirty-eight-year-old overseer, John A. Austen, whose wife and four children also lived on the place. Austen was a trusted employee, having been with Metcalfe for at least seven years. As we have seen, it was one of his youngsters, Benny, who seems to have first revealed the existence of the Plan to other whites. The younger James (W.) Metcalfe probably did most of his own managing, but he may occasionally have utilized the services, or at least the nearby presence, of a Metcalfe family driver, Louis, or of John Austen, who presumably could be called upon if needed. Perhaps his brother Orrick, who owned many more slaves, did the same when he was without an overseer of his own. After all, Austen was a well-established family man and an experienced manager. Before his employment, some of the Metcalfe sons appear to have served as overseers for their father—a natural way for them to learn the business of planting.[31]

30. Dr. James Metcalfe in Census, 1860 Free, household 950; Slave, MS pp. 61–65; Adams Land; Adams Personal; Road Duty, UTA, 85–87, 222–23, 273–74, 337, 338, 379, 381, 494, 495. Hutchins Landing is in *Johnson's Diary*, II, 691. His Kentucky origin, given in Dunbar, *My Mother Used to Say*, 83–84, seems more probable than the census, which found him such a fixture that his birthplace was listed as Mississippi. Henry L. Metcalfe is in Census, 1860 Free, household 1075; Slave, MS pp. 173–75; Adams Land, 1853, 1857, 1861; Adams Personal, 1858, 1859, 1861, 1862; Road Duty, UTA, 278, 362, 432, 515. The Testimony of James Carter Taken by George Tucker, Document M, associated Henry L. Metcalfe with Pine Ridge, but this was clearly a mistake. James W. Metcalfe is in Census, 1860 Free, household 993; Slave, MS p. 134; Adams Land, 1853, 1857, 1861; Adams Personal, 1861, 1862. In Adams County he was not liable for road duty in the mid-1850s, or taxed for personal property before 1861. Although his activities elsewhere are a guess, it is doubtful that at age forty-one he found it hard to support a wife, five young children, and a Scottish gardener. Possibly some of his slaves were old hands at Ingleside Farm, taken over with it from a previous resident: in the mid-1850s, "Ingleside" (probably the same place) had been occupied by Thomas Affleck, owner of only about twenty slaves but well known as a writer on plantation affairs. See Road Duty, UTA, 303, 309, 438, 513. Household numbers can be used as a general though far from certain guide to propinquity.

31. Road Duty, UTA, 337, 379, 433. Louis' ownership cannot be established with certainty, but it seems likely he was a carriage driver and/or foreman owned by Dr. James Metcalfe. In Conner's transcript he may at first appear to be one of the Mitchell slaves, but the crossed-out name of Alfred and the punctuation in Alfred's testimony, as well as Mitchell's owning the driver Big John, suggest not.

Alfred Mosby found it possible to visit Ingleside Farm fairly often. He had established a sufficiently close relationship with one of the Metcalfe slave women that he was in the habit of whipping her—a habit Orange associated with the widespread reign of whipping he promised would stop. In Alfred's case, apparently, the standing example of slaves being whipped combined with common values about proper relations between the sexes to enable him to whip a slave woman (or women) on another plantation at his own pleasure, quite independent of the usual lines of authority in the slave system.[32]

Mas Benny had gone to the Dunbar place, probably in company with Louis. It is also probable that Louis knew John, a driver belonging to James H. Mitchell who may have doubled as carriage driver and slave foreman. Mr. and Mrs. Mitchell, in their early sixties, lived at Palatine, immediately south across the creek from Fair Oaks and Forest. The only other people in the household were two Mitchell girls, Emma, aged ten, and her younger sister, Clara. The Mitchells apparently had no overseer to deal with their forty-seven slaves, and perhaps John served as such. Whether or not he did, at least seven of the Mitchell group—including John—became involved with the Dunbar and Mosby rebels.[33]

Three of the Mitchell men were examined: the driver John ("Big John"), and Dennis and Doctor. Presumably the latter name—which was common on southern plantations—had been acquired from recognized skills, but these did not seem especially pertinent at the examinations because poisoning was not suspected. Doctor admitted meeting two runaways, and admitted hearing John, Dennis, and two other men on his place "talk about it." These latter two Mitchell slaves, Harry Lyle and Philip, "said the fighting would begin in New Orleans." But Doctor also claimed, rather inconsistently, to know "nothing about the neighborhood difficulties," and he failed to mention Little John and Edward, two other Mitchell slaves who were involved. For his part, Big John adopted an elevated view of the matter that comported

32. Harvey's testimony referred to *ongoing* abuse: "Alfred whipping Metcalfe's woman." In the usage of some African Americans, the word *woman* could be plural, but probably the singular was intended here. This woman may have belonged to Orrick or Dr. James Metcalfe, but the connection with James W. Metcalfe seems more likely.

33. Census, 1860 Free, household 1076; Slave, MS p. 178; Adams Land; Adams Personal, all years except 1852 (where a page may be missing) and under S. G. Mitchell in 1862.

with his position as a driver-*cum*-overseer. "Black folks," he said, had been "talking of freedom." He had spoken with the most active of the Dunbar men and with Nelson Mosby. He had learned that George Dunbar "was collecting a company" of Dunbars and Mosbys to "fight the white people."

Dennis Mitchell was both more forthcoming with information and more outspoken about it. He described Alfred as "a soldier" in the battle for "freedom." He quoted Simon as saying "he hoped to see the day when he would blow down a white man who called him a damn rascal." Here was eloquent testimony as to the feeling of outraged dignity harbored by many of the rebels, for the phrase "damn rascal" was a forceful and heartfelt one, lacking its modern tone of staged and playful, even affectionate, reprobation.[34]

At his examination, Dennis went on with his succinctly colorful reporting about what had been said. Two men who cannot be identified other than by the names George Bush and Levi "talked fierce" and "told Big John all what they told me." Simon and George Dunbar, he reported, had predicted that the North would win the war. He quoted them with words that conveyed vengeful delight in the prospect of the downfall of southern chivalry and valor: "Northerners make the South shit behind their asses."

Such vivid language was most unlikely to have been Lemuel Conner's fabrication. Dennis' language rang of youthful bravado, and it is indeed very likely that he was a young man.[35] Obviously, Conner was not so surprised or taken aback by these words that he was unable to record them. Dennis' next statement must have shocked him much more: "Simon said they would have white women as free as black ᵂᵒmen." In setting down this striking remark, it may have been Conner's sheer consternation that led him mistakenly to write "men," but he later added *wo* above the line to correct the word to "women." Whatever the significance of

34. More than today the term implied inferiority of *class.* See William Dwight Whitney and Benjamin E. Smith, eds., *The Century Dictionary* . . . (rev. ed., 12 vols.; New York, 1889–1913), *s.v.* "rascal." The famous free Negro barber of Natchez, defrauded, he thought, in a financial transaction, concluded his summary of the affair, "I pronounce him a Rascal." *Johnson's Diary,* I, 235.

35. He was not listed in Road Duty, MDAH, Pt. 1, p. 31 (1855), and probably he was too young, since James Mitchell was unlikely to have been buying more Negroes in the intervening years. Doctor was not listed as such, but may have been under his other (unknown) name. Little John *was* listed, as was a Harry without the Lyle. John the driver (Big John) and Little John may have been father and son, but sometimes such descriptive terms were used merely for purposes of differentiation, not to indicate blood relationship.

Conner's original slip, Simon's remark was an unambiguous assertion about the freedom of black men.

After the examinations of the three Mitchell slaves, Conner may for some reason have become distracted or even have left the scene for a time. Whatever the case, his handwriting for the next five or six examinations suddenly appears more hasty and the entries much briefer and indented from his customary left margin. The first, "Mitchells boy <u>Harry Lyle</u> says 00 —," might logically be interpreted as the equivalent of the last two, where "<u>Obey</u>— says nothing —" and Billy did the same. Yet zeros and nothings may not have been exactly equivalent in Conner's mind, and it is not entirely certain that these three slaves did not mumble words that seemed to Conner mere nonsense or entirely repetitive of previous testimonies. Interpretation of his transcript is rendered even more problematical by the second and third of these entries: "Hendersons boy <u>Adam</u> says Orange told him what am[oun]ts to nothing——," and Mitchell's Little John "says Orange told him on the Creek, that — 00 —." The only straightforward entry concerned Dr. Grier's Fred, who said that Orange had told him about the general named Scott eating his breakfast in New Orleans.

In the same section of his transcript Conner also entered the name of Isaac Giddings, but it is not clear why. There is no indication of what, if anything, he said, or even if he was examined.[36] Known sometimes as Ike but always with his own last name, Giddings was nearly elderly by standards of the day—a man in his late fifties. He was the father of Adam, who apparently did not inherit the Giddings name. Both slaves lived on A. C. Henderson's Grove Plantation, a substantial place with fifty slaves that bordered For-

36. There are several ways of interpreting this section of Conner's transcript. The location of the name Isaac Giddings suggests that it is either an unadorned addendum to Doctor's testimony or a heading for the indented five entries that follow. The handwriting suggests that Giddings' name was inserted after those entries were made. It is possible that these five were meant to reflect what Giddings said they had said—thus the repeated *says*. But serious difficulties attach to such a reading, and I am grateful to Gerry Anders for pointing them out. My conclusions that Obey and Billy (and perhaps Harry Lyle) refused to say anything are far from being the only reasonable ones. I have been guided partly by the format of the manuscript and more strongly by the string of *Obey*'s near its end. Conner's inattention or absence is presumed because the single best explanation (it seems to me) for this section of the transcript is that he asked some other observer what had been going on during a period when he had not been taking down verbatim responses.

est, Brighton Woods, and Henry Metcalfe's The Grove.[37] According to Conner's record, taken as a whole, the Committee eventually heard that a total of seven Henderson slaves had been in on the Plan. Some of its members may have remembered Nelson saying that Orange and his son Harvey had been meeting at the Henderson plantation on Sundays. During this spate of relative inattention on Conner's part, slaves had been implicated not only there but also at Mosby's, Mitchell's, and Grier's.

Dr. Grier's Fred was thus implicated for the second time, for Nelson had already named him, as well as referring to Grier's Bob and Prince.[38] Nelson also used the name Isaac, referring either to another man belonging to Grier or to Henderson's Ike Giddings.

The assistant marshal had recorded Dr. Samuel L. Grier as a "Farmer" owning sixty-one slaves.[39] In fact, Grier had received an M.D. from New Orleans Medical College and had come to Adams County more than ten years earlier to manage River Place in Wilkinson County for Dr. John C. Jenkins. Later, he may well have had slaves of his own at Elgin, next to the Dunbars' Forest, for he had managed that place when the Jenkinses had gone on tours to "the coast" or the northeastern states, and he had become executor of the large financial estate when Dr. and Mrs. Jenkins both died of yellow fever in 1855.[40]

37. A. C. Henderson in Census, 1860 Free, household 976; Slave, MS pp. 124–25; also John W. Henderson, *ibid.*, household 984; MS pp. 126–27. Comparison of this data with Adams Land, 1853, 1857, 1861 and Adams Personal, 1858, 1859, 1861, shows inconsistencies but suggests that the Mrs. Henderson of Nelson's testimony was probably A. C. Henderson's daughter-in-law, living either at Ellis Cliffs or with him. Plantation names and approximate ages of individuals come from Road Duty, MDAH, Pt. 1, pp. 119, 125; Road Duty, UTA, 91, 167, 263 (1853, the only year "I.[saac] Giddons" and his son Adam were both listed), 264, 361, 372, 432, 434, 484. Grove, which bordered Elgin, Forest, and Brighton Woods, also shared a short boundary with Henry L. Metcalfe's The Grove. A. C. Henderson owned Louisiana lands worth $298,000; see Weaver, *Mississippi Farmers*, 109.

38. The testimony suggests Prince may have been hired out or somehow otherwise living across the creek at Nichols'.

39. Census, 1860 Free, household 985; Slave, MS p. 118.

40. Alternatively, Grier may have owned a town lot and been renting farming land: see Adams Land, 1861; Adams Personal, 1858, 1861. See also Gillis and Gillis, *Adams County Marriages*, 29, and the Jenkins Diary, which has numerous references to Grier. His role as executor appears in Road Duty, UTA, 506. In Mississippi "the coast" still means the land along the northern coast of the Gulf of Mexico.

The Dunbars, whose founding Mississippi father had come to be known as "Sir" William, had earlier intermarried with the Surgets. Elderly Jacob Surget had inherited the Cherry Grove mansion built by the patriarch, Pierre Surget, a French immigrant who had arrived in the late eighteenth century. Jacob's recently deceased brother Francis had been one of the wealthiest planters in the state—a multimillionaire who owned land in at least five counties in three different states. Another brother, James, was the owner of nine plantations and, like Frank, a "4,000-bale planter." He or a James Surget of the next generation owned property abutting Aventine, which was just east of Mitchell's Palatine. By 1860, Jacob had long since moved to New York, but he still owned Cherry Grove. James or his son, in turn, may have been living there in 1861, but more probably it was in the charge of an overseer. Cherry Grove plantation lay next to Forest, just up the creek. None of the rebels suggested targeting any of the Surget families, at Cherry Grove or anywhere else. It seems likely that more than one hundred slaves were living there, though it is possible the number was somewhat smaller. Cherry Grove was not a huge plantation—only 997 acres—but it was the family seat, and the Surgets were very important people.[41]

Many years later an elderly former slave who grew up on a large plantation a mile across the creek from Cherry Grove recalled his owner's marrying into the Surget family: "Dem Surgets wuz pretty debblish fur all dey was de richest fambly in de land." Then Charlie Davenport ran a string of superlatives: "Dey wuz de out fightenist, out cussinest, fastest ridin, hardest drinkin, out spendinest folks I ebber seed. But Lawd, Lawd, dey wuz gentlemen eben in dey cups." As for the Surget women, Davenport's report was both more and less restrained: "De Ladies wuz beautiful wid big black eyes en soft white hands but dey wuz high strung too."[42]

41. Some of the various Surget holdings can be followed in Adams Land and Adams Personal. See esp. Census, 1860 Free, households 795, 1012, 1013, 1014; Slave, MS pp. 11, 22, 76–77, 154–56. For Louisiana, see Weaver, *Mississippi Farmers*, 108–109. A brief incomplete summary of Surget holdings is in D. Clayton James, *Antebellum Natchez* (Baton Rouge, 1968), 153–54, which has James Surget [Sr.] living at Cherry Grove in 1850. But Jacob became the legal owner, as is clear in Road Duty, UTA, 50, 217, 286–87, 363, 433, 491; Adams Land, 1861; and Adams Personal, 1861. Jacob owned no carriage or other household property at Cherry Grove. Abutting is mentioned in Aventine Plantation Diary, November 29, 1859, MDAH. The name Surget was and is variously pronounced, but usually with the accent on the second syllable.
42. Rawick, *American Slave*, Suppl. 1, Vol. VII (Miss. Narrs.), Pt. 2, p. 559, Documents Y and Z.

The old Surget plantation on Second Creek was home to Obey and Billy, to Henry, Steve (Stephen), Wash (Washington), and Ransdell. The role of these slaves, and perhaps as well the Surgets' social position, was sufficiently important that the Examination Committee held some of its sessions there. Conceivably, it may have been sheer cussed pride that caused Obey and Billy to say nothing.

Cherry Grove, where some of the rebels were hanged, was one of at least eight plantations that acted as focal points of the conspiracy—so far as we can now discern. In retrospect we can see the conspirators linked to one another by propinquity and by personal interactions that resemble an intricate tatting now only partially visible in fragments through a screen darkened by time. The conspiracy was wider, perhaps much wider, but the evidence becomes increasingly faint and fragmentary at the edges, consisting as it does, to our eyes now, of floating names and allusions that defy the customary canons of historical re-creation.

On occasion it is possible to make partial sense of a remnant of information on this periphery. Nelson Mosby, who was the first to be recorded in Conner's transcript, named names prolifically, including some twenty-five slaves. One was Prince, who may or may not have been owned by Dr. Grier, but who was described as "at Mr Nichols." P. R. Nichols and his much younger wife, Eliza, had both been born in Connecticut, and they had done well in Mississippi. He owned sixty slaves at Bottany Hill, a two-thousand-acre plantation immediately across the creek from Cherry Grove. One of them, Edward, served as Mrs. Nichols' carriage driver. Nelson Mosby claimed that Edward was the "only" "Strange" Negro off his own place he had spoken with directly, and his claim may well have been correct, since he often played a somewhat passive role in the Mosby fraternity. We do not know whether Edward told some of the other Nichols slaves about the Plan. We may guess that he did. We do not even know whether he was hanged, whether being implicated by Nelson and rather indirectly by Harvey was sufficient indictment to result in his execution. We *do* know that neither Mr. and Mrs. Nichols nor their two teenage daughters were explicitly targeted by any of the rebels who testified. Mr. and Mrs. Nichols may have protected Edward or they may have welcomed his hanging with relief and angry satisfaction. On this score, their Yankee background was all but irrel-

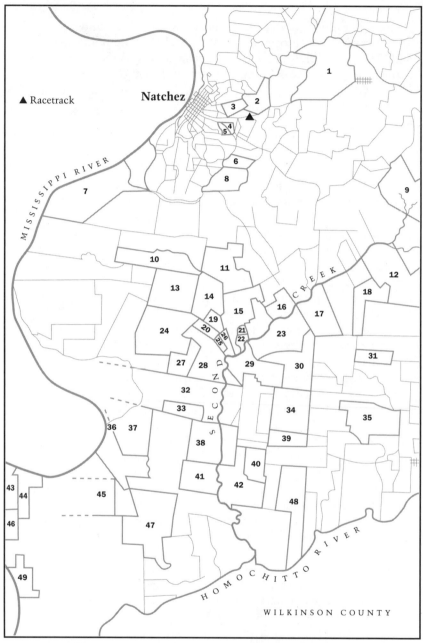

Plantation Map, Central and Southwestern Adams County, Mississippi.
Plantations mentioned in the text are identified by number; see key on
following page.

Anchorage(s) 2, 27	Carthage 7	Fatherland 8	Oakland(s) 1, 33
Avalanche 44	Cherry Grove 16	Forest 15	Overton(s) 39, 40
Aventine 30	Clifford 31	Grove 14	Palatine 29
Beau Prés 22	Cliffs 24	Hutchins Landing 36	Poplar Grove 12
Berkley 42	Concord 3	Ingleside Farm 21	Retirement 17
Beverley 38	Corinna(s) 46, 49	Laurel Hill 32	Saragossa 10
Bottany Hill 23	Dunbarton 9	Linden 5	Spokan 18
Bourbon 45	Egypt 34	Magnolia(s) 13, 35	Springfield 48
Briars 43	Elgin 11	Monmouth 4	The Grove 28
Brighton 20	Ellis Cliffs 37	Montebello 6	Waverly 25
Brighton Woods 19	Fair Oaks 26	Montrose 41	York 47

evant, for life in Mississippi, as in many parts of the South, was remarkably efficient in stamping its cultural imprint on people who were, initially, outsiders.[43]

At this point, with inclusion of the Nicholses, the specific location of the center of the Plan becomes increasingly clear, especially when viewed from the plantation map. That map should not lead to an unwarranted assumption that the Plan was confined to the immediate neighborhood above the creek's southward bend, but it does raise questions about certain places that obviously ought—at least by a crude logic of location—to have been involved.

Beau Prés plantation was situated on the north bank of the creek between Cherry Grove and Forest. Built in 1837, it had been owned by the recently deceased Dr. Benjamin F. Young and was in process of passing to Robert Young. In 1860 there had been eighteen slaves on the 450 acres of Beau Prés, and unlike many other physicians in the county, Dr. Young had probably relied heavily on his income from medical practice.[44] None of the Young slaves were examined while Conner was taking down evidence, but Simon Dunbar said the rebels had planned to "kill Mr Young and take his wife." Frederick Scott, considerably later on in the examinations, suggested as much in his recital of Orange's list of tar-

43. Census, 1860 Free, household 1015; Slave, MS pp. 179–80; Adams Land, 1861; Adams Personal, 1861. However, Adams Personal, 1852, indicates that Eliza J. Nichols owned a few of these slaves in her own right, so possibly Edward belonged to her legally. Edward had been on the Nichols place since 1853 and perhaps earlier; see Road Duty, UTA, 280, 327, 439, 506.

44. The evidence is somewhat inconsistent, but see Census, 1860 Free, household 1080; Slave, MS p. 168; Adams Land; Adams Personal; Road Duty, UTA, 199, 301, 374, 405, 510; *Goodspeed's*, II, 1090; Young, "Tradition of Second Creek Valley," 11; Jenkins Diary, *passim*.

geted plantations: "kill Mr. and Mrs. Mosby, have young ladies to self, kill Dr Scott, then go to Dr Orricks, then go to Dr [sic] Dunbar, then to Mr Young's, then to Mr Metcalfe."

No other slaves on immediately neighboring plantations were mentioned in Conner's record. Thus there are several remaining "holes" on the map where slaves "ought" to have been involved. By process of elimination we may take advantage of the mysterious white road traveler's question, "who was nearest neighbor," and Harvey's answer, "Henderson and Walton Smith"—which was true enough perhaps about A. C. Henderson at Grove but stretching things with Smith, whose Saragossa was immediately west of Elgin. Evidently it was not a large operation, for it had only twenty-eight slaves, and Smith had lived there only five or six years.[45] So far as can be discerned, however, his slaves were not involved in the Plan.

No matter how focused the Plan may seem now, it would be a mistake to assign it geographical limitations merely on the basis of the testimony recorded by Conner. Clearly he did not attend all the examinations, or at least did not write down all the agonized "testimonies" that were extracted. Even in normal times, the threads of verbal contact among the rebels themselves—what today would be called "the grapevine"—could indeed reach far afield. Young Dennis Mitchell told Doctor (Mitchell) about the Plan. Doctor probably also learned from Dennis that Orange had run away. Doctor admitted to having been "away" himself and having met two runaways, one named Davy Williams who "had a gun," and the other a "yaller" man who belonged to the wealthy and socially prominent A. L. Bingaman, who lived at Fatherland, some five miles to the northwest on the outskirts of town.[46] Doctor actually said Bingaman's "boy," using as slaves often did among themselves the same term used by whites when referring

45. Mr. and Mrs. Walton P. Smith had four teenage sons, an elderly Irish gardener, but no daughters. Census, 1860 Free, household 1041; Slave, MS p. 149. He was described as a large planter in *Goodspeed's*, II, 790–91. See also Road Duty, UTA, 431, 508; Adams Land, 1857, 1861; Adams Personal, 1858, 1859, 1861, 1862; and Jenkins Diary, April 27, 1855. Saragossa had previously been in the Conner family, and then sold several times, as indicated in Jenkins Diary, November 21, 1850, and Road Duty, UTA, 98, 172. Almost certainly Smith owned property elsewhere.

46. Owner of 310 slaves in Adams County, Bingaman was the patron of William Johnson; A. L. Bingaman, Jr., probably used some of them, for he was listed in a separate household but not as a slaveowner. Census, 1860 Free, households 897, 862; Slave, MS pp. 46–50. It is very possible that this Davy Williams was in fact the same man as the runaway referred to earlier as Dave Bradley.

to black men. This "boy" was absent without leave and equipped with a "gun and pistol." It seems exceedingly unlikely that Doctor told the two runaways nothing about the Plan. Indeed, it seems unlikely that they did not know about it already, or if they had not heard of it, that they kept the matter a secret from all other slaves as they skulked around the countryside and even the town.

One other plantation was marginally implicated in Conner's transcript. Simon Dunbar, who was more active in the Plan than talkative before the Examination Committee, nonetheless dropped the name Helm. No one else mentioned John Newton Helm, the wealthy owner of 133 slaves at Oakland, a mile or so south of the Mosbys. Helm, a widower, had recently transferred another thirty-five slaves to his son, who was making his way with a plantation in Tensas Parish. Only one of Helm's slaves was named, but Simon quoted him verbatim: " 'If the black folks were turned loose with hoes and axes they would whip the country' Edmond, Helm's driver, said." Edmond (sometimes "Edmund") had been on the place for more than ten years. Yet no matter how long he had been a trusted servant, a report about a remark like that could get a man "hung." [47]

Conner's transcript also included the name of George Marshall, though Marshall's own slaves were not under particular suspicion. Probably he was present at the examinations merely as an observer, or possibly as a member of the Committee. A few years younger than Conner, Marshall had only twenty-two slaves on his own small place, which was not in the immediate neighborhood, but he owned real estate in Louisiana worth at least $119,000. As the eldest son of Levin R. Marshall, a planter of enormous wealth and far-reaching connections, his views necessarily commanded respect.[48] Levin Marshall owned Poplar Grove, only two miles up

47. Road Duty, UTA, 17–18, 500. Census, 1860 Free, household 991; Slave, MS pp. 127–29; Adams Land; Adams Personal, 1858, 1859, 1861, 1862. The transfer is assumed on the basis of a numerical drop between 1860 and 1861. Jenkins Diary, June 8, 1854, makes clear he was a widower. The younger John Newton Helm, who was listed in his father's household, foundered financially in Louisiana after the war; see Michael Wayne, *The Reshaping of Plantation Society: The Natchez District, 1860–1880* (Baton Rouge, 1983), 67.

48. Census, 1860 Free, household 808; Slave, MS p. 33; Adams Land, 1857, 1861; Adams Personal, 1858, 1859, 1861, 1862; Road Duty, UTA, 306, 449, 508; Weaver, *Mississippi Farmers*, 109. George M. Marshall personifies a common pitfall in the assessment of slaveholding status. He was scarcely a second planter. A

and across Second Creek from Cherry Grove, so the son may have been inquiring about his father's slaves. George Marshall was the only planter whom Conner specifically noted talking with at the examinations, and apparently Conner knew him better by reputation than personally, for he referred to him with a formal term of address, noting after Harry Scott's testimony, "(Mr <u>Marshall</u> thinks Dick and Peter are deep in it.)"

Indeed these two Dunbar slaves, father and son, most assuredly were. At the time of that conversation between Marshall and Conner, neither man knew that Dick's brother, George, in his later (second) testimony, would begin by saying, "Kill Mr Marshall."

Some of the names mentioned in Conner's transcript remain far more obscure. The Mrs. King whom Orange kept boasting about to the other Mosbys was not listed in the previous year's census, understandably so since she was a "fortune teller by cards." Given this marginal profession, it is no surprise that this "tall slim woman" had eluded the assistant marshal and apparently had no qualms about talking with slaves.[49] Characteristically, Orange had sought her out and found her. Certainly he had every reason to be interested in her special talents.

Orange's son, Harvey Mosby, named several people not mentioned by anyone else. Some or all of them were "Homochitto Teamsters," who seem to have been the subject of a conversation with Frederick Scott "at Polly's house." Wesley Mosby, unassertive as usual, was "present" at the time. Asked for names, Harvey gave Henry (Mr. Cooper's) and Charles (probably also belonging to Cooper); Wiley Wood (who was either Cooper's or Mrs. Nancy Wood's or Dr. Spencer Wood's or someone else's). He also mentioned Elisha, who probably belonged to Gerard Brandon, a

---

Princeton graduate, he had left his family's suburban mansion in the mid-1850s, several years after his marriage, in order to build his "own residence." In addition to his own wealth across the river, his mother owned an Adams County plantation with 188 slaves. His father, a banker and merchant as well as planter, was one of the largest absentee landowners in Louisiana and owned northern securities as well as residences in Manhattan and the Bronx. See Census, 1860 Free, household 971; Slave, MS pp. 59–61; Road Duty, UTA, 306, 449, 508; Weaver, *Mississippi Farmers*, 108–10; *Goodspeed's*, II, 397–99; Jenkins Diary, May 28, 1852; and Morton Rothstein, "Resistance, Flight, and Adjustment: Some Natchez Elite Planters During and After the Civil War" (Working Paper Series No. 28, Agricultural History Center, University of California, Davis, 1985, Mimeographed), 9–10.

49. Of course her absence from the census could mean that she was a recent arrival in the county. "Fortune tellers" were likely to be peripatetic.

planter who controlled the largest number of slaves in Adams County. Very possibly Elisha was the same "Brandon's teamster" Orange told Alfred he had talked with. Obviously, the teamsters had considerably more mobility than most slaves; Brandon Hall was located some fifteen miles away, in the northern part of the county.[50]

For *his* part, when pressed about whom *he* had actually talked with, Harvey named only Henry, Charles, and Billy. He had, Harvey said, talked with Billy "at breaking up time," referring either to a social event or, more probably, to the work of spring plowing.[51] We do not know, nor will we ever, what was said in those conversations. But we do know that Billy was probably a young man and that he was owned by Mrs. Eliza Sanderson, a wealthy widow and grandmother who owned 174 slaves, most of them on two or perhaps three large absentee plantations, the two Overtons situated to the south and across the creek, an hour's walk from the Mosby place, and Briars, far to the west on the river.[52]

Yet we do know about *some* of what the slaves said. And it is important that we know, for example, that Edmond's assertion "If the black folks were turned loose with hoes and axes they would whip the country" was one of the most optative recorded expressions of any made by the rebels. The words themselves underscore a prevailing restraint of language, an unwillingness to indulge in bombastic bluster about hoards of arms and glittering prospects for victory. Yet in order to assess the measure of the rebels' realism, we need to attend more closely to what they said about their own intentions.

If we judge that they ought to have been better revolutionaries

50. Cooper is not in the census. For Wood(s): Census, 1860 Free, households 825, 1063; Slave, MS pp. 34, 165–66.The names Elisha and Brandon in Conner's record should probably be read to mean Brandon's Elisha. For Brandon, *ibid.,* household 885; MS pp. 87–92, 149 (174 slaves in his own right and 290 as trustee for his wife and children). Weaver, *Mississippi Farmers,* 109, cites the property in Louisiana at more than $250,000.

51. *Breaking up* meant "plowing" in Jenkins Diary, January 9, 13, 1847—an uncommon month for such work.

52. Census, 1860, household 1043; Slave, MS pp. 74–76; Adams Land, 1853 (John A.), 1857, 1861; Adams Personal, 1858, 1859, 1861, 1862; Road Duty, UTA, 157, 210, 288, 339, 346, 381–82, 426, 473, 494–95, 509; Road Duty, MDAH, Pt. 2, p. 30.

than they actually were, we will fail to understand either them or their oppressors. And as always we need to listen to their plans in the contexts that permeated not only the plans themselves but their oral disclosures. Obviously we can eavesdrop only on those plans that a human being within earshot for some reason decided to write down—which means plans revealed to persons who slaves had every reason to think wanted to hear certain things and not others, as people usually want, but in this case with extreme intensity.

That intensity surfaced in different form under different circumstances many years afterward, when the Plan and its aftershocks seemed to have totally subsided. In 1937 the federal government sponsored a project for interviewing "ex-slaves," elderly Negroes who could and would recall and talk about life under slavery and after the Civil War. Partly, the project was intended to generate work for unemployed "writers" during the Great Depression. Except in Virginia and Florida, the great majority of interviewers were white, as were the state office workers who helped with typing and editing the results. Inevitably there was considerable bureaucratic confusion, and as historians have discovered only recently, some interviews were typed up in more than one form. Although a great deal of information about the project has been unearthed, it is usually impossible to trace exactly how specific interviews took the shape(s) that now remain. This is the case with Charlie Davenport.

More pertinent here, he was the only such former slave whose testimony about the crisis at Second Creek is now available.[53] A number of historians have written about the value and use of these narratives in general, but only after the typescripts were made more easily available than when many of them lay unexamined for years (except for their folkloric value) in the Rare Book Room (of all places) in the Library of Congress. Since the beginning of their publication about 1970, they have been widely combed with great profit, and many other typescripts have been found squirreled away in various state offices and even in private hands. Taken as a whole, what is especially striking about this

53. My tally and an unpublished computer list compiled by Lance Walters both show WPA interviews with a total of twenty slaves who had lived in Adams County at some point in their lives. Apart from Davenport's and (as will become clear) Charles Williams', almost all these accounts are nearly useless for the prewar period.

process of collection and preservation of ex-slave narratives is that it was begun in the 1920s by a small number of black scholars and students, especially at Fisk University, well before whites showed much interest in the matter.

Unfortunately, none of the black interviewers seems to have known old Charlie Davenport, and Davenport himself was unaware that what he knew of the Second Creek tragedy was of special interest to anyone, even when in 1937 a white lady came around to his place in Natchez to ask him about slavery times. He told her some of what he recalled, but the Plan apparently seemed to him and to her of no greater importance than many other aspects of his early life.

Reading what emerged from that conversation or conversations is instructive not merely about Davenport's view of the Plan, but about how historical whispers are heard today. We see his testimony rather differently after reading Conner's transcript and other pertinent documents, very differently than if we were to include Davenport's interview merely as one among many perused in a sweep through the mass of ex-slave documents for purposes of discovering what slavery was like in general.

Once again, it is striking that most historians have treated the interviews as *oral* history (with all its promise and problems) rather than as written documents. Yet a moment's reflection suggests the strong cousinhood of the typescripts of the interview(s) with Davenport and the pages of Conner's transcript of the Second Creek examinations. In both cases we have a written record, generated by one person, as to what another person said. With the Davenport discourse, changes in the record were made shortly thereafter, as seems not to have been the case with the words of the Second Creek rebels. Davenport was not being lashed, nor was he under threat of violent death, but he *was* being asked to answer questions by a person in authority.[54] His interviewer, Mrs. Edith Wyatt Moore, was an indefatigable devotee of local history who

54. Some former slaves, if asked about concerted resistance to slavery, heard danger and ducked. Prince Johnson, a former "house boy" born in Yazoo County but raised in central Mississippi, responded to Mrs. Carrie Campbell's query: "I knows all 'bout what slave uprisin's is, but never in my life has I seen anything lak dat. Never! Never! Where I was brought up de white man knowed his place an' de Nigger knowed his'n. Both of 'em stayed in dey place. We aint never had no lynchin's, neither." Rawick, *American Slave*, Vol. VII (Okla. and Miss. Narrs.), Pt. 2, p. 83. A version of the same with sanitized phrasing is *ibid.*, Suppl. 1, Vol. VIII (Miss. Narrs.), Pt. 3, p. 1179.

wrote extensively about Adams County for the Federal Writers' Project and for local newspapers.[55] No doubt she was less demanding of answers than the Examination Committee had been. Indeed, her motivation was probably genuine personal interest suffused with benevolence. But she had her own expectations, just as the Committee and Conner had, and like the rebels, Charlie Davenport had a very good idea about what those expectations were. Both the rebels and Davenport were black, and both were "interviewed" by whites. As with many matters in the past, the contexts were very different yet suffused with similarities, if only because they shared important historical continuities along with important changes—which perhaps is to say no more than that 1937 was not 1861 and that the latter year came before the former and that no year ever begins on a slate completely clean of previous ones.

What Charlie Davenport is said to have said about the conspiracy is interesting partly because we have two versions, one apparently an earlier version of the other or possibly both derived from a third, protoancestral one. The sequence is far from certain, and the exact relationship between the two documents is not entirely clear. Nonetheless, they are not so much inconsistent as different from one another, and very different indeed from other documents concerning the rebel conspiracy. The longer of Davenport's two descriptions of what went on during the 1861 crisis is more vivid, more detailed, and (it will be noticed) introduced as personal recollection rather than as a grandmother's story.[56]

Davenport recited that story succinctly—or at least one version of what he is said to have said is succinct:

> My granny tol' me 'bout a slave uprisin' what took place when I was a little boy. None o' de marster's Niggers 'ud have

55. Mrs. Moore wrote most of the articles on the old mansions in the 1959 Pilgrimage ("Pink") edition of the Natchez *Democrat* (undated but customarily filed between February and March). Many of her draft pieces for the Federal Writers' Project are in Boxes 215–20, Works Progress Administration, Adams County, RG 60, MDAH.

56. Certain set questions originated with the national office of the Federal Writers' Project and then were usually disseminated to various locales from state offices, but often instructions were not followed. The two Davenport versions can best be compared in the longer printed typescripts as cited in their published forms at the end of Documents Y and Z. The question of which came first is more difficult than may at first appear, but it seems likely that Mrs. Moore's original draft was heavily edited by other project workers. It should be noted that Davenport's "granny" may or may not have been his natural grandmother.

nothin' to do wid it. A Nigger tried to git 'em to kill dey
white folks an' take dey lan'. But what us want to kill old
Marster an' take de lan' when dey was de bes' frien's us had?
Dey caught de Nigger an' hung 'im to a limb.

Another, probably earlier, version is more detailed—similar in
many respects to the shorter rendering, but the details sound like
Davenport's own:

When I wuz a little boy they wuz a slave uprisin planned.
Hit wuz befo de wah broke out. De slaves had hit all worked
out how dey wuz goin to march on Natchez aftah slayin all
dare own white folks. Us folks wouldn't jine 'em kaise what
we want to kill Ole Marse fur? One night a strange nigger
come en he harangued de ole folks but dey wouldn't budge.
While he wuz talkin up rid de sheriff en a passel ob men. He
wuz a powerful, big black feller named Jupiter, en when he
seed who wuz comin he turned en fled in a corn field.

My granny tole me next day dat dey kotch him hidin in a
bayou en hung him on a limb. Dey didn't need no trial kaise
he was kotch rilin de folks to murder.

Probably Charlie Davenport was understandably mistaken in
figuring himself "to be nearly a hundred," for that age would have
meant his being in his early twenties at the time of the conspiracy,
and he probably would not have talked about it as either his grandmother's recollection or "when I wuz a little boy." His claim that
"Hit wuz befo de wah broke out" was of course mistaken if read
literally, but not if one supposes that Charlie Davenport felt the
impact of the war only with the arrival of Federal troops in his
neighborhood in 1863.

Yet many parts of his story (or stories) comport with what is
otherwise ascertainable. His owner, Gabriel Shields, was a very
wealthy man and owned more than eighty slaves at Aventine and
fifteen or twenty more at his home place on the outskirts of
Natchez. He may well have been the man of benevolence depicted
by his elderly former slave. He did indeed marry one of the Surgets, and Charlie Davenport's vivid description of the men of that
family—"de out fightenist, out cussinest, fastest ridin, hardest
drinkin, out spendinest folks I ebber seed"—fits very well with
what we often expect from the third and fourth generations of a
large clan with old, abundant money. Aged forty-three at the time
of the conspiracy, Gabriel Shields had an only slightly younger
Surget wife who had borne seven children (stepping-stones every

two years with the oldest twenty-one and the youngest nine) and then had stopped for reasons she no doubt found sufficient. The Surget women may well have been, as Davenport described them, "beautiful" but "high strung too." Shields himself was something of a gay blade, but he seems to have taken his family responsibilities seriously. He had a sword cane (which most Adams planters did not), and A. D. Pickens listed him as Gabe, rather than Gabriel. Pickens recorded the four youngest Shields children in the column that indicated they had attended school within the last year. Not long afterward, tragedy struck the family when son James, seventeen and no longer in school when the war broke out, was killed in defense of his country.[57]

If Davenport was right, the Shields slaves had refused to participate in the Plan, even when urged by a strange black visitor named Jupiter. It would have been surprising if no attempts had been made to recruit them. Charlie Davenport had lived at Aventine, the plantation whose rigid work routine is known from the plantation diary kept by its overseers. Aventine was well across the creek from the center of the most intensive plotting but only a mile from Cherry Grove and next to Nichols' Bottany Hill and Mitchell's Palatine.[58] As a rebel recruiter, Jupiter visited Aventine, was turned down by the slaves, caught, and hanged. But we are left in ignorance as to the identity of Jupiter, since he was mentioned by no one at the time, at least in writing. Conceivably he was Orange disguised with another appellation, but clever as he was, Orange was rather too self-confident and too much the feisty egotist to conceal himself behind another name.

We need to attend Charlie Davenport's testimony with care, partly because of its intrinsic worth but partly because so far as we know Davenport was the only one of the twenty Adams County slaves interviewed by the Federal Writers' Project to so much as mention the Second Creek conspiracy. This is not to say,

57. Census, 1860 Free, household 869; Slave, MS pp. 65–66; Adams Land; Adams Personal. Aventine had either been bought from Francis Surget or received from him as a gift or inheritance about 1856 or 1857. For F. Surget, see Road Duty, UTA, 295, 342, 424, 472; for Shields, 77, 229, 296, 424, 512. For some reason Shields was not listed in 1854. James's death is from Davenport, who did not name him, but he was the only male child old enough to be in the war unless one counts Jacob, aged thirteen in 1861. The marriage was noted June 12, 1838, in *Johnson's Diary*, I, 232.

58. Several entries in Aventine Plantation Diary, MDAH, complicate these boundaries.

of course, that he was the only Second Creek former slave who remembered it. Indeed, that possibility seems unlikely, but 1937 was not a good year for black people to be telling white folks about the Plan and the hangings that had gone on, and besides, it was a long time ago and the physical limitations and pains of old age and the ten-dollar monthly public support check and the youngsters getting out of hand were much more vivid and important.

It is no surprise that word of the Plan should have met with rejection on some plantations. As Charlie Davenport said, "What we want to kill Ole Marse fur?" There was benefit to be had from not doing so, benefit that was solidly evidenced by the fact that he was still alive to talk about it seventy-five years later. For whatever reasons, the Shields slaves, or at least many of them, rejected participation in the Plan.

At least so Charlie Davenport said, and he is to be believed perhaps most of all because of what he did not say. He did not claim that he and his fellows had actively opposed the Plan. Possibly one of the Shields slaves revealed existence of the conspiracy to the white family, but none of them were mentioned in the other documents, nor was Mr. Shields. Possibly Davenport was thinking about the response his own remarks might elicit in other blacks still living, especially on that particular matter.[59]

Less conjecturally, also absent from his remarks—presumably for reasons of deference to his interviewer, Mrs. Moore—were references to linking up with the northern "enemy" and (similarly, but of course much more powerfully) to taking of ladies. Yet there also remains the possibility that the Shields slaves so quickly and vehemently rejected the Plan that Jupiter and perhaps other emissaries thought better of raising such sensitive operational details on a plantation seemingly so little disaffected from authority. From Davenport's accounts, though, it is clear that the "ole Dutch oberseer" (Charles Sauters) was roundly hated. Davenport called him "a big, hard fisted Dutchman bent on gittin riches," and described the slaves' reaction to his departure when the war broke out with the tersely vivid observation: "We wuz powerful glad en hoped he'd git his neck broke." It is also clear, however, from evidence much older than Charlie Davenport's report, that the Sec-

59. Rather oddly, in my opinion, most modern discussions of the former slave narratives do not consider whether interviewees feared their remarks might somehow quickly get onto the local grapevine, or even who else may have been present during interviews. Historians have focused on other difficulties, such as age, memory, and deference to the interviewer.

ond Creek rebels did not make much headway at Aventine. Presumably Major Shields's slaves were not the only ones who received word of the Plan but "wouldn't jine 'em."

As we have seen, Aventine was an absentee plantation. It was far from being the only absentee plantation in the neighborhood and the county, but if we are seeking to generalize about the matter and assimilate the Natchez district to New World patterns as a whole, then it was Concordia rather than Adams where rebelliousness ought to have surfaced. Generalizations about the wider pattern may still stand, though absenteeism is very difficult to disentangle from other factors such as African immigration, black-white population ratios, and the culture of the master class. Even though he did not live on the place, the owner of Aventine kept his domain under an unusually strict regimen. It was run with the kind of regularity one would expect of a man who required complete daily records from his managers. Each day a roll was called of all the hands. Those too sick to work were listed every day. The slaves at Aventine had a week off for "holiday" at Christmas after the cotton was in, but the Fourth of July was a full working day without any celebration. On Sundays they ground corn, without benefit of a plantation mill.

The Aventine Plantation book carried no indications of insubordinate behavior until August of 1859. Then (at least as recorded) Fanny was for five days variously placed "in the jail house," put in the "stock" by the head or by the legs, and finally, on Sunday, given "10 lashes this evening and turned out." Her offense was not specified. Fanny had periodic "fits," and was (in the language of the day, though not in the overseer's record) "insane." Possibly in response to this treatment of Fanny, the day after her release, "Dick Brown complaining and Run away." He was brought back by another slave the next day (Tuesday), placed in the stocks for several days, and finally whipped thirty-nine lashes.

Several weeks later another slave was disciplined, a slave with a name that cannot help but arrest our attention: "Davenport in the stock and gave him 39 lashes with the strop for ~~saucing and~~ being saucy and clinching his hands against the overseer." Clearly there had been a clash of wills and Davenport had challenged Charles Sauters' dignity and authority. Clearly, too, Aventine was not always the idyllic place that old Charlie Davenport described to Mrs. Moore for her benefit and by extension the world of white folks. Whether the saucy slave Davenport was Charlie himself is simply not clear. More probably, the rebellious slave was Charlie Davenport's father.[60]

It may well be, then, that the slaves on Aventine rejected joining the Plan *because* they were kept under unusually rigid and efficient discipline. It was indeed a rare requirement that the overseer call the roll of hands three times every Sunday. Evidently Major Shields was determined not to have his slaves spending their one day off roaming around on other Second Creek plantations. He had better reason than he knew.

As it happened, other men were roaming around the Second Creek area that spring and summer of 1861, some of them without leave from the people who legally owned both the land and the other people who worked it. Charlie Davenport said nothing (that we know of) about these white men. He may or may not have seen them, even talked with them. Why bring up such a matter to Mrs. Moore even if he had? In his old age at least, the former slave was a man of contemplative external expression, however calculating and angry he may or may not have been within. As he looked back on his life he concluded, "Day aint no sich thing ez freedom. Us is all tied down to somethin."

60. Davenport's name was afterwards on the sick roll for several days. The episode clearly does not fit Davenport's self-description in 1937 as being "a little boy" in 1861. But as an elderly man he may have distanced himself from the old pain with this self-description or may for other reasons have deliberately misled Mrs. Moore about his age. The "Davenport" in the Plantation Diary was a grown man, very possibly Charlie Davenport's father or some other relation or someone whose name young Charlie took out of fondness or admiration. The entries of offenses and punishments are in Aventine Plantation Diary, August 17–21, September 18, 1859.

CHAPTER 8

ROAD TRAVELERS

As with many other slave conspiracies in the United States, white authorities at Second Creek suspected that slave discontent had been instigated or at least abetted by villainous white men. Any system of slavery, especially one with such a strong racial component, tends to breed fear among the master class that proper subordination is threatened from above the prescribed line of demarcation as well as from below.

Yet even slave systems based on race have varied greatly in this respect. Different circumstances of time and place and culture have shaped differing patterns of conflict between the two classes and—an important effect—sometimes resulted in the development of more than two classes. In these latter instances, the lines among various classes have tended to become more fluid and indistinct than in rigidly biracial societies; or, most strikingly in Haiti, a third distinct class could emerge, one with powerful political interests of its own. Important aspects of Haitian culture in fact spilled over into a corner of the United States, where the southern Louisiana mulatto ownership of slaves was common and widely accepted. There were "black" slaveholders in all the slave states, but nowhere else was such ownership so widespread and so clearly permeated with racial definitions that were, in a sense, foreign to the rest of the country. Slave revolts could take place in such a culture, and indeed the largest one in United States history occurred not far from New Orleans. That insurrection of 1811 remains the least well documented of all the major conspiracies in the American South as a whole. But (to understate the matter) southern Louisiana was not southern Mississippi.

In some regions of the New World, even those with more fluid racial lines than the United States, such as Bahia and even Jamaica, "black" slaves so vastly outnumbered "white" masters that there was no need for whites to explain slave rebelliousness by resorting to the supposed machinations of white troublemakers. Nor did it make sense to anyone, black or white, that whites should join where blacks were strong. The notoriously successful *quilombo* state of Palmares (populated almost entirely by escaped slaves) in Brazil and the mountain towns of the Jamaica maroons were multiethnic, but not biracial, enterprises. By the early nineteenth century in the United States, ethnic distinctions among African Americans had been largely obliterated by the sheer numbers of whites, by the shriveling of slave importations from Africa, and by the crushing weight of the United States binary racial classification system.

In the United States, particularly after the Turner rebellion in 1831, whites became nearly frenetic in their search for white provocateurs whenever blacks showed signs of discontent. In the seventeenth century in Virginia, where biracial slavery had not yet become firmly entrenched as a rigidly defined institution, there was good basis in fact for suspicions that white and black laborers were taking up common cause. In the eighteenth century whites were given to making cold-eyed assessments rather than peering under beds for nonexistent white agitators. In New York City in 1712, white officials were well aware that they were dealing with a rising by African Coromantees, and it seems not to have occurred to anyone that whites might be involved.[1] By contrast, in the same port town in 1741, a famous plot that was put down with great savagery seems to have involved several whites— at least, the reigning hysteria resulted in their execution on as good grounds as the slaves supposed to be involved. Later, after the Revolution, Gabriel's plot of 1800 in Virginia was not attended by suspicions of white complicity, even though the rebels admitted that they intended to spare white Methodists, Quakers, and Frenchmen. Virginia authorities were not surprised by such disclosures, for they remained heirs to a strong tradition of realistic assessment of slave unrest. They had good reason to suppose, correctly, that Virginia slaves might regard those two religious groups and the French refugees from revolutionary St. Domingo as (in the words of one of the plotters) "being friendly to liberty."[2] In the early nineteenth century, there were a number of smaller incidents supposedly involving white men, but the year 1831 marked a turning point in the United States.

1. *Coromantee* was the English-language New World term for the Akan-speaking peoples of West Africa, especially the Ashanti. At the time, the population of New York City was slightly smaller than Natchez' would be in 1860.

2. The words are from "[Ben] Woolfolk's Confessions," in Box "Negro Insurrection 1800," Executive Papers (September–December, 1800), Virginia State Library, Richmond. Many of these MSS have been printed in *Cal. Va. State Papers*, Vol. IX (p. 152 for the quotation).

After the Turner rebellion, a wave of novel orthodoxy swept the white South. In the wake of the bloodiest slave rebellion in the nation's history, southern publicists began to trumpet the benevolence of slavery and the contentedness of slaves. The new moral posture could be bolstered with the logical corollary that unrest among the black population could come only from outside agitators. Free Negroes could qualify on this head, and to some degree had always done so. But now there was the new specter of abolition, of "northern fanaticism," which if not discouraged was sufficiently insidious to crop up not only in the guise of Yankee peddlers, but even among low white southern men of mean intentions and false principles.

Thus, during the years after Turner, socially marginal white men fell under heightened suspicion as fomenters of discontent in the quarters. Especially in parts of the frontier slave South, purported discoveries of white involvement in black unruliness came to serve a double purpose. Not only did such nefarious activities afford proof of natural placidity and loyalty in the slave population, but they also offered persuasive explanation of deviant behavior among lower-class whites and the welcome opportunity of stamping it out. Perhaps the most striking instance took place in several counties north of Adams in Mississippi itself in 1835, when the famous "scare" about slave insurrections resulted in the hanging or banishment of dozens of purported gamblers, river pirates, steam doctors, horse thieves, and slave stealers, and the whipping and hanging of slaves.

Similar self-confirming processes surfaced in the Texas slave panic of 1856. Sometimes there may (or may not) have been good grounds for such fears, as was suggested a few years later when a white woman in Louisiana wrote privately that "there has been abolihion misonarys in Texas and I would not be surprised if they passt thrugh here for there is a great many Negroes out now and they are verry bold for they try to brake in to some houses in the day on the side of the public Road." In Texas in 1860, exceptionally hot weather combined with the forthcoming election to produce an outbreak of mysterious fires and a witch hunt for supposed arsonists. Slaves came under suspicion; so did whites. Local committees hanged more than a dozen men of both races.[3]

3. Wendell G. Addington, "Slave Insurrections in Texas," *JNH*, XXV (1950), 408–34; Nancy Willard to Micajah and Mary Wilkinson, September 26, 1859, in Micajah Wilkinson and Family Papers, LSU—her spelling of abolition with an *h* perhaps reflecting her pronunciation; William W. White, "The Texas Slave Insurrection of 1860," *Southwestern Historical Quarterly*, LII (1949), 259–85.

Thus many whites of the South's prewar generation were fully prepared and even downright eager to discover that white men were involved in any possible slave conspiracy. Such suspicion could lead, of course, to fanciful creativity and the ferreting out and punishment of completely innocent victims. On the other hand, witch hunts can turn up real witches. Indeed, it seems very likely that at least a few white men sought to stir up slaves—or to aid them, depending on one's point of view. Almost by definition, such whites were regarded by others and by themselves as operating on the margins of the social order, playing what men when faced with crisis often call, revealingly, a dangerous *game.*

Two (or possibly more) such men made an appearance at Second Creek, and the way they were described reads today almost like a casting director's wish list. Their appearance generated considerable confused curiosity and excitement among the slaves and among their interrogators. It would be difficult to account otherwise for the monumental confusion in Conner's record. Even a quick rereading of that record testifies as to sheer bewilderment, and Conner must have felt it when he was attempting to set things down. Yet today, if we deconstruct that record and then reconstruct it, we can get a better sense of the confusion felt by the participants.

In order to do this, we need to resort to a procedure not guaranteed to gain the confidence of all historians, that of making up conversations. More directly expressed, we can attempt to tentatively reconstruct one-half of what was after all a series of dialogues that took place in an atmosphere suffused to the breaking point with fear, anger, and pain.

It is important to be clear about the nature of such an attempt. What follows is decidedly *not* an attempt to re-create the questions actually asked by the Examination Committee. Conner made no such attempt when recording each slave's responses. Though his transcript at times seems remarkably verbatim, he was very consciously keeping a record that would make sense when read on its own. Accordingly, he filled in proper names rather than record the pronouns that no doubt were actually used. Hence his repeated *W. M.*'s (for "white man")—the best he could do for a proper name under the circumstances—in preference to the *he*'s that were actually used in the testimonies. Inserting reconstructed queries into this dialogue—and using a deliberately stilted diction—may well aid our hearing the logic of the responses. This is to say that stiltedness may (at a price) have its uses. Perhaps it should be borne in mind that the supposedly original record is a written transcript of much of what one man thought he heard. It is not verbatim, and it never *was* the original dialogue. In important ways, modern re-creations are scarcely more unreal than Conner's record itself—or than any other dialogues that were written down more than a century ago.[4]

In Conner's record, Nelson Mosby was the first slave to be examined. In response to the opening queries, he talked about the beginnings of the Plan—fishing on the creek, our boys and Mitchell's. Then, almost immediately, he was asked about white men. Rumors about them may well have been ricocheting around the neighborhood, though Nelson's response makes it hard to tell. Perhaps he was asked about them. Perhaps he volunteered the information. So we may surmise, neutrally:

Q. *Who else did you talk to?*
"First talk with W M."

Evidently members of the Examination Committee either did not hear or were totally nonplussed by this response, for Nelson's next reply concerned other Mosby slaves. He did not mention white men again. The subject came up only much later in the grim proceedings, after eleven other slaves were examined with no apparent mention of white men. Then it was Harvey Mosby's turn, and characteristically Harvey proved to be a fountain of information. After he told about the young ladies beating Wesley's sister, a complaint that must have merely bored the examiners:

Q. *Did you all talk about this Plan with anyone else?* (Or possibly, but less likely: . . . *with any white men?*)
"White man and Wesley and Daddy [*i.e.,* Orange] at fence. Daddy in comes Wesley on fence."
Q. *What did the white man say?*
"White man says at 10th of this month Genl Scott wants every second planter to join him and kill white man."

4. In this respect we sometimes underestimate the magnitude of the revolution brought about by electric recording devices. The magnificent sounds of the PBS *Civil War* television series (1990) were created in the twentieth century, no matter how "original" the director and our minds managed to make them.

Q. *Did he ask you any questions?*
"White man asked Daddy who was nearest neighbor—"
Q. *What did you say?*
"Henderson and Walton Smith."
Q. *What else did he ask you?*
"White asked Wesley how master treated him."
Q. *Where was he from?*
"W. M. says from Sugar farm."
Q. *How did he look?*
"Rawboned white man, not tall, like Irishman."
Q. *When were you talking with him?*
"Twas betwixt dark and daylight."
Q. *Where was he staying?*
"W. M. says he was next to Metcalfe's field."
Q. *When were you talking with the white man?*
"The second day it rained."
Q. *When was that?*
"Week before last—Saturday night—"
Q. *When did he say you should do the killing?*
"10th Sep—was Tuesday week."
Q. *Did this white man have a beard?*
"W. M. no beard."

After this last helpful but limited disclosure, the line of questioning suddenly veered. Harvey was as forthcoming as Nelson had been, and before the questioning came back to the subject of white men, he had named some twenty-five other conspirators owned by a half dozen different slaveholders. But then he quoted Louis (the Metcalfe driver) as saying that "Southerners whipping North." This gratifying response seems to have struck a specific chord, since the focus of the questioning immediately returned to the white man:

Q. *What did you say when you talked to the Metcalfe boy?*
"I told Louis what the white man said—that Genl Scott would eat his breakfast in New Orleans."
Q. *Where did you get that idea?*
"This talk of Nelson."
Q. *Was there anyone else there at the time?*
"Benny present."
Q. *What else did you talk about?*
"Blockhead boats."
Q. *What else?*
"White man spoke 'Second planters' to help."

After finishing with Harvey, the Examination Committee next named fourteen slaves to be summoned and then turned to Alfred, the Mosby slave who said his last name was Scott. Alfred proved more talkative than Harry Scott, his father. As the questioning proceeded, having heard from Alfred the interesting revelation that, according to Orange, Alfred's father "would ravish Mrs Scott," the examiners changed their line of questioning:

Q. Did you talk about all this with a white man?
"White man: mother told me Wesley said he came to W. M. who had on dark clothes."
Q. What else did Wesley say?
"Wesley says, 'You are telltale.' "
Q. Did you talk with any of the other boys on your place?
"O. says there was another W. M.—"
Q. Did you speak with any other white men?
"Only talked with one W. M."
Q. What did Orange say about this other white man?
"O. thinks the <u>W. M. was painted, was a white man, tho passing himself as a negro.</u>"
Q. Did the white man have anyone to help him?
"The W. M. says he had relations up the river."
Q. What did this one look like?
"The W. Man had a short foot."

Having had done with Alfred, the Committee turned immediately to a third Mosby slave, Wesley, who proved to have an observant eye for detail and who introduced the possibility that there may have been more than one "white man":

Q. When Orange and Nelson talked with a white man, did you talk with him too?
"I saw W. M. first, behind the quarters."
Q. What did he tell you?
" 'Master good.' 'whips our children' 'neighbors tight.' "
Q. Where did he come from?
"W. M. says he worked on Sugar farm."
Q. How did he look?
"Like a dutchman or Irishman—"
Q. What was he doing around here?
"Road travellers."
Q. Who else talked with him?
"O. present when I was with W. M."

Q. Was anyone else with him?
"I saw another white man behind the fig tree."
Q. Did he have a beard?
"The W. M. clean face."
Q. What did he look like?
"Chunky."
Q. What were these men wearing?
"They had wool hats, linsey clothes, nice shoes."
Q. Road travelers with nice shoes?
"From tracks, one barefooted."
Q. Did they have anyone to help them?
"W. M. says he had friends above Natchez."
Q. Was he going there?
"His home there."
Q. What else did he say?
"Bell rang and I left him and O. talking."
Q. What did you say when you saw Orange later?
"I said W. M. was a nigger;"
Q. What did Orange think?
"O. said W. M. was a nigger painted red."

At this point the line of questioning shifted, and Wesley had to respond to perhaps ten queries on other matters. But toward the end of his interrogation, one of his inquisitors suddenly returned to the subject of the white men:

Q. When were you talking with the white man?
"I talked with W. M. just about dark."

Indeed the phrase "just about dark" may serve as a flag to epitomize these verbal exchanges. Where do they leave us? What may we conclude, other than that the historical record has left us with inauspiciously murky tailings?

The fact that we cannot say a great deal on the basis of such evidence should not preclude drawing certain quite specific and useful conclusions. First, it seems clear that there actually *were* two or possibly three white men lurking about the neighborhood with things to say to some slaves that very much arrested their attention. The details observed and recalled by the Mosby boys sparkle with precisely the kind of specificity that leads us almost inexorably to believe that they were not made up. Under the circumstances of the Examinations, few human beings could have been so imaginatively creative as to be able to invent them on the spot. And clearly the testimonies of Harvey, Alfred, and Wesley lacked the kind of consistency that would suggest prior collusion and rehearsal. The Examination Committee may have itched to find white men involved in the awful business, but the ones they found were real and not of their own invention.

Our sense of verisimilitude is also reinforced by the inconsistencies of the independent descriptions given by Wesley, Alfred, and Harvey. If we lump these depictions together and assume they applied to the same man, they have precisely the quality of inconsistent consistency that we have come to regard as typical of eyewitness descriptions of strangers first seen and later recalled under conditions of great stress. Harvey's "Rawboned white man, not tall" with "no beard" comports completely with Wesley's "clean face" and "chunky." Harvey said he was "like Irishman," and Wesley "Like a dutchman" (that is, a German) "or Irishman." Alfred remembered that the white man had "dark clothes" and Wesley that "they" (in his burst of detail that suggested the possibility of a third white man) "had wool hats, linsey clothes, nice shoes" but that one of them made barefoot tracks in the mud or dust—this latter observation probably indicating that one of them toted his shoes at least some of the time when skulking about the Mosby place, rather than crud them with all the field dirt. Only Alfred noted—and it was the only descriptive detail he offered— "The W. Man had a short foot."

As for the complexion of the "white" man they talked with, the Mosbys' testimony reeks with the complicated ambiguities inherent in a rigid system of status and social definition that hinged so crucially on skin color. In Mississippi and throughout the American Union, racial distinction rested on bifurcated social categories of "white" and "black." Both castes were presumed to be rigid entities, with instances of blurring thought to be the unfortunate productions of intermixtures of "blood."

The twin categories of black and white were not merely summary descriptions of appearance. They had become qualities so internal and so inherent that any alteration was necessarily superficial. Thus when both Wesley and Alfred claimed that Orange used the term *painted,* they were pointing to Orange's feeling that the "white man" was not *really* what he seemed. They accepted Orange's premise about color, though they disagreed about the conclusion he had drawn. For most Americans today, the conclusion is so crucial as to blind them to the importance of the premise. According to Alfred, Orange thought the W. M. really "was a white man." By painting himself superficially the man was, to use Orange's peculiarly Anglo-American term, *passing*—"passing himself as a negro." (Conner's underlinings are omitted here, since they served to indicate the importance that *he*, probably more than the rebels, attached to the phrases in question.) On the contrary, according to Wesley, Orange thought the "W. M." really "was a nigger." He had "painted" himself. Wesley agreed: the "W. M. was a nigger."

Several things may be said about this jumble of wordage. First, any distinction we may detect between *Negro* and *nigger* is of our making and not the rebels'. Slaves used both terms, the latter without embarrassment and often without the inverted affection that is common today.[5] Furthermore, these exquisite assessments of physiognomy were made at dusk or at night or possibly in moon shadows. It is not impossible that these men had painted themselves.[6] In addition, Orange may have been misreported by either Alfred or Wesley, or his own opinion may have vacillated. Finally, many urban Americans today may need to be reminded that to paint a socially black man white in the rural South, one might well use red tint rather than white. A well-known epithet (in most contexts not intended as flattering) derives from the fact that southern whites who labor outdoors often appear to have "red" necks and faces. The words *black* and *white* are no more chromat-

5. As becomes clear upon opening any of the volumes of ex-slave narratives. No special significance attached to the abbreviation W. M.; the free Negro diarist of Natchez used "B. M" for "Black man"; *Johnson's Diary*, II, 671.

6. One contemporary account of the Vesey conspiracy claimed that the rebels got a white barber to make wigs and false beards out of "white" hair, and "with the assistance of these, and by painting their faces, they hoped in the darkness of the night and in the confusion to be mistaken for white men." Lionel Kennedy and Thomas Parker, *An Official Report of the Trials of Sundry Negroes, Charged with an Attempt to Raise an Insurrection in the State of South-Carolina . . .* (Charleston, 1822), which varies slightly from the manuscript in South Carolina Department of Archives and History, Columbia. The published version has been reprinted as John Oliver Killens, ed., *The Trial Record of Denmark Vesey* (Boston, 1970), p. 27 for the quotation. Whites were always more suspicious at times of crisis. In the wake of the Turner revolt, far from the scene, the Raleigh (N.C.) *Register*, September 1, 1832, reported that one of the dead conspirators was a white man who had "blackened" himself; quoted (together with other interesting assertions) in Robert N. Elliott, "The Nat Turner Insurrection as Reported in the North Carolina Press," *North Carolina Historical Review*, XXXVIII (1961), 6.

ically accurate than *red* when used to describe human skin colors, as a glance at human hands on piano keys should remind us.

Actually, the mysterious stranger could conceivably have been a socially black albino. The latter condition was in fact relatively more common among blacks than whites.[7] One or both of the two W. M.'s may have been mulatto in some degree. Then, as today, thousands of American "blacks" lead "white" lives. The entire system of bifurcated classification depended on an agreement shared by everyone. The collective conspiracy of "passing" rested on a silence that was crucial to the system's working at all. One does not safely go around calling white people black or black people white, except—and it is a revealing exception—with intentionally barbed irony wrapped in a safety coating of levity.

Yet the W. M.'s were strangers in the Second Creek neighborhood. Indeed they may well have been Irish or German, since there were numerous such immigrant laborers in the towns and countryside of the lower Mississippi Valley. They were on the loose—"road travellers," in Wesley's pithy phrase—a species of itinerant frequently encountered and commented upon by less aimless northern and foreign visitors, and also by slaves. The one that the rebels talked to came from farther north, "above Natchez," where "he worked on Sugar farm." Sugarcane cannot be cultivated as far north as Adams County, since the growing season is not sufficiently long. Yet in 1854 the United States government had obtained sweet sorghum seeds from Japan, and Mississippi farmers rapidly embraced sorghum as a cheap source of molasses. Cotton planters did not ordinarily give over their land to such production, especially at a time when cotton was so profitable, but they could purchase sorghum molasses for their black families at two to three dollars a gallon.[8] Neither the rebels nor their examiners had reason to puzzle about "Sugar farm."

---

7. The human gene for albinism occurs more frequently in West African than in European populations. It is in this sense that the *frequency* of albinism is a racial characteristic.

8. John Hebron Moore, *Agriculture in Ante-Bellum Mississippi* (1958, rpr. New York, 1971), 143. Moore does not distinguish sweet sorghum from other varieties, or give the price, which is interpolated here from Salt Lake City prices in 1860 given in Mitford M. Mathews, *A Dictionary of Americanisms: On Historical Principles* (Chicago, 1951), *s.v.* "sorghum." Its place of origination is obscure, since it was also often called "Chinese sugar cane." Just before the war, an African variety was introduced that eventually became the dominant kind. See Lewis Cecil Gray, *History of Agriculture in the Southern United States to 1860* (2 vols.; 1933; rpr. Gloucester, Mass., 1958), II, 829. It is not clear exactly what one is getting today when one buys it at a farmers' market in a plain quart can.

These road travelers of course avoided contact with the planters. There were well-founded reasons for suspicion on both sides. At the Mosby place the two (or three) found opportunity to stir up trouble, for they must have sensed very quickly that these men, especially the one called Orange, were already planning on their own and even with some others in the neighborhood. When Orange met one at the fence, the conversation turned serious. Then when Wesley came up he took a back seat, as he usually did. The white man cautiously asked him "how master treated him," a question that probably met with an equally pregnant but carefully noncommital response.

Orange was interested in the war, and he may well have asked about possible sources of support. The white man proved eager to supply information and even outright encouragement. *He* had nothing to lose by pushing the brazen falsehood that the second planters might join the blacks, and probably Orange gave no indication that he had towering doubts on that score. But Orange had little reason to reject the specific information that the Union general named Scott wanted the Negroes and the second planters to rise on the tenth of that September. Probably he had already picked up word from Nelson that General Scott would take New Orleans with such ease that he "would eat his breakfast" there. "Dine" was the word used later. It was a memorable image, this enemy general dining at a sumptuous table set in the center of the world of cotton. It cropped up again and again.

At one point Conner's transcript becomes so cryptic as nearly to defy interpretation. As Wesley recapitulated his conversation with the white man, Conner set down three staccato phrases in quotation marks. Of the first two, "Master good" is immediately followed by "whips our children." We may construct at least the following two possibilities:

> W. M.: *How does your master treat you?*
> Wesley (warily): "Master good."
> W. M. (pressing): *Does he* really *treat you well?*
> Wesley (easing): "Whips our children."

Or:

> W. M.: *"How are you? Do you have a good master?"*
> Wesley: "Master good [but he] whips our children."

Wesley's third quoted phrase, "neighbors tight," must remain awash in uncertainties. It could have been used by either man; it could have referred to neighbors either black or white; and "tight" could have suggested either resistance to scheming or solid backing. If we accept this oversimple bifurcation of three variables, we are left with a total of a mere eight different possibilities to ponder.

We are also left with the fact that the stranger was interested in finding out about the neighbors. He was testing the waters, scouting around, asking Harvey for specific names, and generally behaving in a way that would have confirmed the worst suspicions of the planters. By their lights, he should not even have been *talking* with those slaves. The likes of him should not even have been walking around those places where they had no business. Especially the Mosby place.

There is no evidence that the W. M. or his companion(s) were ever taken up by the authorities. If by some chance he was, there is little doubt he was quietly hanged. But we may more safely conclude by reminding ourselves that the coat of class rebellion can be worn in various ways and has many colors.

CHAPTER 9

OF WOMEN WHITE AND BLACK

The cotton planters found another aspect of the Second Creek revelations much more appalling than the involvement of white men in a slave conspiracy. Blacks rebels intended to take their white women. Of course they did.

At least in 1861 in Adams County, Conner's record *says* they did. The transcript is unambiguous on this matter, except that it leaves room for flexibility as to what "taking" of white women actually meant. Before attending to that meaning, however, we need to confront the issue more generally but nonetheless very much head on. The assertion that black men intended to seize white women for sexual purposes was a highly charged one. At the time, it carried heavy emotional freight. It still does today. Many historians regard it as a patently racist canard. Yet despite the persistence of such tensions, we need to concentrate on the context in which these claims about the young women were actually made.

For nearly two previous centuries in America, British settlers turning into Americans had allowed their own sexual anxieties to intermingle with and to buttress their fears of black insurrection. On a number of occasions, actual slave insurrections or rumors of slave conspiracies were accompanied by charges that the rebels intended to spare the attractive white women "for themselves." Such a charge of course comported with the prevailing view that blacks were inherently lustful. It dovetailed logically with the presupposition that when blacks were intent on overthrowing due social order, they must necessarily be aiming at taking white women. For white men, these women embodied that order because they were its subordinate but integral subjects. Such an unimaginable attack was in fact easy to imagine because it was an assault on the most emotionally explosive component of white male domination.

These assertions about rebellious black men are especially striking because they lacked basis in fact. Even when slaves were able to seize temporary local control, as during several revolts in Jamaica and at Stono in South Carolina in 1739, there were no instances of rape or attempted rape. Indeed, there were no such actual instances during *any* of the myriad excitements over slave plots in the entire history of the Anglo-American colonies and nation. There were dozens of documentable instances of individual black men being convicted of raping white women or girls, but none of them in connection with slave conspiracies.[1] Thus the record points unambiguously to the fears and anxieties of white men rather than the actual behavior of blacks. It was blacks, not whites, who had good reason to fear.

The first known instance in Anglo-America of whites associating sexual attacks with black revolt came after the Barbados slave rebellion of 1676. The allegation was made in a pamphlet aimed at an audience home in England, a promotional pamphlet that reported suppression of a "grand conspiracy" under the unintentionally ironic title *Great Newes from the Barbadoes.* Similar charges were made at even greater distances from the actual events in one of the earliest histories of the British Empire and in a persistently anti-Negro tome by a white Jamaican.[2] Neither writer had been on the scene.

1. There are scattered references to rape and attempted rape by blacks, and also whites, throughout the Anglo-American colonies and states. The most systematic data for slaves derive from records of those executed for capital crimes in Virginia; see U. B. Phillips, "Slave Crime in Virginia," *American Historical Review,* XX (1915), 336–40, and the corrections of Phillips' figures in Herbert Aptheker, *American Negro Slave Revolts* (New York, 1943), 222n; also Philip J. Schwartz, "Forging the Shackles: The Development of Virginia's Criminal Code for Slaves," in *Ambivalent Legacy: A Legal History of the South,* ed. David J. Bodenhamer and James W. Ely, Jr. (Jackson, Miss., 1984), 125–46, and Herbert Aptheker, "American Negro Slave Revolts: Fifty Years Gone," *Science and Society,* LI (1987), 70–71. Despite the execution of some men who were probably innocent, all those convicted received legal trials; it is important not to conflate such trials and punishments with the lynching mob horrors of the late nineteenth and early twentieth centuries. In 1859 in Maryland, a black man was legally sentenced to death for rape of two children, one white and one black, and there was no report of mob vengeance; reported in New Orleans *Daily True Delta,* June 21, 1859, in Dillard Transcripts, Dillard University, New Orleans. As with all negatives, it is difficult to prove the absence of rape in connection with revolts, but to my knowledge *no* such instances have been found. The situation was much the same in the British sugar islands. A thoroughly exceptional case occurred during Tacky's revolt in Jamaica in 1760, when the mulatto concubine of a slain overseer was raped but not killed; Michael Craton, *Testing the Chains: Resistance to Slavery in the British West Indies* (Ithaca, 1982), 129.

2. *Great News from the Barbadoes; or, A True and Faithful Account of the*

In the continental colonies, similar accusations were bandied about, almost always by writers who had no direct contact with the slave plot in question. The usual charge was that the rebels had planned to kill all the whites except those young women whom they "intended to reserve for themselves." A New York jury was less euphemistically informed in 1741 that "the White Men should be all killed, and the Women become a Prey to the rapacious Lust of these Villains!"[3]

The greater the geographical and/or temporal distance white commentators stood from a conspiracy, the more they were inclined to discover sexual aggression among rebellious slaves. In 1757 a writer in the *London Magazine* waxed imaginative about a plot that had taken place in South Carolina more than a quarter century before. The "ring-leaders," he wrote, had been "executed, after confessing the conspiracy, and each of them declaring whose wife, daughter, or sister he had fixed on for his future bedfellow." Yet what seems to have been the only contemporary account of this plot—in the Boston newspapers—made no mention at all of sexual aims on the part of the conspirators. A diary kept by a Hessian officer during the Revolution reported about what was probably the same plot, by this time nearly fifty years after the fact. He had heard that "the entire Negro population, at least the greater part, had conspired to assault their masters on a certain night, massacre all the [male] white population, make the women either their slaves or use them to gratify their desires, and sacrifice the rest."[4]

Grand Conspiracy Against the English . . . (London, 1676), 10; [John Oldmixon], *The British Empire in America* . . . (2 vols.; London, 1708), II, 47, concerning a Barbados plot *ca.* 1687; [Edward Long], *The History of Jamaica* . . . (3 vols.; London, 1774), II, 457n. Winthrop D. Jordan, *White Over Black: American Attitudes Toward the Negro, 1550–1812* (Chapel Hill, 1968), 150–63, discusses these and other such early assertions.

3. New York *Gazette*, March 25, 1734; [Daniel Horsmanden], *A Journal of the Proceedings in the Detection of the Conspiracy Formed by Some White People, in Conjunction with Negro and Other Slaves, for Burning the City of New-York in America, and Murdering the Inhabitants* . . . (New York, 1744), 42. Similar remarks are cited in Jordan, *White Over Black*, 152n.

4. *London Magazine*, XXVI (1757), 330–31; Boston *News-Letter*, October 22, 1730; Boston *Gazette*, October 26, 1730; "Diary of Captain Johann Hinrichs," in *The Siege of Charleston* . . . *Diaries and Letters of Hessian Officers* . . . , ed. and trans. Bernhard A. Uhlendorf (Ann Arbor, 1938), 323. The most accurate account of the latter conspiracy is in Peter H. Wood, *Black Majority: Negroes in Colonial South Carolina from 1680 Through the Stono Rebellion* (New York, 1974), 237,

By itself, the sweeping generality of such statements renders them suspect. These records yield no names. Only rarely do they employ a phrase about a specific intention of the sort that would reverberate at Second Creek. A private letter of 1740, datelined Annapolis, speaks of a long-brewing conspiracy that aimed at destroying "their several families," the "Negro women," and "all except the white women only whom they intended to keep for their wives."[5]

On the basis of Conner's transcript alone, one might conclude that these eighteenth-century claims established a persistent tradition of which the Second Creek rebels were the unfortunate heirs. Ordinarily such emotionally driven allegations do not rapidly dissipate in the course of time. Yet what seems to have happened—and it is indeed something of a surprise—is that the tradition of imputing sexual aggression to slave rebels seems to have weakened somewhat in the years after the American Revolution—until, of course, at Second Creek. Of the hundreds of accounts about slave unrest between the American Revolution and the American Civil War, there were relatively few contemporary reports of purported sexual intentions on the part of slave rebels. Certainly this was the case with the Gabriel plotters in 1800.[6] Allegations about intended sexual assault began a half century after the event with a Virginia historian, Robert Howison, who wrote in 1848 that the Gabriel conspirators planned "to divide the women among themselves." The same assertion surfaced again another half century later, copied nearly word for word from the previous historical report by a budding member of the young his-

---

300. A less widely known conspiracy in South Carolina in 1749 has been profitably studied by Philip D. Morgan and George D. Terry, "Slavery in Microcosm: A Conspiracy Scare in Colonial South Carolina," *Southern Studies*, XXI (1982), 121–45.

5. Stephen Bordley to Matt Harris, January 30, 1739 [i.e., 1740, New Style; there is confusion about the year in the secondary literature], in Stephen Bordley's Letterbook, 1738–1740, Maryland Historical Society, Baltimore.

6. One can make this sort of negative statement with some confidence for previous centuries, when the total number of sources is relatively small. There are so many more historical records from the antebellum period, however, that some such instances have surely been missed. In Gabriel's plot there may have been an exception in the possibly crossed-out words in *Cal. Va. State Papers*, IX, 142, but see other testimony, IX, 171. This was very different from the political view of Ben Woolfolk that they had "intended . . . to spare all the poor white women who had no slaves," *ibid.*, IX, 152.

torical profession.[7] Yet at the time only one of the rebels was said to have made any such claim. Neither the Richmond nor other newspapers seem to have picked up this assertion, though many carried detailed accounts about the appalling state of affairs in Henrico County.

Other such allegations were made in South Carolina, one in a report of disturbances in 1816 in Camden, where a doctor's wife wrote that rebels planned to seize the arsenal and "to murder the men but the women they intended to reserve for their own purposes this is their own confession."[8] During the 1822 trials of the Vesey conspirators in Charleston, one witness claimed that Rolla, a slave of Governor Thomas Bennett's, "said, *'when we have done with the fellows, we know what to do with the wenches.'* " After this testimony, but before it was published in the magistrates' self-justifying summary of the trials, Baltimore's nationally circulated *Niles Register* expanded this assertion by advancing the thrilling rumor that a daughter of the governor had been singled out by one of the rebels. A splendid historical book published in 1990 treated that rumor as fact without documentation. Yet at the time, newspapers in Charleston and elsewhere did not take up this theme.[9]

7. Robert R. Howison, *A History of Virginia, from Its Discovery and Settlement by Europeans to the Present Time* (2 vols.; Philadelphia, 1846; Richmond, 1848), II, 391. (This second volume may have been a revision or reprint of an earlier edition, *i.e.*, Philadelphia, 1846.) According to a published Ph.D. dissertation, the slaves aimed at "seizing the city at night, killing the males, dividing the females, and then arming for extermination of the whites throughout the State"; James C. Ballagh, *A History of Slavery in Virginia*, Johns Hopkins University Studies in Historical and Political Science, extra vol. XXIV (Baltimore, 1902), 92. Other similar sources are mentioned and rightly dismissed by Douglas R. Egerton, "Gabriel's Conspiracy and the Election of 1800," *JSH*, LVI (1990), 203n.

8. R. Blanding to her cousin, July 4, also July 25, 1816, in William Blanding Papers, South Caroliniana Library, University of South Carolina, Columbia. See L. Glen Inabinet, " 'The July Fourth Incident' of 1816: An Insurrection Plotted by Slaves in Camden, South Carolina," in *South Carolina Legal History*, ed. Herbert A. Johnson (1980; rpr. Spartanburg, S.C., 1980), 209–21, which quotes (p. 212) an attorney as referring to "the massacre of all the white male inhabitants, and the more brutal sacrifice of the female."

9. *Niles Weekly Register*, July 13, 1822, p. 320. The quotation is in Lionel H. Kennedy and Thomas Parker, *An Official Report of the Trials of Sundry Negroes, Charged with an Attempt to Raise an Insurrection in the State of South-Carolina* . . . (Charleston, 1822), rpr. as *The Trial Record of Denmark Vesey*, ed. John Oliver Killens (Boston, 1970), 42. A similar but differently worded remark was reported in James Hamilton, Jr., *Negro Plot: An Account of the Late Intended Insurrection*

If ever insurrectionary slaves in the United States had good opportunity for ravishing white women, it was during the Nat Turner rebellion in 1831. For nearly two days in Southampton County in Virginia, Turner and his men proceeded from one farm to another, killing as they went. They met little resistance, and they had taken the lives of some sixty men, women, and children before they, as well as many blacks who had nothing to do with the rebellion, were shot down, hanged and decapitated, or seized for trial. The slaughter of white men, women, and children raised an outcry of public and private indignation across the horrified nation. Yet no source at the time, whether emanating from the scene or from points far distant, so much as hinted at sexual designs on the part of the "banditti." Reports in the Richmond *Enquirer* were replete with shocked denunciations, but they did not even intimate that the blacks had targeted white women for a fate worse than death. That city's *Constitutional Whig* declared, "It is not believed that any outrages were offered to the females." Much of the reporting was remarkably accurate, considering the fears and hostilities raked to the surface by events in Southampton. In Milledgeville, Georgia, readers of the *Federal Union* were not badly misinformed when told that Nat Turner's followers "fully believed, his was a mission of deliverance, and themselves called us [*i.e.*, "as"] the instruments of vengeance"—though no doubt these readers missed the significance of the revealing slip of the author's or typesetter's hand.[10]

Among a Portion of the Blacks of the City of Charleston, South Carolina (Boston, 1822), 13. This latter passage, which does not refer to Rolla but to "one" of the "slaves of the governor," is in Robert S. Starobin, ed., *Denmark Vesey: The Slave Conspiracy of 1822* (Englewood Cliffs, 1970), 86. William W. Freehling, *Secessionists at Bay, 1776–1854* (New York, 1990), 80 and 579n, Vol. I of Freehling, *The Road to Disunion*, 2 vols., adds the assertion about the governor's daughter without citation. Some such rumor was in circulation, as in a letter from Anna Hayes Johnson to her cousin, June 23, 1822, in Starobin, ed., *Denmark Vesey*, 72: "I have a very beautiful cousin who was set apart for the wife or more properly the 'light of the Haram' of one of their Chiefts." At the trial of a white man accused of complicity, the charge about blacks having white wives came up again; Killens, ed., *Trial Record of Denmark Vesey*, 153. See also William W. Freehling, "Denmark Vesey's Peculiar Reality," in *New Perspectives on Race and Slavery in America: Essays in Honor of Kenneth M. Stampp*, ed. Robert H. Abzug and Stephen E. Maizlish (Lexington, Ky., 1986), 15–47. I am grateful to Professor Freehling for his gracious response to my queries on this matter.

10. Richmond, *Enquirer*, all extant issues of August and September, 1831; Richmond *Constitutional Whig*, August 29, 1831; Milledgeville (Ga.) *Federal*

Much later, two commentators revealed the way personal and regional predilections could shape retroactive perception of the facts. In 1861, Thomas Wentworth Higginson, a radical abolitionist from Massachusetts, undertook a brief history of the great crisis in Southampton County. A trenchant and penetrating observer, though with unusual prejudices of his own, Higginson confronted the question head on. "One fear was needless," he wrote, a fear that must have racked "many a husband and father" when faced with the rebellion. "These negroes had been systematically brutalized from childhood; they had been allowed no legalized or permanent marriage; they had beheld around them an habitual licentiousness, such as can scarcely exist except in a Slave State; some of them had seen their wives and sisters habitually polluted by the husbands and the brothers of these fair white women." Yet these same slaves, when "fair white women" were "absolutely in their power," eschewed the opportunity for retaliation in kind. "I have looked," he wrote, "through the Virginia newspapers of that time in vain for one charge of an indecent outrage on a woman against these triumphant and terrible slaves. Wherever they went, there went death, and that was all."[11]

Much later, at the turn of the century, a white southern historian took an opposite view. Since he had interviewed people still alive who purportedly recollected the affair, it is difficult to ascertain whether he was venting his own prejudices, those of his informants, or (most probably) both. "Some say that [the white] victims were murdered and no further outrages committed . . . ," wrote the young Virginia historian William S. Drewry (citing Howison), "but this is an error." "Women were insulted," he continued in the Victorian mode, "and it is said that Nat offered pro-

---

Union, September 8, 1831. Henry Irving Tragle, ed., *The Southampton Slave Revolt of 1831: A Compilation of Source Material Including the Full Text of the Confessions of Nat Turner* (1971; rpr. New York, 1973) provides some newspaper and many other accounts in a very useful though incomplete collection. Many newspapers elsewhere quoted at length from those published in Virginia. As a sampling, the New York *Post,* Albany (N.Y.) *Argus,* Harrisburg (Pa.) *Chronicle,* Mobile *Register,* and Boston *Columbian Sentinel* offered no suggestions about ravishing in their reports about the crisis. See also Robert N. Elliott, "The Nat Turner Insurrection as Reported in the North Carolina Press," *North Carolina Historical Review,* XXXVIII (1961), 1–18.

11. Thomas Wentworth Higginson, "Nat Turner's Insurrection," *Atlantic Monthly,* VIII (1861), 173–87, quotation p. 176. Available also in Tragle, ed., *Southampton Revolt,* 327–49.

tection to one beautiful girl if she would consent to be his wife, but death was to this noble woman a blessing in comparison with such a prospect."[12] Here lay Nat Turner, disinterred and transmogrified, though not for the last time.[13]

Nat Turner may possibly have been a household name in the quarters at Second Creek, but it seems unlikely, and we will never know.[14] The planters had almost surely heard the name—in much the way many people had heard of Toussaint L'Ouverture—but they had no reason to discuss him at the dinner table and, indeed, every reason not to. Yet the parents and grandparents of some of the Second Creek rebels may well have come from the Virginia Tidewater, where considering the havoc he had created Nat Turner was, to say the least, well known. Had his name embodied solely the cause of revolt, the Second Creek rebels might have invoked it at the examinations. They did not. They may have heard it only as a byword of caution—one they had refused to heed—since Turner's killings had been followed by wholesale slaughter of Southampton blacks by panicked and vengeful bands of white men.[15]

Whatever the case with Nat Turner, stories about ravishing remained alive among southern whites, as such fables do when they touch deep feelings. They cropped up in Mississippi in 1835 during the scare about blacks, gamblers, and the Murrell "land pirate" gang, which resulted in the execution of some seven whites

12. William S. Drewry, *The Southampton Insurrection* (1900; rpr. Murfreesboro, N.C., 1968), 117, also published as William S. Drewry, *Slave Insurrections in Virginia, 1830–1865* (Washington, D.C., 1900). Tragle, ed., *Southampton Revolt*, 478–83, gives the curious initial history of this publication.

13. Publication of William Styron's *The Confessions of Nat Turner* (New York, 1967) generated a storm of controversy, much of it ideologically driven (as was the book) and little focused on the author's cavalier approach to historical sources. See John Henrik Clarke, ed., *William Styron's Nat Turner: Ten Black Writers Respond* (Boston, 1968), but in this context especially the trenchantly titled chap. 3 by Vincent Harding, "You've Taken My Nat and Gone." The Introduction to the 1968 reprinting of Drewry's book (pp. iv–v) criticizes Styron from a very different standpoint. The story of this complicated dispute merits separate historical treatment.

14. The ex-slave narratives, read collectively, suggest that Turner's name was not known by many slaves. See especially Donald M. Jacobs, assisted by Steven Fershleiser, *Index to "The American Slave"* (Westport, Conn., 1981). It seems probable, though, that this collective record considerably underestimates the spread of his reputation.

15. The Manuscript Division of the Library of Congress has an anonymous MS autobiography by a black man who grew up in Southampton County (I have managed to lose a more exact citation); its author excoriates Turner for placing the lives of so many black people in danger.

and ten to fifteen blacks. The story was told without circumlocution. One of the nefarious white men confessed that the slaves intended on "murdering all the white men and ugly women—sparing the handsome ones and making wives of them."[16]

Less than a year before the examinations at Second Creek, the Macon *Daily Telegraph* offered the same tale in Georgia, framed in terms that were meant to convey airy detachment along with the shocking facts: "The negroes state that their intentions were, on Tuesday, while the men were gone to the polls, to kill all the married women and children, but to keep the young women for the wives, &c, and kill the [men] on their return home." In such a context, a mere *et cetera* could carry all the weight an imaginative reader might choose to impose.[17]

Such assertions were almost invariably framed in language conspicuously lacking in specifics about exactly who was in danger. It was the *point* that mattered, not the threatened individual women. Indeed it was never (except at Second Creek) really clear exactly who these women were. As two Texas newspapers propounded the formula during a panic there in 1860, "They had even gone so far as to designate their choice, and certain ladies had already been selected as the victims of these misguided monsters."[18]

Such thoughts served not only to gratify individual fantasies, but also to satisfy the social needs of a society that felt itself besieged. The white South's spokesmen (and spokeswomen, in novels and shorter fiction) defensively touted the region's special virtues, puffing them to the point of caricature. They proclaimed with "perfect confidence" that far from being lodged in a backwater, out of the mainstream of the century's flood tide of progress,

16. Quoted in Edwin A. Miles, "The Mississippi Slave Insurrection Scare of 1835," *JNH*, XLII (1957), 51–52. A slave named Jim was said to have "stated, that it was their intention to slay all the whites, except some of the most beautiful women, whom they intended to keep as wives." Quoted in *Virgil Stewart*, 232. The formula could scarcely have been stated more succinctly, but the matter was complicated by the presence of purportedly criminal white men.

17. Macon *Daily Telegraph*, November 9, 1860, referring to Crawford County, Georgia. Strikingly similar language appeared in the same state a half year later: "kill all of the men and old women and children and take the younger ones for their wives"; quoted in Clarence L. Mohr, *On the Threshold of Freedom: Masters and Slaves in Civil War Georgia* (Athens, Ga., 1986), 51.

18. Bonham (Tex.) *Era*, July 17, 1860, and Houston *Telegraph*, July 14, 1860, quoted in Donald E. Reynolds, "Smith County and Its Neighbors During the Slave Insurrection Panic of 1860," *Chronicles of Smith County* [Texas], X (1971), 2.

they stood on the higher ground once occupied by the societies of Greece and Rome, far above the present raging turmoils of fanaticism and licentiousness. Resting as it did upon the piles of due subordination, a slave society provided a firm bulwark against the crashing waves of social and familial disorder.

The mere idea of black men taking white women constituted a double inversion of these values. One measure of the dangers of the times was that in the North, women were "unsexing themselves," abandoning hearth and home in favor of the factory and (worse) the speaker's platform. Out of control, they became "unnatural"—a word used commonly and with a meaning much altered from the previous century. Their natural and proper roles stood protected by slavery—except, of course, upon those extremely rare but all-too-common and appalling and indeed unnatural occasions when slaves themselves got drastically out of control.

A fully accurate measure of this fever would require a battery of quotations, but even one (taken not at all at random) may serve as a gauge of the atmosphere among the rulers of Second Creek. Some of them may well have read, just a year before in the widely circulated *DeBow's Review,* a summary of the problems and the possibilities of their challenging situation—an epitome, to the extent that such important and complex matters could be epitomized. At a convention of southern states at Vicksburg, young Leonidas W. Spratt of South Carolina declaimed in favor of reopening the Atlantic slave trade (as quoted in *DeBow's*):

> I have perfect confidence that, when France shall reel again into the delirium of liberty—when the peerage of England shall have yielded to the masses—when democracy at the North shall hold its carnival . . . when women shall have taken the places and habiliments of men, and men shall have taken the places and habiliments of women—when Free Love Unions . . . shall pervade the land—when the sexes shall consort without the restraints of marriage, and when youths and maidens, drunk at noon day, and half naked, shall reel about the market places—the South will stand, secure and erect as she stands now—the slave will be restrained by power, the master by the trusts of a superior position.

As for the South, he concluded in an astonishing phrase, "She will move on with a measured dignity of power and progress." Here was an arresting spectacle. With a fusion of gender not easily achieved, a female South, imbued with masculine virtues, would assuredly prevail in the highest realm of morals.[19]

It is important to bear in mind that it was primarily the anxieties of white *men* that energized these thoughts. As participants in a male-dominated culture, white women were not immune to the formal proposition that black men lusted after them. Southern bellehood was partially shaped by such concerns, which were incorporated into norms of proper female demeanor. In his own unsympathetic way, the Yankee commentator Frederick Olmsted caught a snapshot of this stance toward life in his description of the occupants of a carriage: "The ladies sat back, good-looking women enough, and prettily dressed, but marble-like in propriety, looking stealthily from the corners of their eyes without turning their heads."[20] Yet clearly these women were less driven than men to expatiate the standard formula about black men, since it lacked for them the coercive emotional fire that propelled the danger from the realm of reality into burning fantasy. Perhaps this is to say that white women, as themselves the objects of sexual aggression from men of their own class, were less likely to invent imaginary perpetrators than were the men who dominated them. White men could protect their own privileges while shifting responsibility for any possible excessive exercise to someone else. They felt more than free—they felt obligated in the deepest sense—to see that the lurking danger was suppressed. If suppression and terror did not work, of course, the most conceivably severe punishment was not merely permitted but required.

It is difficult to bring evidence to bear on this distinction of gender within the master class. Partly, white women were, of course, shaped by and in turn participated in a larger culture, and they could not help but be influenced by its prevailing assumptions, especially on the affectively powerful subject of race. They also did not (at least in the South) spout social formulae in public. It was not their part to do so. Yet even in their diaries, one looks in vain for sustained allusions to the Negro as rapist. In the case at hand, we may instance Susan Sillers Darden of Jefferson County, whose diary mentioned "murder[ing] the whites" but made no reference to rumors of sexual intentions on the part of the disaffected slaves. At the same time, in mid-May of 1861, John D. L. Davenport was writing the governor (who was not, assuredly,

19. *DeBow's Review*, XXVII (August, 1859), 210.

20. Frederick Law Olmsted, *A Journey in the Back Country* (New York, 1860), 36.

a woman) that "such of the females as suited their fancy were to be preserved as <u>Wives</u>."[21]

Profound ambiguity on this matter existed not merely in white southern culture as a whole but within individual participants. The anonymous (but assuredly male) author of *The South Vindicated from the Treason and Fanaticism of the Northern Abolitionists* (1836) contended that "the genial influence of civilization, the advantages of christianity, and a sense of the kindness and protection of the master, render the American-born negro often a domestic friend, and attach him to the family of his master so fondly that he is prepared to defend them with his life rather than assail them." Yet the same writer also warned about slave insurrection: "The inhabitants would be slaughtered with every cruelty which ingenious malice could devise." These cruelties were left to the imagination in the special manner of that age: "The father or the husband would be reserved to witness the violation of the daughter or the wife." Lest the point be left unclear, "Helpless females would be spared to glut the savage and brutal passions of their demoniac captors, amid . . . the shrieks of those reserved for peculiar and lingering torture." Here was the durable portrait: the loyal darky as barbarous fiend.[22]

The slaves of the Second Creek neighborhood saw their society differently. They did not have to invent enemies or multiply them in various guises. The master class was enemy enough and sufficient to explain their worst miseries and dangers. They had no need to dig up whole colonies of nefarious external threats, no need for strange road travelers, strolling organ-grinders, peddlers, gamblers, steam doctors, Black Republicans, abolitionists, free Negroes, unsexed females, religious enthusiasts, free-love fanatics, phalansteries, protective tariffs, Free-Soilers, or Mrs. Stowe.[23]

21. Darden Diary, May 16, 1861, Document C; Jo. D. L. Davenport to Gov. [John J.] Pettus, May 14, 1861, in Governors Papers, MDAH, Document E.

22. *The South Vindicated from the Treason and Fanaticism of the Northern Abolitionists* (Philadelphia, 1836), 43, 247.

23. Most of these references are obvious, but *phalansteries* was the current term for communitarian Fourierist "phalanxes." "Some strolling organ-grinders" came under suspicion in a scare in Georgia in 1856, as quoted in Robert Manson Myers, ed., *The Children of Pride: A True Story of Georgia and the Civil War* (New Haven, 1972), 284. "Steam doctors" were the practitioners of the widely popular Thomsonian medicine, which included hydrotherapy.

In their own real world, slaves faced a relatively monolithic enemy. They sometimes tended to view whites as an undifferentiated mass. In doing so they were no different from whites, who also tended to regard color not merely as a descriptive category but as an inherent condition. In this sense enslavers and enslaved shared in a view dictated by a rigid economic system. But at a time of crisis—perhaps because they were much more accustomed to living with crisis—blacks were more inclined to make discriminating judgments about differences within the other caste. Not only were they well aware of the distinctions between "cotton planters," "road travelers," and "second planters," but the Second Creek slaves were also finely attuned to distinctions among individuals. At least they were recorded as saying so, in effect, when Conner wrote down their words at the examinations.

When we listen to the testimony of the rebels, it is important that we remember that the persistent naming of individual women is unique among the documents of slave rebellion in the United States. On no other occasion were the names of specific white women spelled out in anywhere near such detail. On the other hand, such names had not previously been required at such examinations elsewhere. So far as we know, they were not a requisite of established ritual. What the Second Creek rebels were saying was unique in its detail—unless we embrace the thoroughly improbable proposition that the uniqueness here lay entirely in the amanuensis, a proposition that would make Conner a sport of nature among the scores of white men over the years and throughout the South who undertook to take down what was usually and disdainfully known as "negro testimony."

If we take the rebels seriously, then, we have to accept what they said when they talked of "taking" and "ravishing" certain white women.[24] They had their own reasons that seemed to them entirely sufficient. Even if we do not approbate these reasons, we can understand them on their own terms. As was the case with the rebels' other plans, they felt very strongly about the matter.

At the same time, we need to bear in mind that members of the Examination Committee were horrified but not astounded. Once the matter was broached, it generated sufficient energy for self-

24. The case for treating assertions about the sexual aggressiveness of black men as a function of white insecurities and domination is made in Jordan, *White Over Black*, chap. 4, a case that in my opinion remains valid for that earlier period and indeed as a generalization about the phenomenon in American history as a whole.

continuation. We cannot know who first raised the matter, though we can easily imagine that it began among whites in the manner of many rumors with auto- and external suggestion piling upon and intertwining with each other to produce a self-fulfilling prediction-*cum*-statement of reality.

For some blacks, the reality of their intentions had its own self-justifying independence. They had intended to take certain white women, which is what free men could and did do. Why *explain* such intention when it carried its own justification in the circumstances of their lives? Freedom, after all, was freedom.

On the other side, we can easily hear the snide hostility of the question: *Which one of the ladies was you going to take, boy?* The query was perhaps as much salacious as hostile, though it also smoldered with elements of curiosity, envy, and anger, as well as of flaunted privilege and gnawing self-doubt.

Some of the rebels did not admit or claim to have had white women in mind. John, Mitchell's driver, had nothing to say about ravishing the young ladies or indeed about actually killing anyone. By the time he was examined, five slaves had already talked about "ravishing," so it seems highly improbable that John was not queried about the matter. Next, Dennis Mitchell had interesting things to say about white women in general, but he did not give the name of a single prospect. Mitchell's Little John, Doctor, and Harry Lyle had nothing at all to say on the topic. Neither did Henderson's Ike Giddings or his son Adam, or Dr. Grier's Fred. The two Surget men, of course, "said nothing" at all. The last rebel who we know had nothing to say about the ladies was Wesley Mosby. As the least assertive of the Mosby men, he may not have appeared to the Committee as a likely suspect in the ravishing business, despite his youthfulness. But Wesley was well along on the list of slaves examined. He tended toward self-deprecation, and some of his first words to the Committee were that in the organizational scheme of the Plan he was "to go behind."

With one exception, the rebels who said anything about the "plan of ladies" all belonged to three planters. Talk about ravishing had started with either the Mosbys or the Dunbars, then spread to Scott's. Dick Henderson was the only man from off those three places to testify about the matter, and although he had heard about the entire Plan from the Mosbys, he claimed that "I was against it" and in fact named none of the ladies in question. One of the Mosby men he had talked to was Wesley, who may well have been less diffident with Dick than he was before the Committee.

Thus the taking of ladies was planned, at least primarily or so far as we know, by three rather small groups of rebels. Of the five Mosbys, Orange alone was probably still at large. Evidently his energies went into traveling about, talking with people, and avoiding capture, for he was the only Mosby rebel who had clearly been in on the plan of ravishing but who had *not* picked out a specific young white woman.

The Dunbar rebels had made what sounds very much like their own independent plan about the ladies. Though there was disagreement, it is clear that George, Simon, Dick, Peter, Paul, and Albert had all named their choices. Over at the much smaller Scott place, Harry Scott had picked out his and so had Frederick.

As is scarcely surprising, each of the rebels had his own goals and own modes of expressing his feelings and intentions. According to Nelson Mosby, Harry Scott's son, Alfred, was the "1st man" among the Mosbys "to talk of ravishing." It was Alfred and the older Nelson who first told Dick Henderson about the entire plan. When he talked about the ladies, Alfred had a decisive and clearcut agenda in mind. Whenever he mentioned the matter, he first spoke of first killing the man—in this case, "old Mosas" Mosby; in another, "you kill your master"; and most sweepingly, "the blacks were to kill all the white men and take the young ladies and women for wives."

For some reason Alfred seems to have been the only rebel to make specific distinctions among the white women according to their ages and their correlated standings in the households. At least this seems the best construction of his "young ladies and women" and his forthright "Kill master and mistress. Ravish the girls." In the latter instance Alfred was speaking of the white Mosby household, which had four teenagers, none of them yet eighteen and three of them female. Alfred's and Nelson's testimony agreed that Alfred would have seventeen-year-old Anna Mosby. Yet Alfred insisted that the ladies were to be taken "for wives." According to Harry Scott, "Alfred said he would have one for a wife," and had told him, "You kill your master, Make your Mrs for a wife."

Nelson and Alfred also agreed that "Nelson would ravish Miss Mary"—very probably forty-year-old Mary of the exclusively female Dunbar family (but just possibly young Mary Grier, age fifteen). Miss Mary was a widow, which may account for why Harvey called her one of the "young ladies" even though she was (probably) about his own age. When Nelson asserted he was the "3rd" man at the Mosbys "to talk of ravishing" and claimed he would "take Miss Mary," he clearly had a very specific grievance in mind. Miss Mary was targeted "because she poured water upon his daughter." Harvey had this same abuse but different vindication in *his* mind when he said that the father and son, "Nelson and Wesley[,] would kill the young ladies because they drown and beat Wesley's sister." Apparently such treatment was sufficient to justify deadly retaliation.

Harvey Mosby had been the second "to talk of ravishing." When hauled before the Examination Committee, Harvey began by saying that the planners "would kill Master and Mrs; ravish and kill young ladies." This was his only direct reference to the business, at least as specifically reported, and he was unambiguously direct about killing the ladies after ravishing them. Harvey had nothing to say about making them "wives."

Harvey's testimony was forthright and circumstantial. Like his father he had a pragmatic bent and an eye for the details of the main enterprise. He gave the longest testimony—though Alfred rivaled him in this respect. He also provided some of the most descriptive details about the white man. He spoke with evident pride about his unusually wide contacts off the Mosby place: with the Homochitto teamsters, with Sanderson's Billy, with the Metcalfe driver Louis and some of those men, and with Dick and others of the Henderson plantation. Of course, he had spoken with the Dunbars and Harry Scott, though unlike Alfred he had not discussed business with Scott's Frederick.

Despite or because of this wide acquaintanceship, Harvey seems not to have firmly staked a specific claim to one of the white women. Nelson was uncertain or confused about Harvey's intentions, for he testified that Harvey would take Miss Sarah, only a few breaths after saying that Harvey would have the same Miss Anna Mosby who had explicitly been claimed by Alfred. For *his* part, Alfred claimed that Harvey would have Miss Fanny Mosby, who was actually only fourteen. Harvey himself said nothing about his own choice. There may have been some confusion or conflict about Miss Sarah, since Alfred claimed that Wesley was to take her. Miss Sarah herself cannot now be further identified.[25]

In his own testimony, Wesley was the only Mosby rebel *not* to talk about the plan of ravishing. On this as on other matters, young Wesley was in the habit of deferring to his companions. Yet he evidently voiced no dissent from the plan, for Harvey reported that Wesley's father (Nelson) and Wesley would "kill the young ladies" for drowning and beating Wesley's sister. None of the rebels claimed that Wesley had picked out one of the ladies for his own. When Nelson came to listing who was going to take whom among the ladies, he concluded with a phrase that dripped with a father's disappointment and disgust: "Wesley dont know."

None of the Mosby rebels spoke about taking the youngest Mosby girl, Bessie, who was thirteen years old. Fanny Mosby was mentioned only by Alfred, who said only that Harvey was to have her. Whether these two young ladies had actually grown to womanhood was scarcely the issue. They had at least until recently been mere girls, and probably the Mosby men thought of them as still standing on the edge of that condition and status. Of course, that pivotal point of blossoming could have its own attractions, but especially on a small plantation it could also cause hesitancy. Whatever their perceptions, the Mosby slaves did not universally think of these younger women as suitable or deserving targets for vengeance, at least at an individual level.[26] None of them mentioned young Bessie. Yet Alfred and Harvey (both perhaps in their

25. Of course the rebels could have *planned* to have two or more slaves take the same woman, but the overall pattern and tone of the record clearly implies exclusive claims. This sense of exclusivity could only have been reinforced, but not in my opinion entirely generated, by the assumptions of the white examiners.

26. The matter of age is quicksand for analysis, since rape can be inflicted on people of all ages. In that era, however, the dividing line between girl- and womanhood probably seemed more important to men (both free and slave) than it has become in the late-twentieth-century United States. It also ought to be borne in mind that the age of menarche in the nineteenth century was about two years older than today. Robert A. Margo and Richard H. Steckel, "The Heights of American Slaves: New Evidence on Slave Nutrition and Health," *Social Science History*, VI (1982), 516–38, give 14.5 years as the average age of menarche. See also James Trussell and Richard Steckel, "The Age of Slaves at Menarche and Their First Birth," *Journal of Interdisciplinary History*, VIII (1978), 477–505, esp. 504, a much broader article than its title suggests and which has some data on white women. But in this situation the abrupt biological turning point was of course less important than more visible physical developments and general demeanor.

early forties) talked about ravishing and killing the "girls" or the "young ladies," and they named no one as exempt.

If the situation concerning young ladies was perhaps somewhat confused and confusing at Mosby's, it was entirely clear at the much smaller place belonging to Dr. Scott. Only two of the five adult men belonging to Scott were claimed to be involved. Harry Scott was one of the most active rebels. Nelson had heard only that Harry was to "kill Mrs Scott," but Orange told Alfred that "Harry Scott would ravish Mrs Scott"—though, in context, killing her also may have been simply assumed.

Harry himself said directly, "I kill master and ride Mrs." Customarily terse, Harry always used that vivid term concerning the white women—at least, he did so when speaking of the plans to kill master and "ride the ladies" at Mosby's, Mary Dunbar's (where Mrs. Dunbar would be killed, since there was no Mr.), and Metcalfe's. Even during his second examination Harry Scott insisted that "I will kill old master and ride the ladies." His formulaic language dripped with anger at the whole system, for his master was scarcely "old" at thirty-five (being probably some twenty years younger than Harry himself) and his mistress was the sole white female in the Scott household. For Harry Scott, "the ladies" were a class of beings rather than individuals.

The other Scott rebel, Frederick, was not much talked of by the others, but when he was examined he said—in language strikingly gentler yet more possessive than Harry's—that they were to "have young ladies to self" and "takes possession of the girls here." Frederick was noticeably less filled with hatred than many of the other rebels. He had first learned about the Plan from Orange and Nelson, and as he put it, "At first talk I agreed with Orange." Though temperamentally a follower, Frederick had made up his own mind about which lady he was going to have. Unlike many of the testifiers, he gave no list of who was going to take whom. He confessed, or rather asserted in terms that rang more of infatuation than of anger: "I liked <u>the looks of Julia Dunbar; Miss Julia is the best looking</u>. If things should happen, I would like to have her as a wife." Though others would take possession of the Mosby girls, Frederick claimed again, "I take Miss Julia"—the twenty-year-old Dunbar daughter. Frederick's language about Miss Julia so startled and (surely) outraged Lemuel Conner that he carefully underlined the phrases indicating physical attraction. The phraseology was not, indeed, *pro forma*. For Conner, such human yearning in a black slave was profoundly shocking. Frederick, in his innocence, was truly breaking one of the most basic of the rules.[27]

Of the eight Dunbar slaves implicated before the Examination Committee, five seem to have formed something of an inner circle. Three of these men talked about plans to take the white women, though with less consistency and more confusion than among the Mosby rebels. Some of the confusion was perhaps Conner's, for twice he struck out the name Margaret when evidently the testifier was referring to Miss Mamie Jenkins. The Dunbar family had intermarried with the Jenkinses, and apparently Conner was unfamiliar with all the names of the young women belonging to the two clans. There was in fact a Mamie Jenkins, and there was also a Margaret Dunbar, a young woman of twenty-three.[28] Dick and George agreed that Simon would take Miss Margaret.

Dick and George were natural brothers and respectively the father and uncle of Peter. These three and another Dunbar slave, Paul, kept in close touch with Harry Scott and the Mosbys. Paul had a particular grievance against Mrs. Dunbar because she was overworking his wife: in the only reference to a slave marriage, Harvey Mosby declared that Paul "consented" to join the Plan because "Mrs. D. kills up Pauls wife sewing." There was general agreement among the Dunbar slaves that Mrs. Dunbar would be killed, though Paul's special complaint was probably not the only cause of her being singled out. As something of an afterthought in his testimony, Dick Dunbar said Paul was to take "Mamy" Jenkins. During his first testimony, George himself laid no claim to any of the ladies. Only his brother had picked out someone for him—a Miss Jenkins.

George very clearly gave the impression that taking the ladies and making wives of them was Alfred Mosby's idea. Though he did not profess to having opposed the Plan, George's informative

27. In the transcript the verb *take* is plural in the quotation "takes possession of." The "here" probably means that Frederick was being examined at the Mosby place. The ages of the Scott men were *about* 51, 26, 26, 21, and 16, and today, if forced to take a plunge on the exacta, a betting person might very well say that Harry was the oldest (which is a sure thing) and Frederick sixteen. See Census, 1860 Slave, MS p. 140.

28. Mame or Mamie is mentioned many times in the Jenkins Diary.

testimony was almost entirely about other rebels. He said almost nothing about his own role. When queried about the "dispatch," he characteristically depreciated his own involvement: "I read of it a few words." Then when he was questioned once again later on, he came out with new names, some of them very possibly made up in an attempt to somehow satisfy his inquisitors. He introduced the idea of killing Mr. George M. Marshall.

Then George was asked for names of women. First he came up with the one *he* would take—a Miss "Alie"—who was the daughter of John C. and Annis Dunbar Jenkins.[29] Then he said Paul would have Miss Mary W., whose identity appears to be untraceable, unless perhaps Conner conflated the two Mrs. Dunbars and Mary G. was meant. George named several other women, including Julia for Albert Dunbar and (a few moments later) for his brother Dick, thus ignoring the claim set forth by Frederick Scott. Simon, he said, was the "1st man to talk of ravishing." In this matter as in others, George's second appearance before the Examination Committee—with its terse and jerky catalog of names and specifics about the timing of the Plan—has the nearly unmistakable sound of the lash.

His brother Dick had been dragged up before that, immediately after Obey and Billy Surget had refused to say anything. As recorded by Conner, Dick's testimony has the same staccato quality. After being asked who was at the head of the business, the questioning turned to the matter of white women. Dick claimed that they were "going to take the ladies" and that he would "take Miss. Julia." George would have Miss Jenkins, not Miss Margaret. Peter would take Miss Mary Dunbar. His brother would begin the killing with Mrs. Dunbar (which designation may have meant the same person). As if there had been firm agreement on the matter, "Miss Mamy Jenkins for Paul." Dick's final remark suggests that these assignments had been settled rather recently, long after the beginnings of the Plan. As he put it, "Made plan of ladies two weeks ago."

Peter, Dick's son, seems to have tagged along in the planning, either in his father's wake or because of more generalized temerity or youth. Like his father and uncle, he knew how to read, but he seems to have wielded little influence. Harry Scott named him as one who would "ride the ladies" at the Dunbars. He did not tes-

29. Frequently mentioned in Jenkins Diary, Allie had attended Mrs. Henry's school in Natchez, as referred to October 2, 1854.

tify, at least in Conner's presence, nor was he quoted by anyone who did. He seems almost to have been assigned one of the white women by his father: while claiming the attractive Miss Julia for himself, Dick said Peter would have forty-year-old Miss Mary.

Simon Dunbar, who did testify, was more assertive, yet he made no specific claims for himself about the ladies. (Dick, when pushed on the matter, linked Simon to Miss Margaret, but no one else made that suggestion.) Simon had talked with Orange and especially with Harry Scott, and he used Harry Scott's mixed imagery of killing, taking, and making wives of the white ladies. If at times Simon appeared indifferent about the plan of the ladies, he was scarcely backward in the business. Harry Scott quoted him at one point as if he had lagged behind in the plan to kill Mrs. Dunbar and ride the ladies: " 'Simon be damned if he dont have one too.' " Yet Harry Scott immediately went on to claim that at the Dunbars, Simon was the "head man." Simon may well have developed the kind of leadership in a group that often is signaled by speaking last.

Unlike several of the Dunbar rebels, Simon had apparently not talked with Dick Henderson about the ladies, but he had spoken eloquently to Dennis Mitchell. It was Dennis who cited Simon's and George's colorful language about what the northerners would make the South do "behind their asses." And Dennis went on to quote Simon as offering a remark about men and women that was both ambiguous and utterly clear: "Simon said they would have white women as free as black women." Perhaps the "they" were the "Northerners" in his previous sentence, but perhaps there had been a pause and another question from the committee, and Simon was defiantly declaring the freedom the rebels would have with white women. His equating of white women with black was dramatic enough, but it is also important to note Simon's assumption about the sexes: in both cases the northern soldiers or the rebels—all males—would "have" women freely.

At this point Conner, as amanuensis, must have been disconcerted, for he recorded Dennis still quoting Simon as saying that "the white women would take black husbands run to the black man to uphold them." Then, immediately, the questioning shifted to emotionally neutral grounds. In front of the whole Committee in all its augustness, Simon had suggested an awful possibility, had given voice to the unthinkable. Could white women possibly look to black men for marriage? But husbands always protected their wives. And wives were always subservient to their husbands.

Thus, if listened to closely, the assertion Conner crossed out was immediately repeated in insignificantly different terms. White women running to the black man to uphold them? That was tantamount to having them as husbands. Uphold them against whom? The northerners? That, at least, was what Nelson claimed when he said he had "first heard" about the war "when young missus wanted black to fight for her." Or possibly in a sense were the young ladies thought to want to be upheld by black men against domineering white men? No wonder Conner was taken aback.

As for Simon, riding the ladies *was* freedom. It was a fuller freedom because it was wanted by white women. It would include upholding the ladies whom they would possess and thereby have under their protection. White women would want this because they would be running to really free men, and free men upheld their women. To overturn oppression was to establish true freedom, and true freedom meant the complete inversion of subjugation.

Underlying all the talk of ravishing, taking, and making wives of the young white ladies lay a jumbled collection of thoughts and feelings. They can be disaggregated into discrete elements, but if left combined they make infinitely more sense than when considered separately. While today we recognize the powerful and indeed central element of violence in the act of rape, we greatly oversimplify a complicated mixture if we call it only an act of vicious violence and nothing more, for surely it includes hatred and attraction, aggressive humiliation and sexual assertiveness, brutality, vengeance, lust, eros and thanatos, perverse devotion and devotion to perversity. We know that the "act of love," even in a loving context, can involve a great deal of aggressiveness and that such feelings and behavior are embedded in our mammalian natures.

In considering this matter, it also needs to be borne in mind that marriage had pronouncedly different over- and undertones in mid-Victorian America than today. Marriage among whites involved, perhaps most powerfully in the slaveholding portions of the country, pronounced qualities of possession and protection, of exclusiveness and purity, for men honor and women virtue, and for women everywhere the awful dangers of procreation. The most emphatic and persistent theme in the rebels' testimony was the sheer *possession* of women: *having* someone for a wife was what came after *taking* her for one.

That taking and having and possessing, of course, was exactly what slaveholders did with slaves.

It would be negligent to pass so quickly Nelson's striking remark about his "young missus." He had no reason to fabricate his assertion that she had asked him if he and his fellows would "fight for her"—against the Yankees, clearly, since it was from this conversation he learned about the war. So he claimed, at least. Even had he already heard about the conflict from another source, the point about his informant was one he wanted to make. Conner showed no signs of surprise. Nelson was old enough to be the young woman's father. So far as we know, she had no special reason to distrust him. She felt hc could be asked and counted on for protection against external threat. Throughout the South, such trust was not uncommon, and there was often good basis for it. The ironies of that trust should not lead us to deny its existence.

Yet there were other possible levels of interaction between the daughters and the male slaves of the master class. Underlying her apparently straightforward request there may have been, in fact, a glowing element of toying and teasing with the realities of power. The dynamics of personal interchange between older black men and young white women could be complex (and variable) indeed. Mrs. Susan Sillers Darden's account about the daguerreotype may be taken as one revealing instance. Miss Parker was at the "office" (which may have been a wagon or the telegraph office) of a photographer in Fayette. She was having a daguerreotype taken of herself to give to Mrs. Anna Darden, the Anna who later "said she had trusted her life with [the carriage driver] Davy" when he was hanged for conspiring to insurrection. Susan Darden's report of the incident in her diary was succinct but nonetheless eloquent about what had happened. "Davy came in and Anna asked Miss P. how she would like to see Davy's picture taken." One may imagine what Davy may have thought, with near certainty that his reaction was not unmixed. Mrs. Darden the diarist hastened to add that "they had it taken all in jest," but she was well aware that what had happened was more than a joke. That was how "the report" got started, and she recognized its unseemliness and perhaps even its danger when she wrote, "It is a pity for any thing of the kind to get in circulation." Anything of that kind was potentially explosive. Not fully conscious why she did so, she then turned immediately to the subject of the sixteen girls who had left the school on account of "the excitement" about insurrection.[30] Whatever the power of these sensitivities, though, Anna Darden had started the affair by suggesting taking Davy's picture. No doubt she thought the prospect lots of fun.

In the slave culture of the American South, black women were of course in an entirely different position. They themselves were doubly possessed. They were the legal chattels of their owners, who sometimes otherwise took them. They were also the wives (and sisters, mothers, daughters, and so on) of black men. As wives, in some measure possessed by those who were also possessed, they were not thereby and necessarily twice as much oppressed as slave men by reason of some additive combination of gender and chattel condition. Indeed, the degradation and ownedness of their husbands often served to raise their personal leverage in their own realm and to give them some say as to what that realm was. We need not delve into the measure of that leverage here, and we would do well to avoid altogether the question that is often summarized by the loaded phrase *black matriarchy*. That subject has become an arena of present political debate, swept by ideological winds.[31]

Conner's record contains one general reference to black women and nine brief references to eight different individuals, some of them thoroughly puzzling and none of them helpfully informative about the women themselves. The other records of the Second Creek proceedings are even less informative. Yet even with their severe limitations, these ten instances constitute by far the largest body of references to specific slave women during any American slave conspiracy.

Throughout North American history, slave women were rarely mentioned as participants in the planning of revolts. The only women known to have played active and important roles in Amer-

30. Darden Diary, May 12, 20, 1861, Document C. This was not the first time a photographer had come to the area; *ibid.*, July 29, 1859.
31. Some of the recently growing and increasingly sophisticated historical literature is discussed in Darlene Clark Hine, "Lifting the Veil, Shattering the Silence: Black Women's History in Slavery and Freedom," in *The State of Afro-American History: Past, Present, and Future,* ed. Darlene Clark Hine (Baton Rouge, 1986), 223–49.

ican slave plots were young Peggy Kerry (Sorubiero), from Ireland, and especially Mary Burton, a white servant, during the New York plot of 1741; two slave women in South Carolina in 1775; and two black women, one of whom, Lucy Barrow, was hanged in the wake of the Turner revolt a century later. Slave women were referred to tangentially during the Vesey trials, and as talking insolently about freedom during the Mississippi slave scare of 1835. But they rarely appear to have been implicated in American slave conspiracies.[32]

What is equally striking is that historians have scarcely noticed their absence. As much as has been written about slave women and about slave conspiracies, women seem to have dropped—or rather been dropped—from the scene during occasions of collective plans and action against the slave system. Indeed, historians have customarily passed over a striking instance of outright distrust of slave women on the part of two of the Gabriel conspirators.[33]

This prevailing omission of black women is the more arresting because so many appear so frequently in the myriad original records and secondary accounts that pertain to American slavery—in many roles, to be sure, but including instances of murder, arson, poisoning, running away, feigned illness (including preg-

---

32. [Horsmanden], *Journal of the Proceedings, passim;* Thomas J. Davis, *A Rumor of Revolt: The "Great Negro Plot" in Colonial New York* (New York, 1985), *passim.* A remarkable aspect of the two women in South Carolina is that the report suggests that they may have been preachers; see Thomas Hutchinson to Council of Safety, July 5, 1775, in *The Papers of Henry Laurens,* ed. Philip H. Hamer *et al.* (10 vols. to date; Columbia, S.C., 1968–), X, 206–208, and a recent work that sheds much light on rebelliousness in the Revolutionary era, Sylvia R. Frey, *Water from the Rock: Black Resistance in a Revolutionary Age* (Princeton, 1991), 61. Slave women in the Turner insurrection are discussed in Stephen B. Oates, *The Fires of Jubilee: Nat Turner's Fierce Rebellion* (New York, 1975), 79, 80, 96, 120 (the 1976 New American Library edition is paginated differently). The documentation of this work is hard to follow, and it contains many vivid but untraceable details. A more firmly buttressed account is Herbert Aptheker, *Nat Turner's Slave Rebellion* (New York, 1966). Lucy's hanging is in Tragle, ed., *Southampton Revolt,* 237. For 1835, see *Virgil Stewart,* 223–25. A slave woman was executed for rebellion in French Louisiana in 1732; see Jack D. L. Holmes, "The Abortive Slave Revolt at Pointe Coupée, Louisiana, 1795," *Louisiana History,* XI (1970), 342. Assertions by several historians of female leadership in Louisiana, 1771, based on Helen T. Catterall, ed., *Judicial Cases Concerning American Slavery and the Negro* (5 vols.; Washington, D.C., 1926–37), III, 423–24, seem to me to misread the court documents.

33. *Cal. Va. State Papers,* IX, 162: "The witness enjoined him to keep it a profound secret, which he promised to do; not to mention it to or in the presence of any woman."

nancy), broken tools, trashy picking, and even outright physical fights with mistresses and overseers. Yet they were very seldom mentioned in contemporary documents as active or even passive participants in American slave insurrections and conspiracies.[34]

That historians have not commented on this absence is perhaps understandable if one takes the view that elucidation of what did *not* happen historically is always a sisyphean and fruitless venture. Yet we can scarcely suppose that slave women remained ignorant of plans for revolt, or indifferent to them, or unwilling or unable to participate in meaningful and programmatic ways. Such a proposition seems absurd on its face, so obviously so as to deserve (as it has received) little comment.

Slave women lived in a somewhat different world than slave men, and we should not underestimate the power of gender roles in African American culture and the larger Victorian atmosphere in which, however independently, it shared. But surely black women learned of these desperate enterprises. They may well have found it safest to keep their own counsel on such matters, for too much assertiveness on their part could easily have generated dangerous reactions not only from whites, but also from black men, who in that culture thought of concerted revolt as men's business. As things turned out during the Civil War, former slave men evinced enormous pride when permitted to join the Union army and fight for the cause of freedom. After the war, moreover, many former bondsmen insisted that their wives abandon heavy work in the fields and devote themselves to the tasks of the domestic household.

Surely slave women had a stake—in many cases a very great one—in the outcome of conspiracies against their masters. It was not the *same* stake as their menfolks', even though they shared the same central and overriding commitment to freedom. They suspected if they did not know, after all, that their men might have designs on other women, including even just barely possibly white women, who were not only doubly forbidden to their men but potentially very dangerous to their own security and welfare. No doubt at a time of general danger many slave women were more likely than slave men to have their thoughts recur instantly to the safety of their own children, the more so if some of the

34. Such negative statements make historians apprehensive, since they are so easily disproved. In this instance, no evidence of such participation has been found. It is not known how commonly slave cooks spat in the big-house soup.

older ones were perhaps involved in the business. Unlike their counterparts of the master class, slave women were not completely set apart from men as incapable of becoming warriors, since many of them normally led working lives little differentiated from those of slave men, at least out of doors. They were not enveloped by the thickly patterned curtains of female gentility that so effectively protected and imprisoned white women of the planting classes. Many were thoroughly accustomed to the "axes and hoes" that could serve as weapons, and they were as fully acquainted as men with the terrible threat and pain of the whip. But open physical confrontation with large groups of whites, particularly white men, was another matter.

No matter how fully such values had been internalized, no matter how much they derived from older African value systems, they were continuously reinforced by contacts with whites. It is abundantly clear that slaveholders in the United States did not ordinarily expect that black women would actively participate in plotting and revolts. These expectations had a double effect: they shaped the prevailing pattern of who would be charged by whites with concerted rebelliousness, and they formed a framework of role definition that affected black women in thousands of daily interactions with members of the master class, as well as with other black women and black men.

In this respect, what happened at Second Creek was unusual but not surprising. Early on during the questioning of Alfred Mosby, after sending for fourteen more slaves (owned by Henderson, Scott, Dunbar, and Mitchell), the Examination Committee learned more about the crucial role of Orange Mosby in the Plan. Among other things, Alfred said that "O. would join and got all of us on the place to join." At this point it occurred to some members of the Committee to inquire whether this "all of us" was meant literally, that is, were women included. Conner carefully recorded Alfred's response by adding the word "men" above the words "us on," thus indicating that the Committee had questioned whether the phrase "all of us" was intended to include the (slave) women. In all probability no one on the Committee was surprised by Alfred's assertion that he had meant only the men on the place.

If anyone was surprised during this exchange it was probably Alfred. He may even have thought the question absurd. He had simply used the obvious phrase "all of us" to include the *men* on the Mosby place. It was "us" who "began talking when the war began," and he had felt no need to elaborate the obvious as to who "us" were. They had "not" been talking "in the field" but "about the house"—a reference much more probably to one of the three slave cabins on the Mosby place than to their master's "big house."

It seems very possible that one or several slave women *heard* these conversations, but far from likely that they participated in them. Certainly Alfred did not think of women as having taken part. The possibility of Alfred's testimony stemming from a chivalric desire to exculpate and thereby protect slave women would seem an exceedingly slim one indeed. Several of the rebels who were hauled before the Examination Committee gratuitously referred to slave women as having knowledge of the Plan, but their references were tangential and lacking in specific detail. The examiners did not pursue these allusions. For both slaves and masters, the Plan was men's work.

Thus we need to approach the references to Second Creek slave women with a dual caution. On the one hand, there were not many such references; on the other, there were many more than during other American slave conspiracies. They may be easily culled from the available body of testimony.

All the rebels who mentioned black women came from the Mosby place, with the exception of George Dunbar, who reported that "Orange said he had Mitchell's Caroline Sweetheart." Orange was just the sort of man to have a sweetheart off his homeplace. The Victorian term employed to denote his relationship with a lover was nowhere near as quaint then as it sounds today; it may or may not have been George's rather than Orange's.[35] A very different relationship was referred to by Alfred: that Louis, the Metcalfe driver, had been whipping a woman. It was that observation that provoked Orange's promise and then Mas Benny's question. We can only guess at the inner dynamic of Louis' violence against a slave woman, protected as he was by a master's seal of authority.

35. Caroline was clearly one of Mitchell's slaves, not one of the white family, and her absence from Road Duty, UTA, in 1856 suggests she was young. The census listed Mitchell and his wife, both age sixty-one, with the only other whites in the household being two girls age ten and seven. James H. Mitchell owned forty-seven slaves, nearly balanced between males and females. Census, 1860 Free, household 1076; Slave, MS p. 178. One planter unintentionally made clear that the word *sweetheart* was used by blacks in connection with a fifteen-year relationship between a slave woman in the big house and a white man who frequently visited their place; see A. K. Farrar to H. W. Drake, September 4, 5, 1857, in Alexander K. Farrar Papers, LSU.

In George Dunbar's same first appearance before the Examination Committee, he also provided direct evidence that on at least one occasion several slave women had been included in conversation about what was going on politically. He told the Committee that "Paul came" (presumably back from visiting the Mosby place) "and told my brother[,] Peter and women about the Mosby scrape" (Peter was the son of George's brother Dick).[36] Perhaps George meant the Dunbar slave women generally, though it seems more probable that this was a largely family conversation. At any rate, George apparently saw nothing peculiar in slave women listening to reports about the specific plans made by Orange and by Alfred and his father, Harry Scott. The planters on the Committee seem not to have been surprised. Evidently they felt the information about women not worth pursuing.

Two of the other references elicited under questioning concerned the unnamed slave woman who was both Nelson's daughter and Wesley's sister. She had been the victim of specific abuse—the beating and drowning—at the hands of Miss Mary Dunbar and others of the ladies. Even today, the resentment and outrage of her customarily helpless protectors nearly shouts from Conner's careful pages. Nelson and Wesley were her vengeful kin. It was two of the younger Mosby rebels, Alfred and Harvey, who reported on the atrocious treatment. They may well have been much the same age as the victim.

In the second reference, two of the Mosby rebels were talking about the Plan "with Frederick [Scott] at Polly's house." Polly's identity remains uncertain; clearly she was black, since the rebels uniformly referred to white women with the titular Miss or Mrs.—or at least Conner transcribed them as doing so in accordance with prevailing etiquette. She may very well have been the Polly owned by John S. Mosby.[37] She was head of her house, perhaps widowed or married or perhaps not, but nonetheless a slave. We simply do not know much about who lived in which cabins. We cannot reconstruct slave families at Second Creek.[38] It may be

36. The word *scrape* probably did not refer to an internal quarrel on the Mosby plantation; in Madison County in 1835 it was used specifically in reference to a plan for insurrection, as is clear in *Virgil Stewart*, 229.

37. Road Duty, UTA, 98, 172, 277, 345, 449, 460. The Road Duty books name several different Pollys on nearby plantations.

38. Such reconstruction is possible only in a very small percentage of all southern plantations. Of course it would be helpful to know whom the various cabins were thought to "belong" to, but the evidence is extremely thin. George spoke

said only—and it does not take us very far—that most but not all the larger plantations had a rough numerical balance between the sexes.[39]

At least in all probability Polly was a slave, both because there were few free blacks living out in the county and because Alfred (who mentioned the conversation) would probably have alluded to her unusual status had she been legally free. It is perhaps not mere circumstance that Frederick had been there, given his unusually comfortable feelings about women—at least if his feelings about white women extended to black women and were not inverted by racial concerns. The other two visitors were both younger Mosby men, and the Mosby place was indeed the most likely location of "Polly's house." As it happened, Harvey "talked with Frederick" at Polly's house, but Wesley, with his usual lack of assertiveness, was "present." We do not know what was said. For that matter we cannot even be certain that Polly was there or, if she was, whether she talked or was merely present too.

When Wesley was finally examined, he spoke at some length

---

once about "my house," suggesting his headship, but Simon talked about "our house," which may or may not have been a different one. We are left here, as in so many instances, unable to tell who was living with whom and who was regarded as head of the living units. Familial relations among slaves on Second Creek may have received less sexual interference from white men than in most parts of the rural South owing to the presence of abundant sexual opportunities in nearby Natchez. For such opportunities, see especially D. Clayton James, *Antebellum Natchez* (Baton Rouge, 1968), 142. William Johnson noted a fatal fight "at Some house of ill fame," but it is not entirely clear that the men were white; see *Johnson's Diary*, II, 466. There is a list of slaves at the end of the Aventine Plantation Diary, MDAH, but it lacks any indication of family relationships. Elsewhere in Adams County, a list by family was entered in Springfield Plantation Account Book, Vol. I, in John A. Quitman Papers, MDAH; and an overseer made one at a Ker plantation in Tensas Parish, February 10, 1861, in John Ker and Family Papers, LSU. Grouping by families was common in antebellum plantation books but, significantly, rare in the much less voluminous sources that survive from the eighteenth century.

39. The 1860 census MS slave schedules make this balance clear. The reasons for exceptions are sometimes apparent, sometimes totally obscure. Odell's work force was heavily male, as one would expect with a gunsmith. Brandon's preponderance of male slaves may have reflected his involvement with the teamster business. Yet for some reason males outnumbered female slaves by a three-to-two margin on the Henderson place, and Mrs. Sanderson owned nearly twice as many women as men. Out of chance, small holdings often had distinct imbalances one way or the other, as was the case conspicuously with Dr. Scott, who owned seven adults (and no children), five of whom were men.

about the "white man," as well as Lincoln, two named but unidentifiable other men (Munroe Morris and Bill Chamberlain),
and Orange's getting pistols. Then (as far as the record shows)
out of the blue he blurted, "Howard told Margaret, 'he
murdered the Dutchman.['] " The sentence capped Wesley's
demonstrated propensity for laconic and thoroughly enigmatic
expression.

The pronoun "he" apparently referred to Howard, a person who
today can be identified only as a male human being. Given his
immediately prior and ensuing statements, however, Wesley may
possibly have been referring to Harvey or (even more unlikely) to
Obey. The Dutchman was probably a day laborer or a road traveler
rather than a permanent resident of the neighborhood. In all probability he was a relatively recent immigrant from Germany, and
according to Alfred all the Mosby slaves knew about his murder
by "Henry Brown and Howard." Margaret must have been a black
woman, almost certainly a slave, and very possibly the Margaret
on the Mosby place.[40] Yet why Howard was telling Margaret about
the recent murder remains as mysterious as the murder itself. We
do know that murders, mysterious and otherwise, were not uncommon in Natchez and its immediate environs, and that two
overseers had been killed by slaves near Kingston several years
earlier.[41] The Committee showed no interest in that particular
homicide, for they immediately forced Wesley back to the important matter at hand, the Plan. Still, unless we conclude that Wesley had been crazed by being beaten, we are forced to ponder the
curious scenario of a man named Howard telling a black woman
exactly who had committed the recent murder of a white man.

Finally, we can recover some satisfaction from two very brief
but less murky allusions by Harvey and Alfred Mosby. According
to Harvey, Alfred was "whipping Metcalfe's woman"—though according to Alfred the whipping was being done by Louis. Whoever
was right (presuming this was the same slave woman), it was at
this point in the conversation that "Orange says whipping colored

40. See the sources cited in note 37 to this chapter.
41. A nearly astounding number of killings are referred to in *Johnson's Diary*.
The interesting and complex trial of three slaves for murdering their overseer near
Kingston in 1857 is discussed at length in Michael Wayne, "An Old South Morality
Play: Reconsidering the Social Underpinnings of the Proslavery Ideology," *Journal
of American History*, LXXVII (1990), 838–63, which mentions (pp. 484n, 856n)
still another overseer recently murdered by slaves, a matter Wayne is investigating
further.

people would stop." Orange's comment might perhaps suggest that Alfred had been hired out as some sort of foreman on a Metcalfe plantation, but more probably Alfred was involved in some sort of romantic entanglement and thereby engaged in a running fracas with one of the black men on that plantation. What is most striking about the report is that Orange seized upon it to make a brisk but telling point about the purpose of the Plan. No doubt Alfred's wretched victim would have welcomed hearing Orange's optative assurance that there would be no more whipping. Alfred himself made no reference to any woman singled out for violence, unless perhaps he was ducking his own responsibility when he claimed "Louis whipping woman."

During further grilling about other matters (this was immediately after Harvey's first and longer examination), Alfred was brought round to the subject of the "white man." His reaction was to report on the remarks and observations of others. He began by saying, "Mother told me Wesley said he came to W. M. who had on dark clothes. Wesley says, 'You are telltale.' " Several readings of these remarks are possible, but it appears most probable that Wesley had accused Alfred of making up the story of his learning from his mother about Wesley's supposed contact with the white man. The Examination Committee was understandably not interested in this tangled interpersonal skein, and the planters pressed on with queries about Orange and the white man. What we may note here is that somehow Alfred's *mother* had become involved in at least one aspect of the larger affair.

That is all we know about this otherwise anonymous woman. It is a relief, at last, to stumble across clear-cut evidence that one of the rebels actually had a mother. We are left peering through a dense fog at a part of the peak of the tip of a living pyramid of human feelings, actions, thoughts, words, and gestures that are now lost forever but not the less real and significant for that. We cannot learn much about the black women of Second Creek without wholesale importations of data from outside Adams County and even Mississippi—without, in short, distorting the unique qualities of that particular community. It will be better, then, to turn from gender relationships to more formal ideological matters, since they make up in relative clarity what they lack in the affective power that we know was churning at Second Creek no matter how thoroughly hidden from us now.

CHAPTER 10

OF IDEOLOGIES AND OCCUPATIONS

Especially when large numbers of people are involved, groups re-
belling against established authority often rely upon a common
set of ideas that helps cement their cohesiveness. As is well
known, their members may and usually do disagree about these
ideas in detail. From one case to another, such ideologies differ
markedly in the degree of their formality and rigidity. Larger
groups with long-range and ambitious goals tend to rely on embracive values and articulated views of history that lay claim to universal and timeless applicability. Smaller groups aiming only at a
single programmatic goal usually share mutual cultural norms
but place little or no reliance on ideas about universal rights and
wrongs and about the essential nature (and hence the "origins")
of a good society.

Rebellious groups and their goals may include a broad spec-
trum of activities, ranging from bank robbery to bread riots, from
sit-ins to mutinies in closed systems such as ships and prisons,
and from palace revolts all the way to great colonial and national
revolutions. At the larger end of such a scale in the United States,
one thinks of the American Revolution, when the ideology of the
rebels kept broadening as the conflict became more serious, and
also of the American Civil War, when disagreement focused on
the proper interpretation of a common national ideology that was
being strained by regional divergence in economic, demographic,
and cultural development.

More narrowly, conspiracies and actual rebellions by bound laborers have also varied in the number of people involved and the
degree to which they have been sustained by ideological considerations. These ideologies have taken many forms, many more
than arose in the racially based plantation societies of the New
World. What, for example, are we to make of the conspiratorial
ideologies held by slaves who were not only of the same race as
their masters but enrolled as elite troops in their owners' armies?

Such situations actually arose in a number of societies, including several in West Africa.[1]

In the Americas, slavery developed on a racial basis that became its most distinguishing, though perhaps not most important, feature. Despite the central importance of race in the New World, from the very early years onward the fit between racial and slave status was never perfect, since a few Africans (and most Indians) were not slaves. No Europeans were fully enslaved, but many early European settlers were treated as unfree and often abused accordingly. In this respect, the United States has had a somewhat peculiar history. Intermediate statuses, notably indentured servitude, gradually disappeared over time, giving way under the pressures of economic and demographic change, the growth of racial slavery, and development and institutionalization of ideas about personal rights and liberties for persons of European background.

The entrenchment of racial slavery was not a uniform development even in North America. Very quietly in the wake of the American Revolution, in a major transmutation that is often presumed without explanation, seven of the thirteen original states of the North American national union brought slavery to an end.[2] What did not come to an end, in either these "northern" or "southern" states, were the old invidious racial distinctions. They continued virtually unchanged.

From the very early years of their settlement, Anglo-Americans in the continental colonies had developed an unusually rigid and bifurcated system of racial categorization, in which "blacks" and "whites" constituted two (and only two) discrete varieties of people, with the original inhabitants of the continent treated (by

1. Suzanne Miers and Igor Kopytoff, eds., *Slavery in Africa: Historical and Anthropological Perspectives* (Madison, Wisc., 1977), 40, 47, 170, 338, 344. The editors' Introduction (pp. 3–81) is a fine essay on slavery in Africa. Orlando Patterson, *Slavery and Social Death: A Comparative Study* (Cambridge, Mass., 1982), 308–14, discusses the importance of military slaves in the Islamic world.

2. Suddenly by court decision in Massachusetts but more slowly in other states by means of gradual emancipation acts. New Jersey still had nearly seven hundred slaves in 1846, when the legislature finally passed an abolition act so halfhearted that the census of 1860 listed eighteen slaves in the state. See Arthur Zilversmit, *The First Emancipation: The Abolition of Slavery in the North* (Chicago, 1967), 220–22. The Founding Fathers expected that Delaware would take this route, but that state never abolished slavery by its own action. However, more than two-thirds of its blacks were legally free, as the result of private emancipations, when the Thirteenth Amendment abolished slavery nationally in 1865.

whites) as external to their society and categorized as less racially distinct than blacks. Whites were willing to tolerate, even to advocate, racial intermixture with Indians, but not with Africans and their "black" descendants. Mixed descendants of Europeans and Africans were not considered half-breeds but as belonging fully and inherently to the inferior caste. This inflexible, peculiarly North American system turned out to be remarkably durable and persistent. Often it has received little comment in the United States precisely because it has appeared to white Americans (and to many African and Native Americans) as simply the way the world works, not as an arrangement in any way eccentric—which in light of developments elsewhere in the world it most certainly was.[3]

Given this system, slave conspirators in the United States faced peculiar problems in formulating both strategies and goals for rebellion. Similar problems appeared in somewhat different guises during the mid-twentieth-century movement for civil rights. For slaves, the core of the problem was the accurate definition of authority. Put baldly, did authority lie with members of the slaveholding class or with whites in general? Or with both? If so, in what proportion and with what shadings of power? The answers to these questions had profound bearing not only on choices of tactics but also on the formulation of suitable ideas to support attempts to overthrow the system.

For good reason, American slaves gave little consideration to the legal powers of the state. Slave codes were immensely distant from their experience. What mattered was the local power of white masters and whites generally. At Second Creek the rebels were thoroughly realistic in this assessment. Their masters paid little more attention than slaves did to the requirements of constitutional and statute law. The rules of governance at Second Creek lay *there*, on that ground, not in the courthouse in Natchez or the capital at Jackson, much less in the new national capital that moved from Montgomery to Richmond.[4]

3. Of the many studies of this matter, St. Clair Drake, *Black Folk Here and There: An Essay in History and Anthropology* (2 vols.; Los Angeles, 1987–90) is one of the most interesting.

4. The Confederate government of course had no slave code, since slavery was held to be a matter for regulation only by the several states. The national government in Washington had passed laws bearing only on fugitive slaves and the existence of slavery and slave trading in United States territories and the District of Columbia. This is not to say that slave resistance had no political impact. Clearly

Like most conspirators, slave rebels tended to fuse various idea-tional elements that bore on their condition—immediate pro-grammatic goals, strategies for their attainment, fundamental cultural values, and formal ideologies. Today, the latter seem rel-atively discrete, susceptible of analysis, and likely to have been borrowed from external sources. For these reasons historians have been tempted to search for ideologies at the cost of overlooking less well-articulated systems of values. In doing so, they have often been animated by two unacknowledged purposes. One has been to explain the motivation of the conspirators, on the as-sumption that slave rebels ought to have been revolutionaries and that revolutionaries have to have ideologies. The other has in-volved placing slaves on some sort of scale of sophistication (often "politicization"), a maneuver that itself has been motivated either by a priori, schematic systems of social analysis or by a persistent itch to prove that the lowly victims of oppression were not stupid. Often these latter two motivations have gone hand in hand, and we have been introduced to such terms as *hegemony* and *internal-ization of values* with an air that supposes the reader's utter igno-rance of the dynamics of human domination.

Yet such terms can be useful, and the processes they are in-tended to denote were very much at work around Second Creek. For some reason some slaves wanted to revolt. They thought a great deal about revolting, and they talked about doing so with one another. They made plans that converged into a Plan. But they did not, as other American slaves had sometimes done, borrow formal ideologies to support their efforts. They did not *fail* to in-corporate such ideologies. They simply did not do so. The ques-tion *why* they did not do so is of course ours, not theirs.

Two distinct but not inherently incompatible sets of formal ideas were available to American slaves seeking to change their social

---

"resistance" to the institution by slaves had an effect on state and national govern-ments and their policies, especially during the 1850s and most of all during the Civil War. Yet the impact of a deliberately and successfully localized conspiracy was very indirect and hard to assess with any accuracy. It is suggestive that at-tempts to demonstrate the political effectiveness of slave resistance have concen-trated not on "conspiracies" or outright "rebellions," but on the steady trickle of running away, which mounted to a flood after the great war broke out. See, for example, James Oakes, "The Political Significance of Slave Resistance," *History Workshop*, XXII (1986), 89–107.

condition. One was religion, specifically the special kind of Christianity that was widespread among southern slaves by the time of the American Civil War. That special branch of the Judaic-Christian tradition has been extensively and affectionately explored by historians, especially since the 1960s. For the antebellum period, they have emphasized its distinctiveness from the Christianity that was preached at slaves by white religious enthusiasts, moralists, and conscientious supporters of the slave system. They have stressed the persistence of certain West African expressive styles, a melding of sacred and secular, an affinity for certain books of the Old Testament, the communality of religious practice, the immediacy of salvation and liberation.[5]

These and other qualities in African American religion are often crucial to an understanding of slave life. But so far as the extant records suggest, the Second Creek Rebels were themselves not much interested in religious beliefs or practices. Their questioners were not much interested either, and this indifference may explain in part why the rebels did not mention such matters. The single most important piece of evidence in this connection is Harry Scott's remark that "Dick was religious man." Dick Dunbar was the only man singled out in this respect, and presumably he was exceptional. At least Harry thought so, and although Harry Scott was not a man of conspicuously perceptive or balanced judgment, no one else contradicted him about Dick or so much as suggested that any other rebels were "religious." Some of them may have been religious in a rather conventional sense, but they displayed no signs that an otherworldly belief system was animating their thoughts and feelings about the Plan. None of them referred to God, the Bible, praying, conjuring, funerals, preachers, preachings, or any kind of church meetings.

It is perhaps significant that the most direct evidence of religious practice among Second Creek slaves comes from a plantation whose slaves refused to join in the Plan. Many years later, in 1937, the former slave Charlie Davenport gave brief descriptions of such practices on Aventine Plantation, but the net import of his remarks is not entirely clear. In what was probably an early

5. There has been a large and growing historical literature on the subject. One important early article emphasized the contribution of religion to African American rebelliousness: Vincent Harding, "Religion and Resistance Among Antebellum Negroes, 1800–1860," in *The Making of Black America: Essays in Negro Life and History,* ed. August Meier and Elliott Rudwick (2 vols.; New York, 1969), I, 179–97. Unfortunately, music has usually been treated as a rather separate matter, though there is agreement on its great importance.

version of his interview(s) with the white lady, he was quoted to the effect that Aventine slaves had attended officially endorsed Christian services: "On Sundays us rested en had meetin in a log house where a white preacher tole us 'bout de way ob salvation." (The overseers' journals made no mention of such a practice.) Then, when being asked questions about life after the war, Davenport reported with considerable skepticism: "Us niggers didn't have no secret meetins. All us had wuz church meetins in arbors out in de woods. De preachers would exhort us dat we wuz de chillen of Israel in de wilderness en de Lawd done sont us to take dis land ob milk en honey. But how us gwine to take land what wuz already took?" So-called hush arbors with black preachers in the woods had existed in a great many parts of the South during the antebellum era, but it is far from clear that the arbor meetings Davenport was referring to were not preached to by whites from the North after the war or by other white men unsympathetic to the former slaveowners. What is clear is that his reference to white preachers in a "log house" was for some reason not included in the other typescript version of his remarks. We would stand on very slippery (though not impossible) ground if we concluded that official white preaching at Aventine before the war was responsible for making those particular slaves supinely passive in regard to the Plan.[6]

Evidence of religious beliefs and practices had surfaced during the South's earlier, better-known slave conspiracies. In this respect the Second Creek rebels were aberrant rather than typical. Rather than communicating with one another at a preaching, they talked about the Plan while fishing on the creek. Despite the Examination Committee's disinterest, the rebels could easily have raised religious matters either deliberately or inadvertently. They had to respond somehow to questions about where such-and-such a conversation had taken place, and the answer could well have been at a prayer meeting or a burial.

By contrast, at the legal trials of the Gabriel plotters in 1800, Ben Woolfolk testified, "I told them that I had heard in the days of

6. The two versions of the Davenport interview are in Documents Y and Z. The Aventine Plantation Diary, in MDAH, does not mention religious gatherings of any kind, but the overseers may have chosen to ignore or not report them.

old, when the Israelites were in service to King Pharoah [*sic*], they were taken from him by the power of God, and were carried away by Moses." Yet he went on to caution "that I could see nothing of that kind in these days." He was immediately corrected by Gabriel's brother, Martin (Prosser): "I read in my Bible where God says if we will worship Him we should have peace in all our land; five of you shall conquer an hundred, and a hundred a thousand of our enemies." Later, after most of the Gabriel plot hangings, a note from a conspirator was found in a bottle on a Tidewater roadside; addressed to "dear frind," it promised that "brother X will come and prech a sermont to you soon, and then you may no more about the bissiness." [7]

Twenty-two years later, in Charleston, the Denmark Vesey rebels talked about the Christian God, the Bible, about conjuring with crab claws, about *"prayer meetings at night,"* and about how *"all those belonging to the African Church are engaged in the insurrection."* The extant records of the Vesey plot trials were prepared for publication and included "confessions" made and written down—actually composed—after slaves had been convicted by purportedly legal courts and were awaiting the gallows. Accordingly, they are far more lengthy, articulate, and coherent than the testimonies in Conner's transcript, though of course not necessarily therefore more reliable as to what the rebels really thought. Much of the time, though, the Charleston confessions carry the ring of truth, if allowance is made for the circumstances and animus of their composition. Rolla, a slave owned by the state's governor, denied any involvement at his trial but confessed to a white minister after his conviction: *"He* [Denmark Vesey] *then read in the Bible where God commanded, that all should be cut off, both men, women and children, and said, he believed, it was no sin for us to do so, for the Lord had commanded us to do it."* With such words, offered under such circumstances, we are left wondering in what proportion the language reflected Vesey's,

7. Ben Woolfolk's testimony in *Cal. Va. State Papers*, IX, 151. The note is quoted in full in Gerald W. Mullin, *Flight and Rebellion: Slave Resistance in Eighteenth-Century Virginia* (New York, 1972), 155. Douglas R. Egerton, "Gabriel's Conspiracy and the Election of 1800," *JSH*, LVI (1990), 191–214, esp. 192–93, downplays the role of religion in the Gabriel plot, points out that Martin was not a preacher and Gabriel not a religious fanatic, but disregards these quotations about Israelites. Despite his emphasis on Gabriel's secular ideology, Egerton (p. 210n) says he was "doubtless" the "brother X" in the letter. If this is correct, Gabriel was thought to be planning to communicate at least in the guise of a sermon.

the minister's, and/or Rolla's. Perhaps the minister felt that conspirators against white dominion must necessarily be blasphem-
ers of God and therefore placed words in Vesey's mouth that would
confirm such gross impiety.[8] But perhaps Denmark Vesey actually
said what he was said to have said.

Nat Turner's rebellion is even better known, if only because
those rebels succeeded in killing some sixty whites. A much
larger number of blacks in Southampton County were slaughtered
in the panicked response to the uprising. Turner, who dominated
planning and events with powerful charisma, was widely acknowledged to be a talented preacher. How fully his followers
were influenced by his complex and sophisticated religious beliefs
is open to question. Yet there is no question at all, as his published
Confessions makes clear, that Nat Turner was himself animated—perhaps even driven—by religious visions. Three years
before, he had "heard a loud noise in the heavens, and the Spirit
instantly appeared to me and said the Serpent was loosened, and
Christ had laid down the yoke he had borne for the sins of men,
and that I should take it on and fight against the Serpent, for the
time was fast approaching when the first should be last and the
last should be first." When his prison interviewer, Thomas Gray,
asked him, "Do you not find yourself mistaken now?" he responded cryptically, "Was not Christ crucified." *The Confessions*
was suffused with images of "white spirits and black spirits engaged in battle," the discovery of "drops of blood on the corn as
though it were dew from heaven," as well as finding "on the leaves
in the woods hieroglyphic characters, and numbers, with the
forms of men in different attitudes, portrayed in blood, and repre-
senting the figures I had seen before in the heavens." Some of Tur-

8. Lionel H. Kennedy and Thomas Parker, *An Official Report of the Trials of
Sundry Negroes, Charged with an Attempt to Raise an Insurrection in the State of
South-Carolina . . .* (Charleston, 1822), rpr. in *The Trial Record of Denmark Vesey,*
ed. John Oliver Killens (Boston, 1970), where the passages quoted are pp. 50, 85, 46.
(Here and throughout, italics in quotations derive from the source cited.) Significant excerpts are in Robert S. Starobin, ed., *Denmark Vesey: The Slave Conspiracy
of 1822* (Englewood Cliffs, 1970). At the Gabriel plot trials in 1800, the voluble Ben
Woolfolk claimed that another rebel was supposed to have "intended . . . to enlist
men, partially the *Outlandish* [i.e., African-born] people, because they were supposed to deal with witches and wizards, and of course useful in armies to tell when
any calamity was about to befall them"; *Cal. Va. State Papers,* IX, 153. The quotation reflects in part the fact that by 1800 virtually all the "outlandish" slaves in
Virginia were well along in years, since slave importations effectively stopped in
Virginia with the revolutionary crisis of 1774.

ner's language reads almost as if it had been lifted directly from the Book of Revelation.[9]

In comparison with these well-known and lushly documented slave conspiracies, the evidence from Second Creek is meager and fragmentary. There were no legal court reports, no articles in newspapers, no pamphlets justifying or denouncing anything about the business. Even under their examinations, though, some of the Second Creek rebels could have referred to religious beliefs or practices. They did not. One strains beyond imagination to hear Orange talking about the Israelites or even Harry Scott predicting assistance from the Lord—let alone anyone at Second Creek assuming the mantle of an avenging Christ. Apparently it occurred to no one that the Plan had begun almost exactly on the sixth anniversary of an eclipse of the moon, and no one seems to have attached significance to a bright comet that had appeared early that July.[10] And though we will never know for certain, it seems exceedingly unlikely that the "dispatch" contained much in the way of Scripture.

By way of explanation, we have to resort to the fact that Christianity seems not to have done well in Adams County. Indeed, the census of 1860 showed Adams (including Natchez) to be the least churched of all the counties in the state: it was counted as having only six churches (two Presbyterian, one Baptist, one Methodist, one Episcopal, and the large Roman Catholic church, which served the immigrant population of the town). The average number of Baptist churches in each Mississippi county was nine. A few years earlier a Methodist revival in Natchez was said to have "met with no success."[11] As early as 1800, white Baptists had

9. Thomas R. Gray, *The Confessions of Nat Turner, the Leader of the Late Insurrection in Southampton County, Va. As Fully and Voluntarily Made to Thomas R. Gray, in the Prison Where He Was Confined, and Acknowledged by Him to Be Such When Read Before the Court of Southampton* . . . (Baltimore, 1831), which has been very widely reprinted, including in Henry Irving Tragle, ed., *The Southampton Slave Revolt of 1831: A Compilation of Source Material Including the Full Text of the Confessions of Nat Turner* (1971, rpr. New York, 1973), 300–21, quotations 308–10. In its reverberations elsewhere, the ideology of Turner's rebellion appears not to have been a factor. Its absence stands out implicitly in a private letter from the Union District of South Carolina by Rosannah P. Rogers to her brothers, October 29, 1831, in William W. Renwick Papers, DUL.

10. Jenkins Diary, May 2, 1855; Wailes Diary, July 3, 4, 5, 1861.

11. U.S. Bureau of the Census, *Statistics of the United States . . . in 1860 . . . Eighth Census* (Washington, D.C., 1866), 418–19. The remark about the Methodist revival is quoted in James Oakes, *The Ruling Race: A History of American Slaveholders* (New York, 1982), 205.

founded New Hope Church on Second Creek, but even amidst the cotton boom it soon ran into financial difficulties and was labeled by the Baptist Association one of the "destitute churches." By 1840, New Hope was no longer listed on the roles of the state association. The year before, William Johnson noted, clearly as an unusual event, that a Mr. Bradley had baptized five white women in the river one morning and then sixteen "Darkeys" in the afternoon, adding caustically that the more numerous latter baptisms took the same amount of time as those earlier in the day. In 1846 the Baptist church in Natchez itself seems to have had a membership of well over four hundred, including sixty whites. At some point that church split along racial lines, and by 1861 the whites seem to have withdrawn. The numerous Baptist slaves and free blacks in Natchez may have been spreading the Word of God to slaves who occasionally came to town, but there is no evidence that they were doing so. Given the dangers involved, any such activity would have been hushed, no matter how enthusiastically pursued.[12]

Out in the county, an Episcopal church, St. Mary's, had been built in 1839 at Laurel Hill Plantation, a dozen miles from Natchez on the old Woodville road. Its first rector reported that his chief work was "visiting through the week, the servants attached to the estates." By using that term he marked himself a newcomer to the area. He had some but not notable success with what he called his "principal and most important charge," for twenty-six "colored people" were confirmed in St. Mary's during the whole of 1844. By the end of that decade, the little church was moribund.[13]

12. *Johnson's Diary*, I, 264. This was one of the light-skinned Johnson's more favorable remarks about those who shared his legally free status but not his social position. For New Hope, and the Mississippi portions of the old Natchez district more generally, see T. C. Schilling, *Abstract History of the Mississippi Baptist Association for One Hundred Years, from Its Preliminary Organization in 1806 to the Centennial Session in 1906* (Jackson, 1908), 18–23, 42–43, 57, 67–68, and Richard Aubrey McLemore, *A History of Mississippi Baptists, 1780–1970* (Jackson, 1971), 31, 45, 46, 50, 52–71 (39 for the quotation). For somewhat contradictory information on the Baptist church(es) in Natchez, see David Benedict, *A General History of the Baptist Denomination in America and Other Parts of the World* (New York, 1848), 771; *A. Mygatt and Co.'s New Orleans Business Directory . . .* (New Orleans, 1857), 261; and Patrick H. Thompson, *History of Negro Baptists in Mississippi* (Jackson, Miss., 1898), 24–28.

13. St. Mary's appears in "Inventory of the Church Archives of Mississippi, Protestant Episcopal Church, Diocese of Mississippi" (Typescript, Jackson, 1940, in Mississippi Historical Records Survey Project; available at numerous Missis-

Perhaps even older was a church on Forest Plantation, built probably at the behest of Mrs. Dunbar. Her hiring a Presbyterian minister may have been partly an effort to bring the Word to her slaves. Dr. John C. Jenkins, a Presbyterian himself, noted attending "Forest church" in his diary. Located as it was on the now-long-abandoned "Forest church Road" that cut across the midsection of the plantation, it was near Elgin, and Jenkins (having married into the Dunbar family) gave it financial support. He made no mention of his own slaves attending, but he did note having visiting preachers at Elgin who "preached to the negroes" or to "our people." In January, 1850, he paid one of these ministers $50 for the "past year"—which evidently included occasional preaching at his other two plantations, in Wilkinson County. Yet the preaching seems not to have been very regular. That same year Jenkins paid Elgin's overseer an annual salary of $650. The next, he noted paying $200 for "my subscription to Forest Church" and that his wife had been to town to buy a "sofa or chairs for Forest Church pulpit." Plainly the church was not primarily for the benefit of the Forest and Elgin Negroes. Jenkins also made occasional note of ministers marrying his slaves, usually during the year-end holidays. These few entries in his diary are the only specific references to actual slave marriages in the accumulated sediments of data on Second Creek plantations.[14]

---

sippi libraries and some elsewhere). Without intending to do so, several draft typescript histories of churches in Adams County, mostly done in 1937, give a picture of well-intended but unsuccessful struggle; they may be found in Box 216, Works Progress Administration, Adams County, RG 60, MDAH. The chief successes, besides Natchez, were in the hamlets of Washington, Pine Ridge, and Kingston. During and especially after the war, in a process of separation that was common at the time, black churches multiplied in Adams County, seven in 1865 and eighteen in 1870. Michael Wayne, *The Reshaping of Plantation Society: The Natchez District, 1860–1880* (Baton Rouge, 1983), 138, has details particularly about the Kingston neighborhood.

14. Jenkins Diary, "3d Week," January, 1850, November 24, 26, 1851. Over a period of more than ten years, Jenkins recorded about sixty Sunday visits of ministers at Elgin to "preach" or occasionally "give instructions" to his Negroes. Much of the time he had either the Reverend Mr. Ogden or the Reverend Mr. Brown on annual retainer. But the random irregularity and the number of entries about preaching make it impossible to tell whether the omissions (more than four hundred from what would have been weekly preaching) were actual or the diary's. There is one notation about an apparently uninvited, unpaid visiting preacher, on February 28, 1853. Jenkins noted a named white minister's officiating at a half dozen marriages and two funerals during that whole period—which suggests at

Farther afield, in 1857, Benjamin Wailes tried his hand at bringing the gospel to his Fonsylvania Plantation north of Jefferson in Warren County. He paid a prominent Methodist minister, assisted by another, $20 for christening "some ten or a dozzen young negroes." The assistant attended a sick slave there several months later. Wailes did not mention any such activities again until 1862, when he permitted a "Mr. Lewis missionary to the Negroes sent by the Methodist Conference" to preach at Fonsylvania and at Ivanhoe, a nearby plantation owned by his niece and ward. Wailes thought Lewis "a young and inexperienced preacher and . . . not likely to do the negroes any good." Lewis fared better when he introduced a catechism, but one Sunday his preaching at Ivanhoe was followed "immediately after service" by "a *row*" between groups of "negro girls" from the two plantations—"which proves," Wailes thought, "that they were not favorably impressed by the Sermon and that their moral advancement is nothing to speak of." A benevolent man, Wailes found the situation getting out of hand and himself under compulsion: "This fracas led to a piece of insolence by them towards a member of my family and compelled me to flog five of them." No doubt he thought the whippings very different from the "severity" he had worried about during the crisis at Second Creek, and given the difference in purpose, not to mention his own temperament, surely they were.[15]

The cause of religion seems to have fared better in Jefferson County. Susan Sillers Darden wrote often in her diary about going to various churches and about her husband attending without her. She referred to gatherings of Methodists, Baptists, Presbyterians, Campbellites, and perhaps Roman Catholics. After mentioning specific services she often wrote, "Not many there," but such a comment is scarcely a useful index of the number of people attending. In the summer of 1859 she noted that "Rev. Mr. Sibley is having a 2 days meeting for the blacks at Springhill." Evidently the Baptists were active at least on occasion, for the next spring

---

minimum that many slave marriages and all infant funerals were accomplished by the slaves themselves. Mrs. Jenkins once went across the creek to a "prayer meeting" (August 30, 1854), but both the Jenkinses normally attended irregularly at the Forest church or in Natchez. The doctor-planter made some but less effort to support formal preaching by white ministers at his other two plantations, in Wilkinson County, as indicated for example *ibid.*, May 10, 1853.

15. Charles S. Sydnor, *A Gentleman of the Old Natchez Region: Benjamin L. C. Wailes* (Durham, N.C., 1938), 105–106, the quotations coming from the Wailes Diary.

she noted without comment that blacks and whites had been baptized together in a creek—not a rare occasion in the rural South generally, though not as common as it had once been.[16]

Certainly the rural parts of Adams County seem to have been little touched by revivalism. At least there is no evidence that the slaves of this more aristocratic area were much affected by active servants of Christ's cause, if indeed they ever heard anyone expound the Word. The formalisms of the Presbyterian and Episcopal churches satisfied the planting class, which remained largely free of strong missionary urges concerning their slaves.[17] One exception was the Reverend Mr. Ogden, the Episcopal clergyman who in the past, at least, had supported himself in part by preaching to slaves of such planters as the recently deceased Dr. Jenkins. In 1860 he had boarded with Jenkins' close friend, Dr. Scott, but there is no evidence that his preaching did much to spread the gospel among the slaves at Waverly or elsewhere in the neighborhood. And there had been a Presbyterian minister at Forest, whose proselytizing victories included at least three slaves who could read, one of whom was singled out as a "religious man."

These somewhat ambiguous traces of religious activity need to be set beside countervailing evidence of outright opposition on the part of some slaveholders. More than a half dozen years after the war, a former-slave "stock minder" testified before the Southern Claims Commission about his own experience in such matters. He was deposing legally about the wealthy woman who had owned him at Carthage and its adjoining Blackburn, on the river, a woman who claimed she and her husband and father had been steadfastly against secession from the Union. In addition to that plantation, Mrs. Katherine Surget Minor owned in her own right (by inheritance from her father, James Surget) two others across the river in Concordia, as well as suburban Oakland, which had been bought by her deceased husband, John, with money from *his* father, William J. Minor. When Lee Scott was asked by friendly counsel how he and other slaves at Carthage had been treated by their absentee owner, he responded, "Well sir: Mrs Minor was a

16. Darden Diary, July 23, 1859, April 2, 1860, and *passim*. See also the interview with Isaac Stier in Rawick, *American Slave*, Vol. VII (Okla. and Miss. Narrs.), Pt. 2, pp. 144–46.

17. Though often reliable, the Reverend Mr. Ingraham's remarks on this matter reflected conventional wisdom as to what ought to be happening on Sundays, and seem very wide of actual practice in Adams County. [Joseph Holt Ingraham], *The South-West. By a Yankee* (2 vols.; 1835; rpr. Ann Arbor, 1966), II, 126–28.

pretty close mistress; there were better Mistresses than her." Because Scott was by then known as a preacher, counsel pressed on:

Q Didn't she give you privileges of a church; didn't she have a church on her place?
A No sir: and whenever she catched us asinging of a hymn

———

The legal recorder's pregnant trailing dash may have reflected Scott's hesitancy to continue or the recorder's own reluctance to have the witness' description entered in the public record, but on either assumption there is no mistaking what had gone on. Later during the same proceeding, Thomas H. Spain—the relatively well-to-do overseer-manager of Carthage—testified that Mrs. Minor "didn't allow them to have any church." He also said Scott "has been preaching for 15 or 20 years:—ever since the war—ever since he was allowed to preach." [18] This was in 1873, and Spain's chronological confusion was itself testimony to the hidden powers of what has often been called the "invisible church" of American slaves. But in Adams County that church was much more deeply concealed than in most parts of the South, so much so as to suggest little influence. Or, of course, one could presume the Second Creek rebels found its presence either irrelevant, unimportant, or too dangerous to be mentioned. The fact that they were not grilled on the matter (so far as we know) serves to underline the interactive quality inherent in the available evidence about what they had in mind.

A different kind of evidence comes from Charles Williams, a slave who grew up in Adams County and much later wrote an autobiography. Williams recalled, with a vividness common to many childhood memories but in his own particular eloquence, his early exposure to a Sunday "service" that clashed with values he picked up elsewhere or after the war:

I remember every Sunday Morning after Breakfast, 80 or 90 Slave Had to go eround for the owner Master and make 4 rounce (rounds) singing something. Master a-setting on front

18. Testimony of Thomas H. Spain, May 24, 1873, pp. 21, 32–33, in Claim (No. 7960) of Katherine S. Minor, in Settled Case Files, 1877–83—Mississippi, Adams County, Records of the Southern Claims Commission, Records of the General Accounting Office, RG 217, National Archives. Even later after the war, two of Martha W. Dunbar's former slaves claimed to be Baptist ministers; see Summary Report, March [?], 1880, in Claim No. 19810, Wm. H. McPhecters and Wm. H. Dunbar, executors of Martha W. Dunbar, *ibid.*

Porch with a old Cow Hide in his Hand. Ever one what did not toe the mark and sing to the top of his Voise, he call to him and whip 4 tears deep, all time him a-setting jest Drunk as he cin Be. Bottle Whisky setting Right Bie his Side. Ever now and then reach down and get Him a Drink. I seen this. I know what I talking erbout. This was done on ever Sunday morning Breakfast. Gone was Holy Sabbath Day in folly. Jesus Christ fround upond such act. Mrs. Clarrie Baker was my Mistress and after he done that dirty act toward his slave. He did not allowed them to have no church to exercise they gift what Jesus alowed for them toward service and worship as He demand of them thay do.[19]

So much for the Fourth Commandment.

No doubt this was aberrant and reprobated behavior among the planters generally, but itinerant Baptist preachers would not have been welcomed in the neighborhood of Second Creek, and there is no record of their attempting to seed that ground. There is no evidence suggesting that preachers of either color were present at the examinations or hangings. It is equally clear, and much more surprising, that there are no references—with the exception of Lee Scott—to black preachers on the plantations.[20] Especially after Nat Turner, black preachers were often the first to come under suspicion when there were rumors of slave discontent. Surely there were believers among the Second Creek slaves; but they seem to have been, in Christian terms, a scattering rather than a gathering.

19. Rawick, *American Slave*, Suppl. 2, Vol. I (Ala. [etc.] Narrs.), 236. The seventy-page "Autobiography" of Charles Williams is most unusual among the WPA ex-slave narratives in that he apparently wrote it out himself. His spelling was errant (and hence the occasional interpolations in parentheses by some editor), but he was often eloquent. Williams' master was Louis E. Baker, just thirty years old in 1860, who appears to have been married at least twice; he employed an overseer for only thirty-three slaves on 225 acres, but maintained no carriage; see *ibid.*, I, 237; Census, 1860 Free, household 883; Slave, MS p. 85; and Irene S. and Norman E. Gillis, *Adams County Mississippi Marriages, 1802–1859* (Shreveport, La., 1976), 2. Louis Baker lived near a single woman named Baker old enough to be his mother who owned 116 slaves; in Census, 1860 Free, household 903; Slave, MS pp. 56–58. Thus Williams' recollection of eighty to ninety gathering may not have been wildly off. Baker died within a year of the census, probably from a cause that Charlie Williams may have thought he had sufficiently described in the above passage. See Adams Land, 1861; Adams Personal, 1859, 1861, 1862.

20. There is one laconic notation of a slave "preacher" being jailed in Jefferson County, but nothing about what happened to him, in Darden Diary, May 18, 1861.

Another collage of ideas, at least a mental posture, was readily available to slave conspirators in the American South during and after the Revolution. White Americans had relied upon an ideology of natural rights to justify revolution against British authority and had incorporated much of that philosophy into the process of nation building. The result was to lock the idea of liberty into American nationalism, to make it seem a bedrock of the new republic. At the time, some Americans both black and white pointedly denounced the inconsistency of enslaving men while fighting for the natural right of liberty. This telling argument had considerable impact in the states from Virginia northward, effectively so in those with few slaves.

In Virginia (where there were more than a few) a young lawyer reflecting on the recent Gabriel plot summarized a change he thought had been caused by the Revolution. In 1775, St. George Tucker recalled, hundreds of slaves had responded to the proclamation issued by Virginia's royal governor, Lord Dunmore, who promised slaves freedom if they would abscond from their masters and join the British forces. Now, in 1801, Tucker's pamphlet on the Gabriel plot contended that in 1775 slaves "fought [for (or *sought*)] freedom merely as a good; [but] now they also claim it as a right."[21] At least that is the way the matter appeared to Tucker as a self-conscious heir of the Revolution.

Devoted as he was to that glorious triumph, Tucker failed to recognize the Gabriel rebels' hatred of whites and overestimated their consciousness of Revolutionary principles. The black rebels outside Richmond saw liberty in a different light. As one of them, Jack Bowler, said, he wished to join "a society to fight the white people for their freedom." Bowler did use the word *right*, but in a sense very different from Thomas Jefferson's: his ringing assertion that "we have as much right to fight for our liberty as any men" bore the corollary "that on Saturday night" the plotters "would kill the white people." Another conspirator was quoted as speak-

---

21. [St. George Tucker], *Letter to a Member of the General Assembly of Virginia on the Subject of the Late Conspiracy of the Slaves, with a Proposal for Their Colonization* (Richmond, 1801), 6–7, quoted in Egerton, "Gabriel's Conspiracy," 208. Both Mullin, *Flight and Rebellion*, 157, and Egerton, "Gabriel's Conspiracy," 208n., interpolate the "[for]," but it is possible that "fought" was printed in error for "sought."

ing even more directly: " 'I could slay the white people like sheep.' "[22]

In 1822 some of the Charleston conspirators hoped for assistance from St. Domingo, by then sometimes known as Haiti, the second independent republic in the New World and ruled by black men. Vesey himself had been in the island, and Toussaint L'Ouverture's great black revolution had long since become a byword among American whites as well as blacks. The turmoil there was associated with the broadly revolutionary ideas of the French and (less directly) the American revolutions. According to Jack's gallows confession, Vesey "was in the habit of reading to me all the passages in the newspapers that related to Santo Domingo" as well as many others "that had any connection with slavery." Vesey had brought Jack a speech by Senator Rufus King of New York on the Missouri Compromise—a speech now lost, but apparently marked by pointed references to natural rights and liberties.[23]

Yet the Vesey conspirators, whose testimonies were recorded at great length, dwelt largely on details of their planning. They did not refer directly to the American Revolution, and they seem not to have discussed natural rights. Vesey himself talked about the Bible and St. Domingo, but he placed little emphasis on the failure of the United States to live up to its own ideals. Vesey's interest in the oratory of Senator King suggests his own awareness of national calls for liberty, but he seemed more interested in the (false) rumor that Congress had recently declared slaves free. He resorted to the natural-rights philosophy only in a distinctly religious context. At least this was the interpretation by a white youth who testified that Vesey's *"general conversation was about*

22. *Cal. Va. State Papers,* IX, 152, 160, 162. Egerton, "Gabriel's Conspiracy," 208, adds in his own brackets a modern and slightly distortive interpolation to the words of the Virginia statesman John Randolph, quoting him as observing that many of the rebels showed a "sense of their [natural] rights" and "a contempt of danger." Randolph himself was devoted to natural rights, but he did not think that such rebels were.

23. Killens, ed., *Trial Record of Denmark Vesey,* 88. King's unrecorded speech was apparently never published, but a draft exists in his private papers; he was quoted publicly by Senator William Smith of South Carolina; see Robert Ernst, *Rufus King, American Federalist* (Chapel Hill, 1968), 372–73. In addition, portions of two of King's earlier speeches were published as a separate book, which may have circulated even in the "wrong" hands in Charleston: Rufus King, *Substance of Two Speeches, Delivered in the Senate of the United States on the Subject of the Missouri Bill* (New York, 1819).

religion which he would apply to slavery, as for instance, he would speak of the creation of the world, in which he would say all men had equal rights, blacks as well as whites—*all his religious remarks were mingled with slavery."* [24]

By 1822 the ideology of natural rights was, after all, a fading tradition, though it was far from dead in the nation as a whole. Not only was it fading with time, but it had never been as fully articulated among whites in South Carolina as in Virginia. South Carolina's full-blown commitment to slavery was becoming increasingly strident, and discussion of the natural rights of man seemed subversive of the most central interests of the state's master class. Indeed, an ideology of natural rights now appeared a foolish and dangerous line of thinking for a slave society, and Thomas Jefferson more and more a wrongheaded and wooly philosopher. Ironically, Denmark Vesey's conspiracy accelerated this retreat from the ideals of the Revolution. More than anything, he and his followers talked about killing whites.

A similar but less precipitate ideological retreat was under way in Jefferson's own state of Virginia. In this connection Nat Turner contributed in much the same way Vesey had, though he was a very different sort of man. Turner's religious, mystical vision was so powerful that he had no interest in outside earthly assistance, and he seemed less consumed than Vesey by outright rage at whites. Far less is known about his supporters than Gabriel's or Vesey's, but Turner's own published *Confessions* was nearly devoid of references to the secular ideology of the Revolution. The closest the Turner rebels came to appealing to that tradition was an aborted plan to begin the killing on the appropriate anniversary. After receiving the sign from heaven (an eclipse of the sun), Turner took four other slaves into his confidence. As he described the planning, "It was intended by us to have begun the work of death on the 4th of July last—Many were the plans formed and rejected by us, and it affected my mind to such a degree, that I fell sick, and the time passed without our coming to any determination how to commence." [25]

24. Killens, ed., *Trial Record of Denmark Vesey,* 64. Eugene D. Genovese, *From Rebellion to Revolution: Afro-American Slave Revolts in the Making of the Modern World* (New York, 1979), a fine survey, makes rather too much of the rise in political consciousness among slaves in the United States after the rebellion in St. Domingo.

25. Turner, *Confessions,* in *Southampton Revolt,* ed. Tragle, 310.

The Fourth of July was widely celebrated among southern whites and by many blacks as well. Some Mississippi owners let their slaves make a holiday; as one observer in Madison County reported it, "They are permitted to assemble together from the different plantations, and enjoy themselves in uninterrupted feasting and festivity."[26] In this respect, Gabriel Shields's Aventine Plantation was probably more exceptional than typical in its ignoring the Fourth. Yet even the cordial Dr. Jenkins gave his slaves passes only at Christmastime.[27] As for Turner and his followers, the Fourth of July seems to have meant something, but not, as things turned out, very much. Some American slaves seem to have been vaguely aware of the holiday's irony insofar as it bore on their condition, but the ideology of natural rights was a foreign tradition belonging to their enemies, not to them. It remained for Frederick Douglass, the extraordinary former slave who had escaped into a wider ideological world, to articulate the day's bitterness in a famous, acidic address in Rochester, New York, in 1852: "What to the Slave Is the Fourth of July?"[28]

What indeed? Slaves were more inclined to talk of "freedom" than "liberty." The latter term—nuancedly more political and theoretical—had been used interchangeably with "freedom" by the Gabriel rebels. Yet for them as well as the Vesey plotters, St. Domingo was more vivid, more immediate and relevant than Independence Hall. Throughout two centuries of American slavery, reports and rumors of official actions to abolish slavery sometimes triggered plotting. So did signs that owners faced a crisis with other enemies, whether foreign like the British, the French, or the Spanish, or domestic like the abolitionists.

Most of all, though, for slaves freedom seemed an immediate goal to be accomplished abruptly, not a theoretical condition. At least on Second Creek, it *would* come—however eventually—on home ground. It would bring the end of what seemed to be going on forever. It was "bound" to come, even if it meant killing, which it probably would.

26. *Virgil Stewart*, 227.

27. Jenkins Diary, December 29, 30, 31, 1851.

28. Aventine Plantation Diary, July 4, 1857, in MDAH; John W. Blassingame, ed., *The Frederick Douglass Papers, Series One: Speeches, Debates, and Interviews* (3 vols.; New Haven, 1979–85), II, 359–88, and often reprinted and quoted elsewhere.

The Second Creek rebels did not specifically reject these formal religious and political ideologies. They embraced freedoms that had as many definitions as there were individual conspirators. Certainly their own views were partially shaped by ideologies that had been eloquently articulated and thoroughly absorbed in the culture as a whole. But of necessity and preference they placed their own interpretations on the meaning of freedom, framing it in the contexts of their everyday lives. For the most part they lacked the skills of literacy that would have enabled—or caused—them to adopt a uniform, codified definition of freedom, though of course they had a profound sense of its true meaning. Because the rebels lacked a documentary platform or desire for one, the differences among their individual aims stand out sharply. But so too does their fundamental agreement on overthrowing the authority of their self-appointed owners.

No doubt many, and perhaps all, the rebels had specific grievances they could name—instances where unwritten rules had been violated and thereby injustices done. All plantations had such rules, as indeed did American slave society and slave cultures everywhere. The rules had been hammered out over generations in millions of personal interactions. The planters often read and sometimes wrote down some of the more specific and measurable regulations and guidelines. Essays on "Rules for the Management of Negroes" became so common in manuscript and in published form that they became staples of southern agricultural journals—almost a genre of antebellum literature.[29] For their part, slaves shaped their own literature about how to manage white folks in the form of songs and folktales, and of necessity they wove these rules into their daily etiquette and expressive styles and the way they reared their children. They incorporated rules while whites were writing rules of incorporation.

Of course, rules were constantly being broken by both sides—a phenomenon that was itself an integral part of the rule-making process. For both owners and owned, it was the most flagrant vio-

29. Many so-called plantation diaries, or log books, were kept in printed ledgers available for purchase, the most widely used in Mississippi being various editions written and compiled by Thomas Affleck, Scottish born, previously of Cincinnati, but by the 1840s resident near the town of Washington and at one point in the 1850s at Ingleside near Second Creek. Often these largely blank notebooks included printed "Rules for Overseers."

lations that drew most attention and cried out for specific redress. Allowing for a wide range of personal responses, it was sheer egregiousness that festered most of all.

Thus it is no surprise that slaves under examination did not blurt out long lists of specific grievances. They were not asked for them. And as far as they were concerned, slavery was grievance enough, and no doubt the Examination Committee would have stopped any attempt to catalog injustices. What happened to Wesley's sister was clearly a very special case. It may have seemed so partly because it had taken place at the hands of those who stood farthest from the core of authority and who thereby appeared to be taking especially unwarranted advantage of the system. The "young ladies" (especially Miss Mary) who "drown and beat" Wesley's sister had blurred the customary lines of authority and devastated one of the best avenues for mutual trust and affection between slaves and members of the master class. Miss Mary was white, but she was also both a woman and young. She had no call to abuse the young slave woman, and when "she poured water upon" her, she chose a method that conspicuously snapped the rules. From the language used, it seems clear that this particular humiliation involved not just a single incident, but a habitual pattern. No doubt Miss Mary thought the punishment justified. No doubt Wesley's sister thought the young missus unjust and plain mean. We might see the matter as a personal quarrel. Her father and brother saw it as festering, unforgivable injustice. Thus (according to Harvey), "Nelson and Wesley would kill the young ladies"; or (according to Alfred), "Nelson would take Miss . . . Mary, ravish her." It was in this context that Alfred could claim, "I have no spite against the ladies," immediately after saying that he, Nelson, Harvey, and Wesley each were going to ravish them. He saw a particular grievance as stronger grounds for retaliation than generalized antipathy, or so he said and probably felt at that terrible moment.

Evidently, similar abuse had occurred at the Dunbars' Forest, where overwork—probably of unusual length and at outrageous hours—brought forth the striking language that described Paul's "consent" to join: "Mrs D kills up Pauls wife sewing." As with Wesley's sister, the transgression was not against one of the rebels, but against one of their womenfolk.[30]

30. In the course of reading plantation documents it is striking to find that an unexpectedly large proportion of the incidents of sadistically imaginative torture of slaves were perpetrated by white *women*, with their victims being both men and

From long experience the rebels also had reason for more dif-
fuse anger against whites, and of course some slaves were more
likely than others to feel and express it. Sometimes their expressions were not entirely clear. Young Harvey was the only rebel
who suggested they would kill other colored people: after joining
the northern army, he said, they would "kill whites — and blacks
who would not join." Young Alfred was more ambiguous: after
ravishing at Mrs. Dunbar's, they "would kill those on the road" on
the way to New Orleans, the North, and Natchez.

Others were totally clear about their intentions. Nelson said
flatly that "we planned to kill the whites" and "agree to fight the
white folks." John Mitchell reported that the Dunbar and Mosby
men were "to fight . . . the white people." According to Harvey,
"Obey said, I will join them too to help kill the white folks."
George, during his second examination, claimed that Harry Scott
had talked about "plan to kill the white folks."

By this time, the Examination Committee was perhaps impos-
ing that phrase by its own wording of questions. Certainly in that
culture the feeling of racial difference ran deep within everyone.
Whiteness had become synonymous with authority and oppression, as when the W. M. was reported as saying, with paradox
more apparent than real, "Genl Scott wants every second planter
to join him and kill white man." Only Orange was specifically
nonracial about the enemy. After the crucial conversation that
had taken place with "Benny present," Orange announced "he
would show Cotton planters."[31] It was in exactly the same spirit
that he claimed "he was going to have the country"—a country
that dead cotton planters would no longer possess. Earlier, the
stock phrase about "white folks" had been used in similar but
significantly different form in connection with the plans for ravishing, as when George quoted Alfred as declaring, " 'The blacks
were to kill all the white men and take the young ladies and
women for wives.' "

It remained for Dennis Mitchell—he of colorful phrases—to
strip hostility to its nakedness. Almost at the outset of his ordeal
he spat out, "Kill all the damn white people." Then, in language
that was probably as much his as the man he was quoting: " 'Si-

---

women of all ages. Use of such torture is not suggested in this instance, though no
doubt Wesley's sister suffered pain.

31. Though it is not clear from the immediate context of Alfred's testimony,
the term *cotton planter* ordinarily meant a large rather than a second planter.

mon said he hoped to see the day when he would blow down a white man who called him a damn rascal.' " With these words, though, we are back full circle. Some white man had evidently broken the rules by directly aiming that insulting epithet at a black slave—and, of course, Simon could not have safely replied in kind.

In speaking of their ultimate goals, some rebels also raised the central issue of "freedom." Obviously the men who talked about killing the white folks had freedom in mind, but the fact remains that most of them did not speak of freedom as such. It was a common word among slaves. Years later, hundreds of elderly former slaves recalled talking and especially praying about "freedom."[32] But the great majority of the Second Creek rebels did not use such language in their "confessions." Conceivably the questions and the questioners inhibited their doing so, though it is difficult to see why. It is a virtual certainty that they discussed freedom among themselves. As Simon Dunbar said, "The negroes would be free," and: "Our men talk about it frequently. I too." Nonetheless, the evidence does not suggest that the concept was always central to most of the rebels' thinking. Surely it was always at the back of their minds, but it could easily be crowded from the forefront by specific grievances, by tactical planning, and by a generalized urge for revenge.

Despite the uncommon appearance of the term in Conner's record, some rebels had in fact been talking about freedom. These men were not a miscellaneous group. Not surprisingly, Harry Scott talked about it during one of his loquacious outbursts of enthusiasm at the Dunbars' Forest. According to George (during his first, more coherent set of responses), "Harry Scott said we were all bound to be free." Dennis Mitchell began his laconic but colorful testimony with the words, "First talk of freedom." Probably Dennis had discussed the goal explicitly with Big John, the Mitchell driver. John began *his* brief testimony with the flat, sweeping statement that "Black folks talking of freedom." Edmond, the Helms' driver, was quoted as using language similar to Orange's: " 'If the black folks were turned loose with hoes and axes they would whip the country.' " His remark came, in Simon's account, immediately after discussion of "the negroes" becoming "free."

32. Instances lie scattered abundantly in Rawick, *American Slave*; also in Charles L. Perdue, Jr., Thomas E. Barden, and Robert K. Phillips, eds., *Weevils in the Wheat: Interviews with Virginia Ex-Slaves* (Bloomington, Ill., 1980).

Harry Scott quoted Mrs. Charlotte B. Griffith's (unnamed) driver as saying that " 'freedom was at our door.' "

This pattern of testimony makes clear that of all the rebels, the drivers were the most vocal about freedom, the most willing and able to generalize the goal of the Plan and raise it to a level of universal application. This was Simon Dunbar's view explicitly. He said suddenly, after talking about the taking of the ladies, "The carriage drivers thought the negroes would be free." With all its ambiguities, the record can at times be heard very distinctly.[33]

The carriage drivers had good reason to think of freedom in more general terms than field hands did. They had already tasted of it in their daily routines. Yet caution is needed when we delve into the rebels' occupations and their concomitant outlooks on their condition.

One of the most remarkable aspects of the entire testimony is not the presence of the drivers, but the total absence of any indications about other occupations. Specialized skills were not likely to be found on relatively small places like Mosby's, but they might be expected on large ones like Mrs. Dunbar's. In the agricultural South as a whole, occupational specialization and skills were most common on the larger plantations, especially (owing to the nature of the crops) in the sugar country of southern Louisiana and, less markedly, in the rice and long-staple-cotton lands of the South Carolina and Georgia low country. On the larger upland cotton units, there were often occupational specialists such as wagoners, carpenters, blacksmiths, and among the women, cooks and nurses. Yet there were fewer skilled artisans on these plantations than in earlier years: in the eighteenth century, particularly on the home tobacco plantations of the Virginia aristocracy, slave "tradesmen" had predominated in many skilled crafts, but by the time of the war the growth of cities and towns, better transportation, and an increase in skilled white artisans had combined to reduce the number of slaves who enjoyed specialized occupations

33. And sometimes not. Both because of her distance and eccentric punctuation, it is difficult to weigh the comments made from near Woodville by Mrs. Sophia H. Hunt: "27—have been hung after Monday there had only 5—negro men 4—of them were hung Carriage drivers; and dining room servants of the rich[.] Many are hung[.] They were the ring leaders—" S[ophia] H. Hunt to Jennie [Hughes], October 15, 1861, in Hughes Family Papers, UNC, Document I.

in the cotton kingdom. Aventine was a good example of the many antebellum cotton plantations that made use of some skilled labor by slaves, but more by visiting white men. At Elgin, John C. Jenkins used "negro carpenters" only (so far as his diary suggests) when under the supervision of a white craftsman.[34]

In fact Adams County was marked, so far as can be discerned, by a conspicuous absence of skills among slaves. In 1850 and 1860 the census marshals were required to draw up a list of "Persons Who Died During the Year" preceding the official June date of counting, and this list was supposed to include occupations, ages, and causes of death. The majority of census marshals throughout the cotton South neglected to compile and submit this "Mortality Schedule," but those in Adams County did so. Pickens was as usual particularly careful, and his list of occupations of the deceased was particularly revealing. Of the 152 adult slaves with a named occupation, there were 125 field hands, 22 servants, 3 cooks, 1 teamster, and 1 driver. Ten years earlier, the less accurate census had listed a tinner, a tanner, a carpenter, a seamstress, a cook, a shoemaker, and a plowman.[35]

Besides "driver," the only other slave occupations mentioned at the Second Creek examinations were "printer" and "teamster." Wesley was given the title "printer" by his friends, honorifically as will become clear. For obvious reasons, neither he nor any other Mississippi blacks were permitted anywhere near that craft.[36] In Conner's record the Homochitto teamsters appear as a distinct category, many of them named without indication of being owned by anyone in particular. Probably they worked without close supervision, and many of them may well have been hired out by their owners to entrepreneurs on an annual basis. Indeed, some teamsters were white, as was (almost certainly) the one who came to Aventine to haul bales to town. Yet slave teamsters had mobility and access to the pleasures of town, as was sadly emphasized when a teamster's cause of death was described

34. Jenkins Diary, June 23, 24, 28, 1855.

35. Census, 1850 Mortality; 1860 Mortality. These schedules in the lower South are discussed in Michael P. Johnson, "Work, Culture, and the Slave Community: Slave Occupations in the Cotton Belt in 1860," *Labor History*, XXVII (1986), 325–55.

36. "Hutchinson's Code" of 1848 set heavy fines for any white printer employing black typesetters and the death penalty for free Negroes practicing the craft. See Charles S. Sydnor, "The Free Negro in Mississippi Before the Civil War," *American Historical Review*, XXXII (1927), 771.

by the census marshal as "Excessive Drink," the only slave on his list with that ascription.[37]

Doctor (Mitchell) may perhaps be regarded as having his own special occupation, though it was one that many whites recognized with skepticism if at all—the more so in Adams County because so many of the planters there had formal medical training. "Doctor" was a quite common appellation for slaves in the South, for some slaves practiced medicine with as much good effect, probably, as most white physicians. Such part-time doctors were occasionally called upon to treat whites, despite fears of possible poisoning. The term *doctor* was sometimes associated with conjuring, and some slave doctors practiced it. But Doctor Mitchell was not primarily a conjurer, or accused of being such, as was the famous Gullah Jack in Vesey's Charleston. Mitchell's Doctor, who may perhaps have been a rather young man, seems to have practiced his art at neighboring plantations, since he testified about runaways "I met when away." Still, he seems not to have played an active part in the planning, and he even claimed to know "nothing about the neighborhood difficulties"—a claim that undoubtedly was treated with towering skepticism by the Examination Committee.

Conner's transcript includes the testimony of only one "driver" under examination, Mitchell's John, sometimes called Big John to distinguish him from Little John, who was probably his son. Four other drivers were mentioned or quoted by the rebels: Nichols' Edward, Helm's Edmond, Griffith's unnamed driver, and Metcalfe's Louis. All except Louis were clearly carriage drivers.

Louis was probably a slave foreman, and may well have acquired that status at Montrose, Dr. James Metcalfe's homeplace among several county plantations on which he owned 315 slaves. The overseer there, John Austen, probably had one or several foremen to assist him in supervising the different gangs. Louis stands out for another reason, for he was the only slave mentioned as offering a distinct note of pessimism about the fortunes of the war between the whites. According to Harvey, Louis said "Southerners whipping North." This may have been a careless transposition on Conner's part. Yet Benny was "present," and Louis may actually have offered that prediction with an eye to his own protection in case Benny went back home and talked to his folks.

Apart from their talk of "freedom," the carriage drivers stand

37. Census, 1860 Mortality, MS p. 11.

apart in Conner's record in a subtler way. Though Conner many times recorded a slave as so-and-so's—with an actual or implied apostrophe to indicate ownership—many times he did not. Yet with the exception of Louis, when the drivers were identified their names were given in the possessive mode. Thus the carriage drivers seemed, probably to both blacks and whites, to *belong* to someone in an unusually strong sense. Sometimes only the owner's last name was given, as with "Mitchells John Driver" and "Edmond, Helm's driver." The other two were named as belonging to white women: "Edward — Mrs N's driver" and "Mrs. Griffiths driver." In the latter case there was good legal basis for Mrs. Charlotte B. Griffith's ownership of her driver because she was a widow and hence could legally own property in her own right.[38] Similarly, Edward may have been legally owned by Mrs. Eliza J. Nichols rather than by her husband.[39]

No matter what the niceties of legal ownership, drivers like Edward belonged in a different sense to the mistresses of the plantation households. Edward drove *Mrs.* Nichols and her two teenage daughters when they went visiting. Indeed, the carriage drivers ordinarily drove only women and sometimes children. It was an established, though not invariable, custom among the planters that a gentleman rode his own horse while his wife and daughters rode in the carriage.[40] This practice was not intended as a conspicuous display of manliness; it was merely the ordained style of genteel southrons, at least those of the Natchez district. The planters'

38. Owner of sixty-nine (eighty-four in the census) slaves at Anchorage Plantation, immediately west of The Grove, Mrs. Griffith headed a household with six young people, an overseer from England, and a "teacher of Common School" from Pennsylvania. See Census, 1860 Free, household 953; Slave, MS pp. 114–15; Adams Personal, 1858, 1859, 1861, 1862; Adams Land, 1857, 1861; Road Duty, UTA, 363, 435, 501. Ten years before, she had married a second time, to a man named Field, but by the mid-1850s she was again Mrs. Griffith, with her own property; Jenkins Diary, September 16, 1851; Gillis and Gillis, *Adams County Marriages*, 23. "An Act for the Protection and Preservation of the Rights and Property of Married Women," in *Laws of the State of Mississippi: Passed at an Adjourned Session . . . January 7, to February 16, A.D. 1839* (Jackson, 1839), 72–73, was the first such legislation in the entire country, though it aimed particularly at property in slaves. See Sandra Moncrief, "The Mississippi Married Women's Property Act of 1839," *Journal of Mississippi History*, XLVII (1985), 110–25.

39. She had owned nine slaves in her own name, but their names are not known. There was an Edward on the Nichols place. See Adams Personal, 1852; Road Duty, UTA, 280, 327, 439, 506.

40. [Ingraham], *South-West*, II, 35: "At the north few ride except in gigs. But here all are horsemen; and it is unusual to see a gentleman in a gig or carriage. If his wife rides out, he attends her *à cheval.*" As with most such generalizations, it is easy to find exceptions, as frequently in Jenkins Diary.

wives, moreover, went shopping in Natchez or visiting on their own when their husbands were engaged on more important business. On such occasions the ladies were not without male assistance and protection. They had their own drivers.[41]

That such men should be involved in plotting insurrection was profoundly shocking to their owners. Drivers were trusted. They were carefully chosen for intelligence, reliability, skill with equipage, and often because their fathers had been drivers before them. Many were also trained in the other crafts. Carriage drivers had the sort of prestige that is so often accorded the highest of the lowly in a well-defined caste system.[42] They were dressed well, to the point of finery and even panache.[43] They were clean so far as the standards and opportunities of the day permitted. Customarily they ate in or from the back of the big-house kitchen. The driver's relations with the cook were probably as complicated as any on the entire place. Both had their own realms of allotted dominance, meaningful work, and assorted underlings.

No matter how impressive the cook's and the other house slaves' physical comforts and interpersonal leverage, the carriage drivers had something they did not—mobility. They were men of relatively wide horizons: from Second Creek they had been at least to Natchez, and in addition to the wonders of that city they

41. These arrangements *may* explain one of the most puzzling of all the lines in Conner's transcript, when during his second examination Harry Scott said, "Orange says Mrs Griffith's black man said most time for work." None of her slaves were mentioned except her unnamed driver, so one might conclude that her driver was airily telling Orange that he simply did not have much time because he was so busy. Clearly other interpretations might plausibly apply. The Jenkins Diary is filled with references to his wife, Annis, going in the carriage to shop in Natchez. She bought some things she wanted but also sometimes transacted financial business for her husband. The name of the driver was not recorded.

42. William Johnson was quite clearly taken aback as well as curious when he recorded in 1843 a carriage driver's participation in a public fray involving another slave man and two white gentlemen "in Company with Some Ladies." *Johnson's Diary*, II, 446.

43. Olmsted's description reeks not only of his hostility to the gentry of the area but of patronizing racial stereotypes. After describing the other occupants of a carriage in the "villa district" of Natchez' suburbs, he continued, "But the dignity of the turn-out chiefly reposed in the coachman, an obese old black man . . . set high up in the sun's face on the bed-like cushion of the box, to display a great livery top-coat, with the wonted capes and velvet, buttoned brightly and tightly to the chin, of course, and crowned by the proper narrow-brimmed hat, with broad band and buckle; his elbows squared, the reins and whip in his hands, the sweat in globules all over his ruefully-decorous face, and his eyes fast closed in sleep." Frederick Law Olmsted, *A Journey in the Back Country* (New York, 1860), 36.

knew a good deal about other plantations, about indoor churches, social balls, weddings, important visitors, steamboats, illnesses, and funerals. They also had opportunity to learn about horse racing and elections—and about perfume and crinoline. Not only did they often travel without a "pass," free of that document's humiliating stamp of dependence, but they saw other households and something of how they functioned. When in Natchez they saw, and probably talked with, black men who were actually free. Accordingly, more than other slaves, they had a broad and vivid view of their condition.[44]

Given the privileges of the drivers, many members of white planting families were appalled to learn that any of these trusted slaves could have been so wretchedly ungrateful as to join or perhaps even instigate plots against their benefactors. In Jefferson County that month of May, Susan Darden expressed the matter eloquently. She wrote not long after returning from Sunday services: "Sarah Darden was at church, told Olivia that brother Buckner and Madison witnessed the hanging of Samuel's Darden's car-

44. The carriage drivers' pride was an easy and inviting target for mocking by whites, who nervously ridiculed it as childish pretension. John Ingraham managed to top Olmsted in egregious condescension when he composed the following (much truncated) conversation between two carriage drivers: " 'You know dat nigger, they gwine to sell, George?' 'No, he field nigger; I nebber has no 'quaintance wid dat class.' 'Well, nor no oder gentlemens would. . . . How much you tink he go for?'—'I a'n't much 'quainted wid de price of such kind o' peoples. My master paid seven hundred dollar for me.' . . . 'Seben hun'red dollars!' exclaimed the gentleman upon the coach-seat, drawing himself up with pride, and casting a contemptuous glance down upon his companion: 'my massa give eight hundred and fifty silver dollars for me.' " [Ingraham], South-West, II, 30–31.

It is more than possible that some slaves succumbed to degradation in this manner, but the contemptuousness lay largely on the other side. The so-called pride could be very real, and with the right touch could be used as an effective method of retaliation. A more neutral observer, a distinguished English geologist, recorded an incident in North Carolina in which a driver took advantage of the visitor's presence: "We were proceeding in a well-appointed carriage with a planter, when we came unexpectedly to a dead halt. Inquiring the cause, the black coachman said he had dropped one of his white gloves on the road, and must drive back and try to find it. He could not recollect within a mile where he had last seen it: we remonstrated, but in vain. As time pressed, the master in despair took off his own gloves, and saying he had a second pair, gave them to him. When our charioteer had deliberately put these on, we started again." Sir Charles Lyell, Travels in North America, in the Years 1841–2 . . . (rev. ed.; 2 vols.; New York, 1856), II, 135. By this acute assessment of the social situation, the planter was gently relieved of a pair of gloves, which must have made a nice addition to the pair whose mate was in all probability—if we understand—in the driver's pocket.

riage Driver Davy and P. K. Montgomery's John. He marketed and drove carriage sometimes. Anna said she had trusted her life with Davy, had every confidence in him, did not even want him examined. . . . I feel truly sorry for Samuel and Anna. They have no other negroe that they can trust to drive carriage. He is a Blacksmith and carpenter, too. . . . Davy has been in the family 26 years, poor deluded negro."[45]

No doubt many of these drivers saw things very differently. They were deeply angered, as many people become when they have been forced to absorb a strong whiff of the scent of unattainability. They had good reason to plan revenge.

They also had good opportunity. Indeed, these documents suggest dramatic scenarios. Mrs. Dunbar and her daughter have been driven in their carriage to call upon Mrs. Nichols. The three ladies take cool or even luxuriously iced tea on the veranda and chat about marriage prospects for their daughters and nieces. Down on the hardened drive by the Dunbar carriage, their driver stands with Mrs. Nichols' driver, leaning on the wheels while talking in low and fervent tones about a possible plan—a plan that may include choices about who among them all is going to take which of the daughters of the ladies on the porch.[46]

The lives of the carriage drivers were very different from those of the other "drivers," such as Louis may have been, who were foremen over other slaves and served as agents of discipline. Almost always such drivers were male, though Adams County had at least one exceptional woman who was a driver of women and

45. Darden Diary, May 12, 1861, Document C. The individuals referred to were wealthy, interrelated members of planting families who lived near one another outside the county seat, as sketched in chapter 2 of this book. On the other hand, Michael Wayne, "An Old South Morality Play: Reconsidering the Social Underpinnings of the Proslavery Ideology," *Journal of American History,* LXXVII (1990), 844–45, mentions no special reaction to a carriage driver's turning out to be one of the Kingston murderers in 1857.

46. Women of the planting classes also met for shopping in town; [Ingraham], *South-West,* II, 29; Jenkins Diary, *passim.* Ice was of course a luxury, but its use had become fairly common. At times during some winters it could be found locally in small amounts. More often, block ice cut from northern ponds was brought up from New Orleans or down the river. A hogshead of ice in sawdust was expected to last "about 2 weeks" in summer, at a cost of $4 per week, at least as noted *ibid.,* May 22, 1854. Ice cream was advertised in the newspapers and there was an ice house in Under-the-Hill, carefully listed as a separate business in *A. Mygatt and Co.'s New Orleans Business Directory,* 266. Olmsted quoted another hostile comment about the "swell-heads": " 'Must have ice for their wine, you see,' said Mr. S., 'or they'd die[.]' " in his *Journey in the Back Country,* 26.

children. Charles Williams—the ex-slave autobiographer—wrote that his mother split her time between the big house and working as "a slave driver for her master." She was a strong and forceful woman who "was put over twenty five or 30 heads of women and child to have hoe coton—hoe it right—and chop coton, trim the corn; plant corn and pead (spread) seed." Evidently she was not a woman to be crossed, for her son remembered apparently without resentment his being whipped by her while he was on his honeymoon because he had slapped his bride too hard. Earlier, as a part-time slave forewoman: "She walk erlong with her old cow Hide whip and tell how to do it. She was a Negro slave Driver, pointed by the riding boss."[47] Very clearly she was an exceptional woman and, indeed, raised an exceptional son.

Members of the slave foreman class were chosen on the basis of responsibility, of forcefulness of physique and personality, and sometimes because of conspicuous knowledge and skill with agricultural operations. As suboverseers they compelled the pace of the field gangs and maintained order in the quarters. As a class they had very real power and were accorded special privileges, though both power and perquisites might be withdrawn at any time for offenses such as running away or drunkenness, or for abusing rank, or for ineffectiveness—in short they could be demoted, whipped, or sold at the pleasure of their owner. In Adams County most of these subalterns appear to have remained loyal to what was expected of them in their appointed stations. Perhaps others beside Louis joined in the Plan, but there is no evidence they did so. On many plantations in the South these drivers were resented, feared, and even hated. Yet on others they served as buffers (for some slaves at least) against arbitrary decrees emanating from overseers and owners. At Second Creek the drivers did not play major roles in plotting to overthrow the authority that was, after all, the font of their privileges and power. The field hands may or may not have trusted them to choose the right side in such a dangerous enterprise. Given what evidence we have, we cannot know.

47. Rawick, *American Slave*, Suppl. 2, Vol. I (Ala., [etc.] Narrs.), pp. 200–204. The confusion as to who made his mother a driver may perhaps be laid to the alcoholism of both her owner and her owner's son: *ibid.*, 237–38. Though rare in the United States, it had been common in the British West Indies for female "drivers" to supervise the "grass gang" of slave children on sugar plantations.

CHAPTER 11

OF MEANS AND LEADERS

On first reading, Conner's transcript seems almost hopelessly confusing about the timing of the Plan. In fact we cannot discover exactly when the Plan began and spread. Nor do we know the exact dates of all the examinations and ensuing executions. In early September, word about "great excitement in Adam's County" reached Susan Darden outside of Fayette. "They hung 2 of Henry Swazey's negroes," she wrote, "and have 60 confined belonging to different persons."[1] The rebels themselves had no clear-cut and concerted agreement about when the Plan was to begin and of course no knowledge or choice as to when it would end.

Concerning the beginnings of the Plan, some of the confusion may have been Conner's and the Examination Committee's. Some may well be of our own making, for it is tempting to impose modern standards of organization even on people who would have found them utterly foreign. We should bear in mind, moreover, that we are dealing with a congeries of plans, with portions of parts of a whole that developed over a period of several months and had been gestating much longer.

Each element of the whole had its own internal dynamic. Different and sometimes shifting groups were involved. Obviously the rebels did not all share the same information or intentions, and the "plan of ladies" may (or may not) initially have been a

1. Darden Diary, September 5, 1861. Henry C. Swayse, bachelor planter, owner of fifty-seven slaves, is in Census, 1860 Free, household 1049; Slave, MS pp. 141–42; Adams Land, 1861; Adams personal, 1861. He was not mentioned in Conner's transcript, and he did not live in Second Creek Valley. There are no other references, however, to large numbers of slaves confined elsewhere at the time. He had been involved in the interrogation of slaves concerning the murdered overseer near Kingston four years earlier; see Michael Wayne, "An Old South Morality Play: Reconsidering the Social Underpinnings of the Proslavery Ideology," *Journal of American History*, LXXVII (1990), 849, 854–55. Swayse and his larger family had long-standing interests near Kingston, and it is possible a major investigation took place in that neighborhood in 1861, which, if one did, would explain several otherwise mysterious references in Conner's transcript. But if so, it was kept under much better wraps than the proceedings at Second Creek.

somewhat separate proposition. Most important, we are venturing into a different world, one in which we must deal with now-outmoded ways of conceptualizing time.

These Second Creek slaves and their owners were of course agricultural peoples, guided much more by diurnal and seasonal rhythms than by watches, clocks, and calendars. Watches and clocks were more than mere curiosities in planters' houses, but they did not rigidly govern social and personal activities. Few slaves were acquainted with them or felt the slightest yearning for the precision they offered and, indeed, encouraged. Presumably some household slaves learned how to read time (or as we say revealingly, to "tell" it), though that ability is scarcely mentioned in the voluminous ex-slave narratives. Jane Simpson, who lived for a while near Vicksburg and then in Arkansas, was taught by the white children to read and write, but: "We didn't own no clocks dem days. We just told de time by de sun in de day and de stars at night." [2]

On the other hand, most American slaves were fully participant in their owners' way of counting days. The seven-day week, with its day of supposed rest, had long since been imposed upon their African-born forebears by the Judaic-Christian tradition of English and other western European slave traders and (more especially) purchasers in America. [3] The American-born ancestors of the Second Creek rebels had adopted the customary Anglo-pagan names of the days of the week and names of the months. [4] On occasion they talked in terms of calendar dates. Yet these rebels, and mid-nineteenth-century slaves generally, also thought of time in

2. Most clocks had only two hands, even though a third "second" hand had long been technologically possible. Even in quiet times, slaves were often accused of stealing their masters' property, but timepieces were apparently not special targets. They are not mentioned even in Vesey's plot, which took place in an urban setting. The quotation is in Rawick, *American Slave*, Vol. XI (Ark. and Mo. Narrs.), pp. 313–14. Brass clocks had been advertised in Natchez papers for years; for example, Natchez *Mississippi Daily Free Trader*, January 19, 1841.

3. Many but by no means all West Africans caught in the Atlantic slave-trading net were accustomed to weeks usually shorter but some even longer than the seven days of the European and Islamic peoples.

4. A few black Baptists were still denoting months numerically in their church records (as had been common with early Baptists everywhere and still obtained among Quakers), but for secular purposes this avoidance of pagan names had pretty well disappeared by the beginning of the nineteenth century. So far as can be ascertained, historians have not discussed this matter, not even in the fine study of cultural melding by Mechal Sobel, *Trabelin' On: The Slave Journey to an Afro-Baptist Faith* (1979; rpr. Princeton, 1987).

a somewhat different way than their masters. Given the prevailing cycles of their days and lives—so overwhelmingly dominated by the seasons, the weather, the stars, the moon, daylight, and work—they tended to account for time not by marking duration but by recalling occasions of special human or (less often) unusual environmental activity. It is an open question how powerfully West African cultural conceptions of time influenced their thinking, but their orientation was probably somewhat less linear and more focused on the present than their masters'.[5]

This melding of time and behavior became clear in some of the rebels' answers to the Committee's simple question, when? Often they responded in terms of social, rather than personal, activities or incidents. With the exception of runaways like Orange, slaves were rarely alone by themselves. They had even less personal privacy than the families of their owners. Although hoeing a row of cotton plants is indeed an intensely personal experience because it brutally weighs down one's arms and shoulders and pulls at one's back, it was for slaves a *group* activity. Field work was social in character even though it was forced, no matter whether slaves were permitted (or forced) to labor with song or in silence. Their African-born ancestors had been deeply attached to the social dimensions of work. As slavery developed in the New World, the

5. Much later, two of the few historians who have mentioned the affair misdated it as 1862: Herbert Aptheker, *American Negro Slave Revolts* (New York, 1943), 365–66, citing Clement Eaton, *The Freedom-of-Thought Struggle in the Old South* (Durham, N.C., 1940), 106–107 (pp. which remained the same in Eaton's rev. ed.; New York, 1964). The Eaton version invented details about the conspiracy that carried over into Aptheker's. Armstead L. Robinson, "In the Shadow of Old John Brown; Insurrection Anxiety and Confederate Mobilization, 1861–1863," *JNH*, LXV (1980), 287–88, 297n, gives March 4, 1861, mistakenly assigning the slaves knowledge of the date of the presidential inauguration. On the concept of time, see Eugene Genovese, *Roll, Jordan, Roll: The World the Slaves Made* (New York, 1974), 285–94; G. J. Whitrow, *Time in History: The Evolution of Our General Awareness of Time and Temporal Perspective* (New York, 1988); and Mechal Sobel, *The World They Made Together: Black and White Values in Eighteenth-Century Virginia* (Princeton, 1987), chap. 2 and its references. John S. Mbiti, *African Religions and Philosophy* (New York, 1969), chap. 2, is useful but focuses more on East than West Africa. See also Claudia Zaslavsky, *Africa Counts: Number and Pattern in African Culture* (Westport, Conn., 1973). It ought to be borne in mind that *rhythm* is a way of conceiving time, and thus the persistence of West African polyrhythmic styles into Afro-American music is important in this connection. See especially John Miller Chernoff, *African Rhythm and African Sensibility: Aesthetics and Social Action in African Musical Idioms* (Chicago, 1979). A distinct mode of handling time is evident in the fundamental grammar of American so-called "Black English."

exigencies of the capitalist cotton market reinforced ancient cultural traditions carried over from West African societies. Field labor helped create the kind of camarderie in work that later, in the postslavery era, became obvious on Mississippi's penal road and levee gangs and at Parchman Farm, the state's only prison.

Thus the testimony of the rebels blended different modes of handling time. Their accounts were peppered with references to specific dates and days of the week, to "weeks" and "months" ago, but they also employed clockless diurnal markers such as "at night," "just about dark," and "betwixt dark and daylight." More striking perhaps, was the almost palpable precision of such phrases as "at water melon carrying," "when the war began," "at breaking up time," and "Plan started cutting out cotton." Whites tended to be contemptuous of such thinking: after the war one planter eloquently asserted the superiority of his own learning when he explained, about a former slave, "Like a great many other colored men he don't know anything about what figures is, or amounts or dates."[6]

In Adams County cutting out cotton was done in late April and early May. It is evident that at least the Mosby and some of the Mitchell men began talking about the Plan in the first part of the latter month. Nelson's opening words made this clear: "Plan began on the creek fishing in May. Our boys and Mitchell's." His next response confirmed that they had learned about the outbreak of the war, which of course had begun at Fort Sumter on April 12. As Alfred said, "Began talking when the war began." Harvey confirmed the timing with his "Plan started cutting out cotton." Wesley reported simply, "Heard it in May." All these phrases came from Mosby slaves.

The Dunbar rebels were less specific about timing, and what they did say suggests that they began discussing the Plan somewhat later. It was George who reported about the Friday night dance at which the runaway Dave Bradley promised boastfully to "fetch company tomorrow night." George placed the dance at "about 3 months ago," which would actually have been about the middle of June. Yet later, under examination a second time and clearly under terrible pressure, George claimed, "Started the plan about two months ago." Then, after calling Simon the "1st talker"

6. A. B. Kirby quoted in Brief of the Evidence, December 11, 1876, p. 27, in Claim (No. 7960) of Katherine S. Minor, in Settled Case Files, 1877–83—Mississippi, Adams County, Records of the Southern Claims Commission, Records of the General Accounting Office, RG 217, National Archives.

and the "1ˢᵗ man to talk of ravishing," George denied that someone he named "knew of this plot before we made ours. Taint so."[7] There had been, he said, "new plot two months"—presumably either two months before he had been seized or two months before another early plot. He scarcely clarified this information by adding, "Mosby's three weeks or 4"—more probably intending to convey *before* rather than after the Dunbars' planning. But then almost immediately he described Harry Scott as intending to kill Dr. Scott and "go to the back country," and "then plan to kill the white folks when the Northern army got to Natchez." The only independent corroboration of George's several versions came from Harvey Mosby, a man who took a special interest in the matter of the timing. Harvey claimed, "Saw Mrs Dunbar's people," and then responded "(about 2 months ago)."

If it is correct to suppose that Conner recorded this testimony in mid-September, then the Mosby-Dunbar contact would seem to have been in July, during the less busy period when the cotton was "layed by."[8] Yet it is difficult to believe that it took the Dunbar men as long as two months to learn about what the Mosbys had been discussing in the presence of some of Mitchell's. Simply put, the grapevine worked better than that, especially with matters of such import. And we should bear in mind that men being grilled under that kind of pressure were unlikely to retain and be able to verbalize precise recollections of the exact timing of conversations that had taken place during previous months. Excruciating fear and pain can do strange things to memory of past events.

Conner recorded the testimony of only two other Dunbar

7. It is not clear *who* George was denying knew of the plot earlier, since the first word of his sentence cannot be deciphered. That scribble is one of the very few illegible words in Conner's transcript.

8. Most of the evidence suggests such a time frame. As will be seen shortly, September 10 offers an anchoring reference point. Harvey provided the two most definite assertions from which the exact dates of the examinations might be derived, but his two sets of phrases were utterly inconsistent. Talking about the W. M., he said, "The second day it rained. Week before last — Saturday night — 10ᵗʰ Sep — was Tuesday week." These phrases seem to place the Examination at some time during the week of Monday, September 16. Minor's diary (Document H) appears to confirm such timing. But later in the same ordeal Harvey said (if Conner recorded him correctly), "Northern people would whip us at New Orleans about last month." There are several ways of interpreting this remark, including that the examination was taking place in October or that "last of the month" was intended, meaning the end of August. We are left without a completely satisfactory answer, but mid-September remains by far the most probable time.

slaves. Simon and Dick may or may not have been dodging the question when they claimed "No time fixed for the plan" and that "no time" had been "appointed" for killing Mrs. Dunbar. Yet John, the Mitchell driver, said, "Simon was to tell me when and where they would commence," and Dick muddied matters considerably by asserting, "Made plan of ladies two weeks ago."

The single and most definite point of agreement among the rebels concerned the anticipated capture of New Orleans by General Scott on September 10. Alfred and especially Harvey (two of the younger Mosbys) and Frederick Scott were the most informative on this score. If Harvey's words may be believed, that expectation originated with the "white man" in a conversation with Orange, Harvey's father, "at [the] fence." As Harvey explained it, "White man says at 10th of this month Genl Scott wants every second planter to join him and kill white man." Alfred reported that Orange was going to Mrs. King's and then, "Plan: 'we would begin here — [and evidently in response to a question] 10th Sep.[']" Frederick claimed that "O. first told me Gen Scott would attack New Orleans Tuesday" and that "things" would "Begin after the fuss at New Orleans." The date of September 10 (which was in fact a Tuesday) had evidently spread to other plantations, for Doctor Mitchell reported hearing that "the fighting would begin in New Orleans about Sep 10th," and Dr. Grier's Fred claimed Orange had told him that "Gen'l Scott would be in N O about 10 Sept."

Other rebels were reluctant to jump in immediately as soon as "Gen'l Scott would eat his breakfast in New Orleans." The Homochitto teamsters, perhaps out of caution or because they were more familiar with the nearby town, "agreed to join when the enemy reached Natchez." As usual, Wesley seems to have needed some reassurance: he claimed that as he "heard it in May," the Plan would "begin when they, the enemy got to New Orleans, to Natchez." Harry Scott, despite all his busy visiting at the Dunbars, "would agree when they [the northern army] come to this Country up here." Harry was reported as having said that he "would be here 10th sep after the Northerners got here." The effect of this announcement upon his fellows must have been to confirm him as something of a windbag.

With their timing in considerable disarray, the rebels spoke more consistently about their armaments. They made no attempt to gather a cache of weapons, and with one important exception they planned to rely on what they had at hand.

In this respect their planning was notably different from two other American slave conspiracies about which a good deal is known. Outside Richmond in 1800, Gabriel and other rebel leaders had encouraged the stockpiling of weapons, and they planned to attack the arsenal in the city itself after setting fire to other buildings. In Charleston in 1822, the rebels aimed "to push for the different magazines and Guard Houses."[9] But Richmond and Charleston had long been much larger cities than Natchez was in 1861. There seem to have been no official arsenals or guardhouses in Natchez, except possibly the old "powder magazine" that had been built in 1814 for defense against the British and used after that war for militia musters and the ceremonial cannons on the bluff.[10] Further, both Gabriel's and Vesey's plots were led by skilled artisans, and there is little evidence of such skills among the much more rural Second Creek rebels.

Still, they knew the value of firearms. Harry Scott, who was the only man beside the teamsters to talk about going "on to Natchez," said that "guns" were included in the "Plan at Mrs. Dunbars." Doctor Mitchell claimed that he had met "two runaways," one of them with "a gun" and the other with a "gun and pistol." George Dunbar said simply that "runaways had double barreled guns." Both Harry Scott and Dick Dunbar claimed that George and Simon had "guns." Wesley, who stood in some awe of Orange, testified that "O. got two pistols from Bill Chamberlain. Bill has a 5 shooter pistol." In one of only two allusions to a specific method of killing, Wesley said that Orange "would shoot master."[11]

The most programmatic proposal about firearms had to do with Steve Odell. George Dunbar evidently learned about him (perhaps

9. "The Confessions of Mr. Enslows Boy John," in William and Benjamin Hammet Papers, DUL, quoted in Robert S. Starobin, ed., *Denmark Vesey: The Slave Conspiracy of 1822* (Englewood Cliffs, 1970), 65. The statement, with different wording but the same import, is in Lionel Kennedy and Thomas Parker, *An Official Report of the Trials of Sundry Negroes, Charged with an Attempt to Raise an Insurrection in the State of South-Carolina . . .* (Charleston, 1822), rpr. in *The Trial Record of Denmark Vesey,* ed. John Oliver Killens (Boston, 1970), 111.

10. D. Clayton James, *Antebellum Natchez* (Baton Rouge, 1968), 82. The historical record is oddly subdued on this matter.

11. Bill Chamberlain cannot be otherwise identified. Conceivably he was the slave of a recently arrived planter, or a peripatetic free Negro, or even a white man himself, though none of these possibilities seems at all likely.

through Alfred) from Harry Scott, whose fertile mind and facile tongue had advanced a grand proposal: "said they would kill Steve old Odell — gunsmith." Clearly the name was not readily familiar to Conner and at least some of the other planters. Not only had Conner started to get the name wrong and then corrected himself, but the man's peculiar role also had to be inquired into, as indicated by the pause before his disquieting occupation was revealed. Yet some of the planters on the Committee may well have known his name, for Stephen Odell was the most prominent and prosperous gunsmith in Natchez. Forty years old in 1860 and with a budding young family, Odell was prospering at his trade. He owned twenty-seven slaves, fifteen of whom were children. Of the twelve adults, eight were male, an imbalance of gender that was common among "industrial" slaveholders. Most of the adult men must have worked in his sizable shop, some as highly skilled artisans.[12]

As logical as Harry Scott's proposal may seem, it was actually built on rather thin air. At least so far as is known, crucial details remained to be worked out. How were the rebels to get to Natchez and successfully assault an establishment that presumably had functional firearms and a group of slave men whose enthusiasm for the Plan might well be very cool, considering the relatively privileged positions they enjoyed? The Examination Committee did not pursue the matter. None of the other slaves under examination referred to Odell or his guns.

Although many of the rebels no doubt would have welcomed laying their hands on firearms, they seem to have taken little interest in finding cash. What were they to do with it? Orange was the only man to mention money, but none of the others revealed what, if anything, he hoped to buy. They may well have had nothing but guesses on the matter, for talkative as he was, Orange always played his cards closely. Nelson said merely, "O. says he would kill . . . Mrs to get the money."

Unlike slaves on sugar plantations, the Second Creek rebels had no familiarity with, let alone access to, machetes or cane bills. Yet two of their ordinary agricultural implements seemed adequate, as in fact they probably were. Nelson Mosby put the

12. Census, 1860 Free, household 313; Slave, MS p. 8. Six of the men were in their early to mid-twenties, the other two in their sixties but perhaps not superannuated for a skilled craft. The number of Odell's slaves fluctuated yearly, and he may have been selling some of the many children and later buying adults. See Adams Land, 1853, 1857, 1861; Adams Personal, the last year (1862) being his estate. The rebels did not cause his death.

matter with his customary directness: "The plan they would, with axes and hoes, kill Master and Mrs."

Neither those axes nor those hoes were very sharp, but they were very heavy. A single blow could easily disable or kill. Even a slave not routinely accustomed to employing either could have confidence in them as effective weapons. Edmond, John N. Helm's driver, was quoted by Simon as claiming, "If the black folks were turned loose with hoes and axes they would whip the country." Simon may have been simply reiterating this claim when he said (according to Alfred) that "negroes with hoes and axes would do much damage." At the very end of his examination, after being grilled about the ladies, Alfred must have been asked about weapons, for he asserted without elaboration: "Use hoes and axes for arms."

Nothing was said about knives or making pikes. The Second Creek rebels did not have ordinary access to metalworking facilities or the skills to use them, such as had been the case, for example, with the artisans led by Gabriel in Virginia sixty years before. The cotton gins and presses provided few suitable metal parts, and their maintenance and repair was usually handled by white artisans. In the Virginia conspiracy of 1800, the newly widespread cultivation of wheat and other grains had meant that scythes were in common use, and the blade of a scythe could easily be turned into an effective saber if attached to a short wooden handle or wrapped at the broad end in cloth or rope.

The Second Creek rebels showed similar cultural and technological conservatism in connection with fire. Though they were unaware of the fact, fire had been a major weapon of insurrectionary slaves in most of the sugar island revolts. The Angolan slaves who revolted at Stono, South Carolina, in 1739 had burned houses as they swept through the countryside.[13] Now, in Adams County, gins and houses and other structures could be burned (and well may have been, on a quietly selective basis, in the past), but flames simply would not sweep through ripe cotton fields the way they would cane. Perhaps as important, fires would draw immediate and unwanted attention in a locality where plantations neighbored so closely upon one another. Very possibly, as we will see, arson may have been contemplated, but Conner's transcript

13. "An Account of the Negroe Insurrection in South Carolina" [1739], in *The Colonial Records of the State of Georgia*, comp. Allen D. Candler (26 vols.; Atlanta, 1904–16), Vol. XXII, Pt. 2, pp. 231–36, which James Oglethorpe said should be "inserted in some News papers" (*ibid.*, 231).

leaves no record of its being inquired into by the Committee. As for poison—the other means of slave retaliation most frequently and fearfully suspected by the planters—probably it was too erratically individual and too slow. At any rate, there is no evidence that the subject came up at all.

Guns and hoes and axes might serve well enough, but the rebels were counting on the northern army. In one sense, their assessment of the situation was realistic, since eventually the Union army did bring them freedom. Union forces did in fact take New Orleans and then later did arrive in Natchez. Adams County saw no real fighting in the face of the enemy invasion. Natchez itself surrendered without siege or even a shot. Eventually the presence of Union troops resulted in the freedom for which the rebels struggled. Of course, many did not live to see it. If they had, they would have been among the most eager of the thousands of former Mississippi slaves who joined the Union army, donned its uniform, and shouldered its guns and shovels in the name of freedom and defeat of their masters' own rebellion.[14]

No matter how realistic the Second Creek rebels in the end proved to be about the northern army, they were badly informed about the glacial tempo of its progress. Yet their overly hopeful

14. There is little indication that large numbers of slaves in Adams County took the active initiatives for freedom that were common in many parts of Mississippi and the Confederacy as a whole. See Ira Berlin *et al.*, eds., *Freedom: A Documentary History of Emancipation, 1861–1867*, Ser. 1, Vol. I, *The Destruction of Slavery* (Cambridge, England, 1985); Ira Berlin, Joseph P. Reidy, Leslie S. Rowland, eds., *Freedom: A Documentary History of Emancipation, 1861–1867*, Ser. 2, *The Black Military Experience* (Cambridge, Eng., 1982). It is possible, of course, that the suppression of the conspiracy had drained many Adams County slaves of willingness to push for freedom on their own even when Union troops finally arrived, but there is little direct evidence about the matter. Union forces did not immediately take full control outside Natchez and its suburbs. There was Confederate jayhawking at Mrs. Martha W. Dunbar's, ten miles from Natchez, perhaps partly because that "feeble" elderly woman was known as a Unionist. Of course the raiders did not harm her, but they did single out two slaves at Dunbarton, seize them, and shoot them dead. See testimonies of Oliver Jackson, Harrison Lackey, John Duncan, and Nancy Farrar (all formerly her slaves), July 15[?], 1873, in Claim (No. 19810) of Wm. H. McPhecters and Wm. H. Dunbar, executors of Martha W. Dunbar, Settled Case Files, 1871–83—Mississippi, Adams County, Records of the Southern Claims Commission, Records of the General Accounting Office, RG 217, National Archives.

misassessments were similar to those of a great many other Americans who had far better access to information about the course of the war. Lincoln's first call for troops had been for ninety-day militiamen; and in the Confederate states mobilization was constitutionally fragmented and nowhere geared for a prolonged conflict. The Second Creek rebels were no more optimistic and confused than most people on both sides of the great sectional conflict during those expectant early months. Yet it was clear to them who the "enemy" was, and neither they nor white Mississippians had to deal with the wavering of conflicting loyalties that marked the Border and partially Appalachian states.

Union forces did not in fact occupy New Orleans until May 1, 1862. Federal gunboats accepted the quiet surrender of Natchez on May 13, but almost immediately abandoned it as not worth holding. Federal troops permanently occupied on July 13, 1863. General Scott never got to eat his breakfast in New Orleans. An able but aging soldier whose career went back to the War of 1812, Winfield Scott was the highest-ranking Union officer until his resignation in November, 1861. At Lincoln's request he remained in Washington, but illness, age, and a pushy General George McClellan made even paperwork difficult. It was General Benjamin F. Butler who commanded the Union expedition that captured the largest city in all the seceded states.

Of course, in 1861 the Second Creek rebels had no way of knowing that General Butler would be the one to accomplish this crucial victory.[15] Frederick Scott had at least learned of his name (which came out as "Buttons" in the record of Harvey's testimony). Butler must have been talked about by the planters, for his name appeared early and very commonly in newspaper reports, first as the Massachusetts commander of a successful attempt to get northeastern regiments safely through Maryland by railway, then as nearly losing his regiment in an obscure engagement in western Virginia, and then again as promulgator of the order at Fort Monroe that captured slaves would be treated as "contraband of war."[16] The name of General Winfield Scott was also very much in the news as the ranking general of the United States Army.

15. They would not have been surprised by the wave of slave unrest in the New Orleans area after its occupation. See William F. Messner, "Black Violence and White Response: Louisiana, 1862," *JSH*, XLI (1975), 19–38.

16. The *Dictionary of American Biography, s.v.* "Butler," notes that "Butler was, until Grant took control, as much a news item as any man except Lincoln." The episode about the railway was sarcastically reported in the Natchez *Daily Courier*, May 28, 1861, the editor making very plain the state Butler represented.

Similarly, it is no surprise that the rebel slaves had heard of Lincoln. The new president had been a common topic of conversation throughout the nation ever since his Republican nomination for that office in May of 1860. His name was known to a great many slaves in the South long before September, 1862, when he threatened to draw up an executive order emancipating all slaves in areas controlled by what he called "the Rebellion." Slaves in Jefferson County and Tensas Parish had been talking about him in May of 1861, just after the outbreak of the war. Unfortunately, there is no way of telling whether any of these slaves ever pondered the irony of Lincoln's being a "Black Republican," as he was incessantly called in the southern press.

But there was no question about Lincoln's being an "enemy" of the planters. According to Alfred, "Orange told Mr Lincoln was coming down here." This welcome news had surfaced early on in the planning: Orange had "understood it from" Henry Cooper and "told" the other men "about the house." Alfred then got into conversation with Harry Scott which (as recorded) may be taken in either of two ways: "Says I, 'Harry, let us collect a company and whip old Lincoln out.'" Alfred may have intended to mean that they should clear the way for Lincoln and his troops. Alternatively, he may have been disguising his commitment to the Plan and feeling out Harry's disposition, for his next words were "Harry never told me he would join. O. told me, Harry Sc would join." Young Wesley Mosby was much more direct about the matter—and as usual more passive—when he quoted himself as saying, "Lincoln would set us free."

Only one of the rebels mentioned "abolitionists" at the trials. Nelson used that loaded term during the early part of his examination, immediately after he claimed to have heard about the war when "young missus" asked for protection. Edward and John Mitchell, he said, "would join to fight abolitionists." If Conner's transcription was accurate (and so far as we know, he had just begun writing), Nelson at that point thought that abolitionists were people to be fought—an impression he might very easily have gained from the young missus. But after answering queries about names of the plotters, he said, "O. 1st speaker," and then in response to questioning about what Orange had said, "Plan (when Abolitionists come. O. would join them." If anyone had such matters straight, it was Orange, and Nelson rapidly came round to talk about killing Mr. and Mrs. Mosby and ravishing the ladies. He himself would take Miss Mary. None of the rebels accused him of being on the wrong side about Lincoln.

The Second Creek conspirators may have discussed two other sources of possible outside assistance. Harvey insisted that the white man at the fence had offered very definite suggestions concerning the second planters of the neighborhood. In presenting this wildly unrealistic and dangerous fantasy to Orange and Wesley, the white man clothed it with the authority of the forthcoming conqueror of New Orleans: "White man says at 10th of this month Genl Scott wants every second planter to join him and kill white man." The W. M. may well have suddenly realized that this was not likely to be received as a credible prospect, for according to the next sentence in Harvey's testimony, he then "asked Daddy who was nearest neighbor." Perhaps he was simply trying to get the slaves into trouble, or (much less likely) to test their loyalties, for he went on to pick on the far more vulnerable Wesley by asking "how master treated him"—a question that obviously had only one safe answer, if only Wesley could figure out which one, which was sometimes not easy when talking with white men.

The slaves knew better than to accept the W. M.'s word about the second planters. They could almost instinctively predict the loyalties of that sort of white men at a time of crisis. There is no evidence at all that they discussed the W. M.'s second-planter proposal seriously or even, for that matter, with suspicion or contempt. They let it pass, for what it was worth.

Apparently some of the rebels did discuss the matter of the blockade boats, which represented an unrealistic possibility but not an absurd one. None of the rebels had ever seen one (unless by freak chance from the bluff at Natchez), but neither had most of the planters. By May of 1861, Union ships were beginning to operate in the Gulf, and "blockading" became a topic of wartime conversations.[17] River gunboats deployed from Cairo, Illinois, were ascending the Ohio, the Tennessee, and the Cumberland, and patrolling for some miles down the Mississippi. They were sometimes referred to in the newspapers as "blockade boats," since these specially built armored craft were part of the overall Federal strategy for seizing control of the great river. Few if any Second Creek slaves ever saw the river south of Natchez, and the first and only armed confrontation at the town finally came in a comic-opera battle in September, 1862, when a boat-party from the *Essex* landed in search of ice and was fired upon; the gunboat responded by bombarding Under-the-Hill and the town proper.[18]

17. Natchez *Daily Courier,* May 9, 10, 14, 16, June 1, 1861.
18. One sailor and a little girl were killed. *Official Records of the Union and Confederate Navies in the War of the Rebellion* (30 vols.; Washington, D.C., 1894–

Harvey's reference to "Blockhead boats" is not altogether clear, though the phrase so creatively reproduced by Conner may well have come from the W. M.: it was preceded in Harvey's testimony by his renewed reporting of what the white man had said about General Scott's breakfast in New Orleans and was immediately followed by "White man spoke 'Second planters' to help." Other rebels had been talking about gunboats. Dr. Grier's Fred said it was Orange who told him that General Scott would "Eat his breakfast" in New Orleans but that he "did not know when he would dine. Ships are not satisfactory."

The rebels spoke much more frequently about the northern army, and in doing so showed sober realism. They fully and eagerly expected that the northerners would defeat the South. Only one slave seemed to doubt the outcome. If Harvey's testimony was recorded accurately, Louis, the Metcalfe driver, "says Southerners whipping North." In response, Harvey resorted to the authority of what the white man had said (as reported by Nelson) about the forthcoming success of General Scott in New Orleans.

What is especially striking about so many of the references to northerners is that the rebels continued to use the language of their owners in referring to them as "the enemy." Orange apparently talked about "when the enemy took New Orleans." Wesley said things would "begin when they, the enemy got to New Orleans, to Natchez." The language was not merely an interpolation by Conner. "Us" could mean, for the rebels, the side on which their masters were fighting. As Harvey put it, "Talked to all the negroes on the place — Northern people would whip us at New Orleans."

As so often happens, language had been inappropriately appropriated. Insofar as they were southerners—which was deeply so—the rebels identified the outsiders in the same terms used by their masters. In doing so, they became "us" with the slaveowners they were proposing to slaughter. They were "us" in the larger rebellion against the northern "enemy" even while they were "us" among themselves and would "join" together against "all the white people" closer to home. A powerful sense of place, and of community and commonality under fire, continued to override at

1922), Ser. 1, Vol. XIX, p. 181; Natchez [Daily] Courier, September 2, 3, 4, 6, 9, 10, November 1, 1862; Mary Conway Shields Dunbar, My Mother Used to Say: A Natchez Belle of the Sixties, ed. Elizabeth Dunbar Murray (Boston, 1959), 140–51; John S. Coussons, "The Federal Occupation of Natchez, Mississippi, 1863–65" (M.A. thesis, Louisiana State University, 1958), 15–16.

the verbal level the actual loyalties of race and class. A people of the spoken word, these men had grown habituated to utilizing their masters' terminology, primarily because it was safer to accustom oneself to using the language their oppressors wanted to hear. Such a habit ran deep and could not be easily altered. The rebels lost no clarity by clinging to the old forms. Indeed they may have gained it.

A somewhat different verbal inversion came to light in the rebels' common use of the word *whip*. It conveyed exactly what the rebels hoped and trusted would be the fate of the "Southerners." The whip embodied and summarized the pain and degradation of their own suffering. The term could be turned around. Harvey used it himself ("Northern people would whip us") and quoted Louis as using it. Given the rebels' situations before the Examination Committee, the word reeked of utter defeat and ultimate finality. As George said after talking about taking the ladies and killing Mr. Marshall and Mrs. Dunbar, "No time fixed. When Northerners whip South." That whipping would be a proper one, fully justified and long overdue. Its finality reverberated in Orange's promise that "whipping colored people would stop."[19]

When the rebels would "join [the] northern army," as Harvey said repeatedly, they did not have in mind any possibility of actual enlistment. Rather, they thought in terms of linking forces, of a merger in the cause of freedom. Joining would be on a basis of equality. As one listens to the rebels, there is no major theme of rescue by a superior force.[20] They would link up with the northerners in a common cause.

At the same time, however, the rebels were acutely aware of the martial character of their potential allies. They were acquainted

19. Orange's epitomization of the end of slavery was echoed by several former slaves from Mississippi. Katie Rowe told her interviewer in 1937 some of the chilling details about the whipping on her plantation in Arkansas—about the "cat-o-nine tails" and "den bust de blisters wid a wide strap of leather fastened to a stick handle"—and then added: "Later on in de War de Yankees come in all around us and camp, and de overseer git sweet as honey in de comb! Nobody git a whipping all de time de Yankees dar!" Rawick, *American Slave,* Vol. VII (Okla. and Miss. Narrs.), Pt. 1, pp. 280–81.

20. The single clear exception was Wesley's expectation that the northerners would free them, referred to above.

with military ranks and the principle of hierarchy they exempli-
fied. Some of them were drawn to military terms because such
rankings had long been dangled before them by their masters.
They also had other choices. They intermingled military ranks
with civilian ones, and in doing so they may at times seem merely
confused. Yet we need to recall that in the South during the war,
the customary canons of ranking and authority among governors,
generals, and presidents were in a state of contentious confusion
and flux in the larger society.

The rebels felt need for graded leadership of their own, and
their examiners expected that they would have worked out such
arrangements. Unsurprisingly, there are signs that some of the
rebels vied for positions of rank and precedence. They did so without much pondering about the necessity for organization. Rather,
they operated on the basis of varying assessments of personal prestige, power, and self-worth. In this respect they acted as men usually do when embarked on a hazardous venture requiring cooper-
ation among individuals possessed of diverse temperaments and
abilities. They worked things out among themselves in ways that
reveal a good deal about their own personalities and their roles as
slaves in a world that constrained their thoughts and actions at
every turn.

In order to get at their mutual relationships, it is necessary to
plunge again into the record of the examinations. So far as can be
discovered from Conner's extant transcript, only two groups of
slaves worked out reasonably consistent orders of command (or at
least of rank). These, of course, were the Mosbys and the Dunbars,
the two larger groups about which most is known. It seems unlikely that these two clusters of rebels were the only ones to organize their own pattern of leadership. Much more probably, the apparent lack of rank ordering in other groups was owing to the
sequential proceedings of the Examination Committee and the
incompleteness of Conner's record, in combination with the refusal or inability on the part of some slaves to answer questions
about the leadership. The Committee can scarcely have been interested in such information in the case of some slaves and not
others.

After listening to Nelson Mosby, George and Simon Dunbar,
Dick Henderson, and Harry Scott, the Committee summoned
three of the Mitchell slaves, John the driver, Dennis, and Doctor.
None of these three talked at length, though they furnished some
firm information especially as to names. Then, during the partial

hiatus in Conner's transcript caused by his inattention or absence, the Committee examined two more Mitchell slaves, Harry Lyle and Little John, as well as Dr. Grier's Fred, Henderson's Adam, and perhaps Adam's father, Isaac Giddings. They then tried the two Surget slaves, Obey and Billy, who turned out to be rock-silent. With Conner once again assiduously taking notes, they interrogated Dick Dunbar and Orange's voluble son, Harvey Mosby. At that point, before turning to Alfred Mosby, the committee members paused to consult among themselves and then "sent for" fourteen more slaves—Harry Scott, Louis, five belonging to Mrs. Dunbar, two of Mr. Henderson's, and five of Mr. Mitchell's. The names of several of the Henderson and Mitchell slaves "sent for" suggest that Conner's hiatus may have been caused by recalcitrant answers or perhaps diminished Committee attendance, for Harry Lyle Mitchell had said "00," John (Little) had said "Orange told him on the Creek, that—00—," Adam Henderson had said "Orange told him what am[oun]ts to nothing," and Ike Giddings Henderson's words, if any, had not been recorded at all.[21]

The remainder of Conner's record includes examinations of only three of these fourteen slaves. Unless we assume that the Committee did not bother to follow through or that those men had already been hanged, we are left with the strong likelihood that Conner stopped keeping his record well before all the individual examinations were completed. According to his transcript, neither the Mosby nor the Dunbar men talked in much detail about the Mitchells, so we have no knowledge at all about plans for leadership among the Mitchell rebels. If they had made such plans, as seems probable, we cannot discover what they were.

If the Mitchell men were depending for leadership solely on the Mosbys and/or Dunbars, Conner did not record either John, Dennis, or Doctor as saying so. John and Dennis spoke about the "gather[ing]," "rais[ing]," and "collect[ing]" of "a company"— with the latter term perhaps having at least paramilitary connotations. Dennis said Alfred Mosby was "to be a soldier." Doctor mentioned "gun[s]" and "fighting," but without mentioning ranks or leadership of any sort.

All the rebels who either alluded to or discussed the matter of ranking were Mosbys, Dunbars, and the two Scotts. Of these, Frederick and Harry Scott had the least to say on the subject. Hav-

21. Among the Mitchell slaves sent for was "John," without modification. It seems more probable that Conner would have neglected to add the "Little" (who was examined during the hiatus) than the "Driver" (who had testified earlier).

ing referred to "5 at Mosby's" and "4 at Mrs Dunbars," Frederick went on to reiterate his liking for Miss Julia Dunbar. With his mind still very much on her, Frederick continued in terms that suggest that the matter of the ladies was shaping his perceptions of who among the rebels was taking the lead. He quoted George Dunbar's reassuring "Would be plenty sweethearts," and then immediately asserted flatly, "George head." As for Harry Scott, his fertile enthusiasm led him to spell out military ranks in great detail, so far as the Mosbys and Dunbars were concerned. In order to follow his labyrinthine claims, however, we need first to turn to the plans and perceptions of those two groups of men.

When ranking themselves in military terms, conspirators of any kind rarely opt for lower echelons. They usually emerge top-heavy with brass and marvelously deficient in foot soldiers. The Mosby and Dunbar men proved unexceptional in this respect. At the same time, however, they included five nonmilitary terms in their catalog of rankings—two of them governmental, two others closer to their immediate experiences, and the fifth (and most puzzling) occupational. Clearly they saw nothing anomalous about merging civilian offices with military ranks. As for the latter, they referred to some but not all the ranks of military officers, and they did not employ any of the subrefinements of the principal names—a general was a general without further discrimination. They included no majors and no colonels. Not surprisingly, they employed no naval ranks at all. Altogether, the combined axis of Mosby, Dunbar, and Scott rebels employed eight different titles, which included, in no particular order: captain, boss, president, general, governor, lieutenant, head, and printer. The Mosbys and Harry Scott were especially devoted to such titles, whereas the Dunbar rebels seem to have been largely content with simple untitled rank orders.

Only three of the Dunbar slaves testified. The closest Simon came to mentioning leadership was his statement that "Harry Scott. said, he and Orange was to get the company up." During his first examination George also assigned leading roles to Harry Scott and Orange, but he added (apparently on Alfred Mosby's authority) that "his father [Harry Scott] General." Yet he provided no precise rankings even among the Dunbar rebels.

George's brother Dick was the only Dunbar slave to go into any detail, and he had worked out in his own mind a very clear order of authority among five of the Dunbar men. He used only two titles, and gave himself both. His opening words were "I am Boss."

Later in his very brief testimony, he said, "I Captain." He *twice* gave the following rankings: after himself, George was "2nd," Simon "3rd," Paul "4ᵗʰ," and Peter (with obvious and considerable conviction) "hindmost." He made no mention of the three other Dunbar slaves whose names were brought up by someone else— Nathan, Albert, and Harry Old.

Perhaps the Committee thought George was a vulnerable target. Certainly they put him under terrible pressure when they examined him again, for during this second ordeal he ranked the Dunbar conspirators specifically but with great inconsistency among his several rankings. He gave names in such varying sequences that even members of the Committee must have partially realized that he had been driven past making sense. In response to queries about the ladies, he listed in order himself, Paul, Simon, Albert (for the first time), and Peter, as well as the names of the young women each would claim. Then, when asked about plans for killing, he was still able to maintain some consistency by naming himself, Paul, Simon, Albert, and Dick. After answering a question about timing by implicating Alfred Mosby, he was pushed to be more specific about rank order. His response: "Paul boss, Simon 2nd, George [himself] 3rd, Albert 4th." Then he must have been asked about his brother, for he said "Dick took Miss Julia," a young woman whom he had previously said would be taken by Albert. The confusion continued, with the questions and his answers bouncing from one subject to another; among them was his devastating assertion, "Simon 1ˢᵗ man to talk of ravishing." In all his anguished attempts to respond, George found only one firm and consistent anchor: for whatever reason, his nephew Peter, whom his own brother had called "hindmost," was in his own mind last.

Under examination much earlier in the proceedings, Harry Scott presented a very different picture of the accepted order of leadership. Having received a dime from Dick for the "dispatch," Harry accorded Dick no leading role at all. He began his testimony by saying "Orange head." Alfred (his own son) was next, with the title "Captⁿ," then himself as "Gen[eral]," and finally Wesley as "Lieut." So much for the Mosby men, except that Harry failed to mention either Nelson or Harvey. Later, Harry Scott was asked about the other large group, and he responded, "Plan at Mrs. Dunbars. They would have Captains and guns. Orange captain." The alteration in Orange's title in Harry's testimony is less striking than the fact that Orange *Mosby* was being reported as "captain" of the enterprise at the Dunbars. But Harry Scott went on to rank the planners at the Dunbar place: "Simon head man. Peter next. Paul then." Thus he found Paul farther down the ladder than Dick had, and Peter in a discernibly better position than hindmost. Harry Scott must have had his own reasons for omitting the two brothers, George and Dick. If indeed those two were in positions of leverage at the Dunbars, they may have previously miffed him by not catering to his inflated sense of his own dignity and importance.

Without Orange in their grasp, the Committee examined the other Mosby men. All four gave information at considerable length. Alfred's description of ranking was creative almost to the point of contradiction. He placed Orange both first, as "Govenor," and last, as "Captain," without differentiating between the two roles. Very possibly some member of the Committee inquired what he meant by the rank of "Govenor" and he gave "Captain" as a more acceptable name. Quite clearly he was not attempting to establish two hierarchies of titles, one civilian and the other military, for neither he nor any of the other rebels showed signs of wanting to make such a distinction. At different times during his examination Alfred gave two rankings, one without titles, but he very clearly had a specific and consistent order of precedence in mind. Following Orange in "1st" position came Nelson, who was "2nd" as "President"; then Alfred himself (probably as "Gen Scott"); Wesley as "printer"; and Harvey as "Lieut."[22] Alfred admitted that he, as well as Orange, had talked with Frederick and Harry Scott, which conversation may explain why Harry's testimony began with "Orange head. Captn Alfred." Indeed, Alfred's ranking was identical to Harry's, except for the latter's inexplicable omission of Nelson and much less surprising failure to list Harvey at the end.[23] Alfred's naming himself as General Scott

22. The second of Alfred's two lists can be read another, but less likely, way. His phrase "I, Gen Scott" might be taken to mean two people, himself and his father, Harry Scott, who did in fact claim the title of general. This would have been a very backhanded way of indicating filial obeisance, for Alfred placed himself before "Gen Scott."Such a reading would also be inconsistent with Alfred's earlier list given during the same examination and making no mention of a general or Harry Scott.

23. The most probable reason for the omission of Harvey was Conner's haste at the beginning of Harry's examination and his consequent failure to record "Harvey Lieut., Wesley Printer." With Harvey's name and Wesley's rank dropped, Wesley comes out incorrectly as a "Lieutenant." All the other testimonies refer to him as "Printer" and to Harvey as the lieutenant.

must have come easily, since as the son of Harry Scott he remained insistent that his own last name was Scott. In addition,
the example of the Federal "General Scott" who was scheduled to
take New Orleans may have provided an attractive model for the
title.

Harvey, another of the three younger Mosby rebels, showed
considerable deference toward his father and Nelson, as well as
(much more surprisingly) toward young Wesley. The testimony of
this "son of Orange" was filled with references to what his father
said and did, and at one point he asserted flatly, "Orange spokesman." Yet he also talked about "Nelson and Daddy," "Nelson and
Wesley," and "Wesley and Daddy," and said that "Orange told Wesley and Nelson." Of these three, his father and Nelson, as the two
oldest Mosby rebels, seemed to Harvey the most weighty, as became clear when he claimed at one point in his long ordeal, "First
speakers Orange and Nelson." Yet when Harvey came to produce
an actual ranking of the Mosby men, he gave the following: "Nelson Govenor. Capt Orange. Wesley printer. Lieut Harvey," the latter being himself. Then, by way of expanding the list, "Harry
Scott would join." What is striking here is the omission of Alfred.
Yet Alfred's absence from this listing may have been merely a
lapse in transcription on Conner's part, since Harvey's rankings
followed immediately his remarks about what Alfred had reported
concerning Simon, and about hoes and axes. Given the awful circumstances of the examinations, it is perhaps a wonder that the
historical record has as much logic and consistency as it does.

Nelson Mosby's order of ranking was somewhat similar but not
the same. He named himself first, as "Govenor"; then "O. Captain. Harvey Lieut. Alfred Genl Scott — Wesley Printer." Thus
Nelson's ranking of the top two Mosby rebels was the reverse of
Alfred's but the same as Harvey's, the latter having placed his own
father second after Nelson. According to Nelson, Harvey belonged
before Alfred, not after as the latter claimed. But the striking difference in Nelson's list concerned Wesley, whom he placed last.
Both Harvey and Alfred placed Wesley higher on their lists. Today,
one can think of several possible reasons why Nelson chose to
rank his own son behind everyone else. He was not the first or last
father to treat his son this way.

Wesley's testimony about leaders was succinct, incomplete,
and sui generis. He opened with "Wesley Printer — to go behind,"
thus confirming his father's judgment of his worth. He had "heard
it in May. O. 1st speaker, Nelson 2nd." As far as ranks and leaders

were concerned, this was as far as he got. His relationship with the other two Mosby rebels may be accurately gauged from his assertion that "Harvey and Alfred were all hot for the plan." He may have been given the title "printer" as a way of shoring up his confidence, for the rebels had neither access to printing presses nor sufficient literacy as a group to think in terms of printed communications. There is no evidence to suggest that Wesley or any of the other Mosby men knew how to read, though it is possible that they had picked up the skill from some of their owner's pupils or over at the Dunbars'. It is quite clear, though, that the role of printer carried a certain prestige; possibly the reference was to the hand-lettering that no doubt the Mosby slaves knew about, if not how to do.

Despite some disagreement among the rebels on the Mosby place, it was clear that Orange and Nelson were to head up the business there. And even though they disagreed with one another about the exact order of ranks, the Mosby men had firmly in mind the titles they were committed to. They were inconsistent only with president and governor, the two positions of civilian authority. They seem to have been more easily familiar with military names. Of greater significance, but very hard to weigh, these slaves on a relatively small plantation did not use the terms *boss* and *head*—an omission possibly of no particular meaning but perhaps a reflection of the more vaporous lines and exercise of authority that tended to prevail on smaller places. Such an atmosphere may have been either accentuated or dissipated by the fact that this particular place was owned by a man who had gone into planting by way of teaching school and at least at times was not fully in control of himself.

Unless possibly they had already caught and hanged him, the Examination Committee must have itched to lay hands on Orange. Surely they would have examined him most exactly and strenuously. It is hard to believe that Conner would not have made every effort to include Orange's testimony in his expanding record, and harder still to imagine him (or his heirs) later expunging such crucial and interesting evidence.

Even a casual perusal of Conner's record suggests Orange's prominence in the entire business at Second Creek.[24] On first

24. The origins of Orange's rare but not unique name remain obscure, though orange trees had grown in the county at least earlier in the century; see "Natchez in 1820," in John James Audubon, *Delineations of American Scenery and Charac-*

reading it is tempting to see him as the leader and perhaps even originator of the Plan. Nelson's opening testimony suggests as much. Orange and Harvey (whom we later learn is his son) have been talking about the Plan on the creek with the other Mosbys and the Mitchell boys. Orange and Harvey have been plotting over at the Dunbar and Henderson places. Orange was the "1st speaker" and the "worst man." He was "Captain," a man who could make the vivid promise, "We will be done whipping before long."

As the story in Conner's transcript unfolds, Orange appears in one exploit after another. It becomes evident that he has run away more than once, has talked also with the Scotts and with at least one of the Homochitto teamsters, consorts with other runaways and with a fortune-teller, travels as far as the village of Pine Ridge and to the Swamp, talks with strange white visitors, knows about the murder of the Dutchman, about abolitionists, about Mr. Lincoln, and about General Scott capturing and then dining in New Orleans, has obtained pistols, and has *said* that he "would show Cotton planters" and "was going to have the country." Several rebels spoke of him as "head man."

Yet persistent reading of the record makes clear that Orange was far from being *the* leader of the Second Creek Plan. Most references to his activities and his plans came from other Mosby slaves. Alfred was surely correct in saying that Orange "got all of us men on the place to join," and Orange did indeed talk with many others. But—and here Alfred's words are crucial—Orange had learned about Lincoln "coming down here" from one of the teamsters, Henry Cooper. Having "understood it from Cooper's man," "O. would join." Only then did he persuade "all of us." Indeed, the extant testimony about Orange is laden with what he "said" or what he "told." Given the circumstances of the examinations, some of this reporting was an inevitable grammatical method of indicating future hope as opposed to certainty. Orange

---

ter, intro. Francis Hobart Herrick (1926; rpr. [New York], 1970), 334. A more likely explanation would be that his father or grandfather was a redheaded white man and that he was nicknamed for his hair and/or complexion. An 1855 slave list for a plantation near Jackson included another "Orange"; but a Mr. Orange Clarke of Port Gibson was clearly white. See Thomas E. Helm Plantation Record Book, January 1, 1855, in MDAH; Orange Clarke to Mess. Ballard Frank Cirhea[?], October 6, 1835, in Slavery Documents, UTA.

was not the only rebel to be recorded in the subjunctive mood; the entire record is filled with statements about what so-and-so (including Orange and even the northerners and General Scott) *would* do.

Yet not all the examination statements about future events were wrapped in the subjunctive mode. In this connection it is especially instructive to listen to the more forceful grammar of the white man and the wary teamsters. Harvey's long testimony was filled with *would*'s, but it also included the more directly toned "White man spoke 'Second planters' to help," and the teamsters "agreed to join when the enemy reached Natchez." *Would* could have been used in either of these assertive sentences, but was not. The fact that more active language was chosen is not, of course, a necessary reflection of a different stance on the part of the white man or the teamsters. Rather, it points to the way in which Harvey, as a plantation hand, perceived their intentions and their power to carry them out.

Clearly Orange possessed qualities of leadership, but in net effect he seems more a talker and active protagonist than a strategist or even tactician. His words obviously had great weight on his homeplace, and his energy and daring carried his influence far afield, but he seems something of a gadabout. Certainly he lacked the charisma that could kindle a large and loyal following. He was no Nat Turner, nor should we ask him to be. We know his volubility may have triggered the exposure and hence the ruin of the Plan. After all, it was Orange who talked about it in front of an overseer's son. It was Orange who "said the whipping business would stop" and caused "Mas Benny" to ask why.

Thus the events at Second Creek did not add up to being the Orange Conspiracy. If we look solely at the question of leadership, the Plan looks rather like a fragmented collection of separate plots that centered (so far as we know) on the Mosby and the Dunbar places, with two rebels at the Scotts' scurrying back and forth between. Yet we are dealing with fragmentary evidence. We can earnestly yearn that Conner had recorded all the examinations. Perhaps the planning *was* fragmented, and we may speculate that the apparent absence of commanding leadership prevented the coalescing necessary for unified action. We know that the slaves of at least nine Second Creek planters were directly implicated and another three planters and a gunsmith specifically targeted as victims. A group of slave teamsters and a nearby fortune-teller knew about it, and an itinerant white man (and a companion or two) showed great interest. The prospect of outside help from northerners was not illusory.

We can see parts of the web of interpersonal relationships that might have led to more concerted planning, but we should bear in mind that we cannot see it whole. We can hear some sounds, and listen to them as carefully as we can, while knowing there were many more that are lost forever. Often it is the weakest parts of a web that are hardest to discern, but not always.

CHAPTER 12

THE VOICES OF REPRISE

Most or all of the hangings in Second Creek valley took place at Cherry Grove and close by at Brighton Woods. One of the county's wealthiest planters, William J. Minor, attended the examinations at Surget's Cherry Grove. He had been at one of his Louisiana sugar plantations or in New Orleans on business but returned on Sunday, the twenty-second of September, having received a tele-graphed "dispatch" from his son John informing him that " 'there was trouble among the negroes and I had best come up.' " He ar-rived back home at midnight on Sunday and "found my family all well." It was that same Sunday that Benjamin Wailes, some dis-tance away at his plantation near the village of Washington, re-corded his concern about vengeful "severity" possibly spreading from Second Creek to his own neighborhood. On Monday, Minor rode down to Second Creek, where he found the proceedings al-ready under way at Cherry Grove. Whether this was the first day of the examinations at that plantation is unclear, but it seems probable that Conner had already written his transcript, or much of it, either there or at another place. Two days later, Wednesday, ten "Negro men" were "hung" at Cherry Grove "by order of the Committee." They included "7 of Capt. Jacob Surget's, 2 of Mr. Mosby's and 1 of Mrs. Mary Dunbar's."[1]

1. William J. Minor Plantation Diary, September 23, 25, 1861, in William J. Minor and Family Papers, LSU, Document H. Many of the quotations in the next few pages are from this source. Margaret Fisher Dalrymple kindly transcribed these selections from the original manuscript. Details about Minor are in J. Carlyle Sit-terson, "The William J. Minor Plantations: A Study in Ante-Bellum Absentee Ownership," *JSH*, IX (1943), 59–74, but the article focuses almost entirely on his sugar plantations. See also Morton Rothstein, "Resistance, Flight, and Adjust-ment: Some Natchez Elite Planters During and After the Civil War" (Working Pa-per Series No. 28, Agricultural History Center, University of California, Davis, 1985, Mimeographed), 8–9; and Morton Rothstein, "The Changing Social Net-works and Investment Behavior of a Slaveholding Elite in the Ante Bellum South: Some Natchez 'Nabobs,' 1800–1860," in *Entrepreneurs in Cultural Context*, ed. Sidney M. Greenfield, Arnold Strickon, and Robert T. Aubey (Albuquerque, 1979), 65–88, which has information on other families as well. References to Wailes in this chapter are from Wailes Diary, Document F.

We may guess with some confidence that the seven Surgets included Obey and Billy—unless perhaps their steadfast silence had resulted in their being executed earlier. Surely it did not save their lives. Indeed, they may have died under the lash. Thanks to Minor's diary we know that the Dunbar slave belonged to the younger of the two Mrs. Dunbars, but there is no telling which one he was. We may also surmise that the two Mosbys hanged that Wednesday were either the first or the last of two pairs to die, since Nelson, Wesley, Alfred, and Harvey had all been thoroughly implicated. Orange may possibly have been dead before Minor arrived, but it is much more likely that he was still at large. Yet in all probability Orange was finally taken up: three weeks later a white woman wrote from near Woodville (a long day's ride south of Second Creek) that "the head one is not yet executed[.] They still hope to make him tell."[2]

William Minor wrote nothing in his diary about the Committee making suspected slaves confess, presumably because that grim procedure was what "examining" was all about and needed no elaboration. He may well have been silent on the matter, even in the privacy of his diary, because he found it distasteful or even abhorrent. William J. Minor did not use his diary to vent strong feelings. That Tuesday he remained at Concord, his homeplace on the outskirts of Natchez, and carefully recorded his field hands' cutting of hay in the front yard and the flourishing state of his crop of Quitman peas. This nearly urban home was not the source of his wealth. He owned several productive sugar plantations farther south, in Louisiana, and apparently nothing was amiss among his slaves there or at Concord. The next day, with the weather still cool and dry, he again rode down to Cherry Grove and found the Committee "still engaged in examining witness."

Conner must not have been there, or perhaps he had simply grown tired of writing everything down. Clearly Wednesday's examining was turning up the same sort of evidence he had already recorded. Minor, a conservative man of cool and steady judgment, thought the evidence about the plot was as persuasive as it had been on Monday. On that first day of attending, his summary of what he heard from the rebels comported for the most part with what Conner had written down, though he gave no indication of having talked with Conner. "I came to the conclusion," Minor

<hr />

2. S[ophia] H. Hunt to Jennie [Hughes], October 15, 1861, in Hughes Family papers, UNC, Document I.

wrote, "that some of the negroes who have been arrested had it in view to murder their master and violate their mistressess—their action seems however to be dependent on the 'whipping' of the Southern people by the people of the North, when they thought, they would be made free, then they were to rise and kill their masters etc."

With these words, Minor might as well have been writing a précis of Conner's record, though clearly he had not seen it. Very quietly, William Minor underscored the rebels' intentions about the planting whites: by placing "master" in the singular and "mistresses" in the plural, he accurately reflected assumptions about social roles that were shared by whites and blacks alike. The bracketing of a single owner and many ladies was only in part a reflection of the fact that so many younger white men had gone off to the war. The differentiation between the sexes also reflected assumptions about male ownership and female vulnerability that prevailed in the society as a whole. Minor also placed the word *whipping* in quotation marks when the term had to do with the sectional struggle among white men. The very essence of whipping had for southern slaveholders a dual meaning, but in both cases it meant violence.

Minor's summary of Monday's proceedings added two dimensions that had been lacking when Conner took down his record. Minor concluded his notation, "The leaders were to take possession of the big house and make the rest of the Negroes work for them, the leaders." Very possibly some slave under examination had made such claims. Yet Minor's words have something of the ring of formula, of a perception shaped by his own status as an enormously wealthy planting baron. He had opposed secession largely because he knew he had so much to lose. In seizure of the "big house" he saw insurrection as displacement of himself and his kind, and in the "rest of the Negroes work[ing] for . . . the leaders" he smelled usurpation of proper authority. For him, there was something ultimate about such notions that required no further comment, for he shifted immediately to end that day's entry in his farmer's mode: "Very cool for the season. — rain."

Wednesday's proceedings brought out some old information and some that was startlingly new. Minor was almost judicial when introducing his summation in his diary: from the continuing examinations, he wrote, "It was, I thought, clearly proved that there was a plot" aimed at murdering masters and "tak[ing] possession" of mistresses and property. In Minor's opinion, "They had no definite idea how this was to be done," and he might easily have added "or when." Conner had already recorded what he had heard about the planned methods of the rebels. Now Minor summarized these means by noting, "Some talked of killing with such weapons as they could collect axes hoes and guns." Yet apparently some rebels had gone further, for Minor went on to note: "Others thought of firing the houses at night and burning the sleepers to death before they could get out." On one point, though, the arrested rebels were agreed: "All had the idea in their heads that Capt. Lincoln was to set them free."

As for this central expectation, Minor's wording was not simply a snide swipe at Negro ignorance. The president of the United States was still repeatedly taking the public position that the federal government had no power to touch slavery in the states where it already existed. It is only in retrospect that the ironies of this statement emerge. Lincoln eventually did "free the slaves," even though his Emancipation Proclamation, which became "effective" January 1, 1863, at first actually freed no one at all because it applied to slaves only in areas under Confederate control. Yet Lincoln was later hailed as a deliverer by the freedmen, and of course he became known as the Great Emancipator in abolitionist tradition. And lest we smile condescendingly at the rebels' calling him "Captain," we might recall the moving poem written by Walt Whitman upon Lincoln's death:"O Captain! my Captain! our fearful trip is done."[3]

Whatever the importance of this imagery, Minor's diary noted a dimension of the Second Creek Plan not recorded in other historical sources. The Wednesday examinations unveiled a purported link between the plot at Second Creek "and Negroes in Natchez with a negro named Bill Postlethwaite at their head." Just how the connection was supposed to have worked over some ten miles is not clear. Almost certainly Postlethwaite (who cannot be further identified) was referred to but not present at the examinations at Cherry Grove. According to Minor, some of the Second Creek rebels wanted to hold off any action "till they were freed by Capt. Lincoln when it would be an easy job for them to kill their masters—." But apparently Bill Postlethwaite in Natchez was not so patient, since he was said to have "thought it would be an easy job now as so many [white] men had gone away."

3. Walt Whitman, *Complete Poetry and Collected Prose*, ed. Justin Kaplan (New York, 1982), 467–68, and of course widely anthologized.

With this news, the planters who had gathered at Cherry Grove decided to change their venue. Their adjournment may have been owing to the weather, for it turned from cool to cold Thursday afternoon, and they had been proceeding, in all probability, out of doors.[4] Late that Wednesday or the next day, the Committee "adjourned till after Monday when there will be a meeting in town." That Monday, September 30, an examining committee actually met, but "elected no new testimony." According to Wailes, there was a "very large meeting at the Court House" and "three persons added to the Vigilance or Judicial Committee of the Civty for each of the precincts of Washington and Pine Ridge." Whether or not this cumbersome enlargement was justified by actual danger from blacks, it seemed so. That same day and the next, Wailes "heard nothing" of how things were progressing, but Minor, who lived much closer to the new venue, noted tersely, "Comtee turned up many things." Minor did not record in his diary that he was himself a member of the Committee.[5]

Evidently there were many things to turn up, since for more than two weeks there had been "a great state of excitement" in Natchez itself. Louisa Lovell, eldest daughter of the prominent John Quitman and married to a New York attorney who was now a captain in the Confederate army, wrote to her husband about the matter on September 21. She was living in their suburban mansion situated just across the lane from Linden, which had been bought by the Conner family from the Kers twenty-one years before.[6] "For the last week," she wrote Joseph, her husband, there had been "stories of insurrections etc." Both the new quasi-military groups and the more traditional authorities were at work on the problem: "The Home guard, and Vigilance Committee have been constantly on the alert arresting and confining suspected individuals." They had learned that "a large number of

4. Outdoors is a supposition, but there were probably too many people gathered to pack into a barn, which in any event the committee members would have found unpleasant and unbecoming. The weather is in Darden Diary, September 26, 27, 1861.

5. Wailes Diary, October 1, 2, 1861.

6. Linden's purchase by the Conner family is in Mary Conway Shields Dunbar, *My Mother Used to Say: A Natchez Belle of the Sixties*, ed. Elizabeth Dunbar Murray (Boston, 1959), 82. Louisa was already a widow when she married Joseph Lovell in 1859; see Robert E. May, "Southern Elite Women, Sectional Extremism, and the Male Political Sphere: The Case of John A. Quitman's Wife and Female Descendants, 1847–1931," *Journal of Mississippi History*, L (1988), 254.

plantations on second creek were implicated." Evidently the examinations at Second Creek were reverberating in Natchez among both blacks and whites.[7]

Now, at Monmouth on the outskirts of Natchez, Louisa Quitman Lovell reported, "Many around us have been found guilty and hung, as now for instance as [at] Capt [William T.] Martin's." With surprise and indignation she assured her husband, "Now this state of things never happened here before, and I have never really been alarmed before." But she went on to admit being frightened by the absence of men who had gone off to the army. She obliquely protested his patriotic duties: "It is indeed unsafe and dangerous to be so left alone as we are." She and her family were not literally alone, of course, and she wrote of the "sentinels around us every night and the 'Guard' . . . posted in the lane between Linden and us." Yet she was unnerved by the sounds of all this "excitement": "Every now and then I hear the report of a gun at different points." And just the previous night, "a large fire" in Natchez had burned a "whole square" of buildings to the ground. Wailes, from a distance, thought the fire not connected to Second Creek: rather than being "the work of an incendiary," he felt, it was probably "accidental and the result of carelessness." But Louisa Lovell was truly alarmed. A few days before, a mysterious stranger had been seen lurking outside their house. Perhaps it had been the "miserable, sneaking abolitionist" who was said to be "at the bottom of this whole affair" of the Negroes. "I hope," she wrote in the conventionalized manner of a grande dame, "that he will be caught and burned alive for no torture is too good for the . . . wretch."[8]

Ordinarily Mrs. Lovell's description of the state of affairs in Natchez would not attract our attention, since women and men all over the South were writing similarly at the time and had been for years during other periods of "excitement" about the slaves

7. Louisa Lovell to Capt. Joseph Lovell, September 21, 1861, in Quitman Family Papers, UNC, Document G.

8. *Ibid.* The ellipsis points before *wretch* represent one illegible word. The "whole square" in town was what today would be called an entire "block." Her father had arrived in Mississippi from New York about 1820 and become a vociferous defender of the southern way; see Robert E. May, *John A. Quitman: Old South Crusader* (Baton Rouge, 1985), and especially his "Southern Elite Women," 251–85. Earlier, Susan Sillers Darden had used similar language about *white* scoundrels fomenting trouble among the slaves: "they ought to be hung; burning would be nothing but right." Diary, November 3, 1859. Two days after Mrs. Lovell wrote, Mrs. Darden referred in her diary to the "home Gauard" being called out in Jefferson County: "I suppose it is in reference to the negro rebellion in Natchez."

and lurking abolitionists (as if the former were not also the latter). But now there was a real war going on, and everyone in Adams County was certain what it was about. In addition, as we already know, there was real activity underlying all the worried talk—real heat not caused solely by fevered imaginations.

Two weeks after she wrote, the "Ex. Comtee" (as William Minor noted in his diary on October 3) was "still in session at race track"—Pharsalia, near the bridge on the road east toward Washington.[9] The Committee seemed to be getting to the bottom of matters with a key witness who provided—or so at least is seemed—the answer to how the horrible business had all started. As Minor understood the testimony, it was "proved by Chases man John that the first conversation about the insurrection took place between him and a number of others on the night of the 14th April 1861 — as they came up the Hill after seeing the Quitman Light Artillery off." So preparations for one war would seem to have led directly to plans for another. And those conversations in Natchez now seemed directly tied to the ones that had taken place down fishing on the little tributary early in May. "By the same witness," Minor noted, "was proved the agreement between the town and 2d creek company to the determination to kill, burn and ravish."

His only further entry that day was: "The various drills and other meetings etc. etc." Exactly one week later, on October 10, he noted without elaboration: "Examining Comtee still in session," again without any notation of his own role in the grim proceedings. He then left the area to attend to the sugarcane harvesting on his plantations far to the south. He left behind no record of how many men were hanged at the racetrack.[10] He made no further mention of Second Creek.

Two weeks later still, after long silence on the affair in his diary, Benjamin Wailes noted almost casually about a trip he had taken to town, "Met detachment of Volunteers guarding several negroes who had been condemned by the Judicial or Vigilance Commit-

9. The racecourse had also been known as St. Catherine's (after the creek) and Toll Bridge. Laura D. S. Harrell, "Horse Racing in the Old Natchez District, 1783–1830," Journal of Mississippi History, XIII (1951), 123–37.

10. Even with all the hangings in Adams County, there were no references to public exhibitions of bodies or of heads on poles. Such displays, rationalized by an obvious intent to terrorize the living, had been common in the wake of many but not all earlier American slave conspiracies and even vigilante actions against whites. They dated back to an old but by no means exclusively English tradition.

tee, they were taken out to the Race track and eight of them hung." He wrote nothing more about the matter.

News about all the excitement was of course kept out of the newspapers, but private correspondence was another matter. At some point about the middle of September, Mary S. Ker wrote her brother about what was going on. His regiment was far away in northern Virginia, defending the capital of the new nation against attack by the United States Army. From their encampment near Manassas, spiritedly named "Qui Vive," he responded on October 27. He was happy to learn, he wrote, that she and her friends and family "are moving into and near town." Though he did not say so explicitly, some of those precautionary refugees were probably trusted household servants. At any rate, "it is far safer for all parties concerned, and as you say must make you all more sociable." A potential storm often does just that to neighbors. Feeling badly out of immediate touch with events, William Ker went on to express his sincere hope that "the insurrection has been effectually put down." His sister had written something about the examinations, for he added his hopes that "the trial may be soon over and everything quiet again." He was certain about the root of "this trouble." It "ought to be," he wrote, "a sad lesson to those people about Natchez, who have always allowed their servants to run wild." He wished that "they will not in future, as they have done in the past, heedlessly throw temptation in the way of their servants." One wonders what temptation Ker had in mind. Wandering about? Perhaps fishing on Sundays. He concluded with self-righteous satisfaction, "Thank God that none of ours have been implicated in this sad affair."[11] His remark capsulated a habit of thought among whites that had prevailed for generations: if the Negroes were getting out of hand, it was someone else's servants, not one's own.

But pride of ownership was most easily exercised at a distance. Close to home, what was crucial—and demanded—was a united front among white men against the common danger of "insurrection" by black slaves. In fact, while this defender of the Confederacy was writing his letter from one battlefront, white men at home were busy "examining" enemies on another. Owing to its "domestic institution," the home front had its battlegrounds too,

11. Having heard from her again, William wrote that "I am sincerely rejoiced to know that the last of the wretches have been hung." William H. Ker to Mary S. Ker, October 27, November 7, 1861, in John Ker and Family Papers, LSU. Documents J.

even though in the hands of historians they have remained much quieter. More than most whites, black slaves knew how very long the war had been going on.

Eventually things seem to have quieted down. For planters, the immediate danger from their slaves seemed past. Yet there was a major war on, and the Federals were beginning to penetrate Mississippi.[12] The appallingly bloody battle of Shiloh (known to the enemy as Pittsburg Landing) had been followed by a smaller engagement at nearby Corinth, in the northeast corner of the state. That was six months after the examinations in Adams County, and more than a year before the capitulation of Vicksburg, where Charlie Davenport's father had been with the Union forces. On May 13, 1862, Natchez had surrendered to Federal gunboats, but the town was not occupied by U.S. troops.[13] The impact of this news upon the slaves out in the county is not known. It is clear, however, that by the summer following most of the hangings in October, a considerable number of Adams County slaves were out of hand. Benjamin Wailes noted in his diary that dogs had helped track down some runaways near Pine Ridge. The fugitives had killed a white man; two were themselves killed and three taken alive. "Twenty odd negro men," he added, had taken off from Dr. James Metcalfe's two "tracts" west of his homeplace and "it is said have gone down the River."[14] But we know of such chaos primarily from a letter written to the state's governor two weeks later on July 17, 1862, by the provost marshal in Natchez.

12. For the course of the war in the state as a whole, Edwin C. Bearss, "The Armed Conflict, 1861–1865," in *A History of Mississippi*, ed. Richard A. McLemore (2 vols.; Hattiesburg, 1973), I, 447–91.

13. Rawick, *American Slave*, Suppl. 1, Vol. VII (Miss. Narrs.), Pt. 2, p. 566; C. G. Dahlgren to Brig. Gen. Thomas Jordan, May 17, 1862, in *The War of the Rebellion: A Compilation of the Official Records of the Union and Confederate Armies* (128 vols.; Washington, D.C., 1880–1901), Ser. 1, Vol. XV, pp. 736–38. For the surrender, see *Official Records of the Union and Confederate Navies in the War of the Rebellion* (30 vols.; Washington, D.C., 1894–1922), Ser. 1, Vol. XVIII, pp. 489–91, 494–96.

14. Wailes wrote that Dr. Metcalfe's slaves were ones "he was about to remove from the neighborhood to a place of greater safety." That practice, which was common in the region during the war and landed some slaves in places as far away as Texas, became known as "refugeeing," a term obviously not invented by blacks. Wailes Diary, July 2, 1862. The two "tracts" were Metcalfe's York and Bourbon, not his homeplace at Montrose.

Alexander K. Farrar owned 195 slaves in his Kingston Plantation, near the hamlet of the same name. There, four years earlier, in 1857, he had taken the lead in investigating the mysterious violent death of an overseer at the widow Mrs. Sharpe's Cedar Grove plantation in that neighborhood.[15] Farrar had publicly committed himself to tracking down the person or persons responsible for what he was convinced was a murder. He showed no hesitation in pursuing his investigation among the slaves at Cedar Grove. As he explained in a long letter, the procedure began with hard querying of the cook. She apparently named names without physical pressure. Others were "staked down" and whipped by "Companies of four or five to a negro." The business was done with care, with each Negro tied "separate and apart so that there was no possible chance for them to hear what each other said." Obviously this method of investigation was essential for obtaining the truth—so far as the white investigators could conceive what the truth might be. One slave, the plantation's carriage driver, "received but a few stripes" before admitting his involvement in the murder, but his brother "for a long time held out, but finally confessed." A group of mostly planting men announced their own names in the newspaper as having discovered the true facts of the case. Three of them were participants in the group that was to be brought together in an even more alarming situation four years later at Second Creek.[16]

15. An article that makes a much larger point contains an account of this complex affair; see Michael Wayne, "An Old South Morality Play: Reconsidering the Social Underpinnings of the Proslavery Ideology," *Journal of American History*, LXXVII (1990), 838–63. Farrar is in Census, 1850 Free, household 252; Slave, MS p. 181, which has him age 36, whereas he is 43 in 1860 Free, household 914; Slave, MS pp. 101–103; see also Adams Land; Adams Personal; and as owner of Kingston plantation (which is not on the surveyor's map but was near the hamlet of Kingston) in Road Duty, UTA, 1–2, 179–80, 253, 366, 433, 504.

16. A. K. Farrar to H. W. Drake, September 4, 5, 1857, in Alexander K. Farrar Papers, LSU. These two letters are very similar, with the first probably being a draft of the second. Only the first refers to the slaves being "staked down." There were political rumors, another plantation said to be involved, and accusations against Farrar's motives, which made the affair more complicated than Wayne's broader focus permitted him to discuss. For the list of names, see Natchez *Courier*, July 18, 1857; an accompanying list of seventeen endorsers includes three Second Creek planters: James H. Mitchell, James W. Metcalfe, and Metcalfe's brother Henry. Overseers could have good reason to fear for their lives, and the fear could become self-consuming. Earlier, Dr. Jenkins noted that the overseer on his River Place in Wilkinson County had simply run off after being "seised with mania" that the slaves there were planning to murder him; Jenkins Diary, June 10, 1850.

Under the whip at Cedar Grove, the slaves had accused a certain white man who lived in Concordia, and Farrar had no hesitation in signing (with seventeen others) a newspaper "Notice" warning him never again to set foot in Adams County. The paid announcement emphasized that "the confessions of the negroes" had been "made separately and apart from each other."[17] As things turned out in the complicated case, the white man dropped from view after publicly protesting his innocence, thereby abandoning at Cedar Grove his slave mistress of some fifteen years. Three slaves were given a legal trial, duly convicted, and executed (with a prominent Presbyterian minister in attendance) at the place of the crime.

The indictments and trials were conducted with such scrupulous adherence to prescribed legal procedures that the Natchez *Courier* wished it could have been "seen with a collective eye" by "abolition Massachusetts or fanatic Ohio." This tone of self-congratulation was accompanied by a rising peroration on the lessons to be drawn from the crime and the legal trials. The *Courier* congratulated everyone responsible "upon the laws being vindicated, truth elicited, murder brought to light, the guilty punished, rebellion made an example of, our social institutions rendered more safe, and the negro taught that God has made him in subjection to the white race, and that so he must remain, submissively and cheerfully performing his duty in that situation of life in which it has pleased God to place him."[18]

Such hortatory praise came easily, almost like the natural scratching of an itch, in the wake of a few slaves getting out of control. Yet under graver, more threatening circumstances such as loomed four years later at Second Creek, such rhetoric seemed inappropriate and indeed downright dangerous. So there was none.

A man of inherited wealth and one of the largest cattle owners in the county, A. K. Farrar had proved himself capable of great energy when dealing with affronts to proper social order. When the political crisis came in November, 1860, Farrar, in common with many of the county's planters, at first opposed secession but then rallied

17. Natchez *Courier,* July 18, 1857.
18. *Ibid.* This long account, entitled "An Eventful Drama," may have been based on a letter from Farrar.

to the Confederate cause. Now, early in 1862, as provost marshal of Natchez, he was engaged in trying to hold down a troublesome home front. He appealed to the governor for instructions about handling his difficulties.[19]

At first Farrar referred to "a great disposition among the Negroes to be insubordinate, and to run away and go to the Federals"—whom Second Creek and Natchez slaves could in fact have reached only by boat or by trekking hundreds of miles overland. He explained that he was using militiamen to serve as overseers and patrollers—thus revealing how the shortage of white manpower was fusing mechanisms of social control that had traditionally been quite separate. But his problems stemmed from a more general breakdown of plantation discipline that was, he felt, caused by some masters themselves. As he saw things, effective measures had already been taken with the most dangerous slaves: "Within the last 12 Months we have had to hang some 40 for plotting an insurrection, and there has been about that number put in irons." He now asked how to proceed "against persons who will keep no overseer, and make but little provision for their Negroes, rendering it necessary for them to steal or starve and go naked." It was a measure of changed times that he blamed the owners more than the owned.

As Farrar described the problem he gradually enlarged its scope. "There are some few cases of that kind here," he began, "when negroes seemingly are permitted to forage upon the Community." But then he went on, "The owners will not look after them, will not provide for them, nor will they employ an overseer." Given this laxity, he was not in the slightest surprised at what was happening: "The negroes have such large liberties, they are enabled to harbor runaways, who have fire arms, traverse the whole Country, kill stock, and steal generally, supplying those who harbor them, and send to market by Negro market-men." But then he pulled back, not wishing to describe his district as completely falling apart: "The state of things in consequence to this in a few cases are a serious nuisance as well as dangerous to the Commu-

19. A. K. Farrar to Gov. John J. Pettus, July 17, 1862, in Governors Correspondence, MDAH, Document K. The letter is partially quoted in an addendum by Herbert Aptheker to his famous book: Herbert Aptheker, "Notes on Slave Conspiracies in Confederate Mississippi," *JNH*, XXIX (1944), 76–77. Farrar was one of two Adams County delegates to the state's secession convention, both men having run on the Conservative Union ticket; see Charles S. Sydnor, *A Gentleman of the Old Natchez Region: Benjamin L. C. Wailes* (Durham, N.C., 1938), 295.

nity. Complaints are made to me to remedy the evil. I am however at a loss how to proceed."

Farrar's letter is less important for its figure of forty hanged than as a portrait of traditional relationships breaking down. Social relations seemed to be changing in precisely the direction that many of the Second Creek rebels had hoped for. As often happens, though, the fortunes of war could take unexpected turns, not always to the benefit of some of the "victors." More than a year later, in July of 1863, Natchez was permanently occupied by Federal troops. General Thomas E. G. Ransom reported this bloodless accomplishment to his superiors, asking "what policy I shall pursue with regard to the negroes." His comments on the "problem" were short and, at least to us, revealing: "They flock in by thousands (about 1 able-bodied man to 6 women and children). I am feeding about 500, and working the able-bodied men among them." This was scarcely enough. "I can send you any number encumbered with families. I cannot take care of them. What shall I do with them? They are all anxious to go; they do not know where or what for." [20]

What General Ransom did not say, because it was general knowledge, was that many of the able-bodied freedmen were enrolling in the Union army. Some of the armed men in blue uniforms who occupied Natchez were black, including soldiers of the 58th Regiment of the United States Colored Infantry, who ended up camping on the grounds of the Quitman family's Monmouth. [21] The young mistress of that establishment complained to her husband at the battlefront in Virginia that plans were afoot "to raise 50,000 Negro troops" and that General Ransom was to take over the house belonging to Confederate general William T. Martin. "Were I Mrs. Martin," she wrote, "I would have the house burned down first." [22]

A. K. Farrar could not have foreseen that able-bodied former slaves would be recruited or impressed in Adams County and drilled at the Forks of the Road, next to (or perhaps at) the old slave mart and the Pharsalia racetrack. Those who died of disease were buried on Quitman land nearby. Nor could Farrar or Ransom have predicted the profound misery and awful deaths of many other former slaves—women, children, the elderly, the infirm. William

20. *War of the Rebellion*, Ser. 1, Vol. XXIV, Pt. 2, p. 681.
21. May, "Southern Elite Women," 269.
22. Louisa Lovell to Joseph Lovell, August 17, 1863, in Quitman Family Papers, UNC.

Henry Elder, bishop of St. Mary's Roman Catholic Church, found opportunity in the chaos and baptized more than five hundred blacks, reporting sadly that "many of them were infants." The bishop was horrified by the situation. In the spring of 1864, he reported that "the proclamation of liberty [the Emancipation Proclamation] caused several thousands of negroes to gather in and around Natchez." Although the military authorities did their best to provide food and shelter, "yet great numbers of them sickened and died and they are still dying every day."[23] Neither the bishop, the general, nor the provost marshal specifically mentioned the hundreds of blacks who crowded onto a narrow stretch of land for several miles along the shore up the river from Brown's sawmill. In later years, pedestrian venturers from Natchez-under-the-Hill occasionally came across the bones of these dead as the capricious river from time to time exposed them.[24]

After the war ended, local whites and blacks had to try to adjust to a new world. That adjustment was heroic and tragic in its own right, but it is a somewhat separate story. We will never know what things were like on those Second Creek plantations after the war, though we may very safely infer they were both different and the same as before.

We do know, however, that the Plan and the deaths reverberated in a curious way a few miles north at Natchez and a thousand miles distant in the reunited nation's capital. Those reverberations were generated by the workings of a machine not seen before in Adams County. In 1871 the Radical Republicans in control of the United States Congress provided for a special bureaucracy to handle requests for reimbursement of financial losses suffered by southerners who had remained loyal to the Union. The Southern Claims Commission, as it came to be called, heard thousands of witnesses on both sides, for the claimants and for the govern-

23. William Henry Elder to Mr. Certes, treasurer of the Propagation of the Faith Society, March 22, 1864, in R. O. Gerow, ed., *Cradle Days of St. Mary's at Natchez* (Natchez, 1941), 155–56.

24. Dunbar, *My Mother Used to Say,* 170–71, 183–84; Natchez *Democrat,* Pilgrimage "Pink" ed., 1959, p. [29]. For the mill's location, see *Johnson's Diary,* I, 117n; II, 693. The higher-ranking General Lorenzo Thomas, reporting to Secretary of War Edwin M. Stanton, made no mention of these conditions in his letter of October 24, 1863, extolling the Unionist disposition of the town and county; see *War of the Rebellion,* Ser. 3, Vol. III, pp. 916–17.

ment. The great majority of claims were disallowed, and most of those accepted were pared severely. Over a period of ten years the commission gathered mountainous files of a sort that were conspicuously absent—as we can now see—in the period before the war.

Two of the claimants were Rebecca Ann Minor and Katherine Surget Minor, the wife and daughter-in-law of William J. Minor himself. Rebecca still lived at Concord. Katherine lived at Oakland—a much larger place much closer to Washington than to Natchez—which her husband, John Minor, had bought with money provided by his father. As a Surget heiress, Katherine owned in her own right three other plantations, one on the river and two across in Concordia. The loyalties of William J. and John Minor were very much at issue, even though both were in their graves by the time these claims were creeping slowly through the commission's mill. A large file on Katherine Minor's case survived a later spate of paper junking, so it is possible to learn something about it. At least thirty-three witnesses testified about her claim, mainly white persons of various stations in life, but also a number of blacks. The latter included five of her former slaves, two on her behalf and three (including her former "coachman") "for [the] government." Despite conflicting testimony, the commissioner of claims ruled favorably on Katherine Minor's claim and awarded her $13,072 of the $53,155 she had asked for.[25] In

25. Digest of Evidence to Date, November 22, 1879, Claim (No. 7960) of Katherine S. Minor, in Settled Case Files, 1877–83—Mississippi, Adams County, Records of the Southern Claims Commission, Records of the General Accounting Office, RG 217,National Archives; hereinafter cited as Claim (No. 7960) of Katherine S. Minor. Also, Report on Claim of Katherine S. Minor, December, 1879, *ibid.* Apparently Rebecca Minor's smaller claim was disallowed and its documents therefore thrown out. A printed Geographical List of Claims, giving names, amounts, but not final disposition, by county, is on microfilm in Records of Southern Claims Commission, General Records of the Department of the Treasury, RG 56, National Archives. The list of witnesses in K. Minor's case is clearly incomplete, and not all the listed testimony is in the file. Before it went to the National Archives, the Katherine (Catherine) S. Minor file was carefully utilized by Frank W. Klingberg, "The Case of the Minors: A Unionist Family Within the Confederacy," *JSH,* XIII (1947), 27–45. Klingberg discussed the examinations—and I am enormously grateful he did—but they were not his principal focus. I am also very grateful to Mary K. Jordan for her very generous and skillful assistance with these documents. Apparently the Minor claims originated before William J. Minor's death, at least in connection with two of his Louisiana plantations; for these claims, which began August 19, 1868, see Case No. 3560, William J. and Rebecca A. G. Minor, in microfilm Records of the Court of Claims, 1863–1870, LSU. Kate Surget's marriage to John Minor is noted in Jenkins Diary, March 6, 1855.

effect, she persuaded the commission that she and her family had
been loyal supporters of the Union. Some of the witnesses gave
evidence that may now appear as utterly destructive of her case,
since the matter of examining slaves about a supposed conspiracy
came up. But the commission was far less interested in the fate of
some black men than in the loyalty of her father-in-law and of her
husband.

The examinations were discussed before the commissioners
but were dismissed in their summary report. "It was also
charged," they wrote, "that at one time during the war John Minor
and his father Wm J. Minor participated in the trial and hanging of
negroes at the race course near Natchez. This statement is untrue." Having airily dispatched the matter, they went on to explain, "John Minor took no part in it. His father Wm J. Minor was
opposed to the proceedings: took an active part and exerted himself to prevent the hanging of the negroes." What mattered more
to the commissioners, clearly, was that "it is proved by several
most reliable witnesses, some of them federal officers, that the
Minor family . . . were known and recognized as Union people,
fast and reliable friends of the Union cause, and were accorded
privileges, favors and protection as such."[26]

In light of what they had been told by one of the most persuasive witnesses, the commissioners' report appears entirely reasonable. They had heard from a friend of the family, a lawyer who
had sympathized with William Minor's Unionism but had, when
the choice had to be made, taken a different fork and risen to become a Confederate general. By the time William T. Martin testified in 1877, the commission had already learned of "the hanging of some negroes at the Race Course" and asked Martin
what he knew about it. The general explained that "there was a
vigilance Committee" made up of "people who were disposed
to be lawless." He was nothing if not ingenuous about his own
role in helping to raise money and a military group during those
early days of excitement in 1860: "I wanted a company that I
could control, and composed of men who represented wealthy
families there, in order that I might put down this lawless spirit."
He himself was not present, but he felt sure that John Minor
(William's son) was not present either. "They had my own
negroes there," Martin said, "charged with having some connec-

26. Summary Report, Claim (No. 7960) of Katherine S. Minor, Document R.

tion with it." [27] He did not volunteer that any of his slaves had been hanged.[28]

Investigation of the supposed insurrection, Martin continued, had been pursued with unrestrained vigor. In discussing the investigators, he denied that John Minor had "anything to do with it" but asserted that "the pressure was so great against Capt. Minor and John himself . . . that they insisted" the two men "should join them. They said, 'Come and see for yourself if we are not doing right.'" John, he reiterated, took no part in the proceedings, but "Capt. Minor did go on the Committee and remained there and assented to the propriety of it." General Martin did not explain exactly what the "it" was. Concerning the senior Minor, the general waffled, but in doing so he may well have reflected what was going on in William Minor's mind, if not in his diary. "Capt. Minor finally went off and would not have anything more to do with it, although he thought there was evidence to justify the hanging of some of them, and assented to it." Nothing Martin said about his old friend suggests that Minor's diary was factually wrong. But just as surely the diary did not tell the whole story, which perhaps makes it the more believable rather than less.

General Martin had learned about all this secondhand. He knew what went on, he explained, because "a brother-in-law of mine, who was afterwards on Bragg's staff, was one of the parties who was engaged in that matter. The best men in the county were concerned in it." This brother-in-law was Lemuel P. Conner.[29]

27. Testimony of William T. Martin, December 12, 1877, *ibid.*, Document P. Some of those best men, he said, later became outright Unionists, and he carried on at some length about George Marshall's father, Levin, for whom see Census, 1860 Free, household 1051; Slave, MS. p. 144; Dunbar Rowland, ed., *Mississippi: Comprising Sketches of Counties, Towns, Institutions, and Persons . . .* (2 vols.; Atlanta, 1907), II, 174–75. Martin had commanded the Jeff Davis Legion, of which the Adams Troop became a part, as noted in William H. Ker to Mary S. Ker, October 27, 1861, in John Ker and Family Papers, LSU. Martin was a lawyer and not a planter. In 1861 he owned nine slaves, three carriages, and an eleven-acre "residence"; Adams Personal, 1861; Adams Land, 1861.

28. Louisa Lovell to Capt. Joseph Lovell, September 21, 1861, in Quitman Family Papers, UNC, Documents G.

29. MS sketch of William T. Martin, "Important Personalities," in 2d of 2 "Adams County Biographies" folders, Box 215, Works Progress Administration, Adams County, RG 60, MDAH. Conner's presence was noted in Statement of Pleasant Scott Taken by George Tucker, March 28, 1874, in Claim (No. 7960) of Katherine S. Minor, Document M. Conner seems not to have taken notes there; at

When they talked with General Martin, the commission's agents already had in hand evidence from other sources. Three years before, in 1874, William J. Minor's wife had testified at a hearing, also in Washington, D.C., about her own claim and that of her daughter-in-law. She was asked about events that had taken place eleven to thirteen years before, including the arrival in Natchez of the Union general Ransom, about whom she said—as well she might have—"I recollect the evening that he arrived, very well." Evidently her counsel had already heard something about the racetrack, but he obviously did not yet have things quite straight when he asked, "Do you recollect a trial that took place at the Race Course some eight or ten miles from Vicksburg?" She did not correct him as to the distance or the town but said simply, "Yes sir, I do, with regret." Having made her posture plain, she went on to answer pre-arranged questions about her son's telegraphing her husband at his Terrebonne Parish plantation with the request that he come up "because there was an insurrection feared." "When he came up," she continued, "he heard of the meeting there, and he was then called upon by a committee to act." Accordingly, "He went down to the meeting."[30]

From the dialogue of friendly questions and answers, it is not clear whether Rebecca Minor remembered that her husband had first gone to Second Creek and then, a few days later, to the racetrack. It seems probable that she knew about the two meeting places at the time but had conflated them over the years. But she had his intentions very firmly in mind. "He had but one object" in going there, she said, "and that was to make the punishment as light as possible. He had a great horror of punishment." Her obviously well-primed counsel then asked, "Did he speak of it as a most terrible thing?" and she suitably responded, "He did, as a most terrible thing, and I should think you would find it among

least none survive in the Lemuel P. Conner and Family Papers, LSU. It seems more likely that he did not take any, or none he wished saved, than that they were later culled from his papers by some younger member of his family. The point is of some importance, since it reinforces the supposition that he did not record all the proceedings at Second Creek; yet those at the racetrack had a somewhat different tone, as will shortly become apparent.

30. Rebecca Minor's words here and following are from Testimony of Rebecca A. Minor, in Claim (No. 7960) of Katherine S. Minor, Document O.

his writings for he always kept a diary." Evidently the diary was not at hand or the commission's representative chose to ignore it. Only in retrospect is it clear how greatly she overestimated her husband's willingness to confide his thoughts even to secret pages.

At this point in her testimony, one of the commissioners broke in: "I don't understand yet, what you are talking about.—punishment for what?" Outsiders did not understand such matters, and Mrs. Minor tried to set him straight. "It was said to be an insurrection. The negroes who were engaged in it were some of them a bad set." Then the commissioner wanted to know when all this occurred and was told (with perfect accuracy) "1861 . . . after the war broke out, but before Natchez had fallen." Then she had full reign. "Mr. Minor went down to the track with my sons, and they did all in their power to prevent cruelty, which certainly was administered." Her husband had been "perfectly horrified at what was done there." To be sure, he was concerned with public safety: "He thought if it was proved upon the negroes on trial, that we were in danger of having an insurrection, of course it would be punished and nipped in the bud, but"—and here William Minor's wife unknowingly pronounced her husband more humane and skeptical than had appeared by his own hand—"he was really under the impression that the testimony that was brought forward to him was not as strong as it ought to be, or as strong as they thought it would be, and the only way they could get them to confess, a great deal of cruelty was practised, much to the horror of my son, the husband of that lady."

The final words of Rebecca Minor's breathless sentence point up how conscious she was of her testimony's immediate purpose. Yet her views about her husband were heartfelt. She claimed that his life had been threatened and that "he had to go down armed," accompanied by his son and nephew. Perhaps William Minor's presence did in fact help mitigate "cruelty," though according to a former slave who had been "arrested," "John Minor had a Cowhide in his hand," as did "most" of the other gentlemen he named. But that freedman, Pleasant Scott, had fared relatively well; as he told the commission's agent, "I was put on trial and I proved by witnesses" having been elsewhere at the suggested time "by permission of my master's foreman, and they let me off."[31] Pleasant

31. Statement of Pleasant Scott, Document M.

Scott was fortunate, and his "acquittal" cautions us not to assume that the examinations always progressed with murderous inevitability.

But there was "severity." When Rebecca Minor was asked if she knew "who was the leading prime movers in that barbarity or cruelty?" she was willing to offer two names: "the Metcalfs of Natchez, and Mr. Alexander Farrow—they were the leaders of the cruelty." (As for the first, the Metcalfes "of Natchez" were most probably the Oren Metcalfes—a different family from those of Second Creek. The second name was one that no clerk native to Adams County would have thus misspelled.)[32] But Rebecca Minor's purpose was not to list gentlemen who had participated at the racecourse. Both she and the commission were more interested in her husband's conduct: "It was one of the most unpleasant and disagreeable scenes, I have heard my husband say, that he ever witnessed, and he determined that he would never own a negro afterwards if such barbarity, and conduct, was attempted." She could not hold back on the matter: "He had owned slaves all his life, and his family before him, and a great many of them have been a hundred years in his family, and he was an exceedingly lenient master."

In such social circles, life could seem to go on forever. The Minor slaves might well have agreed, without viewing the matter in exactly the same way. The witness was immediately asked, "What became of your husband, Mr W. J. Minor, afterwards?" Her response said more than she intended: "He left me at Natchez, and went down to New Orleans to take care of his property in Louisiana." In fact William J. Minor's property there consisted of several sugar plantations and hundreds of slaves. Her claims about his "Union" sentiments were as well founded as those sentiments themselves, since the conservative Mr. Minor realized perfectly well and now saw better than ever that a disruption of the Union was very likely to bring disruption to his own world—including the humane and profitable relations that had, of course, existed with all his people for "a hundred years."

---

32. There is no question about A. K. Farrar, but the Metcalfes (a name sometimes spelled without the second e) are more problematical. The phrase "of Natchez" was not an offhand one; locally, at least in certain circles, it provided accurate identification. Almost certainly the reference was to the family of Oren Metcalfe, but Dr. James's son Henry may have been included (as will be seen in a moment).

Three weeks before Rebecca Minor's testimony, a special officer of
the claims commission took a deposition in Natchez from James
Carter, a black man who had formerly been the slave of a druggist
in town. Carter swore that he had been "arrested by the vigilance
Committee here and tried for my life." Neither he nor the agent
taking his testimony thought to name the year in question, but it
was nonetheless entirely clear. He had been about thirty years old
in 1861 when he was taken up on the charge of obtaining "dispatches from the enemy" and reading them "to other colored
people." More specifically, he was accused of communicating
battle news to "certain colored men" who were said to be "in the
habit of meeting in a Bayou called Mrs Boyds Bayou and drilling
for the purpose of rising against the whites." He was "tried," he
said, "at the race course . . . for about three weeks almost each
day." His account was devoid of euphemisms about "severity":

> The final day they carried me out then they whipped me ter-
> ribly. Several of them were whipping me at once. . . . The ob-
> ject in whipping me was to make me confess to something.
> They questioned me first, and I told them I knew nothing
> about it, which was the truth. They said they would make
> me know, and then they whipped me. They would whip un-
> til I fainted and then stop and whip again. Dr Harper sat by
> and would feel my pulse and tell them when to stop and when
> to go on.[33]

Thirteen years after the ordeal, Carter was willing to provide
names. He could recall only two of the four men who all whipped
him at the same time, Mr. A. K. Farrar and Abner Martin.[34] When
asked (probably) about Mr. William J. Minor, he said that Minor
"was there present every day and was one of the leading men in

33. Testimony of James Carter Taken by George Tucker, [Natchez], March 31,
1874, in Claim (No. 7960) of Katherine S. Minor, Document N. The druggist who
had owned Carter was George W. Fox, who also filed a claim (unsuccessfully) with
the commission for, among other things, quinine seized by Union forces; see
Claims of George W. Fox (Nos. 2883, 2884), in Office No. 390, Report No. 2 (1872),
Barred and Disallowed Case Files of the Southern Claims Commission, 1871–
1880, RG 233, National Archives.
34. There is no Abner Martin in Adams County records, though a small farmer
of that name lived in a distant county; Rankin Census 1860, Free, household 707.
Dr. William Harper was a substantial physician-planter, born in the North, resident
in Natchez, and owner of Avalanche on the River; see Road Duty, UTA, 494;
Adams Land, 1861; Adams Personal, 1861; and Census, 1860 Free, households 456,
969; 1860 Slave, MS. pp. 19, 58–59. (Both census schedules listed him twice.)

the trial." Perhaps he was prompted by the man from the federal government, but a few moments later Carter said that "during my trial W. J. Minor sat next to Mr Farrar and questioned me as much as any of them." It was Mr. Farrar who "was the President of the Committee" and who told him "they had decided to hang me." He did not say, nor probably did he know, nor would he have been particularly impressed if he had known, that after the war Alexander K. Farrar had a chapel built on his plantation and brought in a minister fully credentialed by the African Methodist Episcopal Church.[35]

Asked about other committee members, Carter gave ten more names. Only two ring of Second Creek: one was Henry Metcalfe "on the Pine Ridge" (who actually lived at The Grove on Second Creek), and the other the gentleman Conner had talked to there, George Marshall. Carter did not mention Lemuel Conner and evidently was not asked about him, though he did say there were "others that I can not recalled the names of." He was of course asked about John Minor, and responded that he "was there and sat on the Committee with the rest."

In a classic enactment of an old and still very common scenario—not by any means restricted to the slave South—eight of the men who had been "tried one by one" were hanged in front of the others. Carter was among another ten who were taken to the gallows by the "troop of soldiers," accompanied by "all the men of the committee." But: "They then said to me that they had concluded not to hang me but would give me a whipping and send me home." As he explained his last-minute reprieve, a white man who was a deacon at the Baptist church he attended "had interfered and told them that I was a pious man and did not associate with these men who went to the Bayou."

Carter did not say there never were any such men at that bayou. It was not a surprising place for rebel slaves to gather. (Locally, the term *bayou* was used not in the Louisiana sense, but for the many ravines and washes, often dry, that laced the land near the river.)[36] Carter claimed he had never communicated with those men. Fourteen years after that year of 1861, his deposition was being taken for another more narrow purpose, not for the investigation

35. Michael Wayne, *The Reshaping of Plantation Society: The Natchez District, 1860–1880* (Baton Rouge, 1983), 138.

36. [Joseph Holt Ingraham], *The South-West. By a Yankee* (2 vols.; 1835; rpr. Ann Arbor, 1966), II, 88.

of a supposed insurrection. The agent who took his sworn statement wrote the following and signed it in the margin at the end:

> Mrs K. S. Minor or Mrs R. A. Minor
> Statement of James Carter (col)
> Witness who has every appearance of being honest and is
> vouched for by honest colored people.

Each Minor name was preceded by a long case number. Carter's
name was not.

When Provost Marshal Alexander K. Farrar wrote the governor
about mounting chaos in the spring of 1862, he made no reference
to his own role in putting down an insurrection. He had no reason
to announce himself an old hand at such business. The men who
died at the racetrack had been dead for half a year. So had the leaders of the Second Creek conspiracy. The enemy had finally taken
New Orleans (though without General Scott); but for the dead it
was too late. It is hard not to wonder what Nelson and Orange and
Dick and Paul and Harry Scott and Edmond and the rest would
have thought. It is perhaps more profitable to wonder what effect
they all had had on their friends and relatives who were still living, and on the people who had purportedly owned them. We may
guess that their Plan did a good deal to undermine the slavery they
had been born into, but we cannot discern exactly what impact
they had by living, and dying, in a cause they felt was justified by
their oppression. They knew what freedom was for them, but they
would never learn whether those they left after them ever
achieved it. They lived in particular circumstances and they dealt
with particular difficulties. In this they shared with other human
beings the universal trial of living and dying each and all in their
own way.

Note: The reference to Concord on the first page of the next chapter is based
on Laura DeLap, "National Cemetery, Natchez" (Typescript, July 28, 1936, in
folder "Adams County, Cemeteries," Box 215, Works Progress Administration,
Adams County, RG 60, MDAH).

CHAPTER **13**

A SEPARATE PEACE

The killing of human beings by hanging them is a visibly dramatic process, an intentional and effective ritual of finality. The dangling bodies at Cherry Grove, Brighton Woods, the racetrack, and perhaps at other places served as a warning to thc living and a fleeting confirmation of plantation and social order, but also as a reminder to all concerned that oppression and order rested on a bedrock of violence.

Today, some dozen miles north of the bend in Second Creek, on the opposite side of Natchez at the outskirts of town, on land once part of Concord Plantation, there is a United States government cemetery where the bodies of more than a thousand Union soldiers lie buried. Some of those soldiers were black. Now, still, more than a century after the war, many African Americans gather every Memorial Day in Vidalia near the bridge, cross over the river, and walk through Natchez to the cemetery to lay flowers at many of the gravestones.

The bodies of some of the Second Creek rebels were probably buried on Cherry Grove ground. Almost certainly their graves were not marked, at least not right away. Possibly some of the grieving relatives and friends were permitted to bury their dead on their own homeplaces—at a good distance, of course, from both the big house and the quarters. Today at Cherry Grove there is a family graveyard not far from the front of the big house. It is a small square set off only by a post-and-rail fence. Generations of Surgets lie buried there, carefully remembered in spirit and with simple stone monuments.

Obey and Billy and their companions were placed in the ground somewhere else, free at last. There are no traces of any slave burials at Cherry Grove. Treading there today, we cannot hear the moans or the music of either the violent or natural deaths and burials of more than a century ago. Much has been written about slave funerals, especially as occasions of communal unity and vibrant expression, but not at Second Creek. We can assume that in

1861 there were the sounds of grief and lamentation, of weeping and songs of mourning and furious anger and bitterness and resignation, but Cherry Grove is quiet now, except for the birds and the insects and some of the animals and the wind and the rain on a few rooftops and the trees and the grass. There is a silent pall there now, broken at times by human voices and modern machines, but a pall. Nearby, the creek still looks muddy and flows slowly, and it is very, very quiet.

DOCUMENTS AND CAST OF CHARACTERS

NOTE ON THE DOCUMENTS

Historians have not written much about the subject of this book. Some nine secondary works allude very briefly to what happened with some slaves in Adams County around 1861. Most of the authors scented something going on from either Wailes's diary or Conner's transcript, but none has pieced together even a short coherent account. Indeed, most have misdated and/or misquoted the original documents. These references can be found in the footnotes of this book.

There are numerous pertinent secondary works, however, which are not cited in the footnotes at all. The proliferation of truly impressive studies on American slavery has been such that I have made the choice of not including them (except in a very few special instances) in the footnotes. When first setting out, I started to cite some of this now immense corpus, but I was soon overwhelmed by a sense of mercy for the reader and (not forgetting myself) thought better of it. This is not the place for a bibliography on American slavery, which is what full citation of the relevant literature would amount to.

It is with some hesitation that I have included here all the documents I have found that bear directly on the conspiracy. It is a certainty that others exist—somewhere—and I fully expect and hope that publication of this study will help bring them to light, even if they appear in the shape of my being faulted for missing them.

Clearly the transcript made by Lemuel P. Conner is so central that it needs to be immediately available in this book. Inclusion of this document will permit the reader, if so inclined, to refer to the context of the many brief quotations, which are necessarily—as all quotations are—taken out of context. The first, "literal" version is an attempt to replicate in print, insofar as possible, the original manuscript. The second, "augmented" rendering is based partly on internal evidence from the document itself and, to a lesser extent, on other sources, such as the census. Readers are urged to look at the first version—which initially and for a very long time seemed to me downright baffling—before utilizing the second.

My hesitancy about including the other documents stems from concern that some readers may assume that these constitute all that is needed for an understanding of what went on. Even taken together and lumped with all the sources cited in the footnotes, they would make up only a small portion of the evidence necessary to an enterprise of this kind. This is to say that the episode at Second Creek cannot be understood, in my opinion, without drawing on what I will immodestly call a considerable familiarity with other documents concerning American slavery and the culture of the United States in the nineteenth century. Without wide reading in such sources, there is no chance, so far as I can see, of properly evaluating the details and nuances of the documents included here.

Nor is it possible, without such collateral familiarity, to assess the significance of what happened at Second Creek. In fact, the "significance" of any historical episode is not within the competent grasp of anyone. Some readers will disagree with such a gloomy aspersion of the powers of historical analysis and will take the view that in this case the author has been lamentably remiss in assessing the meaning and significance of the story. In response, I can say that at first I had ambitions to set Second Creek in the context of unrest among unfree laborers throughout time and throughout the world. No doubt such an accomplishment would be impressive, but I have concluded to take refuge from criticism by adopting the view that such sweeping comparison would totally swamp this little tale.

In a general way, the historical source materials for the study of slavery may be readily categorized. They include such varieties of sources as have been used by historians in the fruitful proliferation of writing about slavery that has taken place since the 1960s. In addition to more general categories that pertain to southern agriculture, economic development, and politics, they include plantation diaries and account books, letters, autobiographies, travelers' accounts, newspapers, magazines, novels, other polemical publications, interviews with participants (especially former slaves), archeological findings, and extant artifacts that are not usually called "archeological" because they have not had to be dug up. Historians have recently turned increasingly to sources generated by slaves and former slaves and have treated them as evidence somehow "new" because somehow previously "ne-glected." Today, historical practitioners are more aware than they used to be about what was being done. But of course none of them is free from those denigrating assumptions—as the larger culture is not—even though there has been some change in the regarding of African Americans as people who mattered and who ought, like all people, to be taken seriously as such.

LEMUEL P. CONNER'S RECORD

SLAVE TESTIMONY BEFORE THE EXAMINATION
COMMITTEE, SECOND CREEK, ADAMS COUNTY,
MISSISSIPPI, MID-SEPTEMBER, 1861

LITERAL TRANSCRIPTION

[An envelope reads, probably in Conner's daughter's hand:]

there were <u>ten</u> Slaves hung in Brighton Woods and Cherry Grove

Documents about Uprising of <u>Slaves</u> about <u>1860–61</u>

Your <u>Grandfather L. P. Conner's</u> (Senior) own handwriting <u>the</u> <u>testimony</u> of negro slaves.

[The envelope bears the postmark:]

BAYOU GOULA, LA. NOV. 25 3 P.M. 1899 REC'D

[A covering note in the same descendant's hand reads:]

Please <u>take very special care</u> of these four sheets of paper! <u>They</u> <u>are exceed</u>ing interesting, exceedingly important as they are the <u>literal, original. testimony taken down</u> by Lemuel Parker Conner at the time of the trial of some Adams County negro slaves. Tis put down just as these negro men expressed it. This L. P. C. <u>Senior</u>

was the father of L. P. C. Jr (your Dad.— I wish this <u>Kept</u> (— together with open papers and all.

[Then, in the same hand on a new page but perhaps written earlier:] Page 1 Exact copy of Papers in connection with [two words illegible, "the actual"?] uprising of Negroe Slaves near <u>Natchez Miss just before Civil War.</u> This is the testimony as <u>taken down</u> (at the Trial of these Slaves) by Lemuel Parker Conner Sr. [one, or two, words illegible] Mr. Conners <u>own</u> handwriting. Envelope in which paper was enclosed is marked as follows,

L. P. Conner Esq.

Nov. 11, 1861

One envelope — marked

1st days original notes—

2nd days original notes

One envelope marked

"Several day's original notes"

(over)   turn to P. 3

[As things turn out, p. 3 is the second of two pages in the same hand that begins copying Conner's original transcript and then stops. The first of these pages introduces Nelson's testimony with the heading:] Page 2 (Name of Slave). "O." is for man "Orange."

[Conner's record, Adams County, Mississippi, 1861]

Nelson

Plan began on the creek fishing in May. Our boys and Mitchell's. First heard when young missus wanted black to fight for her. Edward would join to fight abolitionists, John too! First talk with W M. O. and Harvey had been plotting at Mrs Dunbars. Simon and Paul — O. and Harvey meet Mrs. Henderson's Sundays. O. 1st speaker — Plan (when Abolitionists come. O. would join them. O. says he would kill master 1st — kill Mrs to get the money. O. worst man. We all joined him in talking. Strange negroes off the place I talked with — only Edward — Mrs N's driver. After we planned to kill the whites, I did not talk with any negroes off the place. Harvey told me and O. that Steve, Wash, Obey and Henry would join — also (Ike Giddings and son and Charles) and (Ed-
                                              Dick   Henderson
mond Wyatt John Henderson) (Dick, George, Peter and Paul. Simon Mrs. Dunbars) (Mr Griers Fred, Bob and Prince) Isaac — (Prince is at Mr Nichols) (Mitchells John Driver, [one word illegi-

ble] Little John and Edward] — All of these agree to fight the white

folks. I was Govenor. O. Captain. Harvey Lieut. Alfred Genl Scott

— Wesley Printer. O. said "we will be done whipping before

long[.]" Alfred said "there will be a resting place in hell[.]" O. was

going to Mrs. King's. She is a tall slim woman. Tells fortunes. O.

said he would get Harvey. The plan they would, with axes and

hoes, kill Master and Mrs. Carry the ladies down the hill, and rav-

ish them. I take Miss Mary, Harvey Miss Anna. Alfred 1st man to

talk of ravishing. Harvey 2nd, I 3rd. Harry said (they told me) they

would kill Mrs Scott and Dr. Scott — I take Miss Ann I take Miss

Mary. Harvey Miss Sarah, Alfred Miss Anna. Wesley dont know.

George

John

Orange and Harry Scott came over to a dance. Orange brot run-

away, named Dave, belong to Bradley. Runaway talked French —

will fetch company tomorrow night. Was on Friday night — about

3 months ago — Harry kept the runaway in his house. The run-

aways had double barreled guns. Runaway stays in Harry's hen

house. Bradley is slim lame man, in left leg. Orange came another

night. Orange said he had Mitchell's Caroline Sweetheart. Alfred

said his father would begin the war soon, said "we would kill old

Mosas and take the ladies for wives." Said he was Scott. "said they would kill Steve ~~old~~ Odell — gunsmith." Harvey came then. Paul came and told my brother Peter and women about the Mosby scrape. Orange was to gather from Mitchell's Surgets — Greers — Hendersons. Alfred said "the blacks were to kill all the white men and take the young ladies and women for wives." Alfred give his name Scott — his father General. ~~Orange~~ talked to Paul, Dick, Simon, Nathan, Albert, and Harry. Every time Harry Scott comes he says, "Hell kicking up." Harry Scott said we were all bound to be free. Last Saturday Scott focht a dispatch. My brother read it. I read of it a few words. Scott said there was "Hell in that paper[.]" Harry Scott runaway, came one night with Orange to my house. [Two or more names scratched out] Alfred wanted me to join him — I told him it was impossible. I talked to no one on the place.

Simon

I heard Orange. (Harry Scott told me) was to start at Mosby's; kill him and take the ladies. Harry Scott. said, he and Orange was to get the company up. Harry Scott would ravish Mrs Scott, then to Mrs Metcalfe, then to our house and kill Mistress, and take the young ladies, and make wives of them. George, Paul and Dick, Simon at our house. Peter, Albert, kill Mr Young and take his wife.

The carriage drivers thought the negroes would be free. Our men

talked about it frequently. I too. "If the ~~white~~ ^{black} folks were turned

loose with hoes and axes they would whip the country" Edmond,

Helm's driver, said. [Three letters scratched out.] No time fixed for

the plan.

Dick.

Mosby's boys talking of the plan. I was against it. Alfred, second

to his father, to begin here killing, then on the ladies — ramm^{ish}age

them — then kill them. Alfred and Wesley talked to me about it.

[Three letters illegible] Harvey, George, Paul, Harry Scott.

Harry Scott

Orange head. Captⁿ Alfred Gen Scott, Wesley Lieut. Dick asked

for a dispatch — gave me a dime. Dick George and Peter all read

it. "They would begin at Mr. Mosby's. Kill him and ride the ladies.

Alfred? said he would have one for a wife. Alfred said, "you kill

your master, Make your Mrs for a wife." Go on to Mrs O. Metcalfe

and Mrs Dunbars and ride the ladies. Then on to Natchez. Plan at

Mrs Dunbars. They would have Captains and guns. Orange cap-

tain. Mrs Griffiths driver said at Mr Moseby's, "freedom was at our

door." Paul, Dick, Simon was going to fight — Harry ^{Scott} Scott too. "I

himself
will go in too." "I kill master and ride Mrs." At Mrs Dunbar's kill

Mrs and ride the ladies. Peter, Paul, Simon, George. "Simon be

damned if he dont have one too." Simon head man. Peter next.

Paul then. (Mr Marshall thinks Dick and Peter are deep in it.)

~~Cont. Peter~~. John, Driver
drivers
Black folks talking of freedom. These boys and Mrs Dunbar's
talked
agreed to raise up and collect all they can. Going to raise a com-

pany. ~~to~~ Simon was to tell me when and where they would com-

mence. I saw Nelson on the creek. Dennis told me George, Dick,

Paul, Simon, told him, he George was collecting a company to

fight — some of Mosby's too — fight the white people.

Dennis

First talk of freedom. Alfred be a soldier. Kill all the damn white

people. Next one was Simon. "Simon said he hoped to see the day

when he would blow down a white man who called him a damn

rascal." George Bush, along with Levi, talked fierce, and told Big

John all what they told me. George said they would gather up a

company. George, Albert and Simon leaders and Bradley a run-

away. Simon and George said the Northerners make the South shit

behind their asses. Simon said they would have white women as free as black ^{wo}men. — the white women would ~~take black hus-~~ <u>run to the</u>

~~bands~~ black man to uphold them. I have talked with Mrs Dunbars

Harry old. Alfred and Wesley talked with me.

Doctor

Dennis told me Monday night. Orange ran away. I met when away

two runaways. Yaller boy with gun and pistol. belonged to Binga-

man. The other boy, black had a gun — his name Davy Williams. I

heard John, Dennis, Harry talk about it. Philip and Harry said the
Paul

fighting would begin in New Orleans about Sep 10th [one word

illegible, and here Conner's handwriting becomes less controlled,

except for the name Isaac Giddings]. Knows nothing about the

neighborhood difficulties[.] Isaac Giddings

Mitchells boy <u>Harry Lyle</u> says 00 —

Hendersons boy <u>Adam</u> says Orange told him what amts to

nothing——

<u>John</u> (Little) belongs to J N Mitchell says Orange told him on

the Creek, that — 00—

Dr. Grier's boy <u>Fred</u> says he talked with Orange, told him Gen'l

Scott would be in N O about 10 Sept. Eat his breakfast there but

did not know when he would dine. Ships are not satisfactory.

Capt Surgets boy <u>Obey</u> — says nothing —

Capt Surgets boy <u>Billy</u> says nothing.

[The handwriting becomes more controlled again.]

Dick.

Says I am Boss. George 2nd. Simon next Paul and <u>Peter</u>. going to
take the ladies. I take Miss. Julia. George Miss ~~Margaret.~~ ^{Jenkins}   Peter

Miss Mary. Simon Miss Margaret. George is to begin killing. kill

Mrs Dunbar — no time appointed. George and Simon have guns.

Harry Scott in quarter. Talked with Alfred and Harvey. Harry Scott

was to fight. Miss Mamy Jenkins for Paul. I Captain. Peter. hind-

most. Paul 4th, George 2nd, Simon 3rd. Made plan of <u>ladies</u> two

weeks ago.

Harvey — son of Orange
[several illegible words]
Harvey says would kill Master and Mrs; ravish and kill young la-

dies; join northern army; kill whites — and blacks who would not

join. Nelson and Daddy said so. Plan started cutting out cotton.

Orange first spoke — would join when the enemy took New Or-

leans. Nelson and Wesley would kill the young ladies because

they drown and beat Wesley's sister. White man and Wesley and

Daddy at fence. Daddy in comes Wesley on fence. White man says at 10th of this month Genl Scott wants every second planter to join

him and kill white man. White man asked Daddy who was near-

est neighbor — Henderson and Walton Smith. White asked Wes-

ley how master treated him. W. M. says from Sugar farm. Raw-

boned white man, not tall, like Irishman. Twas betwixt dark and

daylight. W. M. says he was next to Metcalfe's field. The second

day it rained. Week before last — Saturday night — [three letters

illegible] 10th Sep — was Tuesday week. W. M. no beard. First

speakers Orange and Nelson. I talked to Paul, Mrs Dunbar's boy.

Paul consented — Mrs D kills up Pauls wife sewing. (Dick too

would see about it — and George his brother) and also Peter,

Dick's son.) ~~Harvey said~~ Simon. Alfred says Simon says, with hoes

and axes the negroes would do harm. Nelson Govenor. Capt

Orange. Wesley ~~Lieut.~~ printer. Lieut Harvey. Harry Scott would

join. Orange spokesman. Scott would agree when they come to

this Country up here — saw Mr. Mitchell's Dennis, Doctor, John,

(Edward, Mrs Nichol's carriage driver) Harry, D. D. J and H. agreed

to join. Saw (Henderson) Ike Giddings son Adam. Orange and I

met them at water gap. Ike Giddings agreed to join. Adam would

see about it. Orange told Wesley and Nelson what Ike Giddings

would do. Saw Mrs Dunbar's people (about 2 months ago). Saw

Scott's Harry at water melon carrying. Saw Mitchell's people before. Saw Ike Giddings about 2 Sundays ago — last Sunday too. Talked to all the negroes on the place — Northern people would whip us at New Orleans about last month. First rise here, then Dr Scotts, then Mr Metcalfes, Mrs Dunbar's. Alfred whipping Metcalfe's woman. Orange says whipping colored people would stop. Benny asked why. Alfred said the resting place would be in hell. Louis driver says Southerners whipping North. I told Louis what the white man said — that Genl Scott would eat his breakfast in New Orleans. This talk of Nelson; Benny present. Blockhead boats. White man spoke "Second planters" to help. (Orange says) Scott and Giddings. Never talked with Mose, nor Frederick. Alfred says Frederick said the negroes would rise. Gen Buttons. Talked with Frederick at Polly's house. Wesley present. I said to Homochitto Teamsters. (Henry Mr Cooper's) (Charles. Wiley Wood.) (Sanderson's, Billy) Elisha. Brandon. Talked with Henry, Charles and Billy. They agreed to join when the enemy reached Natchez. Says Orange would stay with Mrs King, fortune teller, "to Pine Ridge, to the swamp. Heard last Wednesday of the trouble at Kingston from Paul — I talked with Billy, Mrs Sanderson's boy, at breaking up time.

Alfred
H   H   Sct —   Mrs D
Ike Giddings and Adam. Harry Scott. (Paul. George. Peter. Simon.

Dick. Dennis. Doctor. John. Edward. Harry — (~~Alfred~~ Louis —)

sent for. Began talking when the war began. Was not in the field

— about the house. Orange told Mr Lincoln was coming down

here — he, O. understood it from Cooper's man. O. would join and
                            men
got all of us on the place to join. O. told me, he had talked with

Harry Scott and Frederick. I talked, only, with Fred and Harry

Scott. Fred says Gen Butler would meet Genl Scott at New Or-

leans — so soon as Genl Butler would get to New Orleans, Fred

would join. Fred says O. had him to join. I started it with Harry

Scott. Says I, "Harry, let us collect a company and whip old
                         and [one word illegible]
Lincoln out." Harry never told me he would join. O. told me,

Harry Sc would join. O. told me, he had got Ike to join — and had
   O
ˆ talked with Brandon's teamster. Louis whipping woman. O. said

the whipping business would stop. Mas Benny asked why. I said

there would be a resting place in hell. O. said, <u>after</u> Mas Benny

left, he would show Cotton planters. Nelson said nothing would

come of it. O. said he was going to Mrs Kings, fortune teller by

cards. Plan: "we would begin here — 10th Sep. O. says Fred said

Scott would be here 10th sep <u>after</u> the Northerners got here — go in the house. (O. 1ˢᵗ Nelson 2nd, I Wesley and Harvey) to Dr Scott's. Dr O. Metcalfe. Mrs Dunbar. To join at Mrs Dunbars — Paul — (Simon said negroes with hoes and axes would do much damage — Fred present). Kill master and mistress. Ravish the girls. Nelson would ravish Miss Mary — Miss Anna. Simon and Paul told my Father, they would ravish at Mrs Dunbar's — would kill those on the road — would go to New Orleans — to the North — to Natchez. O was at Mrs Kings last time he ran off. O. Govenor; Nelson, President; I, Gen Scott; Wesley printer; Harvey Lieut; O. Captain. (Harry would ravish Mrs Scott — so O. says.) White man: mother told me Wesley said he came to W. M. who had on dark clothes. Wesley says, "You are telltale." O. says there was another W. M. — only talked with one W. M. O. thinks the W. M. was painted, was a white man, tho passing himself as a negro. The W. M. says he had relations up the river. The W. Man had a short foot. O. head man. Nelson never talked with us. We all agreed to join at the first talk. I heard, "Henry Brown and Howard killed the Dutchman." O. said so. I knew it a week afterwards. We all on the place knew of the murder. I heard the negroes had got up an army at Kingston. Nelson told me of it. Nelson says Frederick told him. Nelson did not tell me, who told him of the Kingston affair. O. said he was going to have the country. Nelson would take Miss ~~Anna~~ Mary, ravish her. I Miss Anna, Harvey Miss Fanny, Wesley Miss Sarah, Nelson Miss Mary, because she poured water upon his daughter. I have no spite against the ladies. Use hoes and axes for arms.

Wesley

Wesley Printer — to go behind — heard it in May. O. 1st speaker, Nelson 2nd. "If this case should be, would you like it" "Of course I said[.]" To begin when they, the enemy got to New Orleans, to Natchez. I saw W. M. first, behind the quarters. "Master good." "whips our children" "neighbors tight." W. M. says he worked on Sugar farm. Like a dutchman or Irishman — road travellers. O. present when I was with W. M. I saw another white man behind the fig tree. The W. M. clean face, chunky. They had wool hats, linsey clothes, nice shoes; from tracks, one barefooted. W. M. says he had friends above Natchez; his home there. Bell rang and I left him and O. talking. I said W. M. was a nigger; O. said W. M. was a nigger painted red. Harry said "Twas a fine thing for the enemy to be in New Orleans." I said "Lincoln would set us free." Alfred and Munroe Morris proposed a company to be raised. Orange has a

pistol — would shoot master. O. got two pistols from Bill Chamberlain. Bill has a 5 shooter pistol. I heard (<u>Harvey said</u>) Obey
oward
would join us. ~~Harvey~~ told Margaret, "he murdered the Dutchman.["] Harvey and Alfred were all hot for the plan. I talked with W. M. just about dark. Harvey said "Stephen, Obey, Washington and Randsdall, belonging to Mr. Surget." are in it.

George.
George

Kill Mr Marshall. I Miss <u>Alie</u>, Paul Miss Mary W., Simon Miss Margaret, Albert Miss Julia, Peter Miss Mame Jenkins. Kill Mrs Dunbar's at night. No time fixed. When Northerners whip South. I, George, Paul, Simon, Albert and Dick. Alfred told us. Paul boss, Simon 2nd, George 3rd, Albert 4th. ~~Dick~~ Simon had 1st choice, Paul 2nd, George 3rd, Peter 4th. Dick took Miss Julia. Started the plan about two months ago. Simon 1st talker. Simon 1st man to talk of ravishing. Simon, Paul and I present. [One word illegible] knew of this plot before we made ours. Taint so. New plot two months. Mosby's three weeks or 4. Talked with Harry Scott. He told me he was going to have Dr. Scott, go to the back country. Then plan to kill the white folks when the Northern army got to Natchez. Simon and Harry Scott got dispatches.

Frederick

O.

First told me Gen Scott would attack New Orleans Tuesday.
O. said
Call here, kill Mr. and Mrs. Mosby, have young ladies to self, kill

Dr Scott, then go to Dr Orricks, then go to Dr Dunbar, then to Mr

Young's, then to Mr Metcalfe. Orange. I liked the looks of Julia

Dunbar; Miss Julia is the best looking. If things should happen,

I would like to have her as a wife. George, Peter, Paul, Dick

agreed to join; Orange, Nelson, Wesley, Harvey and Alfred; 5 at

Mosby's; 4 at Mrs Dunbars — I — and Harry Scott. Kill Moseby
takes possession of
— excessing the girls here — I take Miss Julia. (Would be plenty

sweethearts, George said.) George head. Harry Scott to join us.
after
First spoke Orange and Nelson. Begin ~~when~~ the fuss at New

Orleans. At first talk I agreed with Orange.

Harvey

Talked to Dennis and Doctor. I talked to Obey next to Mr Met-
will   Obey said
calfe's. Says I, ["]Obey, our folks join the Northerners." I will join

them too to help kill the white folks.

Nelson John O. Fenall. John O. Fenall

~~Harvey~~ Obey, Obey, Obey, John O. Fenall, Obey, Obey, Obey, Obey,

Obey, Obey, Obey, Obey.

end

Harry Scott

Orange

"I will kill old master and ride the ladies." ~~Harvey~~ says Mrs Griffith's black man said most time for work. ~~Alfred~~ [remainder of one-line sentence struck out and illegible]. Dick read dispatch. George too. Dick was religious man. Dick and George and Peter can read. Simon has a gun — George too.

George.

" " " " " " " " " " " " "

Alfred

Dick

[Manuscript ends]

Source: Lemuel P. Conner and Family Papers, LSU.

LEMUEL P. CONNER'S RECORD

SLAVE TESTIMONY BEFORE THE EXAMINATION
COMMITTEE, SECOND CREEK, ADAMS COUNTY,
MISSISSIPPI, MID-SEPTEMBER, 1861

AUGMENTED TRANSCRIPTION

For reference from the text of this book to Conner's transcript, the following is the order of testimony he took down:

1. Nelson Mosby
2. George Dunbar (first time)
3. Simon Dunbar
4. Dick Henderson
5. Harry Scott (Scott's) (first time)
6. John, Driver, (Mitchell's)
7. Dennis Mitchell
8. Doctor Mitchell
9. Isaac Giddings [?] (Henderson's)
10. Harry Lyle (Mitchell's)
11. Adam Henderson
12. John, Little (Mitchell's)
13. Fred Grier
14. Obey Surget
15. Billy Surget
16. Dick Dunbar
17. Harvey Mosby (first time)
18. Alfred Mosby
19. Wesley Mosby
20. George Dunbar (second time)
21. Frederick Scott
22. Harvey Mosby (second time)
   [Nelson Mosby and Obey Surget listed; no testimony recorded]

23. Harry Scott (Scott's) (second time)
[George Dunbar, Alfred Mosby, and Dick Dunbar listed; no testimony recorded]

Conner's text is as follows:

[An envelope reads, probably in Conner's daughter's hand:]

"there were <u>ten</u> Slaves hung in Brighton Woods and Cherry Grove"

"Documents about Uprising of <u>Slaves</u> about <u>1860–61</u>"

"Your <u>Grandfather L. P. Conner's</u> (Senior) own handwriting <u>the testimony</u> of negro slaves."

Nelson [Mosby]

Plan began on the creek fishing in May. Our boys and [James H.] Mitchell's. First heard when young missus wanted black to fight for her. Edward [Nichols, possibly Mitchell] would join to fight abolitionists, <u>John</u> [Mitchell] <u>too!</u> First talk with W[hite] M[an]. O.[range Mosby] and Harvey [Mosby] had been plotting at Mrs [Mary G.] Dunbars. Simon [Dunbar] and Paul [Dunbar] — O.[range] and Harvey meet Mrs [John W.?] Henderson's Sundays. O. 1st speaker — Plan (when Abolitionists come. O. would join them. O. says he would kill master [John S. Mosby] 1st — kill Mrs [Frances B. Mosby] to get the money. O. worst man. We all joined him in talking. Strange negroes off the place I talked with — only

Edward — Mrs [Eliza J.] N[ichols]'s driver. After we planned to kill

the whites, I did not talk with any negroes off the place. Harvey

told me and O. that Steve [Surget], Wash[ington Surget], Obey

[Surget] and Henry [Surget] would join — also (Ike Giddings

[Henderson] and son [Adam Henderson] and Charles [Hender-

son]) and (Edmond [,] Wyatt [,] John Henderson) (Dick [Dunbar],
Dick Henderson

George [Dunbar], Peter [Dunbar] and Paul [Dunbar]. Simon Mrs

Dunbars) (Mr [Dr. Samuel L.] Griers Fred, Bob and Prince) Isaac

[Henderson] — (Prince is at Mr [P. R.] Nichols) (Mitchells John

Driver, [one word illegible] Little John and Edward) — All of these

agree to fight the white folks. I was Govenor. O. Captain. Harvey

Lieut. Alfred [Mosby] Genl Scott — Wesley [Mosby] Printer. O.

said "we will be done whipping before long[.]" Alfred said "there

will be a resting place in hell[.]" O. was going to Mrs King's. She is

a tall slim woman. Tells fortunes. O. said he would get Harvey.

The plan they would, with axes and hoes, kill Master and Mrs

[Mosby]. Carry the ladies down the hill, and ravish them. I take

Miss Mary [Dunbar?], Harvey Miss Anna [Mosby]. Alfred 1st man

to talk of ravishing. Harvey 2nd, I 3rd. Harry [Scott] said (they told

me) they would kill Mrs [Louisa] Scott and Dr. [John T.] Scott — I

~~take Miss Ann~~ I take Miss Mary. Harvey Miss Sarah, Alfred Miss Anna. Wesley dont know.

George [Dunbar]

John
Orange [Mosby] and Harry Scott [Scott] came over [to Mrs. Mary G. Dunbar's] to a dance. Orange bro[ugh]t runaway, named Dave, belong to Bradley. Runaway talked French — will fetch company tomorrow night. Was on Friday night — about 3 months ago — Harry [Scott] kept the runaway in his house. The runaways had double barreled guns. Runaway stays in Harry's hen house. [Dave] Bradley is slim lame man, in left leg. Orange came another night. Orange said he had Mitchell's Caroline Sweetheart. Alfred [Mosby] said his father [Harry Scott] would begin the war soon, said "we would kill old Mosas [Mr. Mosby] and take the ladies for wives." Said he was [named] Scott. "said they would kill Steve ~~old~~ Odell — gunsmith." Harvey [Mosby] came then. Paul came and told my brother [Dick,] Peter [Dick's son — all Mary Dunbar's,] and women about the Mosby scrape. Orange was to gather from Mitchell's [—] Surgets [Jacob and James Surget's] — Greers [Dr. Samuel L. Grier] — Hendersons. Alfred said "the blacks were to kill all the white men and take the young ladies and women for

wives." Alfred give his name Scott — his father General. ~~Orange~~

talked to Paul, Dick, Simon, Nathan, Albert [all Mary Dunbar's],

and Harry [Dunbar, sometimes "Harry old"]. Every time Harry

Scott comes he says, "Hell kicking up." Harry Scott said we were

all bound to be free. Last Saturday Scott focht a dispatch. My

brother [Dick] read it. I read of it a few words. Scott said there was

"Hell in that paper[.]" Harry Scott['s] runaway, came one night

with Orange to my house. [Two or more names scratched out]

Alfred wanted me to join him — I told him it was impossible. I

talked to no one on the place.

Simon [Dunbar].

I heard Orange. (Harry Scott told me) was to start at Mosby's; kill

him and take the ladies. Harry Scott. said, he and Orange was to

get the company up. Harry Scott was to take Mrs [Louisa] Scott,

then to Mrs. [James W. (Jane)] Metcalfe, then to our house and kill

Mistress [Mary Dunbar], and take the young ladies, and make

wives of them. George, Paul and Dick, Simon [*i.e.*, himself] at our

house. Peter, Albert, [all Dunbar's], kill Mr [Robert] Young and

take his wife. The carriage drivers thought the negroes would be

free. Our men talked about it frequently. I too. "If the ~~white~~ black folks were turned loose with hoes and axes they would whip the country" Edmond, [John N.] Helm's driver, said. [Three letters scratched out] No time fixed for the plan.

Dick [Henderson].

Mosby's boys talking of the plan. I was against it. Alfred, second to his father [Harry Scott], to begin here [at Mosby's?] killing, then on the ladies — rammage^(ish) them — then kill them. Alfred and Wesley talked to me about it. [Three letters illegible] Harvey, George, Paul, Harry Scott.

Harry Scott [Scott]

Orange head. Capt[n] Alfred Gen [Harry] Scott, Wesley Lieut. Dick [Dunbar] asked for a dispatch — gave me a dime. Dick George and Peter all read it. "They would begin at Mr. Mosby's. Kill him and ride the ladies. Alfred? said he would have one for a wife. Alfred said, "you kill your master, Make your Mrs for a wife." Go on to Mrs O.[rrick (Helen)] Metcalfe and Mrs Dunbar and ride the ladies. Then on to Natchez. Plan at Mrs. Dunbars. They would have Captains and guns. Orange captain. Mrs [Charlotte B.] Griffiths driver said at Mr Moseby's, "freedom was at our door." Paul, Dick, Simon was going to fight — Harry Scott^(Scott) too. "I will go in too." "I

himself

kill master and ride Mrs." At Mrs Dunbar's kill Mrs and ride the

ladies. Peter, Paul, Simon, George. "Simon be damned if he dont

have one too." Simon [Dunbar] head man. Peter next. Paul then.

(Mr. Marshall [George M. Marshall] thinks Dick and Peter [both

Dunbar] are deep in it.)

~~Cont~~. ~~Peter~~. John, Driver [Mitchell]
  drivers
Black folks talking of freedom. These boys [Mitchell's] and Mrs
    talked
Dunar's agreed to raise up and collect all they can. Going to raise

a company. ~~to~~ Simon was to tell me when and where they would

commence. I saw Nelson [Mosby] on the creek. Dennis [Mitchell]

told me George, Dick, Paul, Simon, told him, he George was col-

lecting a company to fight — some of Mosby's too — fight the

white people.

Dennis [Mitchell]

First talk of freedom. Alfred be a soldier. Kill all the damn white

people. Next one was Simon. "Simon said he hoped to see the day

when he would blow down a white man who called him a damn

rascal." George Bush, along with Levi, talked fierce, and told Big

John [Mitchell driver] all what they told me. George said they

would gather up a company. George, Albert and Simon leaders and

Bradley a runaway. Simon and George said the Northerners make

the South shit behind their asses. Simon said they would have

white women as free as black ^{wo}men. — the white women would run to the

~~take black husbands~~ black man to uphold them. I have talked

with Mrs Dunbars Harry old. Alfred and Wesley talked with me.

Doctor [Mitchell]

Dennis told me Monday night. Orange ran away. I met when away

two runaways. Yaller boy with gun and pistol. belonged to [Col.

A. L.] Bingaman. The other boy, black had a gun — his name Davy

Paul [Dunbar]

Williams. I heard John [Mitchell], Dennis [Mitchell], Harry [prob-

ably Mitchell's Harry Lyle] talk about it. Philip [Mitchell] and

Harry said the fighting would begin in New Orleans about Sep

10th [one word illegible, and here Conner's handwriting becomes

less controlled, except for the name Isaac Giddings]. Knows noth-

ing about the neighborhood difficulties[.] Isaac Giddings [Hender-

son]

Mitchells boy Harry Lyle says 00 —

Hendersons boy Adam says Orange told him what am[oun]ts to

nothing——

John (Little) belongs to J N Mitchell says Orange told him on

the Creek, that — 00—

Dr. Grier's boy <u>Fred</u> says he talked with Orange, told him Gen'l [Winfield] Scott would be in N[ew] O[rleans] about 10 Sept. Eat his breakfast there but did not know when he would dine. Ships are not satisfactory.

Capt [Jacob] Surgets boy <u>Obey</u> — says nothing —

Capt Surgets boy <u>Billy</u> says nothing.

[The handwriting becomes more controlled again.]

Dick [Dunbar]

Says I am Boss. George 2nd. Simon next Paul and <u>Peter</u>. going to take the ladies. I take Miss. Julia [Dunbar]. George Miss Jenkins
~~Margaret.~~ Peter Miss Mary [Dunbar]. Simon Miss Margaret [Dunbar]. George is to begin killing. kill Mrs Dunbar — no time appointed. George and Simon have guns. Harry Scott in quarter. Talked with Alfred and Harvey. Harry Scott was to fight. Miss Mamy Jenkins for Paul. I Captain. Peter hindmost. Paul 4th, George 2nd, Simon 3rd. Made plan of <u>ladies</u> two weeks ago.

Harvey — son of Orange [Mosby]
[several illegible words]
Harvey says would kill Master and Mrs; ravish and kill young ladies; join northern army; kill whites — and blacks who would not join. Nelson and Daddy said so. Plan started cutting out cotton.

Orange first spoke — would join when the enemy [northerners] took New Orleans. Nelson and Wesley would kill the young ladies because they drown and beat Wesley's sister [Nelson's daughter]. White man and Wesley and Daddy at fence. Daddy in comes Wesley on fence. White man says at 10th of this month Genl Scott wants every second planter to join him and kill white man. White man asked Daddy who was nearest neighbor — Henderson and Walton Smith. White [man] asked Wesley how master treated him. W. M. says from Sugar farm. Rawboned white man, not tall, like Irishman. Twas betwixt dark and daylight. W. M. says he was [staying?] next to Metcalfe's field. The second day it rained. Week before last — Saturday night — [three letters illegible] 10th Sep — was Tuesday week. W. M. no beard. First speakers Orange and Nelson. I talked to Paul, Mrs Dunbar's boy. Paul consented — Mrs D kills up Pauls wife sewing. (Dick [Dunbar] too would see about it — and George his brother) and also Peter, Dick's son.) ~~Harvey said~~ Simon. Alfred says Simon says, with hoes and axes the negroes would do harm. Nelson Govenor. Capt Orange. Wesley ~~Lieut.~~ printer. Lieut Harvey. Harry Scott would join. Orange spokesman. Scott would agree when they [the northern army] come to this Country up here — saw Mr. Mitchell's Dennis, Doctor, John, (Ed-

ward, Mrs Nichol's carriage driver) Harry, D.[ennis,] D[octor].
J[ohn] and H.[arry Lyle] agreed to join. Saw (Henderson) Ike Giddings son Adam. Orange and I met them at water gap. Ike Giddings agreed to join. Adam would see about it. Orange told Wesley and Nelson what Ike Giddings would do. Saw Mrs Dunbar's people (about 2 months ago). Saw Scott's Harry at water melon carrying. Saw Mitchell's people before. Saw Ike Giddings about 2 Sundays ago — last Sunday too. Talked to all the negroes on the place — Northern people would whip us at New Orleans about last month [*i.e.*, the last of the month?] First rise here [Mosby's], then Dr Scotts, then Mr [James W.] Metcalfes, Mrs Dunbar's. Alfred whipping Metcalfe's woman. Orange says whipping colored people would stop. Benny [Benjamin H. Austen] asked why. Alfred said the resting place would be in hell. Louis [Metcalfe] driver says Southerners whipping North. I told Louis what the white man said — that Genl Scott would eat his breakfast in New Orleans. This talk of Nelson; Benny present. Blockhead [blockade] boats. White man spoke "Second planters" to help. (Orange says) Scott and Giddings. Never talked with Mose, nor Frederick. Alfred says Frederick said the negroes would rise. Gen Buttons [General Benjamin Franklin Butler]. Talked with Frederick at Pol-

ly's house. Wesley present. I said to Homochitto Teamsters. (Henry Mr Cooper's) (Charles [Henderson?]. Wiley Wood.) ([Mrs. Eliza] Sanderson's Billy) Elisha. Brandon. Talked with Henry, Charles and Billy. They agreed to join when the enemy reached Natchez. Says Orange would stay with Mrs King, fortune teller, "to Pine Ridge, to the swamp. Heard last Wednesday of the trouble at Kingston from Paul — I talked with Billy, Mrs Sanderson's boy, at breaking up time.

Alfred [Mosby]

H   H   Sct —   Mrs D
Ike Giddings and Adam. Harry Scott. (Paul. George. Peter. Simon. Dick. Dennis. Doctor. John. Edward. Harry [Lyle] — [these last five Mitchell] (~~Alfred~~ Louis —) sent for. Began talking when the war began. Was not in the field — about the house. Orange told Mr Lincoln was coming down here — he, O. understood it from
                                                        men
Cooper's man [Henry]. O. would join and got all of us on the place to join. O. told me, he had talked with Harry Scott and Frederick. I talked, only, with Fred and Harry Scott. Fred says Gen Butler would meet Genl Scott at New Orleans — so soon as Genl Butler would get to New Orleans, Fred would join. Fred says O. had him to join. I started it with Harry Scott. Says I, "Harry, let us collect a
                                and [one word illegible]
company and whip old Lincoln out." Harry never told me he

would join. O. told me, Harry Sc[ott] would join. O. told me, he
had got Ike to join — and had $\stackrel{O}{_\wedge}$ talked with Brandon's teamster.
Louis whipping woman. O. said the whipping business would
stop. Mas Benny asked why. I said there would be a resting place
in hell. O. said, after Mas Benny left, he would show Cotton planters. Nelson said nothing would come of it. O. said he was going to
Mrs Kings, fortune teller by cards. Plan: "we would begin here
[Mosby's] — 10th Sep. O. says Fred said Scott would be here 10th
sep after the Northerners got here — go in the house. (O. 1st, Nelson 2nd, I[,] Wesley and Harvey) to Dr Scott's. Dr. O.[rrick] Metcalfe. Mrs Dunbar. To join at Mrs Dunbars — Paul — (Simon said
negroes with hoes and axes would do much damage — Fred present). Kill master and mistress. Ravish the girls. Nelson would ravish Miss Mary — [I take] Miss Anna. Simon and Paul told my Father [Harry Scott], they would ravish at Mrs Dunbar's — would
kill those on the road — would go to New Orleans — to the North
— to Natchez. O was at Mrs Kings last time he ran off. O. Govenor; Nelson, President; I [Alfred], Gen Scott; Wesley printer;
Harvey Lieut; O. Captain. (Harry would ravish Mrs Scott — so O.
says.) White man: mother told me Wesley said he came to W. M.
who had on dark clothes. Wesley says, "You are telltale." O. says
there was another W. M. — only talked with one W. M. O. thinks

the W. M. was painted, was a white man, tho passing himself as a negro. The W. M. says he had relations up the river. The W. Man had a short foot. O. head man. Nelson never talked with us. We all agreed to join at the first talk. I heard, "Henry Brown and Howard killed the Dutchman." O. said so. I knew it a week afterwards. We all on the [Mosby] place knew of the murder. I heard the negroes had got up an army at Kingston. Nelson told me of it. Nelson says Frederick told him. Nelson did not tell me, who told him of the Kingston affair. O. said he was going to have the country. Nelson would take Miss ~~Anna~~ Mary, ravish her. I Miss Anna [Mosby], Harvey Miss Fanny [Mosby], Wesley Miss Sarah, Nelson Miss Mary [Dunbar], because she poured water upon his daughter. I have no spite against the ladies. Use hoes and axes for arms.

Wesley [Mosby]

Wesley Printer — to go behind — heard it in May. O. 1st speaker, Nelson 2nd. "If this case should be, would you like it[?]" "Of course I said[.]" To begin when they, the enemy got to New Orleans, to Natchez. I saw W. M. first, behind the quarters. "Master good." "whips our children" "neighbors tight." W. M. says he worked on Sugar farm. Like a dutchman or Irishman — road travellers. O. present when I was with W. M. I saw another white man behind the fig tree. The W. M. clean face, chunky. They had wool

hats, linsey clothes, nice shoes; from tracks, one barefooted. W.

M. says he had friends above Natchez; his home there. Bell rang

and I left him and O. talking. I said W. M. was a nigger; O. said W.

M. was a nigger painted red. Harry [Scott, Dunbar, or Mitchell?]

said, "Twas a fine thing for the enemy to be in New Orleans."

I said "Lincoln would set us free." Alfred and Munroe Morris

proposed a company to be raised. Orange has a pistol — would

shoot master. O. got two pistols from Bill Chamberlain. Bill

has a 5 shooter pistol. I heard (Harvey said) Obey would join us.
                                            oward
~~Harvey~~ told Margaret, "he murdered the Dutchman.["] Harvey

and Alfred were all hot for the plan. I talked with W. M. just about

dark. Harvey said "Stephen, Obey, Washington and Ransdall, be-

longing to Mr Surget." are in it.

                        George [Dunbar]
                            George
Kill Mr [George M.] Marshall. I Miss Alie [Jenkins], Paul Miss

Mary W., Simon Miss Margaret [Dunbar], Albert Miss Julia [Dun-

bar], Peter Miss Mame Jenkins. Kill Mrs Dunbar's at night. No

time fixed. When Northerners whip South. I, George [i.e., him-

self], Paul, Simon, Albert and Dick. Alfred told us. Paul boss, Si-

mon 2nd, George 3rd, Albert 4th. ~~Dick~~ Simon had 1st choice, Paul

2nd, George 3rd, Peter 4th. Dick took Miss Julia. Started the plan about two months ago. Simon 1st talker. Simon 1st man to talk of ravishing. Simon, Paul and I present. [One word illegible] knew of this plot before we made ours. Taint so. New plot two months. Mosby's three weeks or 4. Talked with Harry Scott. He told me he was going to have Dr. Scott, go to the back country. Then plan to kill the white folks when the Northern army got to Natchez. Simon and Harry Scott got dispatches.

Frederick [Scott]

O.

First told me Gen Scott would attack New Orleans Tuesday. O. said

call here, kill Mr. and Mrs. Mosby, have young ladies to self, kill Dr Scott, then go to Dr Orricks [Metcalfe], then go to Dr Dunbar, then to Mr [Robert] Young's, then to Mr [James W.] Metcalfe. Orange. I liked the looks of Julia Dunbar; Miss Julia is the best looking. If things should happen, I would like to have her as a wife. George, Peter, Paul, Dick agreed to join; Orange, Nelson, Wesley, Harvey and Alfred; 5 at Mosby's; 4 at Mrs Dunbars — I —
takes possession of
and Harry Scott. Kill Moseby — ~~excess~~ing the girls here — I take Miss Julia. (Would be plenty sweethearts, George said.) George head. Harry Scott to join us. First spoke Orange and Nelson. Begin

after
~~when~~ the fuss at New Orleans. At first talk I agreed with Orange.

Harvey [Mosby; son of Orange]

Talked to Dennis and Doctor. I talked to Obey next to Mr Met-
will   Obey said
calfe's. Says I, ["]Obey, our folks join the Northerners." I will join

them too to help kill the white folks.

Nelson John O. Fenall John O. Fenall

~~Harvey~~ Obey, Obey, Obey, John O. Fenall, Obey, Obey, Obey, Obey,

Obey, Obey, Obey, Obey.

end

Harry Scott
Orange
"I will kill old master and ride the ladies." ~~Harvey~~ says Mrs Grif-

fith's black man said most time for work. ~~Alfred~~ [remainder of

one-line sentence struck out and illegible]. Dick read dispatch.

George too. Dick was religious man. Dick and George and Peter
can read. Simon has a gun — George too.

George.

" " " " " " " " " " " " "

Alfred

Dick

[Manuscript ends]

Source: Lemuel P. Conner and Family Papers, LSU.

SUSAN SILLERS DARDEN DIARY

OF CARRIAGE DRIVERS, OTHER SLAVES, AND
WHITE MEN IN JEFFERSON COUNTY, AND
TROUBLES WITH SLAVES IN NATCHEZ AND
SECOND CREEK, 1861

[Even by the standards of her day, Susan Sillers Darden, mistress
of a plantation outside Lafayette, in Jefferson County, was very
sparing in her diary with periods and with capital letters at the
beginning of sentences. Here, some such punctuation and capital-
ization have been silently supplied.]

Thurs Jan 17. . . . Tom and Fed made 7 Bunches Plow Lines; they
had 63 Balls in all. . . .

. . . .

Tues May 7. . . . Allison Ross had a negroe to die from the bite of a
dog; there is 4 more that are badly bitten by dogs. Mrs Richardson
sent for the Dr to day. Martha had Jimmie Baptized at Jack Ross's.
Mrs Ross had her Babe baptized at the same time. It is clear and
cool. I finished Laura's Cape making her under body. . . .
Wed May 8. . . . the little negroes killed one of my largest goslins
and crippled another. Killed a small one also I have only 14 left
out 24 that were hatched. . . .
Thurs May 9. . . . I finished Laura's under body, cut out Sleeves of
Prene's calico Dress. Maryanne made them, Olivia cut out Brown
Plaid Dress for Manda. Prene sewed up the Skirt. Elsy made the
Sleeves. Sue made cake. Ben planted Pumpkin Seed in Stewart
field. It cleared off warm this evening. Mr Darden went to Fayette
did not hear any thing new. Dr Tate came at 5 Oclock; he has
joined the Adams Troop at Washington. Every one seems to be
very warm in the cause of their country.
Fri May 10 cloudy. Ann S[t]uart and Julia got here before 9 Oclock.
Dr Tate staid till after dinner. Mr Darden went to Fayette. Fed had
been talking a great deal about Lincoln freeing the servants. David

Harrison's carriage Driver had been taken up. They had been forming plans about an insurrection. He has a great many carriage drivers connected with it. The Minute men are investigating the matter. They have Bob Adams the Black Smith in Jail. Have Cousin Sarah Howes's Old Thornton in jail. Mrs Terry's negroe that was concerned in it jumped in the well and killed killed [sic] himself. The negroes engaged in it belong to H. Hinds Mrs Shackelford L. Dangerfield G. Torrey. Dr Fox P. K. Montgomery S. Darden and J. H. Darden. He whipped Fed and discharged him. Blount promised to come here to night if he could get off but did not come. It is dreadful to think of it the danger we are in all the time by the Servants besides the Abolitionists. Very warm to night.

Sat. May 11 cloudy. This morning Mr Darden went to Fayette joined the minute men. They marched up to the jail and Bob Adams came praying and crying for the Lord's to have mercy and begging the Minute Men to spare him till he could make his peace with God. Mr Darden said he could not help but feel sorry for him. He thought his time had come that they would hang him. They put him back in jail going to petition to the Govenor for him to go to the Penetentiary. — great many there. There was a meeting of minute men at Ebenezer Church and the Committee said they would hang Mr P. K. Montgomery's John (carriage Driver) and Samuel Darden's Davy (carriage driver). Mr Montgomery left. Blount Stuart thought they were too hasty and would have gone right there if he had not thought it would have been too late. Oh; Horrible; the idea of such a thing taking place in our midst. We got a letter from Buckner. He is low spirits; had so much rain the cotton looks bad and the country so disturbed; the corn looks well. Says they have a home company; he is orderly Sergeant and has a hard duty to perform if it is necessary he has to let the company all know. Charley Scott has gone home; there were only few boys left. . . . Dr Brummell's negros put Cloroform in his whiskey; he took mustard vomited it up.

Sun May 12 Clear and warm. Jim drove Ma to Jacks. Tom drove our carriage to Fayette. Fed was sick. Sarah Darden was at church, told Olivia that brother Buckner and Madison witnessed the hanging of Samuel's Darden's carriage Driver Davy and P. K. Montgomery's John. He marketed and drove carriage sometimes. Anna said she had trusted her life with Davy, had every confidence in him, did not even want him examined. They were only allowed 3 hours after the sentence was passed. I feel truly sorry for Samuel and Anna. They have no other negroe that they can trust to drive carriage. He is Blacksmith and carpenter too. Mr Montgomery Boy is great loss but he is not their only carriage driver and will not miss him so much. Davy has been in the family 26 years, poor deluded negro. Sarah heard their place was to be first attacked to commence in few days. . . .

Mon May 13. . . . Jack came by late this evening; said they brought in 2 more white men this evening one of the Cook's; put them in jail and put one in yesterday that was working on Will Trinble's house. Miss Montgomery was with them when they arrested them; it is dreadful state affairs certain. . . .

Tues May 14 cloudy rained good deal last night; ground wet as can be; hands hoeing. Mr Darden went to Fayette heard they had let old Thornton that belongs to Cousin Sarah Howes out of jail; Cooks will have a trial. . . .

. . . .

Thurs May 16. . . . Mr Darden went to Fayette after dinner. Jeff Cook that was taken for helping negroes to insurrection great many there his wife came in town she has 3 children. Frank Higdon's negroe was hung; they shot him he was advancing on the person that was going to take him; he ordered him not to advance he still kept on toward him. They have had him going through the country. It is horrible to think of. Mr Montgomery told Mr Darden that Davy died with a lie in his mouth; his Boy John acknowledged that they were going to murder the whites but Davy would not say he was going to do it himself. John told Davy to acknowlege and he would die satisfied. . . .

Fri May 17. . . . Mr Darden met with . . . [eight named men] to establish a Home Company and investigate matters; they were there all day. . . .

Sat May 18. . . . Mr Darden went to Fayette; saw Dr Wade; Sam Scott's negroes are engaged in the Rebellion had several Pistols and Knives Put Darden said he was there yesterday they had some powder buried but did not find it, were going to kill their Master. They put John Folkes's Dick (he is a preacher) in Jail at Stephen Hampley's last night. . . .

. . . .

Mon May 20 cloudy and very warm. Mr Darden went to Fayette. Jeff Cook did not have his trial on account some of the parties concerned not being present. Great many there. Samuel Darden was there. He is not satisfied about Davy's being guilty. He did not hear the trial. Brother Buckner was there; he looks better and seems in better Spirits. They had it reported that Miss Parker had Davy's Daguareotype. Samuel says the way it was that Anna was in the office. Miss P. was having her Daguarotype taken for Anna. Davy came in and Anna asked Miss P. how she would like to see Davy's picture taken and they had it taken all in jest and the report strated [sic] from that. It is a pity for any thing of the kind to get in circulation. Laura writes home that 16 of the girls had left and more would in few days on account of the excitement; the School will close on Thursday 13th June. Mr Darden heard that President Lincoln had ordered all the Foreign Ships out the Mouth Mississippi in 21 days. He will have it Blockaded so that nothing can go out nor come in to New Orleans. Dreadful State of affairs that a free and Independent people should have to submit to such an outrage. Oh; horrible; horrible; that we have to submit. . . .

. . . .

Thurs May 23. . . . There was a large company met to try Jeff Cook: 142 in favor hanging him, 165 for confining him in Jail. The testimony was not clear enough to hang him; the people living in his neighborhood were very much dissatisfied because he was not hung. . . .

. . . .

Sat May 25 Clear and cool. . . . Mr Darden was commanded to Patrol to night; he went. Finished moulding his corn at sun down.
Sun May 26 Clear. Mr Darden got Capt Jacob Stampley to excuse him. . . .
Mon May 27. . . . [Buckner's letter] said Bill Peck was trying to get a company of Irishmen, wants to keep them in the South. Says the War excitement very great. . . .

. . . .

Thurs Sep 5 1861. . . . Dr Tate came after 6 Oclock. There has been great excitement in Adam's County; the negroes were going to rise and burn Natchez. They hung 2 of Henry Swazey's negroes and have 60 confined belonging to different persons that were concerned. . . .

. . . .

Sun Sep 22 Clear very cold; had fire; Cate went home. We went to Presbyterian Church in Fayette. Mr Mrer [?] was there from

Natchez. He says there was great excitement there. The negroes had a plot to put poison in the Bread baked for the City. There was a boy belonging to Aldrich and Smith said them Fellows they had been drilling for 3 weeks had 25 of them in jail. . . .

Mon Sep 23. . . . Dr Tate had been ordered out with the home Gauard, I suppose it is in reference to the negro rebellion in Natchez. . . .

. . . .

Tues Dec 31. . . . There was a negroe of Kelly's Struck Mrs Kelly 3 licks with his ax. Cut her several. He had stolen some Meat. His Mistress was talking to him about it. He ran off; they caught him and hung him. This is last day of 1861. How many hearts been made Sad by this dreadful War. How I do hope it was ended.

Source: Darden Diary.

HOW[ELL] HINES TO GOVERNOR

A JEFFERSON COUNTY PLANTER WRITES ABOUT
INSURRECTION, MAY 14, 1861

Gov' J J Pettus
> Dear Sir
>> On my return from Jackson I found the greatest
state of excitement caused by the discovery — of an organization
by the negros for the purpos of riseing on the 4th of July next at
which time they had been induced to believe Lincons troops
would be here for the purpos of freeing them all. This was discovered by Mr Isaac Harrison of Tensas parrish La which lies oposite
Jefferson County. Mr David Harrison, brother to the former, had
sent his children on a visit to their uncle. Being aware that the
negros all knew of the war and what it was for, Mr Isaac Harrison
secreted himself under the house and heared the conversation between his boy and his brothers. The perport of which was about
this. That when Lincons came down each one was to kill his master and that they would later the fine houses and the white
women. Mr Isaac Harrison's boy has paid the penalty. The other is
still in durance vile and has disclosed their plan and on the day I
left Jackson on Saturday two negros one belonging to Mr Darden
(who was captain) the other the property of Mr Prosper K Montgomery 1st Lieutenant were hung by the Gentlemen of the neighbourhood. There are 5 white men and 2 negros now in jail suspected of being in the plot. And the citizens are still investigating
the matter with the view of bring all criminals to sumary justice.
In consequence of this state of affairs I learn from Captain W L
Harper the citizens of Jefferson are not willing any more companys should leave the county. I told him that I considered we
were in honor bound to go and he has consented to go to New
Orleans at Co'lⁿ French's suggestion and take two or three men
with him to learn the drill[.] Now Sir it is with you to say whether
we shall go under the circumstances or not[.] We are anxious to do

so. Whether we will now get that aid from the citizens we had assurances of previously I am unable to say as I have not been home long enough to ascertain their sentiments. We have now about half horses sufficient for the battery and I am well assured we can get men enough[.] After this would it not be adviseable to keep as many of the companys in the river countys at home as possible where the largest negro population is. As for myself I dont apprehend that Lincons forces will ever reach here[.] Still there are many who live in great fear[.] I am a ware there are many in the <u>cow</u> countys who are anxious and willing to go if they could be assured their familys could or would be provided for. I am told some of the wealthiest planters in Adams are going to Europe (I presume for safty.) If such be the fact and they do not subscribe in proportion to their means to protect their property, I hope their property will be confiscated and sold to support those and the familys of those who have little or no interest in the county. Govr Moon of La I am informed has expressly forbiden any more troop from the river parishes leaving and has said if necessary would charter a Steam Boat and put troops on her so that he could send them to any parish on the river where there was an out-break.

You will please share this to Co^{ln} S. G. French. I will advise him when to ship the two guns[.] I should not under other circumstances obtruded myself on your time and patience[.]

accept for yourself — my highest regards &c

your friend,   <u>How Hines</u>

Source: How[ell] Hines to Gov. J. J. Pettus, May 14, 1861, in Governors Papers, MDAH.

JO. D. L. DAVENPORT TO GOVERNOR

A JEFFERSON COUNTY PLANTER STRESSES WEAKNESS IN FACE OF NEGRO PLOT, MAY 14, 1861

Gov Pettus
Jackson, Mi   Dear Sir:
[About eight lines are obliterated from folding. The writer inquires about getting a substitute for his military service.]
A plot has been discovered and [alrea]dy three Negroes have gone the way of all flesh or rather paid the penalty by the forfeiture of their lives. We have at this time five white men and one negro in our jail who will doubtless pull hemp. There are others who we have not yet succeeeded in arresting. In a population of 650 voters surrounded by 11,000 slaves with one company already in the field, of over one hundred men "Charley Clark Rifles" and three other companies mustered into the service awaiting your call. Has set me to thinking where I could be of the most service to my Country, <u>at home</u> or <u>in the army</u>. You will see that nothing but eternal Vigilance will keep down the enemy at home as well as on our frontier and costs [coasts?]. The plans as developed are of the most diabolical character, the white males were all to be destroyed — such of the females as suited their fancy were to be preserved as <u>Wives</u> and they were to march up the river to meet "<u>Mr. Linkin</u>" bearing off as booty such things as they could carry. Notwithstanding all this, we are a brave and fearless people, and will meet this <u>emergency</u> as we expect to meet alothers, as become <u>men</u>, meting out justice to all in the fear of God.
    But I know [three lines illegible].
    Remaining very respectfully your
                        Most Obet Servt
                        Jo. D. L. Davenport

Source: Jo. D. L. Davenport to Gov. [John J.] Pettus, May 14, 1861, in Governors Papers, MDAH.

BENJAMIN L. C. WAILES DIARY

WAILES WRITES ABOUT THE EXAMINATIONS
MAY 19–OCTOBER 23, 1861

Sunday 19 May, 1861

[. . .]

It seems an intended insurrection near Fayette, Jefferson County, planned by some white men, foreigners, Germans it is said has been detected and some two or three white men and as many negroes have been executed. Further discovery has been made extending into Franklin County.

. . . .

Thursday 8 June, 1861

. . . A flag was presented to the "Washington Troop" on the College Campus by the ladies of the vicinity as presented by [one word illegible] Alvarez Gibson who made a short speach on the occasion. The flag was received inbehalf of the Company by the Rev^d Mr. Douglass who made a suitable response and finally the Colour Seargent Calvit on receiving the Standard made his speach promising to defend it &c.

Being invited with a few others not members of the Company by Capt Middleton to be present at a meeting of the Company when a report was to be presented in relation to the establishment of a patroll and formation of a Vigilance Committee all to be appointed by three person the Captain with the power of life and death. Some discussion arose here which seemed indiscreet there being several dozzens small boys present who must have taken away with them some confused views of the state of the County and of some great impending evil in which our slaves were to be involved. When it is considered that these children will mingle before night and converse freely if not indiscreetly with our servants it is to be apprehended that a degree of alarm and restlessness may be produced which it is certainly the part of wisdom and prudence to keep down. The report seemed as temperate guarded and prudent as document of this kind could be.

. . . .

Wednesday 26 June, 1861
... Was notified today by W N Whitehurst Secretary to the "Washington Troop" that I had been appointed one of a "Judical Committee["] of seven constituted by resolution of said Troop to try in cases of immergency and last resort when our courts cannot in consequence of invasion or other unavoidable causes act efficiently, such persons white or black as may be detected in causing or engaged in insurrection. This is a very delicate and dangerous power to exercise but self preservation may justify it[.]

. . . .

Saturday 21 Sept 1861
[...]
    It seems there has been a meditated negro insurrection on Second Creek extending to Natchez and neighborhood[.] [I]t was discovered about Monday last and a Committee of Citizens of different parts of the County composed in part of the Officcr of the two military companies of Pine Ridge and this place have been closely engaged for several days past in making investigation[.] A number of arrests have been made and very positive proof obtained. It is said a number of the Slaves were to be hung today. The City of Natchez was to have been fired as a signal for a general rising—

Sunday 22 Sept 1861
... Owing to the disturbcd State of the County I was advised not to send a Servant in to meet the boat last night[.]
    ... went to the College after three PM to attend a meeting of the Washington troop convened in view of the proceedings of the Committee on Second Creek to claim the right of deciding on cases of accused slaves who may be arrested by our own Committee to secure the innocent from wanton severity and to give the accused the benefit of trial by those to whom they are best known. . . .

Monday 23 September 1861
... Last night a large fire occurred in Natchez. . . .
    Occurring at this time and connecting it with the Second

Creek disturbances, it was thought by a great many to have been the work of an incendiary: But I understand that circumstances connected with the matter go far to prove that it was accidental and the result of carelessness[.]

. . . .

Wednesday 25 Sept 1861
. . . Invited to attend a called meeting of the Washington Troop at which it is proposed to reconsider the resolutions of Sunday, which it seems Capt Middleton and Lieut Roware assumed the responsibility of witholding least some offense might be given to the people of Kingston and Second Creek. . . .

. . . .

Saturday 28 Septr 1861
[. . .]
  The Washington troop had a drill at the College — Excitement about the Insurrection on Second Creek has some what abated[.] Their is said to be a number of arrests in Natchez for examination yet. . . .

. . . .

Monday 30 Sep 1861
[. . .]
  There was to have been a large public or Mass meeting at the Courthouse to day to take some measures about a Committee of Vigilance and in reference to the late attempted or proposed insurrection on Second Creek[.] [H]ave not heard what was done[.]

Tuesday 1 Octr 1861
. . . Very large meeting at the Court House yesterday[.] [T]hree persons added to the Vigilance or Judicial Committee of the Civty for each of the precincts of Washington and Pine Ridge — Committee met today at the Race track engaged in examining the negros arrested in and about Natchez, — Not heard the result. . . .

Wednesday 2 Octr 1861
. . . Heard nothing of the progress making by the investigating Committee at the Race Course today or yesterday —
  Very few persons were seen there or passing[.] It is said that

measures have been <u>adopted</u> to exclude the Crowd or mob and that the investigations are to be conducted privately and without interruption and free from the excitement and influence of the outsiders. . . .

. . . .

Wednesday 23 Oct 1861
. . . [In or near Natchez] Met detachment of Volunteers guarding several negroes who had been condemned by the Judicial or Vigilance Committee, they were taken out to the Race track and eight of them hung. . . .

Source: Diary, Benjamin Leonard Covington Wailes Collection, in DUL.

LOUISA AND JOSEPH LOVELL LETTERS

THE DAUGHTER OF A PROMINENT POLITICIAN WRITES ABOUT INSURRECTION IN NATCHEZ TO HER HUSBAND, IN THE ARMY . . .

Monmouth
Sept. 21, 1861

[. . .]

We have been kept in a great state of excitement for the last week with stories of insurrections etc. There has indeed been some reason for apprehension in N. and the neighbourhood — a large number of plantations on second creek were implicated — The Home guard, and Vigilance Committee have been constantly on the alert arresting and confining suspected individuals — Many around us have been found guilty and hung, as now for instance as [at] Capt Martin's — Now this state of things never happened here before, and I have never really been alarmed before — It is indeed unsafe and dangerous to be so left alone as we are — I wrote you in my last letter how we were frightened a few evenings ago, by a man's showing himself out the front gallery, just before the door. They say, that a miserable, sneaking abolitionist has been at the bottom of this whole affair. I hope that he will be caught and burned alive for no torture is too good for the [one word illegible] wretch — I should not be surprised if it had been he, lurking about here the other night[.] Mr Voor has been very active in keeping up a strict watch — We now have sentinels around us every night and the "Guard" are posted in the lane between Linden and us. Every now and then I hear the report of a gun at different points — and we have taken every precaution out here to be ready for an emergency. It is indeed a tumultuous time — no one is safe — Last night there was a large fire in N — the whole square near Baker's including all Kisee's stables were burned to the ground[.] There was a great excitement in town. . . .

. . . AND CAPTAIN LOVELL REPLIES FROM THE
FRONT IN VIRGINIA

Fairfax Court House
Oct. 6, 1861

[. . .]

I have been greatly troubled by the news you give me of the difficulty among the negroes, but perhaps as the thing has turned out it is well, as no doubt the ones implicated will meet with a fearful retribution, such a one as will put an end to all such attempts for a long time to come, how horrible would have been its success. I am strongly of the hope that the discovery will so awaken the people at home to the possibility of such dangers that they will keep up the necessary vigilance to prevent it in future.

You must charge Mr. Voor to keep careful watch. . . .

Source: Louisa Quitman Lovell to Capt. Joseph Lovell, Monmouth [near Natchez], September 21, 1861, Joseph Lovell to Louisa Lovell, Fairfax Court House, [Va.], October 6, 1861, both in Quitman Family Papers, UNC.

DOCUMENT **H**

WILLIAM J. MINOR PLANTATION DIARY

A PLANTER DISCUSSES THE EXAMINATIONS,
SEPTEMBER 23–OCTOBER 10, 1861

Concord [Plantation, near Natchez] Monday 23d. Sept. 1861. Got
up from N. O. last night at 12 M — having turned back from N. O.
on account of a dispatch from J. M. saying "there was trouble
among the negroes and I had best come up." Came up on the La-
fourche found my family all well — John's daughter continues
better.— Went today to Capt. Jacob Surget's home place to attend
the examination of Negroes said to have an insurrection in con-
templation — From what I could learn I came to the conclusion
that some of the negroes who have been arrested had it in view to
murder their master and violate their mistresses — their action
seems however to be dependent on the "whipping" of the Southern people by the people of the North, when they thought, they
would be made free, then they were to rise and kill their masters
etc and the leaders were to take possession of the big house and
make the rest of the Negroes work for them, the leaders — Very
cool for the season. — rain

. . . .

Wed. 25th
Work as yesterday — Cool — No rain
Examination of Negroes
I again to day attended at Capt Jacob Surget's plantation to witness
the proceedings of the "Examining Comtee" found them still engaged in examining witness — It was, I thought, clearly proved
that there was a plot between a number of negroes on several plantations in the neighborhood of "Second Creek" and Negroes in
Natchez with a negro named Bill Postlethwaite at their head to
rise to murder their master some day this month, and then to take

possession of their mistresses and all property — they had no definite idea how this was to be done[.] Some talked of killing with such weapons as they could collect axes hoes and guns[.] Others thought of firing the houses at night and burning the sleepers to death before they could get out. All had the idea in their heads that Capt. Lincoln was to set them free. — Some thought it would not be best for them to act till they were freed by Capt. Lincoln when it would be an easy job for them to kill their masters—. Bill Postlethwaite thought it would be an easy job now as so many men had gone away.—

Ten Negro men, 7 of Capt. Jacob Surget's, 2 of Mr. Mosby's and 1 of Mrs. Mary Dunbar's were hung yesterday by order of the Committee. From what I learned, I think, the testimony was sufficient to justify the action of the committee.

Thursday 26th 1861
Work as yesterday — Cool — No rain

The Examining Comtee of the Negroes have adjourned till after Monday when there will be a meeting in town.

. . . .

Monday 30th September
Examining Comtee — elected no new testimony —

Tuesday 1st October
. . . Comtee turned up many things —

Concord Wed 2d Octo 1861
. . . Examining Comtee still in session.

Thursday 3d
. . . Ex. Comtee still in session at race track — Proved by Chases man John that the first conversation about the insurrection took place between him and a number of others on the night of the 14th April 1861 — as they came up the Hill after seeing the Quitman Light Artillery off — By the same witness was proved the agreement between the town and 2d creek company to the determination to kill, burn and ravish. The various drills and other meetings etc. etc.

. . . .

Thursday 10th
. . . Examining Comtee still in session. . . .

[After this, the next entry is October 21 at Minor's Waterloo sugar plantation, and he becomes deeply involved with the sugar harvest on his various plantations in Louisiana.]

Source: Plantation Diary, 1858–1861, in William J. Minor and Family Papers, LSU.

S[OPHIA] H. HUNT TO JENNIE [HUGHES]

A WOMAN WRITES FROM A NEIGHBORING COUNTY ABOUT THE HANGINGS, OCTOBER 15, 1861

My Dear Jennie
 . . . They have been threatened with quite a formidable Insurrection in Adams County, Miss. Natchez — 40 miles from here — 27 — have been hung after Monday there had only 5 — negro men 4 — of them were hung Carriage drivers; and dining room servants of the rich[.] Many are hung[.] They were the ring leaders — it is kept very still, not to be in the papers — The investigation is still going on — They implicated two white men — but it is thought they have not named the right ones — The head one is not yet executed[.] They still hope to make him tell — from there they were to come to this County — and go on if successful — don't speak of it only cautiously. Some act very differently[.] Several — have sent in money for the soldiers, they were to kill every Negro that would not join them. Such was their confession under the gallows — . . . .

your affectionate Aunt

Source: S[ophia] H. Hunt to Jennie [Hughes], near Woodville, Miss., October 15, 1861, in Hughes Family Papers, UNC.

WILLIAM H. KER TO MARY S. KER

A MISSISSIPPIAN IN THE CONFEDERATE ARMY REFERS TO THE "INSURRECTION"

Camp "Qui Vive," [near Manassas, Va.], Oct. 27th, 1861

My darling Sister,

Your letter of the 16th came to hand yesterday, and the one of the 13th . . . came today. . . .

I am glad to hear that the people from this [rural] country are moving into and near town, for it is far safer for all parties concerned, and as you say must make you all more sociable. I sincerely hope that the insurrection has been effectually put down, and that, for your sakes and mine, the trial may be soon over and everything quiet again; this trouble ought to be a sad lesson to those people about Natchez, who have always allowed their servants to run wild, and I hope they will not in future, as they have done in the past, heedlessly throw temptation in the way of their servants. Thank God that none of ours have been implicated in this sad affair. . . .

. . . if [Captain William T.] Martin does not meddle too much with us, we will get along very well. . . .

Your aff. brother,

Wm. H. Ker

P.S. . . . Cousin Orrick left Warrenton for home a week ago nearly, and must be nearly home by this time. I believe Mr. [Bob] Young has not given up the idea of going home, but he does not intend returning until all prospect of a battle has been given up. . . .

[Evidently Mary S. Ker wrote her brother October 25 and 30, and he replied as follows:]

"Camp Cooper" Nov. 7, 1861

. . . I am glad to hear that the finishing touch has been put to the investigations of the committee appointed to try the negroes who took part, or were suspected of having taken part, in the proposed insurrection, and I am sincerely rejoiced to know that the last of the wretches have been hung. . . .

Sources: William H. Ker to Mary S. Ker, October 27, November 7, 1861, in John Ker and Family Papers, LSU.

Document K

A. K. FARRAR TO GOVERNOR

THE CONFEDERATE PROVOST MARSHAL OF NATCHEZ ASKS FOR ASSISTANCE, 1862

Provost Marshals Office
Natchez July 17, 1862

His Excellency John J. Pettus
Gov: State of Miss
Sir:
[. . .]
According to instructions which you gave me by telegraph, I have detailed militia men who are overseeing on plantations to do police and patrol duty upon the same. This is a matter of great importance to us here, as there is a great disposition among the Negroes to be insubordinate, and to run away and go to the Federals. Within the last 12 Months we have had to hang some 40 for plotting an insurrection, and there has been about that number put in irons. I appeal to you for assistance, for I do assure you that if the overseers are taken off this County will be left in a condition that will be by no means safe. I do not wish to exempt them from entire service, I only want to keep them until an emergency arises requiring their services, then let them go and do service, but don't let them be taken off as long as it can be helped — I would like your written authority to do this — Also instructions as to the manner of proceeding against persons who will keep no overseer, and make but little provision for their Negroes, rendering it necessary for them to steal or starve and go naked — There are some few cases of that kind here, when negroes seemingly are permitted to forage upon the Community — The owners will not look after them, will not provide for them, nor will they employ an overseer. The negroes have such large liberties, they are enabled to harbor runaways, who have fire arms, traverse the whole Country, kill stock, and steal generally, supplying those who harbor them, and send to market by Negro market-men. The state of

things in consequence to this in a few cases are a serious nuisance as well as dangerous to the Community. Complaints are made to me to remedy the evil. I am however at a loss how to proceed. . . .

Your attention is respectfully asked in these matters at as early a period as possible.

Very Respectfully
A. K. Farrar
Provost Marshal

Source: Provost Marshal A. K. Farrar to Gov. John J. Pettus, Natchez, July 17, 1862, in Governors Papers, MDAH.

VAN S. BENNETT DIARY

A UNION OFFICER HEARS ABOUT SUPPRESSION OF THE SLAVE INSURRECTION, JANUARY 10, 1864

10 January 1864   [Natchez]
 Attended the Presbyterian church again today. Called on Mrs. Henry in the evening and heard her version of the servile insurrection of 1861. The outrages committed on the poor, unfortunate Negroes who were suspected of evil designs surpass any thing I ever heard or read of. The cruelty of the chivalrous gentry of Natchez would put to blush the warmest advocates of the Spanish Inquisition as practiced in the dark ages of Popery. Mrs. H. is a native of this town so the usual cry of "educational prejudice" has no force whatever. We can never know half the evil.

Source: Van S. Bennett Diary, January 10, 1864, in State Historical Society of Wisconsin, Madison.

STATEMENT OF PLEASANT SCOTT

A FORMER SLAVE TESTIFIES IN 1874 ABOUT THE EXAMINATIONS AT THE RACETRACK

My name is Pleasant Scott. I am about 38 years old, I was born and raised in Natchez. I was the slave of Livingston Roundtree. During the war I was arrested and carried to Race Course by the Vigilance Committee as it was called. I was charged with joining a company to kill white people. I was put on trial and I proved by witnesses that at the time they said I joined this company that I was up in Rollence working at my trade by permission of my master's foreman, and they let me off. They had a regular trial there and Mr Farrar was president of the Committee. Besides which I saw other men [one word illegible: "there"?], Mr Metcalf, Mr Revens, Dr. Harper, Mr. Prunalet[?], Lem Conner, Fred Thomas, A Canya Griffin, James Gunsy, Henry Stearns, and John Simon. Most of them had cowhides in their hands, John Minor had a Cowhide in his hand[.]

his
Pleasant **X** Scott
mark

subscribed and sworn to before me the 28 day of March 1874 at Natchez Miss.

George Tucker
Special Com^r

No 4960
  on the Minors.

. . . .

Statement of
Pleasant Scott
a colored witness

who is vouched for
by good men as
truthful.
   G. Tucker

Source: Statement of Pleasant Scott taken by George Tucker, March 28, 1874, in Claim (No. 7960) of Katherine S. Minor, Settled Case Files, 1877–83—Mississippi, Adams County, Records of the Southern Claims Commission, Records of the General Accounting Office, RG 217, National Archives.

STATEMENT OF JAMES CARTER

ANOTHER FORMER SLAVE TESTIFIES IN 1874 ABOUT THE EXAMINATIONS AT THE RACETRACK

My name is James Carter[.] I am about 44 years old[.] I was brought to Natchez Miss. and I came from Richmond Va. and have resided in Natchez ever since. I remained a slave until the war made me free. I belonged to George W. Fox a Druggist in Natchez. During the year I was arrested by the vigilance Committee here and tried for my life. I was charged with getting news from the battles and reading it to other colored people. It was represented that certain colored men were in the habit of meeting in a Bayou called Mrs Boyds Bayou and drilling for the purpose of rising against the whites. I was charged with getting dispatches from the enemy and reading them to these men. I was tried at the race course about two and a half miles from the town, and I was [one word illegible] tried for about three weeks almost each day. The final day they carried me out then they whipped me terribly. Several of them were whipping me at once. Mr. A K Farrar and Abner Martin were two of ones who were whipping me and the other two I cannot recall the names of. The object in whipping me was to make me confess to something. They questioned me first, and I told them I knew nothing about it, which was the truth. They said they would make me know, and then they whipped me. They would whip until I fainted and then stop and whip again. Dr Harper sat by and would feel my pulse and tell them when to stop and when to go on. During the time that I was on trial Mr William J Minor was there present every day and was one of the leading men in the trial. At the end of the trial they decided to hang me. Mr Farrar was the President of the Committee and he told me they had decided to hang me. I was then taken to the gallows to be hung.* ~~When I mounted the gallows I saw eight men hanging dead upon the gallows.~~

[The following is written in the margin:] *with [one word crossed out] others ~~men~~ who had hung and tried at the same time with me, though they were tried one by one. ~~The other~~ eight of the men were hung in my presence. There were eighteen of us, eight were hung and ten of were left.

[Then, in the body of the transcript:] They then said to me that they had concluded not to hang me but would give me a whipping and send me home. I was told when I got back to town by Benjamin Pendleton a white man and a deacon in the Baptist Church that he had saved me from being hung. I belonged to his church and he had interfered and told them that I was a pious man and did not associate with these men who went to the Bayou[.] During my trial W. J. Minor sat next to Mr Farrar and questioned me as much as any of them. They had a troop of soldiers there. When I was taken to the gallows all the men of the committee went with me and the soldiers also. I can remember of the men on that Committee Mr W. J. Minor, Mr A. K. Farrar, Mr Samblar[?], Dr Harper, Mr George Marshall, [?] Lovell[?] and on the Pine Ridge Mr Henry Metcalfe, Henry Sears[?], William Banyon[?], Noble Strickland, Abner Cornellis and others that I can not recalled the names of. I recollect also that John Minor was there and sat on the Committee with the rest.

James Carter

subscribed and sworn to before me at Natchez Miss. this 31st day of March 1874

George Tucker
Special Examings[?]

115496—Mrs K. S. Minor
    or
20489 Mrs. R. A. Minor
Statement of
James Carter (col)
Witness who has
every appearance of being
honest and is vouched
for by honest colored
people.
    G. Tucker

Source: Statement of James Carter taken by George Tucker, March 31, 1874, in Claim (No. 7960) of Katherine S. Minor, Settled Case Files, 1877–83—Mississippi, Adams County, Records of the Southern Claims Commission, Records of the General Accounting Office, RG 217, National Archives.

TESTIMONY OF REBECCA A. MINOR

MRS. MINOR DISCUSSES (1874) HER LATE HUSBAND'S ROLE IN THE EXAMINATIONS AT THE RACETRACK

Q Is your husband now living?

A No sir: he died about five years ago. His name was William J. Minor.

Counsel:

Q Do you recollect whether the officer who first came there was not General Ransom?

A Yes sir: it was General Ransom—he was in command. I recollect the evening that he arrived, very well.

Q Do you recollect a trial that took place at the Race Course some eight or ten miles from Vicksburg?

A Yes sir, I do, with regret.

Q Where was your husband when these exciting times first took place?

A He was down on his sugar-plantation in Terre Bonne parish Louisiana.

Q How was he brought back to check or limit if possible the movements that were going on?

A His son John Minor telegraphed there. Mr. Minor's views on all subjects were conservative and he was a man very much looked up to for his opinions on all subjects, and in cases of difficulty he was frequently called on to decide.

Q He was telegraphed to, to come there?

A Yes sir.

Q For what purpose?

A Because there was an insurrection feared and he thought his father ought to be at home and he telegraphed for him to come up. When he came up he heard of the meeting there, and he was then called upon by a committee to act.

Q   Did he go down to that meeting?

A   Yes sir: he went down to the meeting.

Q   Do you know what object he had in going there?

A   He had but one object, and that was to make the punishment as light as possible. He had a great horror of punishment.

Q   Did he speak of it as a most terrible thing?

A   He did, as a most terrible thing, and I should think you would find it among his writings for he always kept a diary.

Com'r Howell:

Q   I don't understand yet, what you are talking about.—punishment for what?

A   It was said to be an insurrection. The negroes who were engaged in it were some of them a bad set.

Q   When was it?

A   In 1861 I think.

Q   After the war broke out?

A   Yes sir: after the war broke out, but before Natchez had fallen. We were there alone, and as I say, my husband was sent down word to come up and protect us, and see if any means could be brought about that the trial could be carried on in an impartial manner. Mr Minor went down to the track with my sons, and they did all in their power to prevent cruelty, which certainly was administered, but he did all in his power to prevent it. He, however, was perfectly horrified at what was done there. He thought if it was proved upon the negroes on trial, that we were in danger of having an insurrection, of course it would be punished and nipped in the bud, but he was really under the impression that the testimony that was brought forward to him was not as strong as it ought to be, or as strong as they thought it would be, and the only way they could get them to confess, a great deal of cruelty was practised, much to the horror of my son John, the husband of that lady. They had to come down armed to protect Mr. Minor's life from the men who were assembled there, because Mr. Minor took a step directly opposite to their conduct.

[Counsel stated that it appears that one or two of those negroes have made affidavits, which have been returned here, describing this scene, where some of the negroes had been arrested and tried for a supposed attempt at insurrection and the murder of women and children, and one of them testifies that

Mrs Minor's husband, W. J. Minor, was there, and her son and others. He desired to show by Mrs Minor, <u>why</u> they were there, what caused them to go there, what influence they had, and their object in going.] [brackets in original]

Counsel:

Q   I understand you to say that Mr Minor's life was threatened for the part that he took in the matter?

A   Yes sir, he had to go down armed, and they would have been more severely dealt with if Mr. Minor had not taken ~~the~~ a stand against it, and the punishment that was inflicted upon them, was done against his direct wishes, and many of the negroes have thanked him for the part he took.

Q   Do you know who he took down armed for his protection?

A   He took down his son John Minor, and his nephew Mr Richard Chotard.

Q   Any one else?

A   Not any one that I recollect of. They were determined to take a stand against it, as there was nothing but widows and little children living at Natchez.

Q   Did you understand who was the leading prime movers in the barbarity or cruelty?

A   I did hear of some of them. The Metcalfs of Natchez, and Mr. Alexander Farrow; they were the leaders of the cruelty. It was one of the most unpleasant and disagreeable scenes, I have heard my husband say, that he ever witnessed, and he determined that he would never own a negro afterwards if such barbarity, and conduct, was attempted. He had owned slaves all his life, and his family before him, and a great many of them have been a hundred years in his family, and he was an exceedingly lenient master.

Q   What became of your husband, Mr W. J. Minor, afterwards?

A   He left me at Natchez, and went down to New Orleans to take care of his property in Louisiana.

Q   He left the Confederate lines?

A   Yes sir. He was taken prisoner at one time by General Butler, but Mr Minor had requested it, as he wished to be taken before General Butler.

Q   Now will you be kind enough to state anything positive—any act performed by Mrs [Katherine] Minor—in aid of the federal army, and as an evidence of her affection and faith—in that cause[.]

A   Well sir, she entertained every federal officer nearly, who came
to Natchez.

Source: Testimony of Rebecca A. Minor, Washington, D.C., April 21,
1874, in Claim (No. 7960) of Katherine S. Minor, Settled Case Files,
1877–83—Mississippi, Adams County, Records of the Southern Claims
Commission, Records of the General Accounting Office, RG 217, National Archives.

TESTIMONY OF WILLIAM T. MARTIN

A CONFEDERATE GENERAL RECALLS (1877) ALARMS IN 1860 AND THE MINORS' PARTICIPATION IN EXAMINATIONS AT THE RACETRACK

By Counsel:

Q Were Mrs Minor and her husband looked upon as Union people: did they have that reputation before the Federal troops came there?

A Oh, yes sir, before the war began. I can give you an incident to show how the matter stood. In the Spring of 1860, emissaries were found to be in our country there. I call them such, because they were provided with money from some point. They were both white and black, and there was an evident feeling of uneasiness showing itself among the negroes—a feeling of dissatisfaction &c. We captured some of those negroes, but the whites escaped. There was a good deal of excitement manifested about it in Concordia Parish (opposite Natchez) and in Adams County.

In Concordia Parish I suppose there were ten negroes to one white person, and in our own county there were four or five blacks to one white. The people became apprehensive that some servile insurrection might spring up from some quarter, and before it could be put down the negroes might resort to that sort of warfare common to half-civilized people, such as burning, robbing, insulting women, and all that kind of thing, and there was a Vigilance Committee established in the county. Being opposed to mob law, and hoping that we would have not war (and not anticipating it at that time, in fact,) I proposed that a company of cavalry be armed and equipped, made up of the best material that could be obtained in the county—young men of education belonging to the best families—and thus be ready to put down any attempted insurrection in Concordia Parish or Adams county. This organization was formed in the Spring or early part of the summer of 1860. There was a large amount of money subscribed for this purpose, most the wealthier people there contributing—prominent men like Dr. Duncan, L. R. Marshall and others. I destroyed the subscription list because I thought it might at some time be used against them. One wealthy lady, I remember, gave me money enough to buy our sabres—$600. I bought those sabres in Springfield Mass. There was one hundred of them and they cost six dollar's apiece. The men furnished their own uniforms and horses.

By Com'r Ferris:

Q   What time in 1860 was this?

A   It was in the latter part of the Spring or early part of the summer of 1860. Well, when I left home in December to come on here to see what was to be the result, the company then was officered, and we had about 100 men, or nearly that number, although they were not armed as completely as they were afterwards. John Minor was the first Lieut. and Mr Balfour was the second lieutenant. When I got back from the North I called the company together and I told them there was no use of talking about a compromise any more: that the war was inevitable—there was no question about it, and I proposed then to reorganize that company for war purposes, and told those who didn't want to take a part in it to step aside and let us go to work—that there was no use talking about it. Well, John Minor immediately resigned (and so did Balfour) and he made a little Union speech at the time he resigned. I got back there about the 20th of January and our state at that time was about seceding. I was very indignant at the idea of his resigning, and I told him that as far as his own character, and the reputation of his family was concerned, he had better have gone out on one of the bayous and shot himself! Well, I had but little to say to him from that time until I entered the army: but my brothers-in-law—four of them—who were in my company, went to him and talked with him about it, but he persisted in it, and I believe it amounted to almost a quarrel between them, and I don't think the social relations were ever restored. . . .

Q   There is a story about the hanging of some negroes at the Race Course, I believe, in this case. Do you know anything about that fact?

A   Yes sir. That was when I was in the war. Going back to the time that I speak of, when we were getting up this Company, one reason I had for doing it was, that there was a vigilance Committee in that county, and I wanted to deprive people who were disposed to be lawless, of any excuse whatever. I wanted a company that I could control, and composed of men who represented wealthy families there, in order that I might put down this lawless spirit growing out of the excitement there.

Q   We have had a history of that case several times, but I wanted to ask you this. Some one of the witnesses here charged John Minor with being present and aiding in the hanging of those negroes.

A   Whoever said so, is mistaken.

Q   You were not present, but you must have known of the fact.

A   They had my own negroes there, charged with having some connection with it. A brother-in-law of mine, who was afterwards on Bragg's staff, was one of the parties who was engaged in that matter. The best men in the county were concerned in it. John Minor never had anything to do with it, and my brother complained to me about John Minor's conduct; and the pressure was so great against Capt. Minor, and John himself (the people believing that John was influenced by his father) that they insisted upon it that Capt. Minor and himself should join them. They said, "Come and see for yourself if we are not doing right." Capt. Minor did go on the Committee and remained there and assented to the propriety of it, as I have heard since from those who took part in it. John Minor didn't have anything to do with it, so far as I ever heard: on the contrary I think it was a matter of complaint against him that he did take no part. Capt. Minor finally went off and would not have anything more to do with it, although he thought there was evidence to justify the hanging of some of them, and assented to it.

Q   You spoke [outside of the record] [brackets in original] of Mr Levin Marshall; did he occupy something the same position that you did?

A   Yes Sir: he was one of the men who contributed this money in the summer of 1860 to equip this Company. He and Dr Duncan were two of the largest slaveholders and property owners in our country. They afterwards went North. They subsequently got after Marshall and made him give some money to the Confederacy under stress. But there was no question about his being a strong Union man and opposed to the war throughout.

Q   You think he continued his opposition to the end of the war?

A   Oh yes sir

Source: Testimony of William T. Martin, Washington, D.C., December 12, 1877, pp. 6–9, 24–26, in Claim (No. 7960) of Katherine S. Minor, Settled Case Files, 1877–83—Mississippi, Adams County, Records of the Southern Claims Commission, Records of the General Accounting Office, RG 217, National Archives.

BRIEF ON LOYALTY,
KATHERINE S. MINOR CLAIM

IN 1879 ATTORNEYS ENTER A BRIEF TO SOUTHERN
CLAIMS COMMISSION ABOUT WHAT HAPPENED
AT THE RACETRACK

[...]

After the war had been sometime in progress there occurred a panic at Natchez over a pretended conspiracy among the negroes to rise and enter upon a course of murder and pillage, encouraged thereto by the absence of so many men with the army and the progress on the Mississippi of the Federal arms. A vigilance committee was formed; many negroes were arrested; trials were had out at the race-course; some negroes were hung after trial and others cruelly whipped to make them confess. James Carter and Pleasant Scott have testified that they were among the negroes tried at the race-track, and that Mr Minor and his father were both members of the committee and as busy as anybody in the work going on. The other side of the story is told by General Martin and the widows of the two Minors. They say that the elder Mr Minor was over in Louisiana when the proceedings began; that he hastened back when he heard of them; that he protested loudly against what was being done unless the evidence was conclusive; that his protest was resented by those engaged, and he was told to come upon the committee where he could see what the evidence was and use his influence effectually and justly; that he went upon the committee accordingly, and though he admitted that the evidence justified the inquiry, he denied that it was enough to justify the whippings and hangings inflicted, and did all he could to moderate the proceedings until the fright and frenzy died away and the affair came to an end. As for John Minor, it was a matter of complaint against him afterwards that he had not taken part in the work done at the race-track and that if he was present, it was as a spectator merely, and not as a doer or approver.

Source: Brief on Loyalty, Taylor and Wood Attorneys, in Claim (No. 7960) of Katherine S. Minor, Settled Case Files, 1877–83—Mississippi, Adams County, Records of the Southern Claims Commission, Records of the General Accounting Office, RG 217, National Archives.

OPINION ON THE MINORS' ROLE
AT THE RACETRACK

FROM THE SOUTHERN CLAIMS COMMISSION'S 1879
SUMMARY REPORT

It was also charged that at one time during the war John Minor and his father Wm J. Minor participated in the trial and hanging of negroes at the race course near Natchez. This statement is untrue. John Minor took no part in it. His father Wm J. Minor was opposed to the proceedings; took an active part and exerted himself to prevent the hanging of the negroes[.]

Source: Summary Report No. 55116, December, 1879, in Claim (No. 7960) of Katherine S. Minor, Settled Case Files, 1877–83—Mississippi, Adams County, Records of the Southern Claims Commission, Records of the General Accounting Office, RG 217, National Archives.

CHARLIE DAVENPORT INTERVIEW

A FORMER ADAMS COUNTY SLAVE RECALLS [1937] HEARING OF AN UPRISING: VERSION Y

241 – Charlie Davenport, Ex-slave, Adams County
FEC [Final Edited Copy?]
Edith Wyatt Moore
Rewrite, Pauline Loveless
Edited, Clara E. Stokes
[The photographed typescript pages have stamped numbers 34–43 at top right, no repeat of the heading, and are numbered 1–8 at the bottom. The section bearing most directly on the conspiracy is here set in italics. The original of this version of the Davenport interview(s) is about two-thirds as long as the other, Document Z.]

CHARLIE DAVENPORT
Natchez, Mississippi

I was named Charlie Davenport an' *encordin' to de way I fig-gers I ought to be nearly a hund'ed years old. . . .

Aventine, where I was born an' bred, was acrost Secon' Creek. It was a big plantation wid 'bout a hund'ed head o' folks a-livin' on it. It was only one o' de marster's places, 'cause he was one o' de riches' an' highes' quality gent'men in de whole country. I's telling' you de trufe, us didn' b'long to no white trash. De marster was de Honorable Mister Gabriel Shields hisse'f. Ever'body knowed 'bout him. He married a Surget.

Dem Surgets was pretty devilish; for all dey was de riches' fam'ly in de lan'. Dey way de out-fightin'es', out-cussin'es', fastes' ridin', hardes' drinkin', out-spendin'es' folks I ever seen. But Lawd! Lawd! Dey was gent'men even in dey cups. De ladies was

---

* according

beautiful wid big black eyes an' sof' white han's, but dey was high strung, too.

De marster had a town mansion what's pictured in a lot o' books. It was called "Montebella." De big columns still stan' at de end o' Shields Lane. It burnt 'bout thirty years ago (1937).

I's part Injun. . . .

De Choctaws lived all 'roun' Secon' Creek. Some of 'em had cabins lak settled folks. I can 'member dey las' chief. . . .

As I said b'fore, I growed up in de quarters. De houses was clean an' snug. Us was better fed den dan I is now, an' warmer, too. Us had blankets an' quilts filled wid home raised wool an' I jus' loved layin' in de big fat feather bed a-hearin' de rain patter on de roof.

All de little darkeys he'ped bring in wood. Den us swept de yards wid brush brooms. Den sometimes us played together in de street what run de length o' de quarters. Us th'owed horse-shoes, jumped poles, walked on stilts, an' played marbles. Sometimes us made bows an' arrows. Us could shoot 'em, too, jus lak de little Injuns.

A heap o' times old Granny would brush us hide wid a peach tree limb, but us need it. Us stole *aigs an' roasted 'em. She sho' wouldn' stan' for no stealin' if she knowed it.

Us wore lowell-cloth shirts. It was a coarse tow-sackin'. In winter us had linsey-woolsey pants an' heavy cow-hide shoes. . . .

I was a teasin', mis-che-vious chil' an' de overseer's little gal got it in for me. He was a big, hard fisted Dutchman bent on gittin' riches. He trained his pasty-faced gal to tattle on us Niggers. She got a heap o' folks whipped. I knowed it, but I was hasty. . . . .

He snatched me in de air an' toted me to a stump an' laid me 'crost it. I didn' have but one thickness 'twixt me an' daylight. Gent'man! He laid it on me wid dat stick. I thought I'd die. . . .

Den he say to me,

"From now on you works in de fiel'. I aint gwine a-have no vicious boy lak you 'roun de lady folks." I was too little for fiel' work, but de nex' mornin' I went to choppin' cotton. After dat I made a reg'lar fiel' han'. When I growed up I was a ploughman. I could sho' lay off a pretty cotton row, too.

Us slaves was fed good plain grub. . . .

Mos' ever' slave had his own little garden patch an' was 'lowed to cook out o' it.

---

*eggs

Mos' ever plantation kep' a man busy huntin' an' fishin' all de time. . . .

. . .'Course, ever' marster warnt as free handed as our'n was. (He was sho' 'nough quality.) I'se hear'd dat a heap o' cullud people never had nothin' good t'eat.

I warnt learnt nothin' in no book. Don't think I'd a-took to it, nowhow. Dey learnt de house servants to read. Us fiel' han's never knowed nothin' 'cept weather an' dirt an' to weigh cotton. Us was learnt to figger a little, but dat's all.

I reckon I was 'bout fifteen when hones' Abe Lincoln what called hisse'f a rail-splitter come here to talk wid us. He went all th'ough de country jus' a-rantin' an' a preachin' 'bout us bein' his black brothers. De marster didn' know nothin' 'bout it, 'cause it was sorta secret-lak. It sho' riled de Niggers up an' lots of 'em run away. I sho' hear'd him, but I didn' pay 'im no min'.

When de war broke out dat old Yankee Dutch overseer o' our'n went back up North, where he b'longed. Us was pow'ful glad an' hoped he'd git his neck broke.

After dat de Yankees come a-swoopin' down on us. My own pappy took off wid 'em. He j'ined a comp'ny what *fit at Vicksburg. I was plenty big 'nough to fight, but I didn' hanker to tote no gun. I stayed on de plantation an' put in a crop.

It was pow'ful oneasy times after dat. But what I care 'bout freedom? Folks what was free was in misery firs' one way an' den de other. . . .

De marster's sons went to war. De one what us loved bes' never come back no more. Us mourned him a-plenty, 'cause he was so jolly an' happy-lak, an' free wid his change. Us all felt cheered when he come 'roun'.

Us Niggers didn' know nothin' 'bout what was gwine on in de outside worl'. All us knowed was dat a war was bein' fit. Pussonally, I b'lieve in what Marse Jefferson Davis done. He done de only thing a gent'man could a-done. He tol' Marse Abe Lincoln to 'tend to his own bus'ness an' he'd 'tend to his'n. But Marse Lincoln was a fightin' man an' he come down here an' tried to run other folks' plantations. Dat made Marse Davis so all fired mad dat he spit hard 'twixt his teeth an' say, "I'll whip de socks of dem dam Yankees."

Dat's how it all come 'bout.

---

*fought

My white folks los' money, cattle, slaves, an' cotton in de war, but dey was still better off dan mos' folks.

. . . [Experiences during Reconstruction. The following paragraph appears to apply to that time and to outside and/or black preachers, but may possibly have been intended to include times before the war.]

Us Niggers didn' have no secret meetin's. All us had was church meetin's in arbors out in de woods. De preachers 'ud exhort us dat us was de chillun o' Israel in de wilderness an' de Lawd done sont us to take dis lan' o' milk an' honey. But how us gwine a-take lan' what's already been took? . . .

My granny tol' me 'bout a slave uprisin' what took place when I was a little boy. None o' de marster's Niggers 'ud have nothin' to do wid it. A Nigger tried to git 'em to kill dey white folks an' take dey lan'. But what us want to kill old Marster an' take de lan' when dey was de bes' frien's us had? Dey caught de Nigger an' hung 'im to a limb. . . .

De young Niggers is headed straight for hell. . . .

I'se seen a heap o' fools what thinks 'cause they is wise in books, they is wise in all things.

Mos' all my white folks is gone, now. Marse Randolph Shields is a doctor 'way off in China. I wish I could git word to 'im, 'cause I know he'd look after me if he knowed I was on charity. I prays de Lawd to see 'em all when I die.

Source: Charlie Davenport interviewed by Edith Wyatt Moore, 1937, rewritten by Pauline Loveless, ed. Clara E. Stokes, in Rawick, *American Slave,* Vol. VII (Okla. and Miss. Narrs.), Pt. 2, pp. 34–43.

CHARLIE DAVENPORT INTERVIEW

A FORMER ADAMS COUNTY SLAVE RECALLS PLANNED UPRISING: VERSION Z

241–Autobiography of An Exslave
Charlie Davenport–Adams County
FC [final copy?]
(By Edith Wyatt Moore)

[Part of the interview apparently contains responses to questions numbered 1 through 16, but the questions themselves are not indicated. Similarly, superscript numerals in parentheses have no specific references; they almost certainly refer to set questions received by the state field office from the national office in Washington. The section most directly bearing on the conspiracy is here set in italics. The original of this version of the Davenport interview(s) is about 50 percent longer than the other, Document Y.]

—Miss, "I is named Charlie Davenport en 'cordin to de way I figgers I ought to be nearly a hundred. . . .

—Aventine where I wuz bawn en bred wuz across Second Creek. Hit wuz a big plantation wid 'bout a hundred head ob people libin dare. Hit wuz only one ob us Marster's places cause he wuz one ob de richest en highest quality gentlemen in de whole country. Ize telling you de trufe, us didn't 'blong to no white trash. Our Marster wuz de Honorable Mister Gabriel Shields hisself. Ebbery body knows 'bout him. He married a Surget. Dem Surgets wuz pretty debblish fur all dey wuz de richest fambly in de land. Dey wuz de out fightenist, out cussinest, fastest ridin, hardest drinkin, out spendinest folks I ebber seed. But Lawd, Lawd, dey wuz gentlemen eben in dey cups. De Ladies wuz beautiful wid big black eyes en soft white hands but dey wuz high strung too.

Us Marster had a town mansion whats pictured in a lot

of books. Hit wuz called "Montebella" en de big columns still stands yit at de end ob Shields Lane. Hit burned 'bout thirty years ago.

—I iz part Injun. . . .

—De Choctaws lived all round Second Creek. Some ob dem had cabins like settled folks. I kin remembah dare last chief. . . .

—Ez I tole you, I growed up in de quarters. Our houses wuz clean en snug. We wuz bettah fed den I is now en warmer too, kaize us had blankets en quilts filled wid home raised wool. I jist loved layin in de big fat feather bed a hearin de rain patter on de roof.

—All de little darkeys helped bring in wood en us swept de yards wid brush brooms. Sometimes us played together in de street which run de length ob de quarters. Us throwed horse shoes, jumped poles, walked on stilts en played marbles. Sometimes us made bows en arrows too en we learned to shoot like little Injuns.

A heap ob times our ole granny would brush our hide wid a peach tree limb. But us needed hit kaize us stole aigs (eggs) en roasted dem. She show wouldn't stand fur no stealin if she knowed hit.

We wore Lowell cloth shirts. It wuz a coarse tow sacking. In winter we had Lindsey Woolsey pants en heavy cow hide shoes. . . .

I wuz a teasin, mischievous chile en de oberseers little girl got hit in fur me. He wuz a big, hard fisted Dutchman bent on gittin riches. So he trained his pasty-faced chile to tattle on us. She got a heap ob people whipped. I knowed hit but I wuz hasty. . . .

He snatched me in de air en toted me to a stump en laid me acrost hit. I didn't hab but one thickness between me en daylight. Gentlemen! but he laid hit on me wid dat stick. I thought I'd die. . . . Den he say to me:

"From now on you works in de field. I ain't going to hab no vicious boy like you around my wimmin folks".

I wuz too little fur field work but next mawin I went to choppin cotton. Aftah dat I made a regular field hand. When I growed up I wuz a ploughman en could shore lay off a pretty cotton row.

On Sundays us rested en had meetin in a log house where a white preacher tole us 'bout de way ob salvation.[1]

q 12[2] Us slaves wuz fed good plain food. . . .

1. No such sentence appears in the other version.

Nearly ebbery slave had his own little garden patch en he wuz lowed to cook out ob his patch. . . .

Most ebbery plantation kep a man busy huntin en fishin all de time. . . . 'Course ebbery Marster wuzn't ez free handed ez ourn. He wuz shore nuff quality. I've heard that a heap ob colored folks never had nothin good.

q 13[3] I wuzn't larnt nothin in a book. Don't think I'd a tuck to hit no how. Dey did teach de house servants to read but us field hands never knowed nothin but dirt, en weather en how to weigh cotton. Us wuz larnt to figger a little but dats all. . . . [2]

I reckon I wuz 'bout fifteen when honest Abe Lincoln, what called hisself a rail splitter, come here to talk wid us. He went all through de country jest a rantin and preachin 'bout us bein his black brudders. Ole Marse didn't know nothin 'bout hit 'cause hit was sorta secret like. Hit shore riled de niggers up en lots ob 'em run away. Yas ma'am, I shore heard him but didn't pay him no mind.

When de wah broke out our ole Dutch oberseer went back nawth. We wuz powerful glad en hoped he'd git his neck broke.

Aftah dat de Yankees came swoopin down on us. My own pappy tuck off wid em. He jined a company what fit at Vicksburg. I wuz plenty big enough to fight but didn't hanker to tote no gun. I stayed on de plantation en put in a crop. Hit wuz powerful oneasy times aftah dat but what I keer 'bout freedom? Folks what wuz free wuz in misery fust one way en another. . . .

Our Ole Marsters sons went to wah. De one what us loved de best nevah come home no more. Us mourned him plenty kaise he wuz so jolly en happy like en free wid his change. Us all felt cheered when he come around.

Ez to Mr. Jefferson Davis . . . [3] us slaves didn't know nothin 'bout what wuz goin on in de outside world. All us know wuz dat a wah wuz bein fit. Pusonally, I 'bleeve in what Mr. Davis done. He done de only thing a gentleman could do. He tole Mr. Abe Lincoln to tend to his own business 'en he'd tend to hissen. But Lincoln wuz a fightin man en he come down here to run other folks plantations. Dat made Mr. Davis so all fired mad dat he spit hard between his teeth en say:

"I'll whip de socks offen dem damn Yankees."

---

2. The previous four paragraphs, beginning "q 12," actually appear later in this version, and have here been moved up so as to correspond with the other.

3. The ellipsis is in the typescript.

Dats how hit all come about. My white folks lost money, cattle, slaves en cotton but dey wuz still bettah off den most folks. I stayed right wid 'em but they is most all gone now. Marse Randolph Shields is a doctor way off in China. I 'bleeves day would look aftah me now if day knowed I wuz on charity.

... [Various numbered queries. Experiences during Reconstruction. The following paragraph appears to apply to that time and to outside and/or black preachers, but may possibly have been intended to include times before the war.]

q 4 ... Us niggers didn't have no secret meetins. All us had wuz church meetins in arbors out in de woods. De preachers would exhort us dat we wuz de chillen of Israel in de wilderness en de Lawd done sont us to take dis land ob milk en honey. But how us gwine to take land what wuz already took?[4]

q 10 *When I wuz a little boy they wuz a slave uprisin planned. Hit wuz befo de wah broke out. De slaves had hit all worked out how dey wuz goin to march on Natchez aftah slayin all dare own white folks. Us folks wouldn't jine 'em kaise what we want to kill Ole Marse fur? One night a strange nigger come en he harangued de ole folks but dey wouldn't budge. While he wuz talkin up rid de sheriff en a passel ob men. He wuz a powerful, big black feller named Jupiter, en when he seed who wuz comin he turned en fled in a corn field.*

My granny tole me next day dat dey kotch him hidin in a bayou en hung him on a limb. Dey didn't need no trial kaise he was kotch rilin de folks to murder. ...

q 16[5] How I gwine to know 'bout de rights or wrongs ob slavery? Fur ez I is concerned I wuz bettah treated ez a slave den I is now. Folks says hit wuz wicked but fur all I kin see de colored folks aint made much use ob day freedom. Day is all in debt en chained down to somethin same ez us slaves wuz. Dare's dat man what shot de white man. He wuz drunk en toten a gun. Ef he gits cott (caught) he'll be worse off dan any slave cause he'll hab a ball en chain on his foot er else git his neck broke. Day aint no sich thing ez freedom. Us is all tied down to somethin.

---

4. Unlike the other brief passage on preaching, this one does appear in the other version.

Source: Charlie Davenport interviewed by Edith Wyatt Moore, 1937, in Rawick, *American Slave,* Suppl. 1, Vol. VII (Miss. Narrs.), Pt. 2, pp. 558–72.

CAST OF CHARACTERS

BLACK, BY OWN NAME (IF KNOWN)

NAMES KNOWN

[Alphabetization is by last name, if any, otherwise by first name. The name of the owner, if any and if known, is in brackets.]

ADAM [Henderson], son of Ike Giddings; probably examined

ALBERT [Dunbar]

ALFRED [Mosby], son of Harry Scott [Scott] and claimed Scott name; probably whipping Metcalfe woman; examined

ALLEN [Shields], skilled slave at Aventine

ANDERSON, ANDY J. [Haley], former slave in Texas who in 1937 still recalled being whipped

BIG JOHN, *see* JOHN, DRIVER

BILL, *see* CHAMBERLAIN, BILL

BILLY [Sanderson], probably a young man

BILLY [Surget], examined but said nothing

BILLY [?], a Homochitto teamster

BOB [Grier]

BROWN, DICK [Shields], punished by overseer for running away

BROWN, HENRY [?], perhaps white; said to have killed Dutchman

BUSH, GEORGE [?], talked fierce; perhaps free

CAROLINE [Mitchell], purported "sweetheart" of Orange Mosby

CARTER, JAMES, former slave of Natchez druggist; after the war deposed to the Southern Claims Commission about whipping and hanging at the racetrack

CHAMBERLAIN, BILL [?], perhaps white; supplied Orange Mosby with two pistols

CHARLES [Cooper], not certainly Cooper's

CHARLES [Henderson]

CHARLES [?], a Homochitto teamster; perhaps Cooper's

CHARLIE, *see* DAVENPORT, CHARLIE

DAVE [Bradley], runaway who went to the dance at Dunbars; *see also* WILLIAMS, DAVY

DAVENPORT [Shields], slave who chafed under Sauters' regime; perhaps William Davenport

DAVENPORT, CHARLIE [Shields], former slave interviewed by Edith Wyatt Moore for the Federal Writers' Project in 1937

DAVENPORT, WILLIAM [Shields], Charlie's father; served in Union army

DAVY [D. Harrison], carriage driver; thought by some to be innocent but found guilty in Jefferson County

DAVY, *see* WILLIAMS, DAVY

DENNIS [Mitchell], a young man; examined

DICK [Folkes], preacher jailed in Jefferson County

DICK, *see* BROWN, DICK

DICK [Dunbar], brother of George and father of Peter; literate and singled out as a religious man; examined

DICK [Henderson], only slave not from Dunbar's, Mosby's, or Scott's who was said to have talked about ravishing

DIXON [Shields], skilled slave at Aventine

DOCTOR [Mitchell], probably a young man; examined

DRIVER, *see* JOHN, DRIVER

EDMOND [Helm], carriage driver; on the place for at least ten years

EDMUND [Henderson], perhaps same as Helm's carriage driver

EDWARD [Mitchell]

EDWARD [Nichols], Mrs. Nichols' carriage driver

ELISHA [Brandon], a Homochitto teamster; probably same as anonymous Brandon teamster

FANNY [Shields], mentally disturbed and frequently confined on the plantation

FRED [Grier], examined

FREDERICK [?], visitor at Polly's house; probably same as Fred(erick) [Scott]

FREDERICK [Scott], sometimes Fred; examined

GEORGE, *see* BUSH, GEORGE

GEORGE [Dunbar], brother of Dick [Dunbar], and Peter's uncle; had a gun; literate, examined twice and perhaps a third time

GIDDINGS, IKE [Henderson], also known as Isaac and in one source Giddons; father of Adam; mentioned by rebels and may have been examined

HARRIET [Mosby], middle-aged slave with house skills; probably mother of Wesley and wife of Nelson

HARRY [Dunbar], sometimes Harry old

HARRY LYLE, *see* LYLE, HARRY

HARRY SCOTT, *see* SCOTT, HARRY

HARVEY [Mosby], son of Orange; examined twice

HENRY, *see* BROWN, HENRY

HENRY [Cooper], a Homochitto teamster, possibly white

HENRY [Mosby], a Mosby adult slave in early 1850s; gone by 1860

HENRY [Surget]

HOMOCHITTO TEAMSTERS, probably both black and white; worked clearing river and doing related wagoneering

HOWARD [?], perhaps white; said to have claimed killing the Dutchman

IKE, *see* GIDDINGS, IKE

ISAAC [Grier], probably not Grier's but Henderson's Ike Giddings

JACOB [Shields], flogged by overseer for unspecified offense

JOHN [Chase], during racetrack examinations revealed first talks of April 14

JOHN [Henderson]

JOHN, DRIVER [Mitchell], carriage driver whose occupation sometimes was used almost as last name; also called Big John; may have served as overseer; examined

JOHN, LITTLE [Mitchell], perhaps John Driver's son; probably examined

JOHNSON, WILLIAM, prosperous free Negro barber, businessman, farmer, and informative diarist in Natchez; murdered by a man of disputed race in 1851

JUPITER [?], rebel slave otherwise unknown who, according to Charlie Davenport's recollection, attempted to recruit at Aventine

KING, MRS., perhaps white; fortune-teller, perhaps in Pine Ridge; otherwise unknown

LEVI [?], talked fierce; perhaps free

LITTLE JOHN, *see* JOHN, LITTLE

LOUIS [Metcalfe], driver; probably owned by Dr. James Metcalfe but not attached full-time to any single Metcalfe family plantation

LUCY [Shields], noted in Aventine overseer's ledger

LYLE, HARRY [Mitchell], probably examined and may have refused to talk

MARGARET [?], almost certainly a slave, whom Howard told about murder of Dutchman

MARIA [Mosby], middle-aged slave; was substituted for Harriet in debt contract

MORRIS, MUNROE [?], perhaps white; perhaps free

MOSE [Scott], possibly on another plantation; in on Plan

MUNROE, *see* MORRIS, MUNROE

NATHAN [Dunbar]

NELSON [Mosby], father of Wesley and Wesley's sister; examined

OBEY [Surget], examined but said nothing

ORANGE [Mosby], mobile, resourceful runaway and active planner; father of Harvey; perhaps examined

PAUL [Dunbar]

PETER [Dunbar], Dick's son and George's nephew; literate; last as a leader

PHILIP [Mitchell]

POLLY [Scott?; Mosby?; Dunbar?], of "Polly's house," location of which is problematical

POSTLETHWAITE, BILL, slave said to be at head of Natchez conspiracy; presumably owned by some member of the prominent Postlethwaite family of Natchez

PRINCE [Grier], referred to as "at Mr. Nichols," perhaps hired out or working there under an informal arrangement

PRINCE [Nichols?], probably same as Grier's Prince

RANSDELL [Surget]

SCOTT, HARRY [Scott], in his fifties and father of Alfred [Mosby]; examined twice

SCOTT, LEE, stockminder; preacher; testified about K. S. Minor

SCOTT, PLEASANT [Roundtree], tried and released at racetrack

SIMON [Dunbar], examined

STEVE (STEPHEN) [Surget]

STIER, ISAAC, born a slave in Jefferson County; interviewed in 1937

WASH(INGTON) [Surget]

WESLEY [Mosby], son of Nelson; at about twenty-two, probably the youngest of the Mosby rebels; examined

WILLIAM, see DAVENPORT, WILLIAM

WILLIAMS, CHARLES [Baker], Adams County slave who much later wrote an autobiography; owned by Baker and probably not involved in Plan

WILLIAMS, DAVY [?], runaway in Adams County; had a gun; may have been same person as Dave [Bradley]

WOOD, WILEY [?], perhaps free; perhaps owned by Nancy Wood or Dr. Spencer Wood

WYATT [Henderson]

NAMES UNKNOWN

[Alphabetization is by owner's name, if known.]

[BAKER], mother of Charles Williams [Baker]; a house servant and slave driver

[BINGAMAN], a "yaller boy" runaway with gun and pistol

[BRANDON], a Homochitto teamster

[DUNBAR], wife of Paul [Dunbar]; abused by Mrs. D.

[GRIFFITH], a carriage driver

[HARRISON, I.], several unnamed male slaves in Tensas Parish, Louisiana; conversed about the war and Lincoln

[HIGDON], male (probably); shot and hanged for resisting "arrest" in Jefferson County

[MARTIN], one or more unnamed slaves, hanged, perhaps at racetrack

[METCALFE, H. OR J. W.], woman, probably being whipped by Alfred [Mosby]

[SHIELDS], "grandmother" recalled by Charlie Davenport

[?], mother of Alfred [Mosby]; learned some aspects of Plan; possibly lived on Scott place

[?], sister of Wesley [Mosby]; daughter of Nelson [Mosby]; perhaps owned by Mosby, more probably by Mary G. Dunbar

BLACK, BY OWNER'S NAME OR NOT OWNED

BY OWNER

[Name of owner's plantation(s), if known, in parentheses.]

BAKER
    Charles Williams, Adams County slave who much later wrote an autobiography; probably not involved in Plan
    William's mother, a house servant and slave driver

BINGAMAN (Fatherland)
    a "yaller boy" runaway with gun and pistol

BRADLEY
    Dave, runaway who went to the dance at Dunbars; ownership not certain

BRANDON (Brandon Hall)
    Brandon's unnamed teamster
    Elisha, a Homochitto teamster; probably same as unnamed Brandon teamster

CHASE
    John, revealed first talks of April 14 during racetrack examinations

COOPER
    Charles (not certainly Cooper's)
    Henry, a Homochitto teamster

DUNBAR, MARY G. (Forest)
    Albert
    Dick, brother of George and father of Peter; literate and singled out as a religious man; mysteriously absent from Road Duty lists at Forest, perhaps because over age fifty; examined

George, brother of Dick, and Peter's uncle; had a gun; literate; examined twice and perhaps a third time

Harry, sometimes Harry Old

Nathan

Paul

Paul's wife, abused by Mrs. D.

Peter, Dick's son and George's nephew; literate; last as a leader

Polly [?], of "Polly's house," location of which is problematical

Simon, examined

Wesley Mosby's unnamed sister (Nelson Mosby's daughter), may possibly have belonged to Mosby rather than Dunbar

FOLKES

Dick, a preacher jailed in Jefferson County

GRIER (probably Elgin)

Bob

Fred, examined

Isaac, probably not Grier's but Henderson's Ike Giddings

Prince, referred to as "at Mr. Nichols," perhaps hired out or working there under an informal arrangement

GRIFFITH (Anchorage, near Second Creek)

an unnamed carriage driver

HALEY, JACK [Williamson County, Texas]

Anderson, Andy J., former slave in Texas who in 1937 still recalled being whipped

HARRISON, D. [Jefferson County]

Davy, carriage driver; thought by some to be innocent but found guilty in Jefferson County episode

HARRISON, I. [Tensas Parish]

several unnamed male slaves who conversed about the war and Lincoln

HELM, J. N., SR. (Oakland, near Second Creek)

Edmond, carriage driver

HENDERSON, A. C. (Grove)

Adam, son of Ike Giddings; probably examined

Charles

Dick, only slave not from Dunbar's, Mosby's, or Scott's who was said to have talked about ravishing

Edmund, possibly same as Helm's carriage driver

Ike Giddings, also known as Isaac; father of Adam; mentioned by rebels and may have been examined

John
Wyatt

HIGDON
> unnamed slave, probably male; shot and hanged for resisting "arrest" in Jefferson County

MARTIN, WILLIAM T.
> one or more unnamed slaves, hanged, perhaps at racetrack

METCALFE, HENRY L. (The Grove)
> slave woman being whipped by Alfred Mosby; may have been J. W. Metcalfe's

METCALFE, DR. JAMES (Montrose and at least two others)
> Louis, driver; probably not attached full-time to any single Metcalfe family plantation

METCALFE, JAMES W. (Ingleside Farm)
> slave woman being whipped by Alfred Mosby; may have been H. Metcalfe's

MINOR, KATHERINE S. (Carthage and Blackburn)
> Lee Scott

MITCHELL (Palatine)
> Caroline, purported "sweetheart" of Orange Mosby
> Dennis, a young man; examined
> Doctor, perhaps a young man; examined
> Edward
> John, Driver, carriage driver whose occupation sometimes was used almost as last name; also called Big John; may have served as overseer; examined
> Little John, perhaps John Driver's son; probably examined
> Lyle, Henry, probably examined and may have refused to talk
> Philip

MOSBY (Brighton)
> Alfred, son of Harry Scott (Scott's) and claimed Scott name; probably whipping Metcalfe woman; examined
> Alfred's mother, heard about some aspects of Plan; possibly lived on Scott place
> Harvey, son of Orange; examined twice
> Harriet, middle-aged slave with house skills; probably mother of Wesley and wife of Nelson
> Henry, a Mosby adult slave in early 1850s; gone by 1860
> Maria, middle-aged slave; was substituted for Harriet in debt contract
> Nelson, father of Wesley and Wesley's sister; examined

Orange, mobile, resourceful runaway; father of Harvey; perhaps examined

Polly [?], of "Polly's house," location of which is problematical

Wesley, son of Nelson; at about twenty-two, probably the youngest Mosby slave involved; examined

Wesley's unnamed sister (Nelson's daughter), perhaps owned by Dunbar

NICHOLS (Bottany Hill)

Edward, Mrs. Nichols' carriage driver

Prince, probably same as Grier's Prince

ROUNDTREE [Natchez]

Pleasant Scott

SANDERSON (Overton and Briars)

Billy, probably a young man

SCOTT (Waverly)

Frederick, sometimes Fred; examined

Mose, possibly on another plantation; in on Plan

mother of Alfred Mosby; more probably belonged to and lived at Mosby's; learned some aspects of Plan

Polly [?], of "Polly's house," location of which is problematical

Harry Scott, in his fifties and father of Alfred Mosby; examined twice

SHIELDS, GABRIEL B. (Aventine and Montebello)

Allen, skilled slave

Dick Brown, punished by overseer for running away

Davenport, slave who chafed under Sauters' regime; perhaps William Davenport

Charlie Davenport, former slave interviewed about the conspiracy in 1937

William Davenport, Charlie's father; served with Union army

Dixon, skilled slave

Fanny, mentally disturbed and frequently confined on the plantation

a "grandmother" recalled by Charlie Davenport

Jacob, flogged by overseer for unspecified offense

Lucy, noted in same overseer's ledger

STIER [Ownership complex, near Montgomery place in Jefferson County]

Isaac, interviewed in 1937

SURGET, JACOB (Cherry Grove)

Billy, examined but said nothing

Henry

Obey, examined but said nothing

Ransdell

Steve (Stephen)
Wash(ington)

NOT OWNED OR OWNER UNKNOWN

Billy, a Homochitto teamster

Brown, Henry, perhaps white; said to have killed the Dutchman

Bush, George, talked fierce; perhaps free

Carter, James, former slave of Natchez druggist; after the war deposed to the Southern Claims Commission about whipping and hanging at the racetrack

Chamberlain, Bill, perhaps white; supplied Orange Mosby with two pistols

Charles, a Homochitto teamster

Frederick, visitor at Polly's house; probably same as Fred(erick) [Scott]

Howard, perhaps white; said to have claimed killing the Dutchman

Johnson, William, prosperous free Negro barber, businessman, farmer, and informative diarist in Natchez; murdered by a man of disputed race in 1851

Jupiter, rebel slave otherwise unknown who, according to Charlie Davenport's recollection, attempted to recruit at Aventine

King, Mrs., perhaps white; fortune-teller in Pine Ridge; otherwise unknown

Levi, talked fierce; perhaps free

Margaret, almost certainly a slave, whom Howard told about murder of the Dutchman

Morris, Munroe, perhaps white; perhaps free

Postlethwaite, Bill, slave said to be at head of Natchez conspiracy; presumably owned by some member of the prominent Postlethwaite family of Natchez

Williams, Davy, runaway in Adams County; had a gun; may have been same person as Dave [Bradley]

Wood, Wiley, perhaps free; perhaps owned by Nancy Wood or Dr. Spencer Wood

WHITE

[This list includes principally those whites actively or marginally involved with the conspiracies and examinations. Omitted are a number of names, especially from the Darden and Wailes diaries, as being distinctly peripheral.]

ALIE, MISS (probably JENKINS)

ALLIE, MISS, same as Alie

AUSTEN, BENJAMIN H., eight-year-old son of John A. Austen

AUSTEN, JOHN A., overseer with wife and four children; employed by Dr. James Metcalfe

BABBITT [sometimes BABBIT], CHARLES W., stepson of John Mosby; after war was county surveyor for many years

BABBITT, MRS. FRANCES B., widow who married John S. Mosby; mother of Charles W. Babbitt

BAKER, MRS. A. H., plantation owner; perhaps mother of Louis E.

BAKER, MRS. CLARRIE, married to Louis E.; slavemistress of Charlie Williams

BAKER, LOUIS E., thirty-year-old alcoholic owner of Charlie Williams

BALFOUR, WILLIAM S., second lieutenant in troop said by William T. Martin to have been raised in 1860

BANYON [sp.?], WILLIAM, examiner at racetrack

BENNETT, VAN S., Wisconsin army officer in occupied Natchez whose diary noted being told about conspiracy

BINGAMAN, A. L., extremely wealthy planter; owner of Fatherland on outskirts of Natchez; his slaves not deeply involved

BISHOP, ANNA, seventeen-year-old member of Mosby family

BRADLEY, MR., Baptist preacher to both whites and blacks in Natchez

BRADLEY, ROBERT, probable owner of Dave, a runaway; probably a different man from "Mr." Bradley

BRAGG, BRAXTON, general in command of Confederate army unit that included Adams Troop

BRANDON, GERARD, planter of distant Brandon Hall; owned largest number of Adams County slaves; probable owner of Elisha

BROWN, HENRY, accused of having killed the Dutchman; possibly black, either slave or free

BROWN, ALBERT G., able Mississippi Democratic party leader before the war

BROWN, ANDREW, proprietor of lumber mill in lower Natchez

BROWN, HENRY, perhaps black; said to have killed the Dutchman

BROWN, the REVEREND MR., on annual retainer by Jenkins to preach to slaves at Elgin in early 1850s

BUTLER, BENJAMIN FRANKLIN, Union general, highly publicized in early stages of the war

CHAMBERLAIN, BILL, said to have provided Orange with pistols; perhaps black and if so probably free

CHASE, MR., unidentified Natchez slaveowner whose slave John talked before examination committee at racetrack

CHOTARD, RICHARD, nephew of William J. Minor; member of prominent Adams County planting family

CLARK, CHARLES, captain of Charley Clark Rifles in early years of war

CONNER, FRANCES ELIZABETH ("FANNY"), wife of L. P.

CONNER, LEMUEL PARKER, wealthy, well-connected Adams and Concordia planter; wrote down slaves' words at Second Creek examinations

COOPER, HENRY, perhaps white but more probably Henry, slave of Mr. Cooper

COOPER, MR., first name uncertain; probable owner of Henry and Charles

CORNELLIS, ABNER, examiner at racetrack

DARDEN, JESSIE, Jefferson County planter; husband of diarist Susan Sillers Darden

DARDEN, SUSAN SILLERS, diarist, especially of May episode in Jefferson County; wife of Jessie

DAVENPORT, JOHN D. L., Jefferson County planter; complainant to governor

DAVIS, JEFFERSON, Mississippi politician and Confederate president; mentioned by Charlie Davenport only

DUNBAR, DR., a mistaken identification in Frederick's testimony; see Dr. Stephen Dunbar

DUNBAR, JULIA, twenty-year-old daughter of Mary G.

DUNBAR, MAME, perhaps same as Margaret Dunbar

DUNBAR, MARGARET, twenty-three; daughter of Mary G.

DUNBAR, MARTHA W., elderly widowed matriarch at Dunbarton; mother-in-law of Mary G.; Unionist; interested in religious development of slaves

DUNBAR, MARY G., of Forest and Dunbarton; probably widowed; daughter-in-law of Martha W.; slaves heavily involved

DUNBAR, "SIR" WILLIAM, prominent founder of Dunbar clan; died 1810

DUNCAN, DR. STEPHEN, wealthy, prominent physician-planter, resident in the county

ELDER, WILLIAM HENRY, Roman Catholic bishop of Natchez; commentator on wartime conditions

FARRAR, ALEXANDER K., Kingston planter; accuser of slaves charged with 1857 murder; probable head of racetrack examination committee; Confederate provost marshal of Natchez in early years of war

"FARROW," ALEXANDER, mistaken transcription of Alexander Farrar's name

FENALL, JOHN O., mysterious, unidentifiable figure noted toward end of Conner transcript

FOLKES, JOHN, owner of Dick, a slave preacher jailed in Jefferson County

FOOTE, HENRY S., Mississippi governor and U.S. senator *ca.* 1850

FOSTER, DR. JAMES, of Hermitage near Natchez; medically treated slaves at Aventine

FOX, GEORGE W., Natchez druggist; owner of James Carter before coming of freedom; claimed Unionist sympathies

GILLESPIE, HELEN, *see* METCALFE, HELEN

GRIER, MARY S., fifteen-year-old daughter of Dr. Grier; possible target of rebels

GRIER, DR. SAMUEL L., Second Creek physician turned planter; earlier in charge of Jenkins' River Place and sometimes Elgin; perhaps entered claim for Unionist commitment after war

GRIFFIN, CANYA, at racetrack examinations

GRIFFITH, CHARLOTTE B., middle-aged wealthy slaveowner at the Second Creek Anchorage Plantation and a widow for the second time

HALE, JOHN P., antislavery New Hampshire senator

HALEY, JACK, of Williamson County, Texas; owner of Andy J. Anderson

HARPER, DR. WILLIAM, substantial physician-planter, born in North, resident in Natchez and owner of Avalanche downriver; medical adviser at racetrack examinations

HARRISON, DAVID, Jefferson County planter with slaves involved in May episode

HARRISON, ISAAC, brother of David; Tensas Parish planter and discoverer of May plot there

HELM, JOHN NEWTON, SR., wealthy planter at Oakland, south of Mosby's; his driver said to be involved

HELM, JOHN NEWTON, JR., slaves chiefly in Concordia

HENDERSON, A. C., of Grove, toward Natchez from the Creek; some slaves involved

HENDERSON, MRS., probably daughter-in-law of A. C.

HENDERSON, JOHN W., young planter; lived either nearby or with the long-established senior Henderson

HENRY, MRS. L. A., widow (probably of a merchant) and schoolteacher in Natchez; informant of Captain Bennett in 1864

HIGDON, FRANK, owner of slave shot and hanged in Jefferson County

HINES, HOWELL, Jefferson County planter; complainant to governor

HOMOCHITTO TEAMSTERS, probably both white and black; worked clearing river and doing related wagoneering

HOWARD (first name), said to have claimed killing the Dutchman; perhaps black, either free or slave

HUGHES, JENNIE, niece and correspondent of Sophia Hunt

HUNT, SOPHIA H., conveyor of conspiracy news to Jennie Hughes

JENKINS, MISS ALIE (ALLIE), probably the daughter of Annis and John C. Jenkins

JENKINS, ANNIS DUNBAR, married to John; died 1855

JENKINS, DR. JOHN C., wealthy planter, horticulturist, and diarist; native of Pennsylvania; resident at Elgin from 1840 but dead of yellow fever in 1855

JENKINS, MAMY, perhaps same as Margaret Jenkins

JENKINS, MARGARET, initially confused in Conner's transcript with Margaret Dunbar

JONES, MR., shot and killed in Natchez in 1841 by John Mosby

KER, MARY S., daughter of physician-planter of Adams County; sister of William

KER, WILLIAM H., lieutenant in Adams Troop, Jeff Davis Legion, in Virginia; frequent letter writer to his sister Mary.

KILPATRICK, A. R., U.S. assistant marshal for 1860 census in Concordia Parish

KING, MRS., fortune-teller, perhaps in Pine Ridge, otherwise unknown; perhaps black

LAMAR, L. Q. C., prominent Mississippi jurist and politician

LEWIS, MR., young Methodist missionary to slaves, 1862; utilized by Benjamin L. C. Wailes

LINCOLN, ABRAHAM, the man as person and specter as a Black Republican

LOVELL, JOSEPH, captain in Confederate army; born in New York

LOVELL, LOUISA QUITMAN, daughter of John Quitman of Monmouth; wife and correspondent of Joseph

LOVELL, CAPTAIN W. S., commanded Quitman Light Artillery when it left for the war

LOVELL [sp.?], MR., otherwise unidentified; present at racetrack examinations

MARGARET [?], perhaps Jenkins or Dunbar, but probably a slave; told by Howard he murdered the Dutchman

MARSHALL, GEORGE M., Natchez planter and son of an even wealthier planter-businessman; attended both the Second Creek and racetrack examinations

MARSHALL, LEVIN R., extremely wealthy Adams County planter and businessman with strong connections in North; father of George M.

MARTIN, ABNER, active in whipping of James Carter; family relationship to William T. Martin uncertain but unlikely

MARTIN, MARGARET D. CONNER, married to William T. and sister of Lemuel Conner

MARTIN, WILLIAM T., self-claimed organizer of military unit in 1860; prominent Natchez lawyer; brother-in-law of Lemuel P. Conner; general in command of Jeff Davis Legion; testified before Southern Claims Commission after war

MARY, MISS [GRIER(?) but more probably DUNBAR(?)], poured water on Wesley's sister

McGOVERN, PATRICK FRANCIS, overseer of Aventine in 1857; probably Irish-born

METCALFE, HELEN GILLESPIE, grew up at Egypt Plantation; married to Dr. Orrick Metcalfe; no slaves involved, but a proposed victim

METCALFE, HENRY LAURENS, son of Dr. James and brother of Orrick and James W., owner of and probably resident at The Grove on Second Creek; present at racetrack examinations

METCALFE, DR. JAMES, wealthy planter of Montrose, father of Henry, James W., and Orrick; employed John Austen as overseer

METCALFE, JAMES WISTAR, son of Dr. James and brother of Henry and Orrick; at Ingleside (also called Ingleside Farm)

METCALFE, JANE, married to James W.

METCALFE, OREN, sometimes spelled Metcalf and often simply O. Metcalfe; Natchez businessman and county sheriff; not related to Dr. James Metcalfe family of Second Creek

METCALFE, DR. ORRICK, son of Dr. James and brother of Henry and James W.; educated at Yale and professor at Jefferson College before going into planting at Fair Oaks; no slaves involved; proposed victim, but may have been away in army

MIDDLETON, CAPTAIN H. H., officer in Washington Troop

MINOR, JOHN, son of William J. and Rebecca; accompanied father to racetrack; dead of dissipation by time of appeals to Southern Claims Commission

MINOR, KATHERINE SURGET, married to John Minor; daughter-in-law of William J. and Rebecca; owner of Carthage and the adjacent Blackburn in Adams County, two other plantations in Concordia; resident at and owner of suburban Oakland after husband John's death after war; claimant before Southern Claims Commission

MINOR, REBECCA ANN, wife and widow of William J.; apparently unsuccessful claimant to Southern Claims Commission

MINOR, WILLIAM J., prominent, wealthy Natchez and Louisiana planter; diarist, member of racetrack examination committee, and purported Unionist; dead by time of appeals to Southern Claims Commission

MITCHELL, CLARA, younger sister of Emma; granddaughter (probably) of Mr. and Mrs. James H.

MITCHELL, EMMA, ten-year-old granddaughter (probably) of Mr. and Mrs. James H.; older sister of Clara

MITCHELL, JAMES H., planter at Palatine, where some slaves were involved

MITCHELL, SOPHIA G., wife of James H.

MONTGOMERY, PROSPER K., Jefferson County planter, more usually known as P. K.; owned slaves involved in May episode

MOORE, MRS. EDITH WYATT, twentieth-century Natchez local history writer; interviewer of former slaves in 1937

MORRIS, MUNROE, mentioned at Second Creek examinations; probably either white or free black

MOSBY, ANNA, seventeen-year-old daughter of Mr. and Mrs. Mosby

MOSBY, BESSIE, thirteen, the youngest Mosby girl

MOSBY, FANNY, fourteen; sometimes Fanni

MOSBY, FRANCES BABBITT, previously married wife of John S.

MOSBY, JOHN S., schoolmaster and struggling planter of Brighton; most of his few adult male slaves involved

NICHOLS, ELIZA J., wife of P. R.; her driver involved

NICHOLS, P. R., Connecticut-born planter at Bottany Hill

O'FERRALL, JOHN, prominent Natchez merchant; probably not at Second Creek examinations

ODELL, STEVE, prosperous Natchez gunsmith and slaveholder, probably the town's largest gunsmith in the late 1850s; target of rebels

OGDEN, the REVEREND MR. THOMAS A., Episcopal clergyman boarding at Dr. Scott's; may have preached to slaves at Jenkins' Elgin

PENDLETON, BENJAMIN, Natchez Baptist deacon; defender of James Carter, a black fellow-church-member charged at the racetrack with insurrection

PETTUS, JOHN J., governor of Mississippi during war

PICKENS, A. D., Adams County U.S. assistant marshal for 1860 census; also county tax assessor; not wealthy himself

PRENTISS, SEARGENT S., state representative and later congressman for Natchez area before war

PROFILET, EMILE, spelling of name uncertain; at racetrack examinations; possibly the man called "Mr. Prunalet" by Pleasant Scott

QUITMAN, JOHN A., northern-born Adams County planter and prominent state politician

RANSOM, THOMAS E. G., Union general in command of occupied Natchez in 1863

RIVERS, D. L., planter; present at racetrack examinations; possibly the man called "Revens" by Pleasant Scott

ROUNDTREE, LIVINGSTON, owner of Pleasant Scott

ROWARE, [either A. W. or JAMES H.], lieutenant in Washington Troop

SAMBLAR [sp.?], MR., an examiner at racetrack

SANDERSON, ELIZA, extremely wealthy widow and slaveowner at Overton and Briars, not close to Second Creek

SARAH, MISS, family name uncertain; perhaps Surget

SAUTERS, CHARLES, overseer of Aventine in 1859; an immigrant from Württemberg in process of becoming a U.S. citizen; married, with children

SCOTT, DR. JOHN T., small slaveholder at Waverly; owner of rebels Harry Scott and Frederick

SCOTT, LOUISA, wife of Dr. John T.

SCOTT, SAM, owner of Jefferson County slaves said to be involved in rebellion; apparently no relation to Dr. John T.

SCOTT, WINFIELD, army general and former presidential candidate; highest-ranking Union officer at beginning of war; rebels expected him to take New Orleans

SEARS [sp.?], HENRY, examiner at racetrack

SHARPE, CLARISSA, owner of Cedar Grove, where overseer was murdered

SHIELDS, GABRIEL B., wealthy, well-connected planter; owner of Aventine but resident at Montebello; employed McGovern (1857) and Sauters (1859) as overseers; his slaves not involved and were said to have turned down a recruiter for the Plan

SHIELDS, JAMES, teenage son of Gabriel B.; killed in war

SHIELDS, RANDOLPH, absent patron of Charlie Davenport in 1937

SHIELDS, THOMAS R., Adams County planter; brother of Gabriel

SHIELDS, WILLIAM DUNBAR, planter father of Thomas R. and Gabriel B.

SIBLEY, THE REVEREND MR., preacher to slaves in Jefferson County

SIMON, JOHN, at racetrack examinations

SINGLETON, O. R., Mississippi congressman before war

SMITH, WALTON, P., planter near Mosby's, probably at Mag[n]olia, for only about five years; slaves apparently not involved

SPAIN, THOMAS H., prosperous overseer-manager of Katherine S. Minor's Carthage and perhaps Blackburn; testified before Southern Claims Commission

SPRATT, LEONIDAS W., South Carolina advocate of reopening Atlantic slave trade

STAMPLEY, JACOB, captain in charge of slave-patrol duty, Jefferson County

STEARNS, HENRY, at racetrack examinations

STRICKLAND, NOBLE, examiner at racetrack

SURGET, FRANCIS, sometimes Frank; one of wealthiest Surgets; died shortly before the war

SURGET, FRANK, JR., son of Francis

SURGET, JACOB, brother and uncle of James Sr. and Jr.; legal owner of Cherry Grove, where slaves were involved and some hanged

SURGET, "CAPT." JAMES, SR., father of James, Jr., and of Katherine Surget Minor

SURGET, JAMES, JR., son of James, Sr., brother of Katherine Surget Minor; probably supervising and perhaps living at Cherry Grove in 1861

SURGET, KATHERINE ("KATE"), married John Minor in 1855; see Minor

SURGET, PIERRE, late-eighteenth-century French settler in Second Creek valley; founder of Surget family fortune

SWAYSE, HENRY, planter and probably businessman of Natchez and Kingston; owner of two hanged slaves; spelled "Swazey" in Darden Diary

THOMAS, FRED, present at racetrack examinations

TUCKER, GEORGE, "special agent" of Southern Claims Commission; took depositions and investigated throughout Deep South after war

W., MISS MARY, last name uncertain

WAILES, BENJAMIN L. C., diarist, planter, college professor, and author; resident near hamlet of Washington

WOOD, NANCY, possible owner of Wiley Wood

WOOD, DR. SPENCER, possible owner of Wiley Wood

YOUNG, DR. BENJAMIN F., recently deceased owner of Beau Prés; father-in-law of James W. Metcalfe

YOUNG, ROBERT, probably son of Benjamin; inherited Beau Prés; proposed victim

YOUNG, MRS. ROBERT, first name not clear; possibly dead or not living with her husband; a cousin of Conner; proposed victim

INDEX

For many slaves and a few other persons in this book, no last name is known. Such persons are indexed by first name. Where two or more slaves have the same or similar first names, their owners' names are given in parentheses for further identification.